THE CATHOLIC MOMENT

THE
CATHOLIC
MOMENT

The Paradox of the Church
in the Postmodern World

RICHARD JOHN NEUHAUS

1817

Harper & Row, Publishers, San Francisco

Cambridge, Hagerstown, New York, Philadelphia, Washington
London, Mexico City, São Paulo, Singapore, Sydney

George and Joan,
Gwyneth and Monica

FIRST EDITION

Library of Congress Cataloging-in-Publication Data

Neuhaus, Richard John.
   The Catholic moment.

   Bibliography: p.
   Includes index.
   1. Catholic Church—History—1965-
2. Catholic Church—Doctrines.   I. Title.
BX1390.N48   1987   282'.09'04   87-45191
ISBN 0-06-066096-1

87 88 89 90 91 HC 10 9 8 7 6 5 4 3 2 1

Contents

A Word to the Reader

This is a book about the Roman Catholic Church in America and in the world. It is thus about many things: Vatican Council II and what it did to and for Catholicism, Pope John Paul II and where he is trying to lead the church, Joseph Cardinal Ratzinger and responses to theological change, the American bishops and their efforts to relate moral judgment to public policy, liberation theology and conflicts surrounding it, the enthusiasms and despairs of laypeople who are no longer sure what it means to be Roman Catholic. All these subjects are very timely, and they are all addressed in these pages.

But I hope you will see that, in a much deeper sense, this is a book about being Christian, maybe just being religious, in the postmodern world. Being such is not easy. The argument is that the testings and trials going on in the Roman Catholic Church are paradigmatic of the testings and trials of Christianity at the edge of its third millennium. The assumption is that what happens in Catholicism is of enormous importance to the future of Christianity, and of the world. It should therefore be of great concern to all of us—including those of us who are not Roman Catholic.

I will not take it amiss if you begin at the end with Part 6, "The Catholic Moment." In fact, that might be a good idea. Part 6 is a brief summary of the argument and assumptions of the entire essay. Admittedly, it is very tightly packed, but it will give you some idea of where the book is going and where, as they used to say, the author is coming from. Then, when you get to Part 6 the second time around, it will make even more sense than I hope it makes the first time.

What else? There is the matter of gender and language. Terms such as *himself* and *men* should, throughout the book, be taken as abbreviations for "himself or herself," "men and women," and so on. Please note too that the capitalization of the word *church* is not as eccentric as it may seem. It is uppercase when it is the proper name of a church body and when it is used theologically to refer to *the* Church, the Body of Christ. Otherwise it is lowercase. Sometimes it is hard to decide which it should be, but I suppose we can manage to live with that ambiguity.

Permit me one more preliminary: Roman Catholics are not agreed on whether they want to be called Roman Catholics or just Catholics. I have generally written Roman Catholic, and there are three reasons for that. First, in Christian history, catholic is frequently synonymous with orthodox, and it would be both rude and wrong to suggest that Roman Catholicism has a monopoly on orthodox Christianity. Second, many non-Roman Catholic Christians make a point of calling themselves catholics, and we should be sensitive to their convictions on the subject. Third—and this gets into the argument of the book—I suggest that Roman Catholics should not be so hesitant to name themselves as such, for it is turning out, at least under this Pope, that Catholicism is more fully catholic as it is less hesitantly Roman.

But enough of preliminaries. It is, as you can see, a rather big book. It has been a long time in preparation. For the most part, the writing of it was a pleasure, as, I trust, will be your reading of it. My hope is that the book will contribute at least a little to the unity and vitality of the Church of Christ, one, holy, catholic, and apostolic.

RJN

Pentecost, 1987
New York City

The Author's Debts

For more than twenty-five years I have been in formal and informal dialogue with Roman Catholics. It may be because I am by disposition incorrigibly ecumenical. But I expect it has more to do with imperatives issuing from my baptism into the one Christ and his one Church. In any event, to be a Lutheran Christian is to be ecumenical, for Lutheranism is not so much the Lutheran Church as it is a movement of evangelical catholic reform within and for the one Church. For that understanding of what it means to be a Lutheran Christian, my first and greatest debt is to the late Arthur Carl Piepkorn of Concordia Theological Seminary, St. Louis.

Sustained conversation with the following people has powerfully influenced my understanding of Christianity in the modern world, and of Roman Catholicism in particular: Peter Berger, Brigitte Berger, Robert Wilken, Wolfhart Pannenberg, Michael Novak, James Finn, Molly Finn, George Lindbeck, Robert Jenson, John J. O'Connor, William Rusch, John Krol, John Navone, Joe Sobran, John Woolsey, Avery Dulles, George Higgins, Stanley Hauerwas, Raymond Brown, Raymond Schulze, Carl Peter, David Lotz, Bryan Hehir, and George Weigel, to whom, with his gracious family, this book is dedicated. Each bears a measure of responsibility for the views expressed in these pages.

Portions of the book appeared in earlier versions in several journals, including *Commonweal, Worldview, Dialog,* and *This World.* Most of the ideas have been given at least a trial run at numerous conferences, colleges, and universities. I will not attempt to enumerate the many people for whose hospitality, criticisms, and suggestions I am deeply grateful.

Finally, my heartfelt thanks to my colleagues at the Rockford Institute Center on Religion and Society, Paul Stallsworth, Davida Goldman, and Allan Carlson, and to the members of the Community of Christ in the City, with whom I live and by whom I am nourished in body and spirit.

PART I

Beyond the Riddle of Roman Catholicism

This writer is a Lutheran Christian who is certainly but imperfectly a member of the Roman Catholic Church. That, at least, is the official teaching of the Roman Catholic Church. According to the Second Vatican Council's "Decree on Ecumenism," all who are baptized in the name of the Father, Son, and Holy Spirit "are brought into a certain, though imperfect, communion with the Catholic Church."

Such a teaching could be caricatured as a definitional shortcut to Christian unity. One recalls the United States senator who, during the Vietnam War years, said we should just declare a victory and bring the boys home. So Vatican Council II seems to have declared Christian unity an accomplished fact. We are all Roman Catholics, know it or not, like it or not. Admittedly, there is that qualifier "imperfect," but then who is a perfect member of any church? Others might respond to the Council's assertion with a measure of resentment. The claim that all baptized Christians are in communion with the Roman church strikes them as an instance of definitional imperialism all too typical of Rome. They might be inclined to return the compliment, observing that, by the same token, all Roman Catholics are certainly, though very imperfectly, members of the Methodist, Presbyterian, Greek Orthodox, or whatever church.

But these terminological games rather miss the point of the teaching in question. What Vatican Council II did, in a way that the Roman Catholic Church had not quite done before, was to advance an understanding of the Church of Christ that is in no way limited to the Roman Catholic Church. This does not mean that the Roman Catholic Church now claims to be no more than one church among the churches. Far from it. The Council insists that *the* Church "subsists" in the Roman Catholic Church in a most singular manner. But the change is nonetheless of the greatest significance. The comedian Lenny Bruce used to observe, "The Catholic Church is the church you mean when you say 'the Church.'" That is undoubtedly still true for many people. It has never been true for Christians whose first allegiance is to another church tradition. And, officially if not always in practice, it is not true for Roman Catholics today.

There is a reason for beginning with the question of the Church and Christian unity. We begin with it, and will be returning to it in greater detail, because it is important to establish that when we are talking about Roman Catholicism, we are talking about "us" and not (or at least not only) about "them." In establishing this point we are taking up the ecumenical invitation that was, to Roman Catholics and non-Romans alike, one of the most surprising and welcome developments of Vatican Council II. Among the many things that ecumenism means, it means that no church's business is entirely its own. We are, by virtue of our baptism into Christ and our confession of faith, all in this together. We have not only the right but the obligation to question, challenge, and criticize one another. And to do so in love, knowing that we need one another.

The reader will find much in this book that is critical of the Roman Catholic Church. Some Roman Catholic readers may think that an impertinence. In truth, it is testimony to the seriousness of the affirmation that the Roman Catholic Church is also "our church." There is an old saw that an ecumenical zealot, called an "ecumaniac," is someone who thinks every church is wonderful except his own. This writer does not fit the description, for, as will become evident, he believes the Reformation tradition forcefully challenges all the churches today, not least the churches that claim to be in that tradition. But he is convinced that in thinking about "church and world" we must think ecumenically. The subject is Christian existence in the modern world and, more specifically, in American society. To speak of Christian existence is to speak of individual Christians, their beliefs, and their behavior. But it is also to speak of traditions, communities, and institutions. Of all the Christian traditions, communities, and institutions in the world, none is so large, so various, and so influential as the Roman Catholic Church. Every Christian has a steep stake in the Roman Catholic Church. And, to the extent that the future of the world has been and will be influenced by Christianity, so do those who do not call themselves Christian.

The "Constitution on the Church in the Modern World" is by far the longest of the documents coming out of Vatican II. It is probably also the most commented upon, and the most controverted. There are many devout Roman Catholics who, while they do not come right out and say the Council made a big mistake with this document, nonetheless think the Council made a big mistake with this document. Of course the Church is in the modern world as a matter of simple historical fact, but, in their view, the emphasis should be on the Church *apart from* the modern world, *above* the modern world, or even *against* the modern world. Its contrast with the modern world was precisely one of the great attractions of Rome in the past, and many are the eminent converts who went to Rome in order to find relief from the madnesses of the modern world. Francis

Thompson, Ronald Knox, G. K. Chesterton, Graham Greene, Evelyn Waugh, and of course the archetype of this distinguished company, John Henry Cardinal Newman—all have written movingly about discovering in Rome a home in a homeless world, a center of sanity in a world of madness, a refuge from the storms of modernity.

Those who follow these matters, even if only in the general press, know that that is not the picture of the Roman Catholic Church today. To be sure, the visitor standing in the square and looking up at Saint Peter's is likely to find momentarily believable all that has been said about the unchanging majesty of the Eternal City chosen by God to be the center of his Church on earth. Here, it may be thought, is the tranquil core of that constancy and certitude by which the modern world is judged. Protestantism, by pathetic contrast, is in perpetual heat, ever sniffing about for chances to link up with modernity, to innovate, to accommodate, to make itself agreeable to whomever dictates the manners of the time. These were the prevailing stereotypes of Rome and Protestantism, and it is not difficult to understand why, to many civilized believers, Rome came off looking much the better. The stereotypes, or at least the stereotype of Rome, are not easy to sustain today.

There is much loose talk about the "pre-Vatican II church" and the "post-Vatican II church," as though they are really two churches rather than the Holy Catholic Apostolic Roman Church passing and changing through time. The church post-Vatican II, official Rome insists, should be a church renewed, not a new church. A new church is by definition a sect, and Rome is rightly adamant that it is not a sect. Sectarianism is the symptom of "the Protestant disease" of reinventing Christianity to suit the circumstances. It is situational Christianity. Many Roman Catholics fear that the Protestant disease has made alarming headway in Rome since the Council. The Church in the modern world they could perhaps take; it is the modern world in the Church that is so troubling to them. As one Catholic friend remarks, there is something bracing about belonging to a church that dares to be five hundred years out of step, but it is embarrassing to belong to a church that is worried about being five years out of step, and is huffing and puffing in its efforts to play catch-up.

To understand the Roman Catholic Church today, we must understand what it has been, and still is, for many. Rome as the Rock of Ages still has a certain appeal, and not only to the incorrigibly romantic. In 1939, at the beginning of the second catastrophic war of this catastrophic century, Pope Pius XII reflected on the Church in the modern world. "The reason why the principles of morality in general have long since been set aside in Europe is the defection of so many minds from Christian doctrine of which Blessed Peter's See is the appointed guardian and teacher," said the pope. The civilized world had been "welded together" by that doctrine, and then, with the Reformation, it all started falling apart. "When many of the Christian family separated themselves from the infallible teaching of the church," it opened the way to the secular Enlightenment, to pagan nationalisms, to reductive scientism, and to "the general deterioration and decline of the religious idea." Thus men had been "handing themselves over to a capricious ruler, the feeble and grovelling wisdom of man. They boasted of progress, when they were in fact relapsing into decadence; they conceived they were reaching heights of achievement when they were miserably forfeiting their human dignity; they claimed that this century of ours was bringing maturity and completion with it, when they were being reduced to a pitiable form of slavery."

1. AUTHORITY RESPLENDENT

Anti-Roman polemicists (of whom there are still not a few) say that Rome has not changed; Roman Catholic traditionalists say it *should* not have changed. But it has changed and dramatically so. In the view of many, there was no doubt about what Rome was "before the Council." The Rome to which Evelyn Waugh converted was, he thought, the spiritual analogue and guarantor of his view of the world. That view of the world is spelled out in a memorable paragraph from his travel book on Mexico, *Robbery Under Law* (1939). It is well worth a longish quotation:

I believe that man is, by nature, an exile and will never be self-sufficient or complete on this earth; that his chances of happiness and virtue, here, remain more or less constant through the centuries and, generally speaking, are not much affected by the political and economic conditions in which he lives; that the balance of good and ill tends to revert to a norm; that sudden changes of physical condition are usually ill, and are advocated by the wrong people for the wrong reasons; that the intellectual communists of today have personal, irrelevant grounds for their antagonism to society, which they are trying to exploit. I believe in government; that men cannot live together without rules but that these should be kept at the bare minimum of safety; that there is no form of government ordained from God as being better than any other; that the anarchic elements in society are so strong that it is a whole time task to keep the peace. I believe that inequalities of wealth and position are inevitable and that it is therefore meaning-less to discuss the advantages of their elimination; that men naturally arrange themselves in a system of classes; that such a system is necessary for any form of co-operative work, more particularly the work of keeping a nation together. I believe in nationality; not in terms of race or of divine commissions for world conquest, but simply this: mankind inevitably organizes itself into communities according to its geographical distribution; these communities by sharing a com-mon history develop common characteristics and inspire a local loyalty; the indi-vidual family develops most happily and fully when it accepts these natural limits. I do not think that British prosperity must necessarily be inimical to anyone else, but if, on occasions, it is, I want Britain to prosper and not her rivals. I believe that war and conquest are inevitable; that is how history has been made and that is how it will develop. I believe that Art is a natural function of man; it so happens that most of the greatest art has appeared under systems of political tyranny, but I do not think it has a connection with any particular system, least of all with representative government, as nowadays in England, America and France it seems popular to believe; artists have always spent some of their spare time in flattering the governments under whom they live, so it is natural that, at the moment, English, American and French artists should be volubly democratic.

So much for the church in the modern world. While Waugh and others believed that rules should be as few as possible in civil society, in the society that is the church, the more rules the better. After all, so much more is at stake in the realm of the spiritual, and one cannot be too careful. The problem with Vatican II, such people say, is not that it changed this rule or that but that it threw into question the authority behind all the rules. The attraction of Rome for many had been the attraction of unquestioned authority. Some among the psychologically minded "explain" this attraction in terms of "the authoritarian personality" and similar devices. Monsignor Ronald Knox, friend and mentor of Waugh, described his journey to Rome this way:

I did come to wonder whether I had a right to believe in anything—to believe, that is, without being in visible communion with that one visible body of faithful people of whom the prophet foretold, "All thy people shall be taught of God." For authority played a large part in my belief, and I could not now find that any certain source of authority was available to me outside the pale of the Roman Catholic Church. Once inside, I should not care how the authority came to me; I did not crave for infallible decrees; I wanted to be certain I belonged to that church of which Saint Paul said proudly, "We have the mind of Christ."

By what authority? It is the question that must be asked wherever teachings or laws of consequence are involved. And nowhere is it to be asked so urgently as in matters pertaining to the salvation of one's soul. The historian Paul Johnson says the whole of the history of Christianity is a history of dispute over authority. That may be saying too much, but it is not far from the mark, and it is worth noting that most of the more noted disputes within Roman Catholicism today are indeed disputes over authority. In any event, and whether or not it had the authority to do so, Rome once gave an unmistakable answer to the question of authority. And, if Monsignor Knox did not "crave for infallible decrees," others did. These Catholics did not reluctantly obey such decrees; they relished them.

In his engaging 1985 memoir of his parents, *Frank and Maisie*, the novelist Wilfred Sheed describes his maternal grandfather. "Grandfather William, as a Catholic convert, wasted no time flinging himself to the far right corner of his new lodgings, demanding even more papal authority than he was getting. His ideal, he said famously, was a papal bull with his breakfast every morning, along with his *Times*. The term 'ultramontane' referred to this wish of his for orders from 'beyond the mountain,' from the vicar of Christ himself and not from some fly-by-night earthly power. 'Madam, you will find me strong and narrow,' he once said. *'Very* strong and *very* narrow.' '' Infallible decrees with breakfast—now there is someone who knows what authority is about.

But of course Grandfather William did not get his infallible decrees, he did not even get his papal bulls, for breakfast. In truth, there has been only one infallible decree since papal infallibility was declared at the First Vatican Council well over a hundred years ago. And of course Grandfather William was a caricature, although he had and he has company in those, especially converts, who exult in the freedom to submit to authority with wild abandon. To the staunchly Protestant, not to say secular, mind, such an attitude smacks of the pathological. And yet is not authentic Christianity supposed to offend the sensibilities, violate the protocols, and upset the conventions of a world that knows not God? Certainly the great Protestant theologian Karl Barth thought so. After what he viewed as the theological pap of nineteenth-century Protestant liberalism, he fed the Christian world the strong meat of absolute submission to the Word of God. Certainly Saint Paul seems to have thought so: "But we preach Christ and him crucified, a stumbling block to Jews and folly to Gentiles, but to those who are called, both Jews and Greeks, Christ the power of God and the wisdom of God. For the foolishness of God is wiser than men, and the weakness of God is stronger than men"(1 Cor. 1).

More recently the novelist Walker Percy writes about being a Christian in a modern world that is manifestly mad. In *Lost in the Cosmos,* he considers the beliefs of an observant Jew, a fundamentalist Protestant, and a Roman Catholic. What the Jew and the fundamentalist believe is invigoratingly preposterous, but, he concludes, being a Catholic Christian is best of all.

Catholic Christianity is the most preposterous of the three. It proposes, not only [what Jew and fundamentalist believe], but also that the man-god founded a church, appointed as its first head a likable but pusillanimous person, like himself a Jew, the most fallible of his friends, gave him and successors the power to loose and to bind, required of his followers that they eat his body and drink his blood in order to have life in them, empowered his priests to change bread and wine into his body and blood, and vowed to protect this institution until the end of time. At which time he promised to return.

Flaunting his favored preposterousness in the face of a smugly rational modern world, Percy would, if possible, shock that world out of its irrationality. For Paul, the preposterous thing, the *scandolon,* is the cross of Christ. For a certain species of piety that used to be cultivated and is still found among Roman Catholics, any scandal will do. If the sacrifice of intellect would produce the salutary offense, they were eager to sacrifice all the intellect they had, and more if required. A vulgarized version of

Tertullian's "I believe because it is absurd" (*Credo quia absurdam*) was taken to be license for intellectually riotous living. True religion, it was said, should be the jester at the king's court, exposing the self-importance and delusions of the modern world. By the alchemy of religious authority, contradictions are turned into confirmations, and absurdities are said to debunk the measure by which others define what is absurd.

There was something refreshingly defiant in this understanding of the faith. It still has a powerful appeal for all who, with Walker Percy, have come to the perfectly sensible conclusion that the modern world is manifestly mad. By the measures of such a world a sane person might very well seem to be mad. But then there is the troubling distinction suggested by the Protestant theologian Reinhold Niebuhr. It makes all the difference, he said, whether one is a fool for Christ or just a plain fool. To present what in the faith is not foolish as though it were foolish may make for a fun religion, but it is a great disservice to the faith, and therefore to the world. Faith is for flaunting and the world must be challenged, but faith is not to be confused with a religious self-indulgence that ends up challenging not at all a world that has long since learned to tolerate almost anything that does not, as the lady said, frighten the horses. There was, and there is, another Roman Catholicism that is determined to engage the world on its own terms. It is not enough, these other Roman Catholics say, to flaunt and defy, to throw up the preposterousness of the faith against the preposterousness of modernity.

2. TO ENGAGE THE WORLD

The late Jesuit theologian and moral philosopher, John Courtney Murray, who will be reappearing in these pages, championed a form of Catholic wisdom that the modern world could not condescendingly tolerate. Roman Catholicism, he believed, is the keeper of a truth that has everything to do with the right ordering of our lives together in the "City of Man." Murray represents a tradition of "public theology" that takes the world up on its claim to be, above all else, reasonable. In this view the mission of Roman Catholicism is not to be a refuge from the world nor a crusade against the world, but a wisdom for the world. Murray did not want to diminish the distinctiveness, even the *scandalon,* of the Church. On the contrary, it is precisely the distinctiveness of the Church that, by contrast, highlights the distinctiveness of the civil society that we call the modern world.

Murray wrote in *We Hold These Truths* (1960):

Hence the climate of the City [of Man] is likewise distinctive. It is not feral or familial but forensic. It is not hot and humid, like the climate of the animal kingdom. It lacks the cordial warmth of love and unreasoning loyalty that pervades the family. It is cool and dry, with coolness and dryness that characterize good argument among informed and responsible men. Civic amity gives to this climate its vital quality. This form of friendship is a special kind of moral virtue, a thing of reason and intelligence, laboriously cultivated by the discipline of passion, prejudice, and narrow self-interest. It is the sentiment proper to the City. It has nothing to do with the cleavage of a David to a Jonathan, or with the kinship of the clan, or with the charity, *fortis ut mors,* that makes the solidarity of the Church.

Cool and dry, not hot and humid. Murray does not deny the ways of speaking about the Church in the language of the womb, but when the Church engages the modern world, it must employ also the language of the head. In his coolness and dryness Murray stands, of course, in the tradition of Thomas Aquinas. The monumental achievement of that thirteenth-century saint, was, it is claimed, to have made almost the entirety of human knowledge subject to Christ. His critics, Protestant and other, complained that Thomas had taken Christ captive to the mind of Aristotle. In any event, for generations Thomism was the reigning theology and habit of mind in Roman Catholicism. With few exceptions, to be a Roman Catholic theologian was to be a Thomist. That is no longer the case today. Thomas once represented a normative way of relating the Church and the modern world. (If we keep in mind that "modern" means "just now," Thomas's world in his time was as "modern" as ours.) It is part of our argument that that tradition, as interpreted by Murray, has far from exhausted its possibilities in building an ecumenical understanding of the Church in the world.

This is one of "the riddles of Roman Catholicism," how it contains the traditions of both romance and reason in its relation to the world. We considered above instances of romanticism, often articulated by converts of an earlier time. These might be viewed as romanticisms of the Right, of the church *against* the world. We will be considering romanticisms, sometimes revolutionary romanticisms, of the Left, of the church *of* the world. In contrast to these, we will examine a Catholicism of reason that is *for* the world. This option usually does not fit the politically based categories of Left and Right, nor is it entirely separate from the other options. As we shall see, a measure of "againstness" and "ofness," so to speak, is necessary in being effectively *for* the world.

There are other "riddles of Roman Catholicism" to which we must now turn. But before doing so, note that on the far side of the riddle does not lie neat resolution but paradox. A paradox, G. K. Chesterton said, is a truth standing on its head and wriggling its legs, trying to get our attention. There is, as one has come to expect from Chesterton, much truth in that. More pedestrian definitions of *paradox* refer to statements that violate received opinion, or an apparent contradiction that contains an important fact. All these senses are included in what I mean by paradox. But in saying that the manner of the Church's being in the modern world is paradoxical, I mean also something else. I mean that paradox is closely related to promise. The existence of the Church, and indeed of the world, is premised upon a promise, and that promise has not yet been fulfilled in historical fact. The Church is a community ahead of time. It is saying things about itself and about the world that are paradoxical because it is speaking in present time from a point beyond present time.

Once, not long ago, there was a Roman Catholicism that was a "riddle" to those who were not Roman Catholics, and to many who were. The riddle has not been resolved, and indeed it requires and rewards close examination. But the riddle is now giving way to paradox. The Roman Catholic Church is no longer an "other" that needs to be explained. It is increasingly the premier church in *the* Church's understanding of its relationship to the world, a relationship that is essentially paradoxical. Thus, in trying to understand Roman Catholicism we are trying to understand the Church of which we are all certainly but imperfectly part, and therefore trying to understand our own paradoxical relationship to the world. Admittedly, for many non-Roman Catholic Christians the Roman Catholic Church is still viewed as an "other" and still as a "riddle." We must therefore pass through "the riddle of Roman Catholicism" before getting beyond the riddle to the paradox in which we find ourselves, and find one another.

3. WHEN CATHOLICISM BECAME ROMAN

Jaroslav Pelikan's justly acclaimed *The Riddle of Roman Catholicism* was published in 1959. Pelikan is a Lutheran church historian then at the University of Chicago and now for many years at Yale University. In 1959, John XXIII was pope. John F. Kennedy was running for the presidency. The last fact was pertinent to Pelikan's purpose, as is evident in his extended and sympathetic treatment of the prospect of a Roman Catholic president. The religious world was abuzz with word that the pope was to convene a council, and some said that ecumenical observers would play an important role in it. Although Pelikan's book was widely and appreciatively read by Roman Catholics, it is clearly addressed to Protestants and others for whom Roman Catholicism was decidedly "other."

Pelikan was writing in the last glow of the dusk of the old-line Protestant establishment in American culture. The old line, represented by such as the National Council of Churches, was then still the religiocultural main line. Among Pelikan's intentions was the intention to allay the anxieties of mainline Protestantism about the growing strength of Catholicism in American life. The book is irenic throughout. Pelikan was attempting to follow Martin Luther's counsel with respect to the eighth commandment, namely, to "put the best construction on everything." Even the title was irenic. Three decades ago many, perhaps most, non-Roman Christians spoke about the "threat" or the "scandal" of Roman Catholicism. Jaroslav Pelikan called it the riddle of Roman Catholicism.

We must step back for a moment to remember how very Protestant the American ethos once was, and therefore how alien Roman Catholicism seemed. Our first step back is a big one of two centuries. John Adams, later to be second president of the United States, was no nativist bigot. But in 1774, he was of a Sunday visiting various churches in Philadelphia and happened into a Roman Catholic mass. He wrote to Abigail:

This afternoon, led by curiousity and good company, I strolled away to mother church, or rather grandmother church. I mean the Romish chapel. . . . [The] entertainment was to me most awful and affecting: the poor wretches fingering their beads, chanting Latin, not a word of which they understood; their pater nosters and ave Marias; their holy water; their crossing themselves perpetually; their bowing to the name of Jesus, whenever they hear it; their bowings, kneelings and genuflections before the altar. The dress of the priest was rich white lace. His pulpit was velvet and gold. The altar piece was very rich, little images and crucifixes about; wax candles lighted up. But how shall I describe the picture of our Saviour in a frame of marble over the altar, at full length, upon the cross in the agonies, and the blood dropping and streaming from his wounds! The music, consisting of an organ and a choir of singers, went all the afternoon except sermon time, and the assembly chanted most sweetly and exquisitely. Here is everything which can lay hold of the eye, ear, and imagination—everything which can charm and bewitch the simple and ignorant. I wonder how Luther ever broke the spell.

One can almost hear some reader remarking that, for contemporary Roman Catholics, the spell was broken not by Luther but by the Second Vatican Council. To which a traditionalist Catholic might add that that is much the same thing, for it is no secret that "the spirit of Vatican II" was the lively ghost of the renegade monk from Wittenberg. Be that as it is not, it is a different dispute to which we will come in due course. The question at hand is the perception of Roman Catholicism in Protestant America. Adams's perception was not as dramatically different from that of the 1950s as we might like to think. The 1950s were a time of religious self-confidence and presumed good feeling marked by interfaith amity around the true faith of the American Way of Life, as so brilliantly described in Will Herberg's *Protestant, Catholic, Jew* (1955). In 1959 Jaroslav Pelikan stepped back to a nineteenth-century figure and wrote: "Though their prose would be less high-flown, most American Protestants would still describe Roman Catholicism with Macaulay as: '. . . a complete subjection of reason to authority, a weak preference of form to substance, a childish passion for mummeries, an idolatrous veneration for the priestly character, and, above all a merciless intolerance.' "

Pelikan, then, was not only unravelling a riddle but was countering a prepossession of passionate force. His book begins at the beginning, examining how Christianity became Catholic and then how Catholicism became Roman. That is still a subject of lively debate, and will continue to be so. For some Roman Catholics there is no debate at all, for the

Church was Roman from the start. It is a matter of direct and mechanical succession from Peter to today's bishops and pope. It has been "palm upon pate" all the way. For them yesterday's ruling on canon law is but our Lord's latest gloss on the commission he gave to Cephas, the rock and first pope on whom he founded his Church. Those who have thought about the matter more carefully recognize that the development is somewhat more complicated than that.

Nineteenth-century scholars of Protestant liberalism viewed the "catholicizing" of the Church as "the fall" of the Church from its New Testament purity. It is a view that was earlier propounded by some in the left wing of the sixteenth-century Reformation who were determined to repristinate the "authentic Christianity" of the primitive community. They believed that, after the New Testament period, it had been downhill all the way. The descent was from spontaneity to institutionalism, from freedom to subordination, from moral purity to laxity, from equality to hierarchy, from simplicity to establishment, from faith to superstition, from revealed doctrine to man-made rules; in sum, from Jesus of Nazareth to the pope of Rome. Those who embrace this view subscribe to what the historian Robert Wilken has described, in a book by the same title, as "the myth of Christian beginnings." The "myth" is the notion that what we call Christian orthodoxy was established from the beginning rather than being a consequence of historical dispute and struggle. Those who want to be orthodox Christians say it was a struggle guided by the Holy Spirit, but it was a struggle nonetheless, a matter of contingencies that in historical judgment could have gone in quite different ways.

It went the way of Catholicism, and it went the way of Rome. The meaning of this is still an urgent matter for ecumenical discussion. Curiously, one finds among some Roman Catholics today, usually among those who deem themselves very progressive, the view that the path of renewal is the path of return to the New Testament Church. Thus it is not unusual to hear a bishop say that economic life should be designed "according to the Sermon on the Mount," or that the question of nuclear deterrence is the question of "What would Jesus have done?" This way of thinking might almost be seen as a new fundamentalism, an appeal to the Bible unmediated by reason, experience, tradition, or institutional authority. But, of course, this is not the official and predominant view of the matter in Roman Catholicism.

The predominant view is that of more or less direct succession, as mentioned above, in which the authority that Christ gave his Church "subsists" in the Roman Catholic Church today in a most singular manner. Many Roman Catholics are genuinely puzzled why other Christians do not recognize the self-evident truth of the claims of their church. They do not understand, for example, that, in the view of Eastern Orthodox Christians, Rome became, at most, another church among the churches with the break between East and West, usually dated from the eleventh century. Within the church of the West, they are puzzled by those who claim that Lutheranism became a distinct ecclesial communion with the Augsburg Confession of 1530, and Anglicanism with the Convocation of 1532, while Roman Catholicism defined itself as a distinct communion only with the Council of Trent (1545–63). In point of historical fact, and despite its ambitious claims to the contrary, Roman Catholicism became a church among the churches, as in the United States it has become a denomination among the denominations.

Also in point of historical fact, Roman Catholicism is the bearer of the marks of present catholicity and historical continuity far more impressively than any other church. For instance, in the ecumenical dialogues of recent years, it is recognized that Christ may have willed a "Petrine ministry" for his Church, an office of collegial and authoritative leadership. That office might be a "papacy reformed under the Gospel," which would be a papacy quite different from that of post-Reformation history to date. But the point is that, in a reunited church, there is no believable institutional candidate for that Petrine ministry other than the bishop of Rome. Roman Catholicism has been in this and other ways a kind of "baseline," a known quantity that serves as a "control" for further developments in the entire Church's ordering of its life together. The churches of the Reformation can claim and do claim that the entirety of pre-Reformation Christian history belongs to them as much as it does to the church of Rome. They can claim and do claim that Rome bears at least equal responsibility for the divisions of the sixteenth century. (After all, it was not Luther who broke communion with Rome but Rome that presumed to excommunicate Luther.) Nonetheless, after all such claims and counterclaims are argued through, Roman Catholicism remains the institutional baseline for the presence of Christ's Church in history. The reunion of the churches depends in large part upon Roman Catholicism becoming less of a riddle to those who are not Roman Catholic.

Pelikan observed thirty years ago that some people were not prepared to wait for or to work for such reunion. These, as we have seen, were the converts who, as it were, crossed the Tiber for various reasons. Some, wrote Pelikan, were romantics who "went limp at the sound of Gregorian chant" (not a very likely motive for conversion today in view of the almost total desuetude of Gregorian chant in contemporary Catholicism). Others were in search of certainty, or at least of an authority that could stifle uncertainties; yet others, stifled by Protestant parochialisms, sought the spiritual spaciousness of catholicity; and some were devoted to a renewal of Western culture that they believed could only happen through Roman Catholicism. Pelikan wrote sympathetically of the converts, but he rejected "the way of conversion." Conversion, he said, is finally "an individualistic solution to a church problem."

The road to a "solution" that would bring together the truth of Protestantism and the truth of Roman Catholicism, Pelikan wrote, is through mutual understanding, study, and witness. "That road is longer and slower than the way of conversion, but it is the only road on which we have a right to travel. As we travel along this road, we must shoulder our responsibilities and bear together the burden of our separation." Thirty years later, that road seems still to stretch as far as the eye can see. But much has happened along the way that could not have been anticipated in 1959. Then Rome was prepared to accord a certain churchly or ecclesial status to the Orthodox, but Pelikan was doubtful that this same attitude would be adopted toward the other churches of the West. "The present voice of the [Roman] church and its past record both say no, and that seems to be the only possible answer; for a different approach to this heretical and schismatic group [Protestantism] within the Western church would require a redefinition of the church, and that would mean a repudiation of the Roman Catholic heritage." What Pelikan viewed as almost impossible for Rome has now happened to a large extent, but by no means completely. In the teaching of Vatican II, this change is not an instance of repudiation but of renewal leading to reunion.

Pelikan assumed back then that the very idea of reunion between Rome and Protestantism would scandalize both Roman Catholics and Protestants. He was undoubtedly right, and some on both sides of "the breach of the sixteenth century" are still scandalized by the idea today. He also assumed that any ecumenical initiative would have to be taken from the Protestant side, for no one could have anticipated Rome reaching out ecumenically as in fact it did at the Second Vatican Council, and has continued to do so since. Rome had said before the Council that it was in favor of ecumenism. But Pelikan and others who were equally sympathetic viewed that claim with deepest skepticism. Finally, wrote Pelikan, "Rome's eagerness for reunion comes in the form an invitation—'Return to Mother Church.' " Nearly three decades later, in 1985 at the Extraordinary Synod in Rome, Jan Cardinal Willebrands, head of the Secretariat for Christian Unity, declared, " 'Return' is not a word in our ecumenical vocabulary."

But in 1959, even assuming the best of goodwill on all sides, the "riddles" of Rome posed awesome obstacles to reconciliation. It was hard, if not impossible, to see how Rome could modify its exclusivist claims to being alone the Church of Christ, or its imperial claims over all matters spiritual and temporal. The last point touches on the critical question of religious freedom and Rome's view that "error has no rights." In that official way of thinking, other churches and religions were to be tolerated reluctantly and as a matter of necessity in those situations, such as in the United States, where the government could not be induced to support the true faith. This position, too, was dramatically changed by the Council, notably in the "Declaration on Religious Freedom."

Another Roman riddle that appeared to be an insurmountable barrier was a Mariology that was "out of control." Pelikan wrote, "More and more, the attributes ascribed to her seem closer to those of Christ than to those of common mortals. She was conceived in a special way, she performs miracles, she intercedes for us, she was assumed into heaven. All that is needed yet is to say that she is co-mediatress and co-redemptress with Christ. That, apparently, is not very far off." And surely Pelikan was right, for it seemed that Rome was caught in a process of elevating Mary to the point where she increasingly competed with, and even threatened to displace, Christ in popular teaching and piety. But, again, the Council supplied the corrective. Efforts to issue a separate document on Mary were successfully resisted. Her role in the economy of salvation was rightly situated in what the Council had to say about the Church (*Lumen Gentium*). This does not mean that Mary is neglected in Roman Catholicism, as in fact she is sorely neglected in most Protestant piety. The present pope, John Paul II, is emphatic in his devotion to Mary, but that devotion is carefully articulated. She is presented not as a goddess alongside or above the God-Man, but as the model of the Church's faith-filled response to the saving work of God in Christ.

4. TEMPTATION TO IDOLATRY

The many riddles of Roman Catholicism finally came down to Rome's willingness to baptize anything and everything, so long as the authority of the church structure itself is not challenged. Father Carl Peter, a theologian at Catholic University, puts it this way: "The temptation of Protestantism is to blasphemy; the temptation of Roman Catholicism is to idolatry." Protestantism, so insistent upon the worship owed to God alone, tends to neglect or despise the holy that is less than the Absolute. Roman Catholicism, so sensitive to the myriad manifestations of the sacred, tends to worship the holy that is less than God. That temptation is most lethally triumphant when human holiness is elevated to the point that it competes with, or even displaces, the absolute grace of God in the work of salvation. This was the critical argument in what Pelikan calls "the tragic necessity" of the Reformation. The Reformation was tragic because it occasioned the further division of the Church; it was necessary because the truth had to be declared that finally it is the Gospel of God's saving grace that creates the Church, not the Church that creates or controls the Gospel.

Pelikan believed that the continued existence of the Reformation churches is necessary because Rome had not really heard the Reformation message. Thirty years later it is still very much a question whether Rome has really heard and is really proclaiming the word of God's justifying of the godless, of salvation by "grace alone" and by "faith alone." There are, of course, encouraging signs. In the 1980s, for example, the official Lutheran-Roman Catholic dialogue produced *Justification by Faith* (1985), a remarkable convergence document on the core argument of the

Reformation. Similar convergences have occurred in dialogue between Roman Catholics and Anglicans. But the understanding reached in these dialogues has yet to be "received" (the somewhat technical term in ecumenism) or internalized by either church. Some Lutherans, for example, are unhappy with the dialogue's statement because they believe it portrays "justification by faith" as but one legitimate way of understanding the Gospel, rather than as *the* understanding of the Gospel that must be normative for the entirety of the Church's teaching and life.

The claim that reunion depends upon Rome's acknowledging that "justification by faith" (or, as some prefer, justification by grace through faith) is the controlling norm or rule for everything else may constitute an upping of the ante on the part of the heirs of the Reformation. For example, in subscribing to the Smalcald Articles, a key confessional statement of the Reformation, Philip Melanchthon, Luther's closest aide, wrote: "Concerning the pope I hold that, if he would allow the Gospel, we too may concede to him that superiority over the bishops which he possesses by human right, making this concession for the sake of peace and general unity among the Christians who are now under him and who may be in the future." The great good news in the latter part of the twentieth century is that the pope certainly "allows" the Gospel. In the opinion of many, he not only allows it but proclaims it with as much force as any Christian leader of our time.

Pelikan wrote that "we Protestants must discover what made the Reformation possible, while Roman Catholics must discover what made the Reformation necessary." What made the Reformation possible was the catholic substance of the pre-Reformation centuries that all share. What made the Reformation necessary was the eclipse of the Gospel of unqualified grace, which gives saving form to that substance and prevents it from becoming an undifferentiated accretion of religiosity. The alternative to both Protestant and Roman Catholic distortions is an embracing evangelical catholicity that neither blasphemes against the myriad appearances of the holy nor equates any such appearance with the Holy One. Three decades ago Pelikan hoped that the witness of Roman Catholicism would provoke Protestantism into reappropriating the catholic substance, and argued that Protestantism had in fact provoked Roman Catholicism into reforms much more than Rome was prepared to admit. "If Protestants and Roman Catholics ever recognized their mutual needs and their mutual debts," Pelikan wrote, "they might develop a concern for the total church and an awareness of the consequences of their actions for the total church of Christ."

More than two decades after the Second Vatican Council, what Pelikan envisioned has to a very large extent happened. Ecclesial communion, the actual reunion of churches, is still a goal, perhaps a distant goal. But there is, especially in America, a growing awareness of what Pelikan called "the total church." A taken-for-granted Protestant America no longer looks upon Roman Catholicism as a riddle, an alien body to be viewed with curiosity or alarm. And Roman Catholicism no longer sees America simply as a country riddled by heresies and in need of conversion to the true church. Skeptics in the several worlds of Protestantism and of Roman Catholicism may think this change is not all to the good. At what price, they ask, have the old tensions been relaxed? There is a connection between tension and truth, they correctly note, and perhaps tension has decreased because truth has been subordinated to a style of tolerance that is in fact indifference to the importantly different ways of understanding the Christian reality. Such skepticism is not unwarranted. At the same time, however, those who are serious about Christian existence in the world are increasingly asking the relevant questions in a way that encompasses the entire Church. And that is a welcome advance. Admittedly, this advance that is to be welcomed may have been brought about in large part by unwelcome developments that have forced all Christians and all churches to recognize the precariousness of Christian existence in this kind of world.

In speaking about Roman Catholicism today, we are not talking about "them" but about "us." At least that is true with respect to the questions of most immediate concern in this study. Beyond the riddle of Roman Catholicism is the examination of how the Roman Catholic Church, as the premier church among the churches, is pointing the way toward a new understanding of the Church in the world. And here we are returned to the matter of paradox. The image of "Church and world in paradox" is drawn from H. Richard Niebuhr's influential study, *Christ and Culture* (1951). In his survey of Christian history, Niebuhr argued that "paradox" is one of the five major models or "types" by which Christian have understood the relationship between Christ and culture. Scholars have been arguing about the accuracy of Niebuhr's "types" almost since the day the book was published, but the very liveliness of the argument is evidence of the usefulness of the models he proposes. In the remainder of this first section, we look briefly at the models proposed by Niebuhr and then ask whether there is reason to believe that the Roman Catholic Church may be moving toward an understanding of itself, and of "the total Church," as "Church and world in paradox."

5. CHURCH AND WORLD IN PARADOX

A note on terminology is in order. H. Richard Niebuhr spoke of "Christ and culture," whereas we are speaking of "Church and world." A pleasing alliteration may have had something to do with his choice of terms. How Christ is related to anything and everything, however, is a subject considerably larger than "Church and world." Of course Christ and his Church cannot be separated, since the Church is his Body. But neither can Christ and Church be equated. A doctrine of the Church that says that the Church *is* Christ is a doctrine of the Church so "high" as to be heretical. Also, as Vatican II made clear, the Church is not exhaustively any one church. It is not true to say, for instance, that the Church *is* the Roman Catholic Church. As Christ is more than the Church, although the Church participates in Christ, so the Church is more than any church, although such a church participates in the Church, some churches no doubt more than others. In encountering the Church, we encounter Christ; in encountering a church, we encounter the Church and therefore encounter Christ. But the interpenetration between these realities does not destroy the distinctions between Christ, Church, and church. In sum, our subject is how to think of the relationship between the Church—as actually expressed in the life of the churches—and the world. On the use of "world" rather than "culture," suffice it that "world" is more comprehensive. In saying this, we do not deny that culture—meaning the ideas, customs, and traditions by which we order our lives together—may be the most important thing about the world.

The five types suggested by H. Richard Niebuhr are these: the Church against the world, the Church of the world, the Church above the world, the Church and world in paradox, and the Church as the transformer of the world. There is considerable truth in each of these types, and, because they are only "ideal types," it is understood that they are often intermixed in historical fact. Almost no church or Christian theological tradition is "purely" one type or another, although some are more purely one type than are others. But, for the most part, when we consider a particular church or tradition, it is a matter of saying that it is, on balance, more like this type than like another type. Not surprisingly, within a church as large and various as the Roman Catholic Church, we find all five types and variations on each; and some of the variations may even lay claim to being additional types in their own right.

The Church against the world is sometimes called the "sectarian" model. It is also evident in monasticism, however. Here the sharpest possible distinction is drawn between Church and world. The logic is sometimes expressed in the command, "Come out from among them and be ye separate." Here a high premium is placed upon purity and particularity. As we have mentioned, the "Radical Reformation" produced communities of this type, such as the Hutterites and Mennonites known to most Americans. And, as also mentioned earlier, some converts to Roman Catholicism resort to that church as a refuge from the modern world. A sect may be very big, very grand, and very old, but it is still a sect. A sectarian way of thought was sometimes evident in Roman Catholic claims that the church is a "perfect society" surrounded by the manifestly imperfect societies of the world. Today the sectarian option is proposed by some Roman Catholics, even Roman Catholic bishops, of a pacifist persuasion who contend that the church should be a "peace church," perhaps on the model of the original Quakers. Sectarianism of all forms generally gets a bad press. It is frequently accused of being "escapist," of abandoning Christian responsibility for worldly tasks, of refusing to risk the moral ambiguities involved in those tasks. It is also accused of being exclusivist, the opposite of catholic. It establishes "purity tests" for membership and thus encourages self-righteous pretensions of moral superiority. Or so the charge reads.

And yet all serious Christians must, at different times and in different ways, be attracted to the model of the "Church against the world." In fact there is an inescapable "againstness" built into Christian existence. Those who are not strongly against anything are not strongly for anything. That might seem to be an obvious truth, but Christians are ever in need of being recalled to it. Jesus gave definition to his community by antinomies of light and darkness, sheep and wolves, love and hatred; such are the contraries that are not to be resolved but contended for. Those who say Jesus is Lord must at the same time say that neither Caesar nor anyone else or anything else is Lord. Richard Niebuhr, who was critical of the "Church against the world" model, nonetheless contributed to an important volume in the 1930s that was titled *The Church Against the World*. The 1975 ecumenical "Hartford Appeal for Theological Affirmation" produced a volume similarly titled *Against the World for the World*. The latter captures the *sic et non* quality of Christian existence.

Contemporary thinkers such as the Methodist theologian Stanley Hauerwas argue that the Church makes its greatest contribution to the world precisely when it most clearly distinguishes itself from the world. Thomas More was not being ironic when at the block he declared himself the king's good servant. Precisely in being God's servant first he served the king best. It is not surprising that the king, representing the world, did not appreciate the truth of that. Thus also to flaunt what Walker Percy calls the preposterousness of the faith can be a loving provocation that invites the world to question its unexamined presuppositions. Thus also a Mother Teresa's doing of her "beautiful thing for God" is an explosive assertion of "againstness" with respect to prevailing notions of the beautiful life. Indeed, the entire tradition and idea of sainthood is pervaded by a saving negativity toward the world. It is a negativity logically derived from an intense realization of the way God intends the world to be and the way the world is not. Thus the most rigorous withdrawal from the world can be *for* the world. It is a dull and uninteresting worldliness of mind that claims, for example, that a contemplative order of Carmelite sisters is "escaping from reality" in devoting itself to prayer for suffering humanity. One does not need to watch the evening news to know who and what needs praying for. The model of the "Church against the world" must constantly be present in thought and erupting in practice if Christians are to be kept alert to the truth that our contribution to the right ordering of the world begins with the right ordering of our lives in that part of the world that is the Church.

A second "type" of Church/world connection is the *Church of the world*. Such a formulation would seem to be illegitimate on the face of it. After all, we know that we Christians are to be "in but not of" the world. And yet we are told that "God so loved *the world* that he gave his beloved Son," and surely we ought to emulate God's love for the world. Or again, "God was in Christ reconciling *the world* to himself." The Eastern churches most intensively, but the Western ones as well, emphasize the cosmic dimensions of redemption. The biblical vision includes not only the salvation of individuals or of the community of faith, but proposes an entire creation yearning for its fulfillment. As Saint Paul writes, "The creation itself will be set free from its bondage to decay and obtain the glorious liberty of the children of God (Romans 8)." There is in Christian history a venerable strain of devotion to the world that translates into devotion to particular parts and periods of "the world."

For example, Eusebius, the "father of church history," espied a wondrous convergence between the rule of the Emperor Constantine and God's redemptive purposes in history. As a subway graffito near Columbia University puts it, "God loves Constantine." Nineteenth-century liberal theology frequently promoted a "culture Protestantism" in which religion was to be placed at the service of the best in the evolution of society. So also the Protestant social gospel movement in this country envisioned "the Americanization of Christianity and the Christianization of America" as the stirring goal of reform. Reading "the signs of the times," liberation theologians today argue that the mission of the Church is to "get on the right side of the revolution." As we shall see, Vatican Council II undeniably gave a great boost to this way of thinking with its somewhat roseate reading of the modern age. The great thing, the redemptive thing, is happening in the world, and the Church must get with it. In vulgarized forms this led to much talk about "the secular city" in which "man come of age" would direct religion to do its duty by going out of business. A religion truly devoted to the human project would result, it was said, in "religionless Christianity." All dissonance between Church and world would be overcome, and the authenticity of religion would be proven by the absence of religion.

In truth, it would be the greatest disservice to humanity for the Church to go out of business, for the Church is that part of humanity that bears witness to the truth about humanity, that truth being Christ. According to the Scriptures, he is the new humanity, and therefore the Church is never so radically "of the world" as when it is gathered in response to him, the Word in whom and through whom the world has its being. The problem with the model of the "Church of the world" is that it so easily falls prey to letting the world define itself apart from Christ. The crucial issue is finally not one of how we posture ourselves in relation to the world; the crucial issue is, What is the truth about the world? The world does set the Church's agenda in that we are called to live in loving response to the needs of the world. Such needs seem nearly infinite, including everything from the search for peace and justice to the care of the sick and the elevation of culture. But the greatest need of the world is to know and believe the truth about itself. In bearing witness to him who is both the truth about God and the truth about the world, the Church exposes the world's delusions and directs it to a destiny that it would not have dreamed to think of as its own.

Of the five he proposes, Richard Niebuhr's favored model is that of *Christ the transformer of culture.* That the Church should transform the world is an idea that is bound to create uneasiness among many contemporary Roman Catholic thinkers. It smacks of a "triumphalism" that was presumably discarded with Vatican II. At the same time, the transformation model has a powerful hold among many progressive Catholics today, whether they promote a reformist or revolutionary course of transformation. More than one observer has noted that among some Roman Catholics who most deride the old triumphalism, there is a new triumphalism. The old triumphalism of the Right, it is said, has become the new triumphalism of the Left. In the new triumphalism, however, the goal is not that the Church as an institution should dominate society; the goal, rather, is the establishment of a Just Social Order. In that New Order, which is the work of God, the Church itself may well be subordinated. Some say it will disappear altogether as an institution because in a truly just society there will be no reason for the transcendent longings to which the institutions of religion now minister.

This view has radical implications for ecclesiology, the way we think about the Church. Now the forces that are actually transforming society become the new Church, so to speak, replacing what used to be called the Church. What used to be thought of as the Church is now dismissively referred to as the "official church" or "institutional church." In other words, it used to be thought that the Church is in some singular manner the agency of God's saving work in history. Now it is claimed by some that the forces of social transformation are that agency. Until those forces have completed their mission, the Church has a provisional role in providing a "revolutionary hermeneutics" or interpretative framework by which we are helped to understand what God is doing apart from the Church and, if need be, against the Church. Elements of the "religionless Christianity" approach are to be discovered here, combined with a version of "the Church against the world," except the latter now appears as the Church of worldly transformation (the authentic Church) against the church (the institutional church). Aside from being confusing, which they admittedly are, these permutations remind us that none of the types proposed by Niebuhr appear in a pure and uncomplicated form.

Niebuhr's idea of the Church transforming the world was not of the variety sketched above, a variety commonly set forth by those who, as they say, "do theology employing Marxist analysis." And yet it would seem that his transforming model is susceptible to that interpretation, which he would surely deplore as a distortion of what he was intending to say. But upon closer examination, it is not clear that "Christ the transformer of culture" is all that different from the "Christ of culture." The difficulties with the transformation model have to do with both direction and verification. The model would seem to assume that there is a known direction in which culture, or the world, should be moving. It is far from evident that this is the case.

In addition, it is far from evident that the direction of history assumed by Niebuhr is defined by any truth distinctively related to Christ and the Church. If this criticism has merit, it would then seem that Christ and the Church are turned into a motor force for historical dynamics that may not be consonant with, and may indeed be opposed to, a Christian understanding of history and its *telos*, or destiny. Moreover, there is the problem of verification. If, in historical fact, Christ and Church do not transform culture at all, or do not transform it in the manner prescribed, does that mean they are not "true" in some important sense of the term? The transformation model provides little support for an understanding of the Church in historical distress, persecuted, driven, and marginalized, yet gathered by twos and threes in his name, to whom he appears with the promise, "Fear not, little flock, it is my Father's good pleasure to give to you the kingdom." Niebuhr's transformation model hinges upon a "redeemability of the world" that is quite different from the manner in which the world has been redeemed by the cross and Resurrection of Christ. Ultimately, eschatologically, in the promised End Time, the truth of the Gospel will be vindicated and the world redeemed in a manner that all will be compelled to acknowledge. At least that is what Christians assert. But until then, the life and witness of the Church is, in relation to the world, a life and witness of paradox directed toward a promise.

6. THE PROVISIONALITY OF IT ALL

Niebuhr's fourth type is that of *Christ above culture, Church above world.* Here the foremost example is Thomas Aquinas and his formative influence on a Roman Catholic way of thinking aimed at "synthesizing" Christ and culture, Church and world, faith and reason, grace and nature. We pass over this model quickly for the moment, since we will be returning to it. It is a type that, seen and described so often in the same way, has become a stereotype. The stereotype of Thomism is sharply antithetical to, totally incompatible with, the paradoxical model that is here being proposed. Thomism is often depicted as being deadeningly smooth, flattening, static, and rationalistic. The paradoxical model of Church and world, on the other hand, is depicted as being maddeningly spontaneous, existential, arbitrary, and finally incomprehensible. As is the way with stereotypes, there is a degree of justice in both of these. And a greater degree of injustice.

With some hesitation, Niebuhr calls *the paradoxical model* "dualism." He thinks there must be a better word for it, and there is. The better word is *paradox*. From among the major thinkers in Christian history, Niebuhr sees paradox as the controlling paradigm in Paul, in Marcion, to a lesser degree in Augustine, and above all in Luther. (In a later and, he believes, debased form, it appears in Kierkegaard's individualistic existentialism.) In this way of thinking about Christian existence, the Christian lives, as it were, in different worlds, different realities. Nature, reason, law, culture—all these mean one thing in relation to one reality, and quite another in relation to another. For example, if the reality under discussion is the question of how we are justified or declared righteous before God, then nature, reason, and human achievements are utterly useless. They are worse than useless, since their claims can only serve to obscure and deny the utterly gratuitous gift of Christ's righteousness. Here we are justified by faith alone, and faith itself is the gift of God.

Our limited suggestion at this point is that paradox as it relates to the core question of justification has its analogies in how we think about the Church in the world. Niebuhr describes the style, the "feel," of the life of paradox. The person living such a life, he says,

is standing on the side of man in the encounter with God, yet seeks to interpret the Word of God which he has heard coming from the other side. In this tension he must speak of revelation and reason, of law and grace, of the Creator and Redeemer. Not only his speech is paradoxical under these circumstances, but his conduct also. He is under law, and yet not under law but grace; he is sinner, and yet righteous; he believes, as a doubter; he has assurance of salvation, yet walks along the knife-edge of insecurity. In Christ all things have become new, and yet everything remains as it was from the beginning. God has revealed Himself in Christ, but hidden Himself in His revelation; the believer knows the One in whom he has believed, yet walks by faith, not sight.

The person living in such a situation can easily become a paradox-monger, a multiplier of paradoxes for the sheer maddening delight of the thing. In the face of that temptation, we should remember that the only paradox to be trusted is the paradox that cannot be honestly escaped. As before God we say that we are at the same time both righteous and sinner *(simul iustus et peccator),* so we say of the Church that it is both spotless Bride of Christ and shameless streetwalker. We have God's own word on the first part of each of those propositions and massive empirical evidence in support of the second. It is not a question of one being true and the other false, or even of one being "more true" than the other. If we try to cover up or belittle the second truth that we do not like, we betray our lack of confidence in the word that supports the first truth. We are then implicitly suggesting that God's word cannot bear the weight of evidence.

It is not adequate to say that paradox is produced by the conflict between faith and reason. It is not as though we "know" some things by faith and other things by reason and, when these things appear to be contradictory, we hold them together in paradoxical existence. It is rather that, in all the reasonable ways of knowing that we possess, things do not hold together, they do not jibe. The saving purposes of God in Christ, we can agree with Thomas, are not contrary to right reason, although reason could not attain such truth if God had not revealed it. But the same saving purposes, we can agree with Paul and Augustine and Luther, are contrary to the unright, and unrighteous, reason that is endemic to fallen humanity. It is false to say that Luther, for instance, despised human reason. As many scholars have pointed out, Luther recognized reason as a mark of man's being the crown of creation. True, he called reason a whore. And so it is, because it so habitually directs itself and sells itself to something other than its proper end, which is God. Augustine and indeed Thomas said as much. Luther's was but an extension and deepening of Paul's understanding of the startling contrast between the "wisdom" of man and the "foolishness" of God.

The model of "paradox" has promising ecumenical possibilities today and is not so locked into the conflict between traditions as Richard Niebuhr seemed to believe. The paradox that is inescapable is not the product of conflicts between nature and grace or between revelation and reason. Paradox is not irrational. Paradox, rather, is the product of careful and relentless reason; we arrive at the paradoxical situation when we discover that the things that we think we know do not fit together. Truths that, as rational beings, we are convinced are true do not jibe. Between them are tensions and apparent contradictions. We cannot in intellectual conscience, we cannot in good faith, trim the truths in order to produce a cognitive consonance that denies the dissonance between pieces of what we think we know.

Put differently, escapable paradox is the product of faulty reasoning. Inescapable paradox is the result of the incompleteness of the world in which we reason. That is why it is said that paradox is directed toward promise. It is one of the greatest obligations of the Church to remind the world that it is incomplete, that reality is still awaiting something. The something for which the creation waits, for which it longs, is in biblical language the Kingdom of God. The Church is that part of the creation that anticipates the future of the entire creation. In anticipating that future by faith, in speaking and acting now on the basis of what is to be, the Church actually participates in that future. Actually, but still partially, for the Church is still part of the longing creation; it is the part of the creation in which the longing is intensified to its highest pitch as we cry, "Maranatha! Come, Lord Jesus!" Christian faith is, in this light, not the satisfying answer but heightened dissatisfaction with all available answers. The explanatory force of Christianity is evidenced in its making sense of our dissatisfaction with all explanations.

Church and world in paradox, then, is not a model chosen by us but an acknowledgement of a situation forced upon us. It is not a matter of our preference but of our provisional moment so far short of the Consummation. Christian existence is marked by "in-betweenness," for we live "between the times" of what is and what is to be, convinced that what is to be has already happened in the Christ event and is awaiting its fulfillment in universal history. Such a Christian existence is inescapably paradoxical. And it should be lived unapologetically, even boldly, but we must never succumb to the love of paradox for the sake of paradox. We should, for instance, press the work of "synthesis" between dissonant truths as far as we possibly can. And here Protestants have a particular responsibility to critically retrieve and resume ambitious synthesizing projects such as that represented by Thomas Aquinas. We have an intellectual duty to do so, which is to say we have a duty to the truth that is in all truths. It is the same duty that forbids us to trim truths in order to force truths into a false fit.

All the models or types mentioned above, and others that might be devised, come into play with the "Church and world in paradox." The Church is at points against the world, but always for the world. It is above the world by its participation in the transcendent, and it is ahead of the world by its anticipation of a future time, yet it is always of the world. And it is transformer of the world, not merely by providing spiritual energy for existing goals of change but, most importantly, by reminding the world of its incompleteness, by preventing prideful or despairing acts of premature closure, by keeping the world open to the promised transformation that is the destiny of Church and world alike. Authentic paradox is not like a riddle or puzzle that can be solved by greater understanding or the application of more careful reasoning. Authentic paradox, the paradox of the Church in the world, cannot be solved; it can only be superseded. It will be superseded, we have reason to believe, by the fulfillment of the promise, by the coming of the Kingdom.

7. JOHN PAUL AND THE NEW ADVENT

We have moved, then, from the riddle of *their* existence as Roman Catholics in a divided Christianity to the paradox of *our* existence as Christians in the modern world. That movement is not of much importance, however, if it is no more than a movement of ideas within these pages. The question is whether there is such a movement within the life and self-understanding of the churches. If there is, there are further questions: Does such a movement hold ecumenical possibilities for the churches in their relationships to one another? Does it have the potential of strengthening their shared apostolate as Church in the world? This writer believes that all these questions can be answered in the affirmative. We have already touched on the ecumenical transformations that have turned questions about Roman Catholicism and "them" into questions about Christian existence and "us." In addition, the thinking of the Roman Catholic Church about itself is not only compatible with, but calls for, a new appreciation of paradox. In this connection, Father Avery Dulles's masterful *Models of the Church* (1974) can readily be translated into "models of the Church in the world."

Dulles affirms the way in which his church at Vatican II recovered the themes of eschatology, promise, and provisionality in thinking about the Church. During the Counter-Reformation era, the dominant notion of the Church, hammered home at every opportunity, was that of the authoritative institution. It was a church that presented itself as a refuge from change, and as such it had a distinct appeal for those who liked the idea of papal bulls with breakfast. A more historical understanding of the Church, however, does not necessarily mean that the Church is conceived in more this-worldly terms, with a consequent loss of transcendence. On the contrary, the Council's "Constitution on the Church" *(Lumen Gentium)* devotes an entire chapter to "The Eschatological Nature of the Pilgrim Church and Her Union with the Heavenly Church." According to Dulles, the idea of the heavenly Church had been almost entirely neglected since the late Middle Ages, so eager was the church institution to establish its claims in the here and now. At this point, as at other points still to be examined, there are intriguing parallels between the pre-Vatican II church of the Counter-Reformation and varieties of "political theology" current in Roman Catholicism today.

The Council's renewed understanding of the Church in historical terms was protected from a loss of transcendence because of its recovered focus on the *telos* of history, the Church in the glory of the Kingdom. The Church is everything that it appears to be in history, and much more. It is both the Church militant *(ecclesia militans)* here in time and the Church triumphant *(ecclesia triumphans)* in glory. As Augustine viewed the Church on earth as the lesser and inferior part of the Church, so we too can see the Church as a pilgrim community on pilgrimage to what it truly is. We say "truly is" and not simply "truly will be," for all things most truly are their "end in the process of becoming." Only in this light may believers say such extravagant (preposterous?) things about the Church. Said now, such statements are paradoxical, but it is paradox that will be superseded and vindicated in the fulfillment of the promise at the conclusion of the pilgrimage.

Dulles sees significant ecumenical convergence in such an understanding of the Church and cites a 1961 statement of the World Council of Churches that speaks of "the Pilgrim Church, which goes forth boldly as Abraham did into the unknown future, not afraid to leave behind the securities of its conventional structure, glad to dwell in the tent of perpetual adaptation, looking to the city whose builder and maker is God." In this pilgrim model of the Church, all depends upon our eyes being fixed upon that transcendent city. It is not a city that is beyond this world or beyond history but is, in ways beyond our understanding, the fulfillment of all that is and has been. If our eyes are not so fixed, "perpetual adaptation" inevitably becomes the perpetual conformation to the world against which Paul warned in Romans 12. Apart from that transcendent destiny, the extravagant things said about the Church are not paradoxical but simply prideful, self-serving, and finally ridiculous.

It remains for this chapter to examine briefly whether in fact the model of "Church and world in paradox" is at work in Roman Catholic self-understanding today. To be sure, Roman Catholicism is so various, also theologically, that almost any idea can be found at work somewhere within its commodious borders. So it is useful at this point to stay with theologians who are definitely not mavericks, who may even be viewed as establishment theologians. Karol Wojtyla and Joseph Ratzinger, for examples. Wojtyla, of course, is better known as Pope John Paul II, and Cardinal Ratzinger is head of the Congregation for the Doctrine of the Faith, an office that has the difficult task of directing the theological border patrol, so to speak, of the Roman Catholic Church.

In his first encyclical, *Redemptor Hominis* ("The Redeemer of Man," 1979), John Paul pondered the end of the second millennium and looked toward a "new advent" of the Church in a world yearning for its fulfillment. He cites Romans 8 and its words about the world being "subjected to futility" and observes the curious and ominous fact that there seems to be a connection between man's progressive "dominion over the world" and that deeper subjection to futility. "The world of the new age, the world of space flights, the world of the previously unattained conquests of science and technology—is it not also the world 'groaning in travail' that 'waits with eager longing for the revealing of the sons of God'?" John Paul rejects a smooth culture-Christianity that suggests a neat synthesis of forces portending a happy outcome. Rather, hope is derived from the surprise of the Gospel, which, in Christ, reveals man to himself in a manner contrary to appearance and expectation. "In reality, the name for that deep amazement at man's worth and dignity is the Gospel, that is to say, the good news. This amazement determines the Church's mission in the world and, perhaps even more so, 'in the modern world.'"

Already in this first encyclical, John Paul cautions against our being taken in by lesser amazements than the amazement of the Gospel. More particularly, quoting Vatican II, he cautions against the enticing amazements of the political. "The Church must in no way be confused with the political community, nor bound to any political system. She is at once a sign and a safeguard of the transcendence of the human person." That transcendence is derived from the "mystery" of the Christ in whom every human being participates by virtue of being "called and destined for grace and glory." All of humankind "has become a sharer in Jesus Christ, the mystery in which each one of the four billion human beings living on our planet has become a sharer from the moment he is conceived beneath the heart of his mother." It is of that amazing truth that the Church is "sign and safeguard."

As sharers in Christ we share in his kingship, a kingship that is expressed in servanthood, the servanthood of the cross. John Paul's paradoxical assertion that "being a king is truly possible only by being a servant" is reminiscent, of course, of Luther's similar statement that the Christian is lord of all and servant of none, and, at the same time, he is servant of all and lord of none. This is not paradox for the sake of paradox. Rather, each factor requires the other. Being a servant, says John Paul, requires such self-mastery and spiritual maturity that it must be described as "being a king." And to be a king, in the model of Christ the King, is demonstrated and fulfilled in being a servant.

The oddity of Christian truth that upsets the applecart of conventional wisdoms seems to have a special attraction for John Paul. It is conventionally thought, for example, that religion is either anthropocentric, focused upon man, or theocentric, focused upon God. Not so, says John Paul in the encyclical *Dives in Misericordia* ("Rich in Mercy," 1980). "The more the Church's mission is centered upon man, the more it must be confirmed and actualized theocentrically, that is to say, be directed in Jesus Christ to the Father. While the various currents of human thought both in the past and at the present have tended and still tend to separate theocentrism and anthropocentrism, and even to set them in opposition to each other, the Church, following Christ, seeks to link them up in human history in a deep and organic way." This, he suggests somewhat boldly, may be the "most important" principle of the Second Vatican Council. While some theologies tend to collapse anthropocentrism into theocentrism, and others collapse theocentrism into anthropocentrism, thus forcing a choice between the two, John Paul insists that both can and must be asserted simultaneously in a Christocentrism that finds *the* center in the God-Man Jesus the Christ. The mystery of Christ's own being is the ultimate paradox by which the Church lives and speaks hope to the world.

Because that paradox is historically grounded in cross and resurrection, it is possible for the Church to live and speak hope in the face of death. John Paul, like his predecessor Paul VI, is frequently depicted as being dour and gloomy in his assessment of the modern world. In fact, he sometimes seems almost naively optimistic in his statements about the possibilities of social, political, and economic change for the better. He appears at times to temper his more buoyant assessments of human possibility primarily for theological rather than temperamental reasons, lest people be tempted to place in themselves the trust that is rightly placed in the "mystery" of the promise. This is dramatically stated in *Dives* where he urges that finally we must "call upon the God who cannot despise anything that he has made, the God who is faithful to himself, to his Fatherhood and his love." Far from relying upon the assumption that things will necessarily change for the better, the Church must live and speak a hope that is convincing "even if in the world evil should prevail over goodness, even if contemporary humanity should deserve a new 'flood' on account of its sins, as once the generation of Noah did."

In the conclusion of this encyclical, John Paul is carried by paradox to doxology. No matter what, it "is not permissible" for the Church "for any reason to withdraw into herself." The very "reason for her existence" is to assert the mystery and the promise even in the face of every evidence to the contrary. "No matter how strong the resistance of human history may be, no matter how marked the diversity of contemporary civilization, no matter how great the denial of God in the human world, so much the greater must be the Church's closeness to that mystery which, hidden for centuries in God, was then truly shared with man, in time, through Jesus Christ." In that adamant fidelity, the Church is doing nothing less than "revealing God" by holding up to the world the Christ in whom God has made himself visible.

The Pope seems almost to exult in contradictions. In a 1984 "apostolic exhortation" to men and women in religious orders (*Redemptionis Donum*), he even touches on such apparent trivia as the wearing of clothes that signify religious consecration. It is not the dress that matters in itself; what matters is that the world be confronted by the consecration and by the contrast between that radical devotion and the ways of the world. This is not said to condemn the world but to call "people of the world" to their own unrealized potential for consecration. The contrast is a "contradiction," and that contradiction should be flaunted, so to speak. It is as though the world needs even to be taunted, albeit tenderly taunted, and, in so taunting the world, religious consecration provides "an unceasing stimulus of salvific renewal."

We will have occasion to consider the theological and philosophical formation of Karol Wojtyla, a formation that he brought with him to the papacy. There are so many tasks involved in being pope that it is easy to overlook what should be obvious, namely, that this pope understands himself to be a "man of ideas," an intellectual. Ideas, words, language— to this pope these seem to matter with a striking sense of urgency. The ideas, the words, must be said again and again, in defiance of every hint of ideological or structural determinism. Finally, words, the Word, this is all the Church has in the confrontation with the "principalities and powers." At the risk of stretching a point, and without presuming to understand the childhood formation of Karol Wojtyla, this writer is impressed by Robert Coles's study of Polish children in *The Political Life of Children* (1986). That John Paul is Polish is hardly incidental, although too much is sometimes made of the fact by those who want to dismiss his positions in a reductionist way. (Even after all that has happened in recent years, Polish jokes die hard.) But the thing that struck Coles most forcefully is that nowhere in the world—not even in South Africa among blacks—had he encountered such "fierce, intransigent estrangement" from the government of their country as he encountered among Polish children. For a people historically oppressed by Germans on the one side and Russians on the other, language becomes everything, and it is the language of the Church. Simply to speak is to sustain hope, to keep open a possibility beyond plausibilities.

Josef, thirteen years old, tells Coles: "We've been a big country once, and we've had to keep the Russians out, and it was always hard. But we prayed and fought—that's what you have to do. And we talked! My grandmother always tells us to remember that every time we open our mouths to say something, we're telling the Russians we're *Polish,* and the Germans, and anyone who's listening. It's *our* language, not theirs." Again, it may be stretching a point, but Josef's sensibility would seem not too different from that of John Paul. Except of course, beyond Poland, the Pope is speaking of the "country" of the Church and its own language that must be "talked" in words and symbols, despite everything to the contrary. And if the result is paradox, so be it. One might stretch the point a little further and note that this is a sense of the power of words— some might carpingly say "the magic of words"—combined with nationalism and religion that strongly marked Luther. If the analogy suggested has any merit, it is not untouched by this irony: that the bishop of Rome, shaped in part by the hostility between Poland and Germany, should share with the German Reformer an understanding of the connections between historical placement, words, and the Word that was once set forth in resistance to the Bishop of Rome.

But that is an aside that could not be explored systematically without an intimate knowledge of the mind of Karol Wojtyla. Indeed, John Paul might well be embarrassed were he to discover that a Lutheran writer intuits such a similarity between him and the Reformer. Or he might welcome it as one of those happy ecumenical convergences that could never have been charted by human calculation. In any event, supporting evidence for the intuition can readily be drawn from his writings before he became Pope, and from his much writing and speaking as Pope. (So much writing and so much speaking. "This pope is drowning us in words," complains a high Vatican official. "And we talked!" says young Josef to Robert Coles.) What is more than intuition, what is evident beyond doubt, is that to this Pope mere words are not mere. "The word shall not return empty," says the prophet Isaiah. That is sometimes taken to be a counsel of consolation for unsuccessful communicators. It is in fact a word of vibrant faith. It would seem to be the faith of this Pope that the words must be said again and again, even if they do not seem to be effective, even if their practical implications may be unclear, even if they just stand there in stark and embarrassing contrast to the way things seem to be.

A 1984 "apostolic letter" on the meaning of suffering *(Salvifici Doloris)* decisively puts aside any effort to "explain" suffering and evil in the manner of conventional theodicies. Suffering and evil can only be addressed in a "strictly evangelical" manner and "by reference to the cross and resurrection." "The Gospel paradox of weakness and strength often speaks to us from the pages of the letters of St. Paul, a paradox particularly experienced by the apostle himself and together with him experienced by all who share Christ's sufferings." John Paul cites Saint Paul: "I will all the more gladly boast of my weaknesses, that the power of Christ may rest upon me." The "scandal" that should catch our attention is not that I, or humanity in general, should be subjected to suffering. The scandal to which the Church directs attention is the cross of Christ, and the answering word of the Resurrection.

8. O FELIX CULPA

John Paul returns to this motif in his fifth encyclical, "The Holy Spirit in Church and World" *(Dominum et Vivificantem,* 1986). ("Pope Extols Holy Spirit," declared the heading of the story in the *New York Times.*) At the very heart of the Trinity, which heart is love, is paradox, writes the pope. "Thus there is a paradoxical mystery of love: In Christ there suffers a God who has been rejected by his own creature . . . but at the same time, from the depth of this suffering—and indirectly from the depth of the very sin of [our] not having believed—the Spirit draws a new measure of the gift made to man and to creation from the beginning." The encyclical includes the vision of the third millennium as both "judgment" and "new advent," a recurring vision that combines warning and promise. And here again, as so frequently in his writing, John Paul lifts up the exquisite paradox of the "felix culpa," the "happy fault" of humanity's fall. It is from the familiar exclamation in the liturgy of the Easter Vigil: *"O felix culpa, quae talem ac tantum meruit habere Redemptorem,* O happy fault which has deserved so great a Redeemer!'"

These citations represent more than the Pope's personal penchant for the paradoxical. They represent a spirit and direction in official Roman Catholic theology, a spirit and direction with important ecumenical potential. We earlier mentioned Joseph Cardinal Ratzinger. The close collaboration between Ratzinger and the Pope has been frequently remarked, and frequently lamented. There is no more controversial theologian than Ratzinger in the Roman Catholic world. Indeed, some would deny him the title of theologian altogether, depicting him as the Grand Inquisitor and scourge of true theology. As both patrolman of, and participant in, Roman Catholic theological discourse, his position is, to put it gently, somewhat ambiguous. Yet Ratzinger is a theologian and, next to John Paul, the most influential theological voice in the Roman Catholic Church. Admittedly, many theologians in the Roman Catholic academic societies think that influence is almost entirely negative. "I find it a good rule," says one professor friend, "that if Ratzinger is for it I'm almost certainly against it." But whether his influence is for good or ill, or is a combination of both, it is impossible to speak believably about Roman Catholic theology today without reference to Joseph Ratzinger.

Joseph Ratzinger was a theologian of high standing in both church and academe before he became archbishop of Munich and then prefect of the Congregation for the Doctrine of the Faith. He was considered to be very much "a man of the Council," as it is said in Roman circles. With John Paul, he is suspicious of a spirit of accommodationism that would obscure the scandal or blunt the edge of Christian teaching. In Toronto in 1986 he urged theologians to embrace "a theology which knows itself to be in service to the faith and which runs the risk of making itself appear ridiculous by trying to put tyranny and arrogance back in its place." Walker Percy would be pleased. In remarkably candid interviews, which we will come to soon, Ratzinger derides what he depicts as a lickspittle theology that toadies to intellectual and cultural fashions. Sometimes he has seemed to include "ecumenical dialogue" among the forms of the accommodationism that he opposes, and therefore Ratzinger is sometimes criticized for being a braking influence upon the quest for Christian unity.

There is reason to believe, however, that Ratzinger, with John Paul, is contributing to an understanding of "Church and world in paradox" that might elicit broad ecumenical agreement. In Ratzinger's own statements, and in documents bearing his mark, the Church and the Church's faith are typically described in terms of "mystery." This use of "mystery" is usually compatible with, often synonymous with, the idea of paradox we have been discussing. An earlier Ratzinger—the theological professor before Munich and before the Congregation for the Doctrine of the Faith—was emphatic about the paradoxical existence of the Church in the world. The evidence indicates that the shape and substance of his argument remains the same today, although, to be sure, his present position forces greater attention upon church structure and discipline.

"One could actually say," Ratzinger wrote, "that precisely in its paradoxical combination of holiness and unholiness the Church is in fact the shape taken by grace in this world" (*Introduction to Christianity*, 1970). The apparent contradiction between what the Church claims to be and what it seems to be has become for many "the main obstacle to belief." "The dreadful words of William of Auvergne, Bishop of Paris in the thirteenth century, seem perfectly comprehensible," wrote Ratzinger. "William said that the barbarism of the Church must make everyone who saw it go rigid with horror: 'Bride is she no more, but a monster of frightful ugliness and ferocity. . . .'" The arguments for repudiating the Church cannot be overcome by "any theory in existence" or by "mere reason." The empirical unholiness of the Church, combined with the fact that "the one Church is divided up into many Churches," makes it impossible for many to say, as we do say in the creed, that the Church is one and holy.

But we can say such things of the Church by faith, writes Ratzinger, and by a hope that looks for vindication through the fulfillment of promise. "The Church is not called 'holy' in the Creed because its members, collectively and individually, are holy, sinless men." Such an idea of the Church, the sectarian notion of a pure "believer's church," is a "dream which appears afresh in every century" but it "has no place in the waking world of our text [the creed]." Ratzinger is sympathetic to that dream and knows how "movingly it may express a human longing which man will never abandon until a new heaven and a new earth really grant him what this age will never give him." But some of us, Ratzinger notes, are not prepared to wait and work and pray for that eschatological fulfillment. Here one finds the seed of Ratzinger's later criticism of forms of liberation theology. People who have a "dream Church" in their heads try to force into existence that pure community that will be marked by unambiguous rigor, whether moral, political, or ideological. Others entertain that dream and, when it is disappointed, turn their backs on the Church. According to Ratzinger, "The sharpest critics of the Church in our time secretly live on this dream and, when they find it disappointed, bang the door of the house shut again and denounce it as a deceit."

The alternative is to live with the paradox, indeed to live within the paradox; the alternative is to live by faith. "The New Covenant no longer rests on the reciprocal keeping of the agreement; it is granted by God as grace which abides even in face of man's faithlessness. It is the expression of God's love, which will not let itself be defeated by man's incapacity but always remains well-disposed towards him, welcomes him again and again precisely because he is sinful, turns to him, sanctifies him and loves him." Reading Ratzinger on the Church, an heir of the Reformation can hardly help but be put in mind of Martin Luther's explanation of the third article of the creed in the *Small Catechism*.

I believe that I cannot by my own reason or strength believe in Jesus Christ, my Lord, or come to Him; but the Holy Ghost has called me by the Gospel, enlightened me with His gifts, sanctified and kept me in the true faith; even as He calls, gathers, enlightens, and sanctifies the whole Christian Church on earth, and keeps it with Jesus Christ in the one true faith; in which Christian Church He daily and richly forgives all sins to me and all believers, and will at the Last Day raise up me and all the dead, and give unto me and all believers in Christ eternal life. This is most certainly true.

This is most certainly true, says Ratzinger too, and he says it especially against those who view the Church simply as religious institution or "political instrument." In 1970, those who saw the Church merely as "political instrument" usually viewed it as being either "pitiable or brutal." Fifteen years later, Ratzinger would be contending with enthusiasts who seized upon the Church as a political and ideological instrument in the revolutionary creation of "the New Man in the New Society." All of these, according to Ratzinger, miss the point that the mission of the Church is not to advance this cause or that but to confront humanity with the grace of God in Word and sacrament. Even Christian unity must not be seen merely in terms of an organizational cause. "This unity is first and foremost the unity of Word and sacrament: the Church is one through the one Word and the one bread." Ratzinger does not belittle the institutional dimensions, such as the organization of bishops, but such organization "stands in the background as the *means* to this unity." The organization, including "the function of the Bishop of Rome," is to assist this unity. "One thing is clear: the Church is not to be deduced from her organization; the organization is to be understood from the Church."

And the Church is constituted by the grace of God in Word and sacrament. "So to the faithful the paradoxical figure of the Church, in which the divine so often presents itself in such unworthy hands, in which the divine is only ever present in the form of a 'nevertheless', is the sign of the 'nevertheless' of the ever greater love shown by God." Ratzinger does not employ the Reformation text of *simul iustus et peccator* (at the same time righteous and sinner), but the melody comes through clear and strong. "I must admit," he writes, "that to me this unholy holiness of the Church has in itself something infinitely comforting about it. Would one not be bound to despair in face of a holiness that was spotless and could only operate on us by judging us and consuming us by fire?" The infinite comfort is in "the interplay of God's loyalty and man's disloyalty [which] is grace in dramatic form, so to speak, through which the reality of grace as the pardoning of those who are in themselves unworthy continually becomes visibly present in history." And so he returns to the gravamen of his argument, "that precisely in its paradoxical combination of holiness and unholiness the Church is in fact the shape taken by grace in this world."

Of course all this is pious obfuscation in the judgment of those who understand the Church in instrumental terms, who see the Church's internal life and external influence primarily, even exclusively, in terms of power relationships. In his 1970 reflection, Ratzinger anticipates such a reaction. He notes the concrete historical facts that militate against the claim that the Church is one and holy. Among such facts is the Church's failure "in so uniting rich and poor that the excess of the former becomes the satisfaction of the latter—the ideal of sitting at a common table remains largely unfulfilled." In the face of these and other contradictions, the Church must strive "not only to profess catholicity in the Creed but to make it a reality in the life of our torn world." Yet the stark contrast between faith's profession and empirical fact does not negate the fact that this is the holy Church, albeit the unholy holy Church. The truth of holiness established by the grace of God is "the sign which the Church is to erect in the world." The contrast will never be completely overcome short of the *parousia,* the final coming. The grace of God in Word and sacrament demands our obedience but is not contingent upon our obedience. The courage to live paradoxically is to say, and to say at the same time, that the Church is holy and unholy. The paradox is relaxed and thereby lost if we say that the Church is holy to the extent that it is not unholy, or that it is unholy to the extent that it is not holy. In the final analysis (and "the final analysis" is always the beginning and end of Christian reflection on this matter), holiness belongs to God alone, and it is by his gift alone that the Church is holy. Or, as the Reformers were fond of saying, it is *sola gratia* all the way.

In this first section, then, we have indicated a movement "from riddle to paradox." It is not suggested that all the riddles of Roman Catholicism have been unravelled. Roman Catholicism is still and undeniably "other" to many Protestants, and Roman Catholics are still and undeniably "them." In the next section we will look at the Second Vatican Council and some of the riddles it poses to Roman Catholics themselves. The debates in contemporary Catholicism are in large part debates over the interpretation of Vatican II, and over whose interpretation is authoritative. Nor is it suggested here that Roman Catholic leadership, represented by such as Pope John Paul and Cardinal Ratzinger, is in agreement with all the cardinal points of the Reformation. This writer would not be surprised if the Pope and the Cardinal were surprised, and perhaps made uneasy, by the degree of convergence proposed here. One might hope, however, that they would also be pleased by the possibilities of ecumenical understanding implied here.

While there is much that is tentative in the present argument, this one thing seems clear: of the various models proposed for understanding the relationship between Church and world, "Church and world in paradox" possesses great explanatory force and high ecumenical promise, and is at least consonant with developments in official Roman Catholic teaching. Again, it is necessary to keep in mind that no model or type appears in a "pure" form. It is a strength of "Church and world in paradox" that it is able to include and sustain the truths in alternative models, as they are not able to include and sustain the essential truth of "Church and world in paradox." I take that "essential truth" to have several parts. The single and most important part is the utterly gratuitous existence of the Church, by the grace of God alone. What the Church is declared to be by the Word of God is to be declared and acted upon by us in the face of impressive evidence to the contrary.

The evidence to the contrary is not to be denied. Such a denial would be blasphemy against God's good gift of reason by which we recognize truth, and recognize dissonant truths. Rather, we say this is true and that also is true, and the resulting paradox simply reflects the limitations of our understanding at this provisional moment in time. And this brings us to the second most important part of "the essential truth" of the model of "Church and world in paradox." It is simply this, that Church and world will continue in paradox for the duration. We cannot resolve it, and we must not deceive ourselves into thinking that we can resolve it, before the End Time. Christian thinkers must continue to exercise the "analogical imagination" in seeking connections between nature and grace, creation and redemption, present and promise. This must be done in order to better communicate the Gospel proposition, not to resolve the Gospel paradox. The paradox can only be resolved by being superseded. If this is understood, we are better equipped to understand the many problems posed by the Church and by the world to one another. "Church and world in paradox" does not make the problems any less complicated; it may in fact make some problems more complicated. It does help us to understand the nature of the complication, and for the duration to contend for all the truths that we know.

PART II

The Councils Called Vatican II

Perhaps the Second Vatican Council is the most important religious event of the twentieth century. The claim that it is the most important religious event of the twentieth century is frequently made. There is no way of knowing whether the claim will stand up in the historical judgment of, say, a hundred or two hundred years from now. Pope John Paul has on several occasions called it "the council of the century." That is no doubt a safer claim, if a somewhat obvious one. Since this Pope will quite possibly be pope until the end of the century, and since he shows no inclination to call another council, and since no other church or combination of churches can convene anything comparable to the Second Vatican Council, it will likely retain secure title to being "the council of the century."

Against its being the most important religious event of the century, however, one has to consider some other weighty claimants: the revival of militant Islam; the Holocaust and the subsequent, perhaps consequent, rebirth of Judaism and its growing spiritual communion with its Christian branch; the explosion of "independent churches" in Africa; the German "church struggle" under Hitler; Russian Orthodoxy's accommodation to the Soviet regime; the amalgam of Marxism and Christianity in various liberation theologies; the ecumenical movement and its expression in such as the World Council of Churches; the vibrant convergence of Asian religion and Western liberal democracy since World War II; the decline of American liberal Protestantism and its loss of theological and cultural confidence; the growth and cultural aggressiveness of conservative evangelical and fundamentalist Protestantism in America and its dramatic spread throughout the poor nations of the world. These are but some of the developments of the twentieth century that compete with Vatican II for the title of "most important."

But we should not quibble. It might also be argued that, unlike the claimants mentioned above, Vatican II was a specific event and not a broad religiohistorical development. It was called and convened at a specific time; there was a specified agenda, and a ceremony to open it and another to close it. But today when we say "Vatican II," we do not mean just that circumscribed event. Today "Vatican II" means the churnings, confusions, and inspirations within and around that event, and it means the shaking of the foundations triggered by that event. We encounter no event in history entirely on its own terms as the "thing in itself." Every event is mediated by interpretation, and even the most "objective" reports are partially interpretative, if only in their selection of what to include and what to omit. These are truisms of historical study, but they are truisms because they are true. And they become more true as the event in question recedes in time.

A rapidly decreasing minority of the currently active bishops in the Roman Catholic Church actually participated in the Council, and even fewer in all the sessions of the Council. At the Extraordinary Synod of 1985, it was implied by authorities at the highest levels that only a fraction of today's bishops had even studied the documents issuing from Vatican II. Be that as it may, there would be no unanimous interpretation of Vatican II even if every one of today's bishops had been involved in the Council and had read, marked, learned, and inwardly digested its every document. There was no unanimity at the time of the Council. Imagine, on a given Thursday morning, walking into a Council session and asking, "What's going on here?" The answers would have been perplexingly diverse. We know that because we have the minutes recording quite different, and frequently contrary, notions about what was going on. And we know it because we have mountains of books and monographs written by bishops, theological experts, ecumenical observers, and journalists, all telling us what really happened at Vatican II.

Therefore we speak of "the councils called Vatican II," for we live not in the event but in the interpretations of the event. Something happened, there is no doubt about that. By ordinary historical judgment, what happened would seem to be the most important happening in Roman Catholicism in this century. If that church is the premier church among the churches, and if the Church of Christ is in some sense the "lead event" in world history, then a plausible case might be made that Vatican II is not only the most important religious event of the twentieth century but the most important event, period. A plausible case, be it noted, not necessarily a convincing one. But, whether or not one thinks that even slightly plausible, Vatican II certainly demands the attention of anyone who wants to understand Christianity or religion in the modern world. And that is much the same thing as saying anyone who wants to understand the modern world, for one of the surprises toward the end of the second millennium is that the modern world is turning out to be exceedingly and confusedly religious. Christianity, and the large part of Christianity that is Roman Catholicism, is very much part of that confusion. This is the context in which we try to understand Vatican II, keeping in mind that Vatican II is still happening.

Something happened called Vatican II, and there is general agreement on much of what happened. Everyone agrees that it came as a great surprise when on January 25, 1959, Pope John XXIII announced the convening of a council. It had not occurred to many people that a council was needed. The prevailing feeling was that the church was in robust condition. Certainly there was no perceived crisis at hand. In the view of top officials in the Vatican Curia, a council not only was not needed, it most definitely was not wanted. There is no record that any curial cardinal had actually said, "Who will free us from this turbulent pope?" But it seems there were certainly those who thought it, and prayed devoutly for Angelo Giuseppe Roncalli's prompt and blessed departure to a happier place where he could do less damage. According to the received story, Roncalli, who was already an old man, had been elected as an interim pope. The hope was that he would provide a short breathing space in which the church leadership could collect its thoughts before deciding on the direction to be taken after the long pontificate of Pius XII. Publicly expressing surprise and undisguised delight in finding himself pope, John XXIII promptly started being turbulent. Perhaps it was when he chose the name of a very questionable fifteenth-century pope who ended up being deposed that some first wondered whether in electing Roncalli the college of cardinals had not made a very big mistake.

It was as though the name John XXIII had just been lying around for five hundred years, never having been given a proper chance. The new John XXIII was a great one for exploring unexplored possibilities. Casting aside the weary image of the pope as the "prisoner of the Vatican," John XXIII set out to pay pastoral calls in the hospitals, old age homes, and prisons of Rome. Every day he celebrated mass in the then new "dialogue" manner, with the people responding. On Holy Thursday he washed the feet of the faithful, and on Good Friday he led the procession bearing the cross. Eschewing the princely appurtenances of his position, he repeatedly described it as a "very humble office of shepherd." And he laughed, also at himself. He is known to have enjoyed a cocktail and occasional cigarette (which may have indicated a measure of ecumenical insensitivity to more abstemious sectors of the Christian community). Many thought all this quite unpopely. It was not clear how anyone, including the pope, could laugh at the pope without being guilty of laughing at the church, which was decidedly un-Catholic. Nonetheless, it all made, as they say, great press.

Style always matters, but that was a time when the style was to talk about how much style matters. Especially for Roman Catholics in America, things seemed to be coming together in those days. John F. Kennedy had come to Washington as president. Some compared it to the dawning of a new Renaissance, others said it was more like the Borgia brothers taking over a previously respectable city in northern Italy. But these others were in a distinct minority. The dominant view was that, with the "two Johns," there was Camelot by the Potomac and *aggiornamento* by the Tiber. After the allegedly dull, gray years of Dwight Eisenhower and Pius XII, it suddenly seemed that all things might be possible. It is hard to say where style ends and substance begins. At the beginning of the Council there were those who feared what it might mean for the substance of Roman Catholicism. Nobody knew, nobody had been trained to think about what a council might do. Indeed, many had been trained to think that there would likely never be another council. As canonist P. Hinschius wrote in 1883 after Vatican Council I, "The general council has become unnecessary and superfluous for the Catholic Church. Since the Vaticanum it no longer has any independent legal significance alongside the papacy."

In one current telling of the story, there were enormous pressures building up that required a council to "let off steam" and to chart new directions. But this strikes one as an after-the-fact explanation. True, there were movements—theological, scriptural, liturgical, ecumenical— for reform. But before January 25, 1959, few people noted any signs of "crisis" in Roman Catholicism, and there were no voices of influence calling for a council. John XXIII spoke of the Council as a sudden inspiration that came to him, and he explicitly discouraged any notion that the Council was a response to threat or crisis. On the contrary, he seemed to suggest that the church was in such vibrant condition that it could well "afford" a council, that it could risk "throwing open the windows" and letting in the tunes of the times. One can today talk with very conservative members of the Roman Curia who insist that, even if the Council did not seem needed at the time, and even though it has been followed by such massive confusions, the church is nonetheless stronger than if there had been no council. One listens sympathetically while keeping in mind that a council is presumably the work of the Holy Spirit and it would therefore pose serious theological problems for such officials to say that Vatican II was a mistake.

At the solemn opening of the Council in October 1962, John XXIII spoke ebulliently about its prospects. It would, among other things, demonstrate the vibrancy of Roman Catholicism, further reconciliation among Christians, advance the human enterprise, and contribute to world peace. He complained about those in the church's leadership who, "though burning with zeal, are not endowed with much sense of discretion or measure. In these modern times they can see nothing but prevarication and ruin." Such people, he said, are "prophets of gloom, who are always forecasting disaster, as though the end of the world were at hand." For his part, the pope was sure that "Divine Providence is leading us to a new order of human relations." The Council, he said, must not discard the past, "the sacred patrimony of truth received from the Fathers." "But," he insisted, "at the same time she must ever look to the present, to the new conditions and new forms of life introduced into the modern world which have opened new avenues to the Catholic apostolate."

"The substance of the ancient doctrine," he asserted, "is one thing, and the way in which it is presented is another." He explicitly cautioned against negative thinking or indulging in condemnations. The Counter-Reformation is over. This was not to be a "counter" council but a "pro" council. Of course there are errors abroad in the world, he seemed to acknowledge almost reluctantly, but the church deals with them by "demonstrating the validity of her teaching rather than by condemnations." "The council now beginning rises in the Church like daybreak, a forerunner of most splendid light. It is now only dawn." And by the Potomac they spoke of the New Frontier, and few observers failed to make the connections.

The *New Yorker,* a self-consciously sophisticated magazine not noted for its interest in matters theological, would for years carry lengthy reports on the Council by the pseudonymous Xavier Rynne. The author, who is thought to be in a more real life Father Francis X. Murphy, depicted the Council in terms of almost perfect symmetry with enlightened American opinion of the time. By his account, the Council was the tale of good liberals against bad conservatives, good progressives against bad traditionalists, and the good guys were winning every round; well, almost every round. As to the meanings of terms such as *liberal* and *conservative,* they were self-evident. It was not required that the reader of the *New Yorker* make any mental shift from "The Talk of the Town" or the "Letter from Washington." The dramatis personae changed, but it was the same drama playing in Washington and Rome. And of course Father Murphy was hardly alone in giving definition to "the spirit of Vatican II."

Today there is considerable unhappiness over the liberties taken in the name of the spirit of Vatican II. Those who are unhappy tend to agree with T. S. Eliot's version of Paul, "The spirit killeth but the letter giveth life." They call us to attend to the text, and not to be carried away by a vague "spirit" of unbounded permissiveness. But it is a question of interpretation, of finding the hermeneutical key. If the hermeneutical key is the stated intention of John XXIII in convoking the Council, those who bend the letter to the spirit would seem to have the better part of the argument. Of course it is said in response that if John XXIII had lived to see what the Council produced, he would have had the same second thoughts that have occurred to Paul VI and John Paul II. The question has been made moot by his death before the Council ended, but it is at least arguable that John XXIII, assuming he still follows church affairs, has enjoyed the last two decades enormously.

While the idea of the Council may have come to John XXIII as a sudden inspiration, when it was actually gathered, it became obvious that the way had been theologically prepared by a number of major figures. Yves Congar, Karl Rahner, Edward Schillebeeckx, Joseph Ratzinger, Jean

Danielou, John Courtney Murray, Hans Küng—all had an inestimable influence on Council deliberations as periti, or theological experts. All were deemed to be progressives or, as it was more commonly said, liberals. (Of that distinguished group, Murray was the only American, and his greatest contribution was in connection with the Council's "Declaration on Religious Freedom.") In the years following the Council, all the above except Schillebeeckx and Küng would become, to varying degrees, critical of the "progressive" interpretation of the Council. Küng finally had his credentials withdrawn as an official Roman Catholic theologian, and Schillebeeckx would be in regular and delicate conversation with the Vatican about his orthodoxy.

For these theologians and others, however, the Council was a heaven-sent opportunity to bring the administrative leadership of the church into conversation with theological scholarship as it had been shaped in ecumenical collaboration. Before the Council many of these theologians had been viewed as suspect because of their challenges to the "manual theology" or "textbook theology" that had typically been equated with Catholic orthodoxy. Some, such as Murray, had been effectively silenced for a time, and were being inhibited from addressing questions on which their views were considered dangerously controversial. Today it is only with some difficulty that one can recall the sense of elation and freedom sparked by the Council. In its four sessions, from 1962 to 1965, the Council brought together more than twenty-six hundred bishops from all over the world. Counting their theological experts, more than three thousand people formally participated in the actual deliberations of the Council (although of course many fewer actually spoke up or exercised any discernible influence). Then there were about a hundred ecumenical observers from Orthodox, Lutheran, Anglican, and Protestant churches, plus Roman Catholic lay auditors.

It was called an ecumenical council, although technically it was not that, since it was the council of but one church. In another sense it was ecumenical, however, in that it represented the *oikumene,* or inhabited world, more impressively than any deliberative gathering of this century, perhaps of any century. The Council was certainly larger, and probably more representative, than the General Assembly of the United Nations, for instance, and was unquestionably more serious in its deliberations. In September 1962, John XXIII declared that "by virtue of the number and variety of those who will participate in its meetings [this council] will be the greatest of the councils held by the Church so far." In his opening address the next month, he said the Council would ready "the path toward the unity of mankind which is required in order that the earthly city may be brought to the resemblance of that heavenly city." There were many at the time who looked out over that august assembly and thought the very coming together of the Council itself was a portent of that coming resemblance between earth and heaven.

9. THE CHURCH BECOMING THE CHURCH

Changes in thinking about the nature of the Church had prepared the way for the Council. "An event of incalculable portent has begun: The Church is being reawakened in souls." Romano Guardini wrote that shortly after World War I, and it is recalled by Joseph Cardinal Ratzinger in a 1985 reflection on the thinking about the Church that led up to, and made possible, the Second Vatican Council. Speaking to a conference in Foggia, Italy, Ratzinger said, "If the Church had until then been viewed above all as structure and organization, now, finally, awareness was aroused that: We ourselves are the Church; it is more than an organization; it is the organization of the Holy Spirit, something vital, which takes hold of us all, beginning from our innermost selves." The movement was away from talking about the Church as a hierarchical, juridical institution, a perfect and independent society possessed of full legislative, judicial, and coercive power. Now it became the manner to speak of the Church as "the mystical body of Christ."

The first and most important change involved here, says Ratzinger, is "the Christological definition of the concept *Church.*" In the past the impression had sometimes been given that Christ was chiefly important for having founded his Church, and he then sat back on his heavenly throne and let the Church carry on. But now, says Ratzinger, it is understood that "the Church is Christ's presence. He is our contemporary and we are his contemporary. . . . So the Church's first word is Christ and not itself. The Church is sound to the degree to which all its attention is given to him." (At the 1985 Extraordinary Synod, there would be several episcopal interventions insisting that the Church should talk more about Christ and less about itself. There was general assent, and then the synod went back to discussing the Church. Admittedly, it is hard to keep the subjects distinct if "the Church is Christ's presence.")

The entire catholic tradition, including the Roman Catholic tradition, aims to counter the individualism and "Jesusology" that drives a wedge between Jesus and the Christ, and that makes the Church a matter of indifference. As Ratzinger puts it in discussing the importance of the concept of the Church as the body of Christ: "The liberal attitude whereby Jesus is an interesting figure, but the Church an unhappy affair, differs completely in itself from such a growth in awareness" as was taking place in Roman Catholic theology. Following the lead of Henri de Lubac, awareness grew that the mystical body, *corpus mysticum,* was inextricably tied to the Holy Eucharist or Holy Communion.

"That," says Ratzinger, "gave rise to a eucharistic ecclesiology which is also often called the ecclesiology 'of communion.' This ecclesiology 'of communion' became the real core of the doctrine on the Church of the Second Vatican Council, the new element which the council willed to give us: new, but at the same time wholly linked back to the origins." Ratzinger is, in passing, scoring a polemical point here. In the years after Vatican II, two theological publication programs were established, *Concilium* and *Communio*. The first is viewed as left of center, the second as right of center. *Concilium*, meaning a meeting or gathering, underscores the dimension of human decision making in the Church. The second, of course, lifts up the "mystical" dimension of the Church's being a divine creation. The distinction may seem slight, but it is of continuing importance, and in this address Ratzinger is staking out his claim with respect to what was "new" and the "real core" of Vatican II teaching on the Church. This is, as it were, Ratzinger's understanding of the hermeneutical key.

The question of collegiality, of how pope, bishops, and others are to deliberate and work together, is not one "regarding the share of power each has in the Church," says Ratzinger. Collegiality can "degenerate" into disputes over power, juridical forms, and institutional structure, but collegiality "is essentially ordered toward that service which is the Church's true and proper service," namely, the Eucharist. In other words, it is a question not of *concilium* but of *communio*. "The Church cannot be produced, but only received, and it is received from where it already is, from where it is really present: from the sacramental community of Christ's body passing through history." Or again: "The Church is not something which we make up today, but something which we receive from the history of believers and which we transmit to others as something as yet incomplete which will be accomplished only with the Lord's return." In addition to stressing again the eschatological, Ratzinger is establishing the sharpest possible contrast with certain ways of thinking about the Church in liberation theology. The arresting title of a recent book by a leading liberation theologian is *Ecclesiogenesis*. Its point is that the only authentic church is precisely the church "produced" by us in the "praxis" of liberation.

And yet, says Ratzinger, the concept of the Church as the mystical body of Christ is not without its problems, especially if that body is almost equated with the Roman Catholic Church. As noted above, despite all the talk about Christ being the center, such a concept has a tendency to end up being ecclesiocentric rather than Christocentric. If the Church is described as Christ's continuing life and ministry on earth, or as the Incarnation of the Son, then every criticism of the Church may be perceived as a criticism of Christ. The danger, says Ratzinger, was that "a definitiveness was attributed to every ministerial utterance and act of the Church which made every criticism appear like an attack on Christ himself and which simply forgot the human—the all too human—aspect of the Church."

In addition, and critically important, that notion of the "juridical church" as the body of Christ excluded other Christians. They are unquestionably baptized into Christ, and there is no baptism into Christ except baptism into his body, the Church. It was for this reason, says Ratzinger, that theology leading up to the Council and then embraced by the Council emphasized the Church as "the People of God." "Thus it may be said that the concept of the 'People of God' was introduced by the council above all as an ecumenical bridge," Ratzinger argues. And in so arguing, he is attempting to counter the common claim that the idea of "People of God" was intended to downplay the divine and mystical dimensions of the Church and to lift up the Church as a sociological and historical community. Ratzinger's claim is that precisely the opposite is the case: "People of God" is intended to acknowledge baptismal incorporation into the mystical body of Christ beyond the boundaries of the "all too human" historical reality that is the Roman Catholic Church.

Then and now it must be emphasized, says Ratzinger, that "the Church is not identical with Christ, but stands before him. The Church is a Church of sinners, which always has need of purification and renewal and which must always become the Church anew. . . . So it was," he continues, "that the idea of reform became a decisive element in the concept of People of God," an idea that "could not be developed so easily from the idea of the body of Christ." And the idea of reform, in turn, logically invited another emphasis, namely, that the People of God is the *Pilgrim* People of God. Taken over from Protestant New Testament studies, this idea was embraced by the Council to underscore that "the Church has not yet reached its goal. It has its real, true hope still before it." In this way it is possible "to express the unity of the history of salvation, which includes both Israel and the Church, along the way of its pilgrimage." There is an internal unity here that is "beyond the boundaries of sacramental states of life."

Ratzinger contends that all temptations to premature closure must be resisted. Although he does not here use the terminology, premature closure is a synonym for what used to be called "triumphalism." And it makes little difference whether it is the old triumphalism of the exclusive salvific mission of the Roman Catholic Church or the new triumphalism of the Church equated with revolutionary praxis, psychological fulfillment, or some other human project. What must be accented, says Ratzinger, is "the eschatological dynamic, that is, the provisional and fragmentary character of the Church always in need of renewal, and finally the ecumenical dynamic, namely, the various ways of being joined or related to the Church which are possible and real, even beyond the confines of the Catholic Church."

It is important to have spent a little time on Ratzinger's understanding of the ecclesiology of Vatican II, and especially his understanding of what is meant by the People of God. The model of People of God is frequently used to accentuate the empirical, sociological nature of the Church. It is posited against both theological and hierarchical concepts of the Church that, it is said, only obscure the very human questions of authority and power that are in dispute. But this is entirely to miss the point, according to Ratzinger. He expresses himself very strongly on the point, which may have something to do with the fact that he did his doctoral dissertation in the early 1940s on the concept "People of God" and believes he is something of an authority on the subject. He discovered that the concept "People of God" in the Scriptures refers chiefly to Israel but "does not simply indicate Israel in its empirical reality." "At the purely empirical level," Ratzinger declares, "no people is the 'People of God.' To claim God as a seal upon a line of descent or as a sociological distinction could never be anything more than an intolerable act of presumption, ultimately a blasphemy." Blasphemy is, in this case, yet another word for an act of premature closure.

What Ratzinger believes he learned is this: "Israel is indicated by means of the concept of the people of God inasmuch as it turned to the Lord, not only in itself but also in the act of relationship and of going beyond itself. This alone makes it what it is not, in and of itself. Therefore the New Testament continuation is consequential: it concretizes this act of turning to another in the mystery of Jesus Christ, who turns to us and in faith and in the sacrament draws us into relationship with the Father." If the Church claims to be the People of God chiefly, or exclusively, in a sociological and historical sense, the Church is not only not very interesting but it is unspeakably presumptuous. "From an empirical point of view, [Christians] are a non-people, as every sociological analysis can rapidly show," Ratzinger says. The Church is only People of God by virtue of the promise of Christ, who is present to his Church in the sacrament, making his Church a sacrament present to the world.

The Church is ever becoming the Church as it is generated anew. Ratzinger concludes on a Marian note. "Even at its beginning the Church was not made, it was generated. It was generated when the *fiat* arose in Mary's soul. This is the council's most profound will: that the Church arise in our souls. Mary shows us the way." Some Protestants will undoubtedly be put off by the Marian reference, but the conclusion is thoroughly amenable to Reformation insight: the Church is the consequence of God's initiative in his Word, through whom he generates the response of faith. The Church remains always, and paradoxically, both what God declares it to be and what we empirically experience it to be. It is not one reality to the extent that it is not the other reality. The one reality of the Church is simultaneously both realities. The Church that claims our allegiance is the People of God when, however falteringly, we respond with Mary, "Let it be to us according to your word."

This does not mean that, either for Ratzinger or for the classical Reformation traditions, the Church is sheer "event." It is not simply the on-again, off-again event of faith that just "happens" to be accompanied by water, bread, wine, sacred texts, and ordered ministries. All these are not merely incidental; they are constitutive of the community called Church that passes through history on its pilgrim course. And, as one might expect, Ratzinger insists that all that is constitutive "subsists" in the Roman Catholic Church in a singular manner. But with the Reformation it is declared that everything, absolutely everything, is in the service of *the* event, who is Christ. The Church is the community in time and ahead of time that participates now, through the anticipation that is faith, in the consummation of that event that is Christ's return in glory. Only then will the paradox of People of God/Not People of God be superseded. Short of the Kingdom Come, the Church is in paradox with itself as it is also in paradox with the world.

10. THE HERMENEUTICS OF THE NEW

This understanding of Vatican II's teaching about the Church and its relation to the world is by no means universally shared by students of the subject. It was the very ambition and sweep of the Second Vatican Council that produced a situation in which twenty-five years later there appear to be "the councils called Vatican II." Unlike some earlier councils of the pre-Reformation Church, Vatican II was not designed to counter a specific heresy or clarify a few doctrinal questions in dispute. It really was, as John XXIII indicated, to be a wholesale reassessment, redefinition, and recommitment of the Christian reality as we approach the third millennium. And not only of the Christian reality, but indeed of the human enterprise and the entire world. Of the sixteen Council documents, "The Pastoral Constitution on the Church in the Modern World" *(Gaudiam et Spes)* is the longest and most sweeping of the documents and almost subsumes the entire Council, or so it has seemed to many commentators. What was the Council about? The answer, it might well be argued, is summed up in the phrase "the Church in the modern world." Some say it was a Council on the Church. Others suggest it was a Council on the world. Those who like what the Council said on the Church often do not like what it said on the world, and vice versa. But, allowing for ambiguities both deliberate and inadvertent, there is an integral connection between what the Council said about Church and about world.

Among the ecumenical observers at the Council there was no more astute analyst than the Lutheran theologian George A. Lindbeck of Yale University. After the Council ended, Lindbeck wrote *The Future of Roman Catholic Theology* (1970). Almost twenty years later it stands up very well both as a delineation of what were seen to be the controlling themes of the Council and as a prescient look ahead to the developments and dilemmas of the "post-Vatican II church."

Lindbeck wrote as one deeply committed to Christian unity, and most particularly committed to what I have elsewhere described as "the healing of the breach of the sixteenth century" between Rome and the Reformation. And he wrote in unabashed sympathy with the "progressive" currents in Roman Catholic thought, represented by such as Edward Schillebeeckx.

Lindbeck quotes Schillebeeckx, who wrote immediately after the Council: "As in the life of humans, so in the life of the Church also there are initially more or less unconscious basic intuitions which guide the entire seeking and thinking; it is only in the result that this basic intuition can be thematised or made consciously reflexive." Lindbeck subscribes to that proposition, in which is to be found the seed of the hermeneutical approach that invokes "the spirit of Vatican II." It is the "intuition" that is normative, it is the music that matters, to which words and notes are subordinate. Lindbeck wrote that after the Council conservatives tended to interpret all its ambiguities in closest conformity with what had been established teaching before the Council. "My own view, in contrast, is that because the Council is part of a dynamic, ongoing process, it is the *new* theological emphases which are likely to prove most significant as a basis and guide for further developments." It is an important hermeneutical assumption.

"The correctness of this hermeneutical procedure," Lindbeck writes, "is confirmed when one considers past councils and doctrinal pronouncements. Their import has been determined by what is new in them, by the redirection they have given the thinking of the church." He cites as an example the Council of Trent in which "the fundamentally new fact . . . was that in it the Reformation had been dogmatically rejected." Post-Tridentine Roman Catholicism, he notes, was far more adamant in its rejection of Reformation insights than was Trent itself. "Something like this seems likely to happen as a result of Vatican II—though now, we may hope, in the reverse direction." Without surveying all the pre-Reformation councils in order to test the hypothesis in Lindbeck's "hermeneutical procedure," one might at least wonder whether it is true even of Trent. The case might be made that the "fundamentally new fact" about Trent was the incorporation of so many Reformation insights and the correction of so many abuses protested by the Reformers. That Rome moved in such a schismatic direction after Trent may have had more to do with political and other historical circumstances that led to the theological and ecclesiological hardening of the Tridentine church. Without rejecting Lindbeck's hermeneutical assumption of twenty years ago, it is necessary to register at least a small measure of skepticism.

A measure of skepticism is required on commonsensical grounds. Surely institutions, like persons, frequently say or do something "new" without inviting the inference that everything they have said and done before is to be subordinated to the new thing. On the contrary, it is more commonly the case that "course corrections" and responses to new questions are to be understood in continuity with the past of persons and institutions, unless the intention to break with the past is explicitly stated or the evidence of such a break is logically undeniable. Nowhere does

Vatican II, even with all its abstract reference to the need for continuing reform, explicitly break with or repent of past teaching. Nonetheless, there are undeniable breaks. It is, for example, very difficult to reconcile the Council's teaching on religious freedom with past Roman Catholic teaching on the subject. What is Roman Catholic teaching on this subject? The answer is to be found in the Council's "Declaration on Religious Freedom." That is the answer because the Second Vatican Council is the authoritative voice of Roman Catholic teaching, and it is the answer that has been subsequently supported by the authoritative interpreters of that teaching. It is somewhat inaccurate to say that it is the answer because it is "new."

Admittedly, the question of "newness" is not irrelevant. It is possible that another council or infallible pronouncement could supersede what Vatican II and subsequent popes have said on religious freedom or on other questions. That would then be the new teaching, but it would be authoritative not because it was new but because it was authoritatively taught. I am suggesting that in interpretation such abstractions as the "hermeneutical priority of the new" should at least be kept in tension with the facts of historical contingency. We should attend to what Vatican II said and to what voices of varying authority make of what it said. There is no necessity, certainly no determinism, that dictates that what was taken to be the "new" will turn out to be the normative and controlling idea. One might want to say that such contingencies are guided by the Holy Spirit, but it was certainly historically contingent that Paul IV and John Paul II were elected pope. That, as it in fact happened, has everything to do with the interpretation of Vatican II. There is no "hermeneutical principle" that would have prevented, say, Joseph Cardinal Bernardin of Chicago from being pope, or Edward Schillebeeckx from being prefect of the Congregation for the Doctrine of the Faith. In that case, the authoritative interpretation of Vatican II and its influence upon "the future of Roman Catholic theology" would no doubt have been quite different. The most striking contingent event—call it accident, serendipity, or divine intervention—bearing upon the future of Roman Catholic theology was, of course, John XXIII's calling the Council in the first place.

When it comes to the interpretation of the Council, there is a "party of discontinuity" and a "party of continuity," the former speaking of the pre-Vatican II church and the post-Vatican II church almost as though they were two different churches, the latter affirming the continuity of the church in a manner that comes close to suggesting that not much of consequence happened at Vatican II. Each party has its own hermeneutical principles for interpreting Vatican II, and the principles are frequently employed in a way that is reminiscent of what in literary criticism is called "deconstructionism," an approach that tends to end up by denying the reality of the text.

In retrospect, and precisely with an eye to Christian unity, one recognizes the dangers in giving hermeneutical priority to what was "new" in Vatican II. Especially when what is declared "new" is so elusively gossamer as Schillebeeckx's "intuitions," ecumenical dialogue becomes exceedingly difficult. Intuitions, hunches, directions, and dispositions are important. But ecumenical agreement and disagreement depends critically upon the clarity of words expressing what, as the Reformers were wont to put it, the churches "believe, teach and confess."

The "hermeneutics of the new" has in the last quarter century sometimes been carried in antiecumenical directions. Cardinal Willebrands of the Secretariat for Christian Unity has insisted that ecumenical progress depends upon all the churches becoming more "confessional." That is, ecumenical dialogue requires churches that can engage one another with respect to the substance of what they believe, teach, and confess. Exploring the pathways opened by the "hermeneutics of the new" may be of great intellectual interest to academic theologians, but it may also be quite irrelevant to, it may even be an obstacle to, the reconciliation of communities of faith. Lindbeck's subsequent contributions to reconciliation between Rome and the Reformation give striking testimony to his own awareness of the importance of working with continuing traditions in the search for Christian unity.

Twenty-five years ago Lindbeck was also keenly aware of how the "new" was in many ways an appeal to the old. In liturgy, for example, renewal meant a return to the patristic era of the first centuries of the Church's life, not always to recover particular forms but to reestablish the normative models and principles of that earlier period. And of course the elevation of Scripture at Vatican II was designed to give biblical studies a greater purchase in relation to later tradition. In addition, ecumenism itself posed the task of *re*union, of restoring a communion that had been broken. Only by reference to the tradition can the tradition be criticized and redirected. Finally, the conflict is not between conservatives and progressives, between traditionalists and innovationists. It is rather a question of which aspects of the tradition are to be conserved and renewed to sustain the progress of the pilgrim Church. A church that is really a "new church" is a sect; a church that is not "new" each day is dead.

11. COSMIC REDEMPTION

The theological atmosphere of the Council, one might almost say the spirit of the Council, is wrapped up in what some have called a "realistically futuristic eschatological" view of Church and world. Some of the most influential periti were in sympathetic conversation with Protestant voices such as those of Wolfhart Pannenberg, Jurgen Moltmann, and even the more popular Harvey Cox. Although few wanted to be associated with him publicly, the work of Teilhard de Chardin was a powerful presence in background conversation surrounding Council deliberations. The proponents of a "realistically eschatological" vision urged the necessity of coming to terms with "the modern worldview." We no longer live in a two- or three-tiered universe of the natural and supernatural, of God "up there" and history "down here." Rather, we live in a unified, developmental, and evolutionary cosmos; new things are happening with ever-accelerating speed, and it is all going somewhere, although it is impossible to say quite where.

In the seven hundred pages of Council documents, one can find passages in support of sundry interpretations, but the controlling progressive interpretation tended to translate "transcendence" into "the future." The transcendent is not above us but ahead of us, the future toward which we are rapidly rushing and that is rushing toward us. The early church fathers saw the world's philosophies in terms of *praeparatio evangelica,* preparing the way for Christ. So this new view sees history in all its ambiguities as the *praeparatio eschatologica,* preparing the way for his Kingdom. Some Protestant theologians, who had been burned by nineteenth-century liberalism's optimism about history, were uneasy about the Council's striking of this note. Other more liberal Protestants drew new life from what they perceived as Roman Catholicism's assent to their worldview. All were surprised, however, by the apparent rapidity with which Rome abandoned the "classical" worldview. Only rarely in the Council's hundred thousand words is the distinction between natural and supernatural even implied, and the terms themselves do not appear even once in the major documents.

The texts of the Council suggest that a new theological epoch had been entered. The "Church in the Modern World," in a typical assertion, says that "the human race has passed from a rather static concept of reality to a more dynamic, evolutionary one." There is a worldwide growth of "human interdependence" and of demands for a social order consonant with "human dignity," and "God's Spirit who with a marvelous providence directs the unfolding of time and renews the face of the earth is not absent from this development." The Christian Gospel is described as the "ferment" that arouses in the human heart "the irresistible requirements of his dignity." The "Constitution on the Church in the Modern World" describes the Christian hope, as Lindbeck puts it nicely, "in remarkably this-worldly terms."

John Paul, Joseph Ratzinger, and others have repeatedly, if obliquely, indicated that the Council fathers were too sanguine in their reading of historical contingencies. The same message came through loudly from the Extraordinary Synod of 1985. This is not the same as saying that the Council was wrong. There is no way back to the tradition that bypasses the Council, nor is there any way the tradition can live today except by passing through the Council. But it is important to understand why it has been such a rough passage to date, and equally important to understand what has been gained on this part of the Church's journey. Again, scholars disagree over whether the confusions to which the Council gave rise have more to do with what it said about the world or with what it said about the Church. The Church is described variously as the pilgrim people of God, a sacrament to the world, and as an agency of salvation. We have seen how Cardinal Ratzinger attempts to bring these themes into a kind of coherence, ending up with a contrast between the theological definition of the Church and the empirical experience of the Church that is paradoxical.

For many theologians, the idea of the Church as agency or institution of salvation poses serious difficulties. It smacks, they say, both of "supernaturalism" and of the "triumphalism" that Vatican II was supposed to have discarded. According to Lindbeck and others, Vatican II abandoned four monopolistic claims it had customarily made. First, there are now secular and not only religious ways to God. Second (notably in "The Relationship of the Church to Non-Christian Religions"), the Church should aim not to convert non-Christians from their religious commitment but to encourage them in it. Third, the Roman Catholic Church is no longer the only form of true Christianity or even of truly ecclesial Christianity. Fourth, it is no longer claimed that the hierarchy and its ordered ministries are the exclusive channel of the gifts of the Spirit. Theologians in the "party of continuity" point out, no doubt correctly, that these claims were not so unequivocal before Vatican II, nor were they so totally abandoned by Vatican II.

But, again, we live in the interpretation of the event, and the interpretation of Vatican II has undoubtedly given rise to confusion. The claims made before the Council, whether advanced in a nuanced or rude manner, gave certain answers to questions such as What is the Church for? What is the purpose of my ministry? Why am I a Roman Catholic Christian rather than some other kind of Christian? Why am I a Christian at all? The earlier answers left no doubt that the mission and raison d'être of Roman Catholic Christianity was to save people from the world in order to so live in the world that they might participate in the world to come. The spirit and the letter of Vatican II were very hard on this multidimensional understanding of "the world."

The shadowed and demonic side of what Paul called the principalities and powers of the present age gave way to the endlessly bright possibilities and promises of present and future. Those Roman Catholic theologians who claim that, after Vatican II, it is no longer the Church's mission to save the world but to be of service in the world's salvational projects— which are finally, ultimately, somehow, also God's projects—can find generous support in both the spirit and the letter of Vatican II. Theirs may not be the "correct" interpretation of Vatican II, but one would not know it simply from reading the documents.

There continues to be lively dispute about what John XXIII and the Council fathers meant by *aggiornamento*. The self-consciously progressive party, joined by the general media, then and now insists that it means accommodation to culture—an opening to the world, an updating, a coming to terms with modernity. The party of continuity, generally viewed as conservative, has been reluctant to give the term canonical status but, if it must be used, prefers that *aggiornamento* be understood in terms of a reappropriation and renewal of the tradition. Mediating souls are eager to point out that the difference is a matter of emphasis, but in fact it is more than a matter of emphasis. On the basis of the Council documents themselves, it would seem that the progressive party has the better case for its interpretation of the tone and substance of Vatican II. Few commentators at the time would have disagreed with Lindbeck's judgment that Vatican II made clear that "the Roman Catholic Church has now joined what might be called the 'Western liberal consensus.' "

On social and political questions, that consensus is evident in a wide range of Council themes: the conditional character of the right to property, the almost unlimited promise of technological and scientific advance, the obligation of massive aid to poor countries, the urgency of disarmament, and the central role of the United Nations in shaping a new world order. As Lindbeck notes, "The views expressed are consistently progressive—more or less similar to those which, in the United States, are held by somewhat left-of-center liberal Democrats." (To be sure, this was written before the "radicalization" of the Democratic party in the 1960s and the "McGovern revolution" of 1972.) In discussing the Council's "move to the left," three important considerations must be kept in mind. First, the Council was largely following the lead of John XXIII's "progressive" encyclicals, *Mater et magistra* (1961) and *Pacem in terris* (1963), and of course John XXIII was in turn following the lead of one plausible reading of Catholic social teaching since *Rerum novarum* (1891). (*Mater et magistra* provoked William Buckley's memorable editorial in *National Review*, "Mater Si! Magistra No!") The second consideration is that, in joining the consensus expressed, for instance, in the pronouncements of the World Council of Churches, Vatican II was hardly making a prophetic breakthrough, although the posture struck and language employed was frequently prophetic in tone. As Edmund Schlink, a German Lutheran theologian remarked at the time, "The church does not go before mankind as a leader, rather it adapts itself in the essential points to that which many men already recognize as necessary quite apart from having any Christian convictions." Lindbeck puts the third and most important consideration this way: "It is not the Council's specific proposals for the solution of the world's problems which are of primary long-range importance, but rather the new theologically based engagement in the world which it recommends."

A church that many perceived as old, outdated, and ossified was in

Vatican II discovering another youth. This was then occasion for almost unqualified celebration by all except a few "diehards" in the Curia. However, the world with which Roman Catholicism was linking its hopes for rejuvenation was already riddled with self-doubt and confusion. Well before Vatican II George Santayana wrote in *The Life of Reason* (1905–6) about change and memory in terms that can readily be translated into today's contentions over the interpretation of the councils of Vatican II. The following includes his often quoted, and misquoted, caution about being condemned to repeat the past:

Progress, far from consisting in change, depends on retentiveness. When change is absolute there remains no being to improve and no direction is set for possible improvement: and when experience is not retained, as among savages, infancy is perpetual. Those who cannot remember the past are condemned to repeat it. In the first stage of life the mind is frivolous and easily distracted; it misses progress by failing in consecutiveness and persistence. This is the condition of children and barbarians, in whom instinct has learned nothing from experience. In a second stage men are docile to events, plastic to new habits and suggestions, yet able to graft them on original instincts, which they thus bring to fuller satisfaction. This is the plane of manhood and true progress. Last comes a stage when retentiveness is exhausted and all that happens is at once forgotten; a vain, because unpractical, repetition of the past takes the place of plasticity and fertile readaptation. In a moving world readaptation is the price of longevity. The hard shell, far from protecting the vital principle, condemns it to die down slowly and be gradually chilled; immortality in such a case must have been secured earlier, by giving birth to a generation plastic to the contemporary world and able to retain its lessons. Thus old age is as forgetful as youth, and more incorrigible; it displays the same inattentiveness to conditions; its memory becomes self-repeating and degenerates into an instinctive reaction, like a bird's chirp.

The question, then, is whether Vatican II represented a juvenile regression, a church in its dotage imitatively repeating the bromides of a largely discredited modernity, or a mature community demonstrating "plasticity and fertile readaptation." Almost all Roman Catholics prefer to think that Vatican II is best described by the third, adding only that, whatever the human errors of emphasis there may have been in the Council, the whole thing was nonetheless under the guidance of the Holy Spirit. The Council participates, it is believed, in that infallibility (some prefer "indefectibility") by which the church's teaching authority is divinely protected from substantive error in faith and morals. That claim can hardly be questioned by anyone who wants to influence the interpretation of the Council. And yet participation in the mainstream of Roman Catholic thought does not require uncritical approval of everything said by Vatican II. Human limitations are not precluded by providential guidance. While it is theologically problematic for an orthodox Roman Catholic to say that Vatican II made errors in what it said about faith and morals, there is no problem in saying that the Council fathers might have expressed themselves more clearly in order to avoid the errors of others in interpreting what they said.

It would be a mistake to depict even the "Constitution on the Church in the Modern World" as a Pollyanish document devoid of any awareness of the darker side of human history. But the references to the darker side usually do appear as asides. These are the asides that are frequently highlighted by John Paul II. For example, in his second encyclical, *Dives in misericordia* (1980), the Pope ponders Council statements about the "deeper conflicts" within human nature and history. In a very gentle acknowledgment that the Council fathers may have been less than entirely realistic in "reading the signs of the times," John Paul II writes: "In the span of the fifteen years since the end of the Second Vatican Council has this picture of tensions and threats that mark our epoch become less disquieting? It seems not. On the contrary, the tensions and threats that in the council document seem only to be outlined and not to manifest in depth all the dangers hidden within them have revealed themselves more clearly in the space of these years; they have in a different way confirmed that danger, and do not permit us to cherish the illusions of the past." He does not say that the Council fathers indulged illusions, and he does tend to exculpate them by suggesting that the problems that concern him have become more evident, indeed have "revealed themselves," since the Council; and yet all the dangers and terrors he addresses were surely to be seen in, say, 1964 by those who had eyes to see—materialism, nuclear armaments, callousness toward imperiled human life, myriad forms of political tyranny, and on and on.

If it is true that we do not so much live in a place and time but in the description of a place and time, the description is provided in large part by the *Zeitgeist,* the spirit of the age. The axiom that he who marries the spirit of the age will soon find himself a widower cuts in all directions. Conservatives who are critical of the "trendiness" of Vatican II and the attitudes it produced need to be reminded that they too may be, in their very criticism, captive to a different *Zeitgeist.* Such captivity becomes evident whenever the analysis is monothematic, whether the theme be that of Pollyanna or of those whom John XXIII chided as the prophets of gloom. The Christian analysis must go deeper, holding truths in tension; it must go to the cross.

In the cross John Paul II recognizes the "antiworld" and "antitruth" dynamics that constitute, as II Thessalonians puts it, the mystery of iniquity *(mysterium iniquitatis)* in human history. And yet precisely here is also the hope. According to his fifth encyclical, *Dominum et Vivificantem:* "If sin caused suffering, now the pain of God in Christ crucified acquires through the Holy Spirit its full human expression. Thus there is a paradoxical mystery of love: In Christ there suffers a God who has been rejected by his own creature. . . . In the depth of the mystery of the cross love is at work, that love which brings man back again to share in the life that is in God himself." Here, once more, John Paul II appeals to the "felix culpa" of sin and salvation. It is a realism of paradox that is largely absent from the documents of Vatican II but is repeatedly asserted in this Pope's interpretation of Vatican II.

If the Council tended to be implausibly high on the possibilities of the modern world, it was, if that is possible, even more exuberant about the potential of the Church in actualizing those possibilities. "There was," Lindbeck writes, "a widespread expectation that if the church would only become faithful to its mission it would be able to mobilize the forces for good in modern secular developments in order to transform humanity." There were tactical and strategic considerations that inhibited the Council fathers from warning against the enthusiasm and utopianism that the Council may have helped to generate. The majority was fighting an almost Manichaen version of the classical outlook for which nothing new and nothing outside the church are good. Public cautions or acknowledgments of limits would mean giving an inch to the "prophets of gloom," who would promptly take everything a mile backward. Or at least so it was feared.

Beyond the seductions of the *Zeitgeist* and beyond the perhaps understandable tactics of church politics, however, the above enthusiasms led to severe confusions about both Church and world. At times the Council and its leading interpreters seem to suggest that the real work of God is being done in the world and the Church's chief task is to "get with it." At other times, while the above premise is accepted, it is suggested that what God is doing in the world can only be done with the cooperation, even the leadership, of the Church. At yet other times, we are instructed that the main thing God is doing in the world is the life and mission of the Church. The faults of the Church are acknowledged. Indeed, notably in the "Decree on Ecumenism," the Council probably went further than any other church body has in confessing its institutional sins. But such confession is nearly eclipsed by the repeated suggestion that the people who are the Church are the finest flowering of humanity, possessing singular wisdom and other resources for resolving the world's problems. Most disturbingly, the distinction between the Church and the Kingdom of God seems at times to be almost erased. To advance the Church, one is led to believe, is to advance the Kingdom. Eschatological references in the document almost always underscore hopes of historical fulfillment but barely touch on the question of judgment; certainly they have little to say about the judgment of the Church.

The "Decree on Missions" asserts that through the mission of the Church "the Mystical Body of Christ unceasingly gathers and directs its forces toward its own growth," and, at the same time, through this mission "the plan of God is fulfilled . . . according to which the whole human race is to form one people of God, coalesce into the one body of Christ, and be built up into one temple of the Holy Spirit." In other Council documents, the same scheme is presented except that the emphasis is on the Church assisting the divinely directed course of history. But the basic scheme is one of wondrous synchronicity, if not identity, between the course of the Church and the course of the modern world. The result is a new church-centeredness or ecclesiocentrism that is as pronounced as the late and unlamented ecclesiocentrism of the Tridentine church. A critical difference is that now the "salvation" of which the Church is the essential, although not exclusive, agent is mainly defined by projects of this-worldly fulfillment rather than otherworldly hope. A Texas bishop, recently asked for his response to fundamentalist Protestant teaching about the imminent return of Christ and the "rapture" of believers, remarked, "We Catholics do not believe in the judgment of history. We believe in the fulfillment of history." That, of course, is not what Vatican II said. But the way Vatican II said what it did say might understandably invite that interpretation.

12. THE CHURCH SUPERFLUOUS

The Council fathers did not address a question that has been keenly felt since the Council. If the pervasiveness and power of the working of "anonymous grace" in history are everything the Council claims, what, if anything, is so urgently necessary about explicitly Christian proclamation, worship, and practice? The Council's posture would seem to be one of great modesty, but there is yet another intriguing twist here. It may seem like a posture of modesty on the part of the church to say that "anonymous grace" is at work in the world even where the formal ministry of the church is not present and the forces in question are indifferent or even hostile to the church. It may seem like a generous act of courtesy to suggest, along with the late Karl Rahner, that those who are not Christians, or even declare themselves opposed to Christianity, are nonetheless "anonymous Christians." The working of anonymous grace among anonymous Christians, it is suggested, is a kind of preevangelization that eventually leads people to explicit faith in Christ. But in fact there is little evidence that this actually happens. Moreover, attributing to people a Christian disposition that they themselves do not recognize may be viewed as an act not of modesty but of spiritual imperialism. Denying to the secular realm and to unbelievers their own reality, even integrity, within the order of creation may be viewed as an act of ecclesiastical hubris. In short, it becomes a species of that old "triumphalism" that Vatican II presumably brought to an end. The classical Christian view is that the order of creation has its own God-given worth quite apart from the order of redemption. Or, as Thomas Aquinas would say, while grace fulfills and transforms nature, it does not deny to nature its integrity apart from grace. It is not necessary to declare that what is non-Christian is really Christian, albeit anonymously, in order to recognize our obligation to respect and serve the world.

In his intellectual autobiography, *A Margin of Hope* (1982), Irving Howe tells about an encounter with the Protestant theologian Paul Tillich.

At one of Tillich's seminars where the theologian, charming as the devil and at least as slippery, spun out his notions about faith, those of us listening felt that the idea of a personal God—the God we had rejected, the only God we knew—kept fading farther and farther into the distance. I asked Tillich: "You say religion rests upon a sense of awe before the 'fundament of being.' Does that mean that if, on a starry night perhaps out at sea, I find myself overwhelmed by the beauty of the scene and become acutely aware of my own transcience before the immensity of things, I am having a religious experience?" My intent, of course, was to distinguish between mere cultivated sensibility and religious belief; but Tillich, suave dialectician that he was, seized upon my question and said, yes, even though I called myself a skeptic I had provided "admirably"—he grinned—a description of a religious experience. He had turned the tables on us, and we sat there uncomfortably—until from the back of the room there came the (Edmund) Wilsonian rumble: "Mr. Tillich, you're taking away our rights!"

The spirit of Vatican II, not without considerable support from the documents, may be seen as a deprivation of rights; the right of unbelievers to be unbelievers, of the secular to be secular, of the world to be the world, of history to decline its destiny, and of individuals to go to hell. Salvation is salvation from something; if everything is salvation, there is nothing from which to be saved. (In fairness to Rahner, it should be noted that "anonymous Christian" usually means not that everyone is a Christian, whether they know it or not, but that humanity is so constituted that all are accessible to the word of radical invitation and grace.)

The distinguished Hans Urs von Balthasar—before he had second, fifth, and tenth thoughts about the enthusiasms engendered by Vatican II—allowed that while damnation is theoretically possible, we should not pretend to know whether the theoretical possibility is ever actualized in fact. To affirm its actualization, he suggested, is to subvert the Gospel by making bad news part of the good news. Certainly, in the Church's proclamation the accent must be on the hope, presenting as winsomely as possible the way to life now and forever. But there is another way that people may go and, at least according to the scriptural witness, it may be the road more traveled.

Before Vatican II it was taught that there are "ordinary" and "extraordinary" means of salvation. The "ordinary" means was incorporation by Baptism into the sacramental life of the Church. The maxim "no salvation outside the church" was popularly thought to mean that non-Roman Catholics, wonderful human beings though they may be, were nonetheless going to hell. Admittedly, the official teaching was a great deal more nuanced than that. But the official and popular understanding of the ordinary means of salvation was a powerful impetus to mission work. Over the centuries, hundreds of thousands of Roman Catholic missionaries have given up their lives in going to the far reaches of the earth to "save souls" from eternal damnation. Vatican II, no doubt inadvertently, gave significant support to those who say those missionaries were wasting their time. Worse than wasting their time, they were engaged in a course of cultural imperialism. The Council's "Declaration on the Relationship of the Church to Non-Christian Religions" *(Nostra Aetate)* has been interpreted to mean that, for non-Christians, non-Christian religions are the ordinary means of salvation. Thus the whole scheme of things is radically reversed, with conversion to Christianity becoming the "extraordinary" means of salvation. Not surprisingly, this apparent reversal has had a dampening effect upon enthusiasm for the missionary enterprise.

There is no compelling need, in this view, for the whole world to become Christian, never mind Roman Catholic Christian. Catholics should not worry or feel guilty about failing to win converts or about the minority status of Christianity in the world. In fact the Church is called to be a minority, a remnant, salt of the earth and leaven in the loaf. Obviously, there is powerful support from Scripture and the larger tradition for this understanding of the Church. Not so obviously, the idea of the Church as remnant can be taken in both a "liberal" and a "conservative" direction. The liberal reading is that the important thing is for the Church to witness to and support the saving work that God is doing in the world quite apart from the Church. On this reading, the Church is to read the signs of the times and then lose itself in service to the ascent of the secular, whether that ascent is perceived in terms of Teilhardian evolutionism or Marxist class struggle.

On the conservative reading, the Church does not determine to be a remnant but is quite prepared for that role in history, at least for a time, short of God's final vindication of his promise. This view is well represented by Henri de Lubac in a 1985 interview with the Italian monthly *30 Giorni.* De Lubac, it will be remembered, was one of the progressive theologians who prepared the way for Vatican II, and is also one of many who are now critical of the directions in which "the spirit of Vatican II" has been carried. In a fascinating manner, and in determined fidelity to Vatican II, he employs the concepts of the Council to ends quite different from those of many of today's liberals. Asked what he thinks is the outlook for the Church at the end of its second millennium, de Lubac responds:

I'm no prophet, even in the short run, and the year 2000 does not impress me the way the year 1000 supposedly affected all Christendom. To judge from history, from the present situation, from Christ's mysterious question, I suppose that the Church must still pass through difficult trials, persecutions, as well as times of weakening—"crises" of every kind—and that many unpredictable changes will renew her human side. I think it's fortunate for her that she doesn't appear in any way "triumphant." At the same time I firmly believe that she will remain faithful to the Lord from whom she has received the Spirit—that she will

perhaps have, in various places, periods of wide expansion; but that, even reduced to a small flock, she bears the hope of the world. She has the words of
eternal life, and she will live, transfigured, in the heavenly Jerusalem.

Father de Lubac leaves no doubt that, to his way of thinking and
believing, one of the crises through which the Church is now passing is
the influence of theologies that teach that the mission of the Church is
exhaustively defined by its service to projects of this-world transformation. His critics, needless to say, deplore the "regression" of this distinguished peritus of the Council to the "other-worldly spiritual escapism
of the pre-Vatican II church." Both can affirm the idea of the Church as
remnant. But for one, it is the remnant of saving truth opposed by the
forces of falsity; for the other, it is a remnant because it is obediently
emptying itself in service to those same forces that, it is believed, are the
forces of fulfillment. Between these two understandings of the Church
and its mission, a great gulf has opened since the Council. Both can find
support in the documents of the Council. Indeed, both can find support
in two millennia of the Christian tradition. What one party calls fidelity,
the other calls loss of nerve. Those who look to the heavenly Jerusalem
for the only satisfactory fulfillment of human aspirations are accused of
abandoning the human project here and now. Those who deride the
heavenly hope as escapism are accused of having succumbed to the soul-
stifling secularism of a world in revolt against its transcendent destiny.

13. THE COUNCILS IN CONFLICT

We have been emphasizing the ambiguities and contrasting accents
within the documents of Vatican II. To many it seems that Vatican II is
much like a jumble of notes, occasional disconnected bars, snatches of
tunes new and old, from which one can pick and choose to compose
whatever song strikes one's fancy. In the United States, the *National
Catholic Reporter* on the Left and the *Wanderer* on the Right both invoke
the authority of Vatican II. It frequently seems that the self-consciously
progressive and the self-consciously traditionalist have more or less settled into a state of trench warfare, with most Roman Catholics and most
of the hierarchy wanly searching for a "middle ground." The party of the
Reporter invokes the authority of Vatican II chiefly as an official reprieve
from authority, while the party of the *Wanderer* tends to reverse the
aforementioned "hermeneutics of the new," implying that only what was
not new in Vatican II is really authentic.

The prestige media of the country, which appear to have an insatiable
appetite for intra-Catholic wars, generally cheer on the progressives.
Dissenting nuns and theologians are the stuff of front page reports, no
matter how familiar the basic story line has become by repetition. Hardly
a season passes on Broadway without plays, often written by embittered

ex-Catholics, depicting the Fascist politics and sexual repression perpetuated by Sister Perpetua or whomever. In the 1980s, particularly with the arrival of John Cardinal O'Connor in New York, the *New York Times,* from which much of the national media takes its cues, has taken a most notable interest in matters Catholic. Beginning in 1984, the *Times* became the promoter, announcer, referee, and judge of the long-running O'Connor versus Cuomo fight, marking the end of each round with a magisterial editorial that declares Cuomo the winner. Governor Cuomo gave every appearance of being the willing proxy in the effort of the *Times* to advance its interpretation of Vatican II. The media story line is indeed about Vatican II. The good guys are depicted as those who truly embrace Vatican II and seek to advance its spirit, while the bad guys reluctantly accept the Council and are ever-interpreting it in a way that would "turn back the clock." Belligerents in the Catholic wars express mixed feelings about such lively attention being paid by non-Roman Catholic institutions and persons. On the one hand, it is always nice to be made to feel important; on the other, especially when the attention is not favorable, it can look very much like "interference" and "meddling."

No doubt many other Catholics are neither particularly pleased by nor resentful of the public attention given intra-Catholic disputes; they are simply puzzled. But the attention is not surprising. The cultural, intellectual, and political leadership of the country is interested in American Catholicism because it has a stake in American Catholicism. The Catholic wars are surrounded by, and indeed are part of, the larger cultural warfare within American society. Those who view with anxiety the resurgence of fundamentalist and evangelical religion in the public arena view with undisguised alarm the possibility that that resurgence may converge with similar directions in American Catholicism. For such people "Vatican II," however vaguely understood, has become a totem, the last remaining and institutionally most formidable redoubt of a liberalism under conservative assault. Similarly, those who are leading the assault, whether Roman Catholic or not, are keenly aware of the stakes in bringing over to their side the world's oldest and most inescapable symbol of moral legitimation, not to mention the more than fifty million Americans who profess allegiance to it. To be sure, there are more than two sides, and the many currents and countercurrents within Catholicism cannot be subsumed under such loose and volatile categories as liberal and conservative. But then the same complexity and confusion of alignments prevails in the general culture. In all the changing definitions of sides and alignments, the contest over the interpretation of Vatican II constitutes a critical battlefront in our society's continuing cultural wars.

But all this, it may be objected, is fearfully inflated. Surely most Roman Catholics are not aware of, and could not care less about, contestations over the definitions and directions of Western culture. Vatican II has made a difference to them in quite different ways. Perhaps in the most palpable way, it means it is no longer a sin to eat meat on Fridays. Then too, the priest now faces them over the altar and speaks in English, they are encouraged to sing those Protestant hymns at mass, the nuns who haven't declared themselves liberated to whatever no longer wear traditional habits, marriages are easier to have annulled, one goes to confession infrequently or not at all, novenas are almost unheard of, parents wonder what they did wrong if their son wants to enter the priesthood, Father O'Hare says there is really no difference between Christianity and Buddhism, Sister Trixy says Che Guevera is very like Jesus, and the bishop seems embarrassed when you try to kiss his ring.

Being Catholic in America has become a quite different thing. Now the accepted confession of faith, according to the sociologist John Murray Cuddihy, is that one "happens to be" a Catholic. It is less a matter of conviction or conversion than of accident, although it is affirmed as a more or less happy accident. The idea of the "communal Catholic" has gained a certain currency. That is, in order to be Catholic one need not be a liturgical Catholic who actually participates in the sacramental life of the church, nor a doctrinal Catholic who agrees with Catholic teaching on this or that, nor an ethical Catholic who tries to keep the rules (if rules there still be); it is sufficient to identify with the community that calls itself Catholic, much as a Jew is thought to be a Jew by virtue of identifying with the community that calls itself Jewish. Recently a newspaper columnist who approves of sleeping around, supports abortion on demand, is very doubtful about whether it is meaningful to talk about God, and is glad to say she has not been to church for years adamantly insisted that she was, is, and ever will be a Catholic. Against the strictures proposed by "patriarchal pre-Vatican II church authorities," she asserts her civil right to be a Catholic. "Nobody can take that away from me," she declares.

The above is admittedly extreme, but it is an extreme that is not so rare. And yet there are millions of other Roman Catholics who do want to be Catholic in every sense of the term—communal, liturgical, doctrinal, moral. From Stamford to Sacramento and from Milwaukee to Houston, one finds parishes with thousands of the faithful packing the masses of a weekend. More than a quarter of the Roman Catholics in the country are Hispanics from various countries of origin. They in particular are not engaged in, and seem to be unfazed by, the contretemps over the meaning of Vatican II. The devotion to the Virgin is undiminished, the effectuality of holy water undoubted, and professed obedience to the Holy Father unwavering. At least this is "the other side of American Catholicism" that is appealed to by those who say the crisis is exaggerated. As America itself looks to immigration to renew popular belief in the work ethic and democratic ideals, so some claim that American Catholicism will be revived. The immigrants and the native traditionalists, it is said, will keep the faith and resist the corrosive influence of sundry elites of "accidental Catholics." It seems a forlorn hope.

The theological questions about the nature and mission of the Church leave nothing untouched and seep through every line of resistance. This is notably true of the most regular and immediate experience of the Church for most Roman Catholics, namely, the liturgy. Immediately after the Council, George Lindbeck wrote about the long struggle for liturgical renewal that had finally been vindicated by Vatican II. The "Constitution on the Liturgy," he noted, opened the possibility of "radical" changes, such as putting the entire mass, "including the words of consecration," into the vernacular, revising the text, "even its central canon," distributing both host and chalice to the faithful, and the disappearance of private masses. "It will take generations," Lindbeck wrote, "simply to train the priests in the meaning and the spirit of the new liturgy. And then follows the task of training the people. But at the end of thirty to sixty years, a type of worship, a piety, and a religious experience very different from the present one might well be common even among ordinary Roman Catholics." Lindbeck observes that thirty or sixty years is not a long time for fundamental transformations of worship and piety to take place. In fact, what Lindbeck envisioned, and more, had within ten years taken place, even if the "meaning and spirit" of the changes have not yet taken root.

To put it differently, what may be taking root is very different from the liturgical renewal envisioned by the "Constitution on the Liturgy." The Council vindicated a movement pioneered by figures such as Dom Odo Casel, Father Louis Bouyer, and, in this country, Monsignor Martin Helriegel of St Louis. What the Council, or those who spoke for the Council, brought about was something very different. The movement for renewal prior to the Council is classically described in Ernest B. Koenker's *The Liturgical Renaissance in the Roman Catholic Church* (1954). It was a movement of rediscovery and reappropriation of the biblical and patristic understandings of the Church as organic-sacramental community. It was premised upon the "Mysterientheologie" of Dom Odo Casel, which articulated the Christian life as participation in the divine mystery, and was to find solemn expression in the revival of Gregorian chant and the congregational singing of, for example, the great Lutheran chorals. Non-Roman Catholics in the more liturgical traditions, scholars such as Koenker, looked expectantly to Rome to provide the lead in renewing worship that is both catholic and evangelical, if only the official church would unloose the chains binding the vitalities of the liturgical movement.

Monsignor Helriegel was among the leaders of that movement who lived to excoriate what they viewed as the movement's betrayal after Vatican II. Popular liturgy had become, in the worst sense of the word, vulgar liturgy; reflective solemnity had given way to mindless spontaneity; corporate mystery had been displaced by individualistic self-expression; sacramental community by chumminess, devotion by entertainment, and art by general tackiness. Of course that is too broad an indictment of Roman Catholic worship today. And of course it may be that some of the pioneers of the movement turned into curmudgeons who outlived their time. And yet there is no mistaking the dramatic discontinuity between the "liturgical renaissance" that sought and received the blessing of Vatican II and what has subsequently happened in the name of liturgical renewal. A personal remembrance may be in order here. This writer was in the 1960s the token non-Roman Catholic board member of the National Liturgical Conference, which for many years sponsored annual "Liturgical Weeks" that involved tens of thousands in the renaissance described by Koenker. Within a few years, invoking the spirit of the recently completed Vatican II, the Liturgical Week had become a religious Woodstock of balloons, guitars, nuns on the town, psychobabble, and politicobabble, all under the official motto, derived from e.e. cummings, "damn everything but the circus." And then the Liturgical Weeks were not held anymore. They were not necessary. You could get it all on television. And Monsignor Helriegel was joined by many others as he sadly shook his head and said, "That's not what we had in mind. That's not it at all."

Not a few Roman Catholic observers have noted that if today one wants to see what the liturgical renaissance in the Roman Catholic Church once had in mind, the most likely place to find it is in a more liturgically inclined Episcopalian or Lutheran parish. The question of why the liturgical renewal urged by Vatican II did not take root is deserving of more careful inquiry. To be sure, one must be cautious in generalizing about thousands of Catholic parishes, and it is true that, at least here and there, renewal is thriving. But it would seem that the great majority of Roman Catholic liturgies today are marked by the engineering of spiritual spontaneities, by recruitment to causes for improving the world, by charismatic enthusiasms, or, most typically, by the assembly line distribution of sacramental favors. It is all as far removed from the liturgical renewal envisioned by Vatican II as is the huddled gathering of "traditionalists" in masses of mumbled Latin guaranteed not to intrude upon one's praying of the rosary.

The question of liturgy has everything to do with the relationship between Church and world. Liturgy is, among other things, the ritual articulation of the community's identity. The importance of liturgy was apparently not recognized by all at Vatican II. This seemed to be especially true of those who thought of themselves as conservatives. Discussing the "Constitution on the Liturgy," Lindbeck writes: "Oddly enough, the conservatives have not resisted these changes as violently as one would expect. In part, this is because the new approaches have not yet been put into practice fully; but in part it is because the conservatives' emphasis on doctrine and on law makes them think of changes in worship patterns as unimportant. A good many Protestants seem to have a similar view." The last observation is not without an ironic twist, since conservatives have subsequently, and tirelessly, complained about the "Protestantizing" of Roman Catholic worship. A more discriminating conservatism, a conservatism that does not confuse the defense of the familiar with the defense of what Russell Kirk calls "the permanent things," might have embraced the liturgical movement envisioned by Vatican II. On this and other issues, the dominant species of Catholic conservatism has seemed eager to earn the nineteenth-century denegration of conservatism as "the stupid party." Drawing back from the various mandates for renewal—in liturgy, ecumenism, and social responsibility—conservatives have surrendered these tasks to others, thus helping to produce the fatuities and infidelities they so loudly deplore. The observer of post-Vatican II Catholicism cannot help but be astonished at the manner in which so many who call themselves conservatives have cooperated in their being depicted as a choleric band of dim-witted regressives. Many of them believe that now, at long last, they have found friends in high places, notably Pope John Paul II and Cardinal Ratzinger. That is probably another of their serious misreadings of reality.

14. THE OPENING TO THE CHURCH

Religion, Peter Berger has written, is humanity's waving of its banners of defiance in the face of death. Liturgy is the corporate form of that defiance on parade. Of course *Christian* religion and liturgy are more than that, but they are very crucially that too. It has become tedious to complain about those who are always talking about making worship "relevant" to this or that. Yet the problem does not go away simply because we weary of discussing it. Even among liturgical scholars today there is frequent comment on liturgy that "works" and liturgy that does not "work." By reference to what, toward what end, we should define "working" is often left quite unclear. Too often it would seem that the controlling frame of reference is self-expression, creating a feeling of community, or enlisting people in some project of social transformation. In all these, worship is centered in what it "does" for people. It is, in other words, anthropocentric in a manner pitted against the theocentric. Father Avery Dulles tells about preaching in a parish where he noticed a banner in the chancel that declared, "God is other people." He says he very much wished he had at hand a Magic Marker so that he might have put a comma after "other."

Christian liturgy should intensify the "cognitive dissonance" between the community of faith and the world surrounding it. Cognitive dissonance is closely related to paradox. That is to say, what Christians believe they know about reality is radically out of sync with the definitions of reality that prevail in the world apart from the community of faith. In the Christian view, ritually articulated in liturgy, the world is both more important and less important than it thinks. It is more important in that it is involved in the divine "mystery" of eternal judgment and salvation; it is less important in that its aspirations and projects are trivial and futile apart from that mystery. Much of the search for "relevance," for liturgy that "works," is an effort to relax rather than to intensify the necessary cognitive dissonance between Church and world. Collapsing the tension between secular and sacred, the secular triumphs under the auspices of the sacred, or at least under the auspices of religion. Except for a few hard-core "traditionalists," no one wants a return to the days of a vulgarized and mechanical view of *ex opere operato,* a view in which the automatic operation of divine grace is affirmed in determined disregard of the understandings, feelings, and responses of the community. But the alternative to such a mechanistic view of worship is not liturgy that is confined to the canons of individual experience and group dynamics. It is to be feared that not only in the Roman Catholic Church have many of us today become in worship so practiced at rejecting the "magical" and viewing with suspicion the "mystical" that we have closed the way to participation in the mystery that challenges prevailing definitions of reality.

At the time of Vatican II, misgivings were expressed about whether in fact a firm foundation had been laid for the reform of a pattern of worship that authentically reflects the Gospel of reconciliation. The intervening years have amply justified such misgivings. What almost nobody seemed to anticipate at the time, however, is the degree to which popular Roman Catholic liturgy would be marked by a loss of transcendence. The exaggerated emphasis upon liturgy as "the work of the people" frequently eclipses the understanding of worship as response to an initiative that is not our own. All our salutings and pledges of allegiance are only of ultimate interest if they are in response to our being saluted by the one who has pledged eternal allegiance to us in the Christ who is present to the community gathered in his name. Apart from that, we are only, as they say, doing our religious thing.

At the end of Vatican II, many shared the high hopes for a renewal of Catholicism that would extend far beyond the boundaries of the Roman Catholic Church. It is not accurate to say that those hopes have been dashed, but the subsequent years have sharply tempered the more exuberant expectations of that earlier time. There can be no question but that, in the view of other Christians, it is much better that Vatican II happened than that it had not happened. More precisely and modestly— since we do not know what would have happened if Vatican II had not happened—the situation following Vatican II is better than the situation that preceded it. Prior to the Council, the problems of Roman Catholicism were "their" problems; now they are our problems. And, conversely, many of our problems have become theirs. The nature and mission of the Church, the relationship between Church and world, the role of Scripture and tradition, the question of teaching authority (the "magisterium") within the Christian community, the connection between teaching authority and theological exploration, the meaning of doctrine and dogma—the Roman Catholic Church is working through these questions on behalf of the entire Christian community. Of course there are other Christian communities addressing these questions. Some communities, however, are not capable of that. Much of liberal Protestantism has lost the points of reference, even the vocabulary, required for deliberation and debate on such questions. Most of conservative Protestantism, especially fundamentalist Protestantism, is not aware of the questions.

After Trent's reaction to the Reformation, Roman Catholicism was presented, so to speak, as a package deal. One bought into all of it or none of it. This totalist proposition still has a powerful appeal to many, and not only to those who like papal edicts with their breakfast. But Vatican II undid the package. The undoing of the package has understandably led to a large measure of confusion. Most of the subsequent confusion and controversy has been over what the Council did or did not say about authority in the church. The most critical move of the Council, however, was in what it said about the nature of the Church itself. *The* Church "subsists" in a singular manner in the Roman Catholic Church, but the Roman Catholic Church is not alone or exclusively *the* Church. In that move, Roman Catholicism opened itself to the entire Christian community, and that, in the long term, is probably of greater historical consequence than the Council's much vaunted "opening to the world." Had the Council declared an opening to the world without redefining the Church, the meaning of "the Church" would have remained intact, and institutional Catholicism would have remained in control of how it chooses to relate to everything beyond its borders. The package might be reshaped and redecorated, but it would remain a package.

That is not what happened. At the risk of being misunderstood, one might say that Vatican II "relativized" the Roman Catholic Church. However superior it may be to all other churches, however qualitatively different it may be from some other churches, it finally is a church among the churches within *the* Church. With this move, it entered into the maelstrom of pan-Christian disputations and confusions about what constitutes the Church. A much bolder risk than anything the Council said about the world is what the Council said about the Church. That is to say, there is no truth about the modern world that is constitutive of the Church. Whether the world is on an evolutionary spiral of Teilhardian progress or at the edge of apocalyptic judgment, the Roman Catholic Church is still the Church. Such different readings of the world might affect what that church does in the world but it would not affect what that church claims to be in the world. An opening to the Church beyond this church, however, makes this church vulnerable. It moves this church into a broader deliberation of truths that are constitutive of being the Church.

It is not accidental that the Council's striking statements about the "hierarchy of truths" occur in the "Decree on Ecumenism." "When comparing doctrines," the Council said, "[we] should remember that in Catholic teaching there exists an order or 'hierarchy' of truths, since they vary in their relationship to the foundation of the Christian faith." The drafters of the document explained why this is so: "It seems to be of the greatest importance for the ecumenical dialogue that both the truths in which Christians agree and those in which they differ should be weighed rather than counted. Although all revealed truths are undoubtedly to be held by divine faith, their importance and 'weight' differ according to their connection with the history of salvation and the mystery of Christ." Counting truths is the appropriate procedure if you want to make sure they are all in the package, or if you want to compare your ecclesiastical package with the packages of others. ("We have more truths than you do!") Weighing truths, on the other hand, is the way of participation—of accountability and vulnerability—in a larger conversation.

Father Thomas Stransky, a Roman Catholic ecumenist, explains the hierarchy of truths this way: "Grace has more importance than sin, sanctifying grace more than actual grace, the Holy Spirit more than Our lady, the resurrection of Christ more than his childhood, the mystical aspect of the Church more than its juridical, the Church's liturgy more than private devotions, baptism more than penance, the Eucharist more than the anointing of the sick." This is not to say that all these truths are not connected. One might go further and argue that, upon closer examination, it becomes evident that they are necessarily connected. Some might want to go even further and say that they begin to look very much like a package. But, whatever conclusions might be reached about the interconnections of truths, what we are weighing is truths and not packages. It is a great sadness of our time that the disputants on all sides of the Roman Catholic controversies typically revert to the package theory of truth. Those called conservatives tend to say it is "all or nothing." Although the "all" is frequently reduced to one, namely submission to official authority, even though their own submission may be somewhat selective. (Mater Si! Magistra No!) Those called liberals, on the other hand, rustle through the package, picking and counting, separating out the "ordinary" truths from the "infallible" truths, weighing authority rather than weighing truth.

Admittedly, maintaining a disciplined conversation for the weighing of truth and truths is no easy matter. The other churches are not doing it very well, or are not doing it at all. In sorry truth, some churches have given up speaking about truths at all and only count opinions. That is another reason why what is happening in Roman Catholicism is so important to all Christians. Catholic liberals and conservatives agree on one thing: John Paul II, Cardinal Ratzinger, and others are trying to put the package back together and wrap it up tightly so that it does not come undone once again. Conservatives call it a belated restoration and liberals call it a renewed oppression. For the sake of Roman Catholicism and the entire Church, one must hope they are both wrong. The hope is that the Roman Catholic Church is attempting to sustain a disciplined conversation about the nature and mission of the Church in the world. It is a conversation opened by Vatican II and impossible to close without repudiating Vatican II. It is a conversation, like all good conversation, in which not everybody participates with the same authority, intensity, or influence. It is a disciplined conversation in that there are some rules (the fewer the better) about who participates and how. It is a conversation in which non-Roman Catholics are not merely listening in but are, directly and indirectly, taking part—as Roman Catholics have the right and obligation to take part in the conversations in our communities of the one Church. There is no guarantee that the Roman Catholic Church is going to be any better at such conversation than are the other churches. One very much hopes it will be, but at present there is more confrontation than conversation, more cacophony than coherence, more matching of conflicting authorities than weighing of truths. Or so it often seems.

15. A CLUTCH OF CRISES

In the years since Vatican II few dispute the proposition that there is a "crisis" in Roman Catholicism. The church's leaders carefully insist that, while the crisis erupted *after* the Council, it is not *because of* the Council. In an ecumenical context it can more candidly be acknowledged that the Council undoubtedly contributed to the crisis. One may wish to absolve the Council fathers of substantive error and simply say that the law of unintended consequences has been working overtime. While there is near-unanimity on the existence of a crisis, there is no consensus on what caused the crisis, how it is to be defined, and what it portends. For some, the crisis is all catastrophe, for others, it is all opportunity, and yet others view it as the normal aftermath of a transformative event in the church's history. The last view deserves more attention than it usually receives. Historians remind us that extended periods of confusion and conflicting interpretation typically followed the great councils in the early centuries of Christian history. In the actual life of the churches and in disputations between theologians, the great controversies over Christology, the Trinity, and the place of human works in the economy of salvation continued long after they had presumably been settled by councils. The maxim proposed by some, "Rome has spoken, the matter is settled," was always clearer in theory than in fact. In this light, the fairly rapid consolidation that followed the Council of Trent in the sixteenth century should be seen as the exception rather than the rule. And, of course, that exception was made possible because with Trent the Roman Catholic Church went into separation, simply removing itself from the contentions that threatened its cohesiveness.

Roman Catholicism, it is commonly said, thinks in terms of centuries rather than of years. It is a way of thinking that might usefully be cultivated in considering the present crisis. Admittedly, the habit of thinking in terms of centuries can be an expression of smugness, a buffer against change, or mere passivity in the belief that "this too shall pass." And, no matter how comprehensive one's historical perspective, the crisis following Vatican II will not go away soon because the most important action of the Council was not its much-discussed opening to the world but its opening to the Church. In this sense, Vatican II made precisely the opposite strategic move from that of Trent. Far from removing itself from the source of continuing challenge and contestation, Vatican II set forth an understanding of the Church that makes any church, including the Roman Catholic Church, continuingly vulnerable. Now, within the entire Christian community, the Roman Catholic Church must contest and persuade; it must exemplify in its life that preeminence that it theologically claims for itself. The combatants on all sides within the Roman Catholic Church who believe that the critical question is the exercise of authority in their church are, I believe, missing the point. That essentially in-house dispute is a regression to Trent. Organizational lines of authority are important in any enduring institution, to be sure. But the great question posed by Vatican II has to do with the nature and mission of the Church and, ultimately, with the meaning of the Christian Gospel. Institutional authority is important chiefly in ordering the ways in which that great question should be explored and that Gospel proclaimed.

Surveying the various explanations of the present crisis, one cannot ignore that center of popular Catholic intellectuality, Notre Dame University. And at Notre Dame one must listen to Father Richard P. McBrien, head of the Department of Theology and a spokesman much favored by parties progressive. McBrien's two-volume *Catholicism* (1980) has become a standard reference in Catholic schools. It is to a large extent an engaging catalogue of uncertainties designed to nurture the continued allegiance of Catholics whose main dogma is the rejection of dogma. McBrien is in no doubt about the reality of a crisis following Vatican II and cites numerous evidences of such a crisis: attendance at mass and vocations to the priesthood and religious life are in sharp decline; divorce and remarriage are way up; theological dissent is rampant; there is widespread confusion and doubt about the church's official teaching; there is agitation for the ordination of women and resistance to priestly celibacy; ecumenism challenges Roman Catholic identity and distinctiveness; young people seem alienated from the church; science, technology, and materialism have for many people replaced spiritual explanations and motivations; and Christians are divided in the struggle for justice between rich and poor, oppressed and oppressor.

With respect to the reality of a crisis, the list can readily be extended, and regularly is extended by people on all sides of the debates over the councils of Vatican II. In *Catholicism,* McBrien ponders the "proximate causes" of the crisis and suggests that they come down to three. The first is the cause emphasized by the prolific sociologist and fescennine novelist Father Andrew Greeley. What happened, according to Greeley, is Paul VI's 1968 encyclical on birth control, *Humanae Vitae*. He contends that American Catholicism "has suffered a severe trauma brought on not by 'enlightenment' or secularization or acculturation or even by the revolt against authoritarianism. The disaster for American Catholicism was the result of a single decision made because of the decrepit and archaic institutional structure of the church, a structure in which effective upward communication practically does not exist." His demurrer notwithstanding, Greeley's description does seem very like a revolt against authoritarianism.

The second explanation of the crisis entertained by Richard McBrien is that advanced by writers and thinkers such as Garry Wills, Wilfrid Sheed, and Daniel Callahan, all of whom are Catholics in varying senses of the term. Such figures, writes McBrien, argue that "Catholicism just could not survive the twin modernizing pressures of the Second Vatican Council and the acculturation of the immigrants." As Roman Catholics became better educated, more successful, and therefore more at home in American society, they began to think for themselves, also on matters religious. The process of acculturation had been going on long before the Council, and many Catholics had been able to make a successful accommodation between thinking for themselves on everything except those questions marked "religion." On those questions they gladly submitted to the church's authority. Contemporary literature on the Catholic experience in America, often written by ex-Catholics or marginalized Catholics, frequently emphasizes that the main thing about Vatican II is that it revealed the very "humanness" of the church's authority.

The church turned out to be an institution like other institutions; the battles between liberals and conservatives, progressives and traditionalists, were like similar battles in other institutions and other fields of endeavor. What the church had to say was no longer "privileged" but was susceptible to the same canons of criticism applied to other claims about what is true and right. For many thoughtful Catholics, the sense of disillusionment, even of betrayal, was so severe that the benefit of the doubt previously given to church authority was now given to whatever and whomever challenged that authority. Although they could not get the church out of their system, so to speak, many were now content to be communal Catholics, hanging around in the courtyard of Catholicism, restraining their nostalgia for the days when they entered the holy of holies.

In the charming memoir of his parents mentioned earlier, Wilfred Sheed describes the requiem mass for his father at Saint Patrick's in New York and allows that, just for a moment, he once again found himself believing the whole thing. But then, with a knowing wink to the reader, he resumes his adulthood and we are assured that it was no more than a moment's sentimental indulgence of a credulity long since outgrown. Michael Harrington, the inveterate socialist writer, is another case in point. Declaring himself an atheist, he is nonetheless vocal in his criticisms of what has happened to his church since Vatican II. It is as though he might someday want to come back and wants to be able to come back to a church that believes something significantly different from what he is able to believe as an atheist. In any event, Richard McBrien seems not to be impressed by this second explanation of the crisis that says it is the result of "the twin modernizing pressures of the Second Vatican Council and the acculturation of the immigrants."

The third explanation, which is favored by McBrien, may represent simply another direction that acculturation can take. It is an acculturation that does not lead away from the church but is compatible with full participation and even a role of leadership within the church. Neither *Humanae Vitae* nor the cultural maturation of American Catholics would have had the effects they did "if something more basic had not already occurred at a more profound level of Catholic consciousness." In explaining that more basic something, McBrien cites the dean of liberal Protestant theology, Langdon Gilkey of the University of Chicago, who in 1975 addressed this question in *Catholicism Confronts Modernity: A Protestant View.* According to Gilkey, what happened to Roman Catholics is hardly unique. It is the common experience of religious believers in the modern world, namely, the experience of "the dissolution of the understanding of the supernatural as the central religious category."

"In the span of a generation," Gilkey writes, "the absolute authority of the church regarding truth, law, and rules of life, has suddenly vanished. . . . The collapse of this authority has not occurred because certain church doctrines, papal decrees, bishops' rulings and so on were at last found to be in error, or obviously 'wrong' or 'old-fashioned' in relation to the mind." The collapse, rather, is due to the loss of a sense of the supernatural. People feel free to reject teachings not because they are wrong but because they no longer believe that the church speaks with the authority of God. McBrien writes, "There has been, in Gilkey's terms, a 'geological shift' in values, away from the supernatural and to the natural, and he calls this a modernizing of the Catholic mind."

McBrien continues:

If "the collapse of the supernaturalistic forms of Catholicism . . . is the key to understanding both the effect of modernity on traditional Catholicism and the current crisis in Catholic life . . . then the task for twentieth-century Catholicism calls for the reinterpretation of the transcendent, the sacred, and the divine—the presence of God to men—into worldly or naturalistic forms of modern experience rather than in the supernaturalistic forms of Hellenic and medieval experience." Among the symbols to be reinterpreted, says Gilkey, are God, revelation, authority, salvation, law, and hope for the future. The reinterpretation must be done in such a way that the historic Catholic values of community, tradition, grace, and sacrament are not only preserved but given powerful new expression "so that a new birth can take place. For on the creative resolution of this contemporary challenge to Catholicism depends the health of the whole church in the immediate future."

McBrien recognizes the radicality of this "geological shift" from the supernatural to the natural, from the transcendent to the immanent. He cautiously advances this "deeper" explanation of Catholicism's crisis employing the words of Langdon Gilkey, but he clearly accepts it as the explanation without which other explanations are superficial. The more than twelve hundred pages of *Catholicism* and its treatment of Catholic teaching and practice reflect the "geological shift" described by Gilkey. McBrien writes that his purpose is to maintain the elements of traditional Catholicism "without prejudice to the twin values italicized, but not patented, by the Enlightenment, namely, freedom of inquiry and freedom of decision." This means that "Catholics and others" should "explore, understand, and exercise their faith in freedom without prejudice to our abiding responsibility to reconcile our understanding, our judgments, and our decisions with the theological criteria embodied in Sacred Scripture, the writings of the great Fathers and doctors of the Church, the official teachings of the ecumenical councils and the popes, the liturgy, and the *sensus fidelium,* or 'consensus of the faithful' maintained through the centuries, everywhere and at every time."

McBrien realizes that he has set himself a difficult task, since the tradition that he would not prejudice is suffused with belief in the supernatural that is presumably no longer plausible. In attempting this task, McBrien is, of course, walking a much-beaten path. He is himself not noted as an explorer but as a marvelously accomplished retailer of the findings of others. His *Catholicism* reflects a consensus, certainly not of the faithful but of the theological professoriat. When he and hundreds of other Catholic theologians publicly protest, as they regularly and understandably do, any Vatican "interference" in the theological enterprise and claim that alleged dissenters are in fact in "the mainstream" of Catholic theology, there is considerable justice in their claim. Moreover, the enthusiastic reception of *Catholicism* throughout the Catholic educational system is further evidence that this "mainstream" theology is hardly limited to the circle of professional theologians.

16. COLLAPSE OF THE SUPERNATURAL

The familiar path traveled by these theologians was blazed and well beaten by Protestant liberalism in the nineteenth-century. In the Roman Catholic Church it was followed for a time by those associated with the "modernist movement," which was condemned by Pius X in 1907. The modernists were a talented and varied lot and their condemnation, in the form of the decree *Lamentabili* and the encyclical *Pascendi,* cast a terrible pall over Roman Catholic theology for half a century. While no reputable Roman Catholic theologian today would call himself or herself a modernist, there is no doubt that Vatican II is perceived as having lifted that pall and as having issued an invitation to resume the broken conversation with the modernists. Much of what is acclaimed or derided as "new" in Roman Catholicism today is exceedingly familiar to students of Protestant liberalism. It is not surprising that many Roman Catholics bridle at such an observation, and there is indeed an element of the patronizing in much Protestant comment on Roman Catholic theology.

When in 1966, shortly after the Council, Leslie Dewart of St Michael's College, Toronto, published *The Future of Belief: Theism in a World Come of Age,* it was hailed by Harvard's Harvey Cox, author of *The Secular City.* "A mature, highly erudite, and utterly radical book. It could be epoch making," raved Cox. The implication was hardly disguised: at long last, "they" are emerging from the night of authoritarian obscurantism and are coming over to our side. The same message is conveyed in the title and gravamen of Gilkey's *Catholicism Confronts Modernity.* There is a piquant touch in McBrien's appreciation of Gilkey's acknowledgment that Roman Catholicism brings some special strengths to the ecumenical mix, such as a sense of community, ritual, and historical continuity. But, having bought into the controlling theological presuppositions of liberal Protestantism, it is not surprising that the resulting mix offered in *Catholicism* is liberal religion, however enriched by traditional elements of Roman Catholicism. One can even imagine the emergence of a kind of high church Ethical Culture Society. In fact, small sects calling themselves "Liberal Catholic" and claiming to combine liberal religion with Catholic ritual have been around for many years. What is new is that variations on such a synthesis should now be entertained within the "mainstream" of American Catholicism.

One hastens to add that there is no evidence whatsoever that Father Richard McBrien intends to be anything other than a faithful Roman Catholic. His work is important in the present discussion precisely because he is not a theological deviant but an exceedingly reliable indicator of trends within the progressive theological establishment. In truth, his tenure at Notre Dame has coincided with a "re-Catholicizing" of the theology department. Distinguished non-Roman Catholic scholars have been replaced by faculty members who are officially Roman Catholic, thus assuring alumni that Notre Dame intends to remain a Catholic University. The significance of the kind of thinking represented by Richard McBrien is that it is so very representative of key leadership directions in the American church. It is not for nothing that the secular media routinely go to Father McBrien for a quotable response to initiatives by Cardinal Ratzinger or others identified with the redirections favored by

Pope John Paul II. Unlike some others, McBrien is not a "dissident" but a theologian fully ensconced and certified at a university that, together with its football team, is in the minds of many synonymous with the best in American Catholicism. In addition, McBrien is responsive, even obedient, to church leadership. For example, some American bishops have raised questions about points here and there in *Catholicism* that are unclear and may lead to misunderstandings of official church teaching. McBrien is reportedly working on a revision that will be responsive to the questions raised. Making adjustments here and there poses no great problem so long as the controlling presuppositions remain unchanged. Those presuppositions suggest that religious language and symbols, even doctrine and dogma, are marvelously flexible and may be variously expressed in order to accommodate the essential religious truth. McBrien is, in sum, an excellent representative of the "liberal tradition" so carefully analyzed by George Lindbeck in his *The Nature of Doctrine,* to which we will be returning in due course.

The controlling presupposition is a general loss of belief in the supernatural and a radical "turn toward humanity." It would seem that traditional Christian belief cannot survive a "plausibility collapse" with respect to the supernatural and the transcendent. But, in fact, it is suggested that the supernatural and transcendent can, with hermeneutical acumen, be retranslated into the framework of the naturalistic and immanent. This retranslation was the great achievement of nineteenth-century Protestant liberalism from Friedrich Schleiermacher onward. It was taken to an extreme, and finally anti-Christian, expression in the work of Ludwig Feuerbach, for whom all talk about God and the supernatural was but a projection of human frustrations and delusions. In a similar vein, Karl Marx was not entirely unsympathetic to religion. While he could condemn religion as the opiate of the people, he could also speak of religion as the sigh of an oppressed humanity. For those who accept the plausibility collapse of traditional belief, a further decision is in order. One can simply discard all traditional reference to the supernatural and, in doing so, discard the forms of traditional religion, or one can "creatively retranslate" references to the supernatural in order to employ them in the service of our human projects. Such projects can be as various as social and political change, psychological well-being, or aesthetic fulfillment.

Whether one decides to discard or to deploy the elements of traditional Christianity that are no longer plausible on their own terms, so to speak, may depend on a number of factors. Those who urge discarding traditional religion may plead a rigorous intellectual honesty, or may simply have arrived at the conclusion that religion nurtures a "false consciousness" that distracts attention from urgent worldly tasks. Those who urge deploying traditional religion may themselves be personally attached to the forms and communities of faith in ways they are reluctant to abandon. The attachment may be occupational, or it may have to do with a debased utilitarian version of Pascal's wager in which they attempt to cover their bets, just in case the traditional talk about God really turns out to be about God and not merely about humanity's religiosity. One cannot, after all, close off the possibility that our human talk and ritualizing about transcendence may turn out to be in response to signals of transcendence sent from somewhere else, even from Someone Else. But the usual explanation given by those who would retranslate and deploy the supernatural referents of traditional religion is that these referents have such a powerful hold upon the bulk of humanity that it is futile to set the course of human progress in opposition to them. More than that, the enlistment of traditional doctrines and forms of religion can add immeasurable depth and passion to commitment to our human projects. And, of course, it can win to our causes the support of the masses who have not been successfully educated to the recognition that belief in the supernatural is no longer plausible.

Whether one elects to discard or to deploy religion, the presupposition is the same; namely, religion is a purely human phenomenon and theology is, after all is said and done, anthropology. Human talk about God is really talk about man in his religious mode of being. From Gibbon's description of the aristocracy's attitude toward religion in ancient Rome up to today's, usually conservative, proponents of a "religious revival" in order to preserve Western civilization or liberal democracy, many who are themselves not believers have recognized the usefulness of belief. Religion is the "noble lie" that is required to secure popular support for sustaining or creating the right social order. Thus, among those who would deploy rather than discard traditional religion, another distinction is called for.

Those who would use the compelling falsehoods and noble lies of traditional religion in order to secure the acquiescence of the unenlightened masses to the existing order are not particularly interested in the retranslation of religious symbols. To put it differently, retranslation through hermeneutical legerdemain is to be used only to the extent it is necessary to maintain the allegiance of the credulous. There is, to put it gently, an element of cynicism in this strategy. By contrast, those who would deploy religion for purposes of radical change in the social order are typically more candid about what they are doing. Liberation theologians such as Juan Luis Segundo or liberationist-cum-feminist theologians such as Rosemary Radford Ruether have no patience with the noble lie. They are eager to bring the masses in on the secret about traditional religion, namely, that it is not about what most people have thought it was about. It is not about God and angels and heaven and hell "out there" or in the distant future but about radical change here and now. "God-talk" and the piety, teachings, and rituals surrounding "God-talk" are all "symbols" of almost infinite malleability. The Exodus is the revolutionary struggle, the cross is sacrifice for the struggle, the Eucharist is solidarity in the struggle, the Resurrection is the triumph of the struggle, and so forth. Such retranslations and transpositions may seem simplistic when stated so baldly, whereas in fact they are worked out with great sophistication and at great length by the partisans of the radical wing of the party favoring the deployment of religion.

What all members of the deployment party share is the presupposition that while traditional religion may no longer be true, it is still useful. A critical difference between the conservative and radical wings of the deployment party is that the liberationists believe that the tradition can be made to be "true" in a manner quite different from the way in which believers have in the past thought it to be true. The deployment party shares with those who would discard religion altogether the assumption that theology is anthropology. "God" is the noblest creation of the human mind and "soul," but it is important to keep in mind that when we are talking about God we are really talking about the human mind and "soul." Theology is the language of human aspiration and projection. To speak of the transcendent is to speak of man's effort to transcend himself.

As we might expect, there are "hard" and "soft" versions of the proposition that theology is anthropology. Soft versions tend to be less intellectually rigorous. They are also less straightforward. They do not say that assertions about the supernatural are not true, only that they are true in a different way, in a way that usually turns out to be quite natural. Richard McBrien in *Catholicism* represents a soft version that does not jar the sensibilities of most American Catholics. Accepting Langdon Gilkey's presupposition that in the modern world what once was believable is no longer believable, he also agrees with Gilkey that "the reinterpretation must be done in such a way that the historic Catholic values of community, tradition, grace, and sacrament are not only preserved but given powerful new expression." The use of the distinctly contemporary word *values* is noteworthy. Values are, of course, quite different from truths. Truths, like facts, are there quite apart from ourselves; they are there to be acknowledged as true but are not true by virtue of our acknowledgment. *Values,* on the other hand, is a term derived from economics and market theory; values are the creation of human valuing. What we deem valuable is, by definition, a value. A great "geological shift" has indeed taken place when our attention is turned from Christian truths to religious values.

In his soft version of theology as anthropology, McBrien writes that "one cannot understand the reality of God unless one also understands what it means to be human, for God is perceived as the source of humankind's perfection, the ultimate fulfillment of human potential." But one must ask whether such a perception of God is in fact a hypercharged perception of man. To be sure, the union of God and man is a classic theme in Christian theology. It is expressed in terms of man's true "end" being perfect union with God and, most importantly, in the Incarnation, in God becoming man in Jesus. Muslim thinkers, for example, have routinely objected that the Christian teaching that God became man must of necessity turn all further theology into anthropology. Union, or perfect communion, between God and man is not confusion or identification, however. It is, according to orthodox Christian theology, accurate to say that Jesus is God; it is not accurate to say that God is Jesus. With respect to the relationship between God and humanity, there is always the need for that comma that Father Dulles saw missing from the parish banner: "God is other, people." The conflation of the human and divine, the transcendent and the immanent, the supernatural and the natural, is pervasive in "mainstream" academic theology today, both Roman Catholic and liberal Protestant. McBrien writes, "To propose the final meaning of human existence is to propose a 'doctrine' of God. In the end, anthropology and theology converge." One is forced to suspect that it is only an absence of intellectual rigor and the fact that *Catholicism* is a middlebrow theology aimed at a general Catholic market that prevent the last sentence from reading, "In the end, anthropology and theology are the same thing."

17. THE NEW GNOSTIC CLASS

Henri de Lubac, in a 1985 interview, looks back upon what he views as the misadventures of Roman Catholic theology since Vatican II and suggests that some errors are not very new at all. He suggests that the "gnosticism" that Irenaeus contended against in the second century is strikingly pertinent to today's disputes.

I find in his description of gnosticism the same content as in certain contemporary works. It always involves a superior knowledge of an active character—different in this respect from mysticism, which is supposed to be nothing but pure passivity. (Human pride never wants to receive anything, but only either to find or create.) The "gnostics" of all times . . . share the same presupposition (though it isn't always clear from the outset): The heart of what the Bible, the Church and Tradition have to say is not faith in a transcendent God, but the true discovery of man. In their eyes, the mysteries of Christianity are nothing but a superficial covering, pure superstition, so long as one hasn't penetrated into the gnosis that they, the initiates, obligingly translate for weaker minds.

Father de Lubac's criticism may seem harsh, but the question is whether it is accurate. I believe that it is a fair assessment of much of contemporary Roman Catholic thought. The "gnostics" are to be found on the Right as well as the Left. On the Right, there are those who "know" that the real purpose of the church is to firm up "traditional values" and secure the existing social order. The difference is that they do not need to "obligingly translate for weaker minds," for they are convinced that they are basically at one with the weaker minds. One must quickly add that there are many "traditionists" who do not belong to what we have called the party of deployment. Their concern truly is for the classic understanding of the truths of the faith, quite apart from any social, political, or cultural "agendas" they may have. It is on the Left that there is a felt need to translate, obligingly or otherwise, for weaker minds.

The task of translation requires the production of articles, books, seminars, and conferences without end. Also for this reason, it is not surprising that the project of the Left is of much greater interest in academic circles. Between reaffirming the faith and reconceptualizing the faith, reconceptualizing wins hands down. It is the very stuff of the academic and publishing industries. If there were no need for thorough reconceptualizations, fundamental reexaminations, moral transvaluations, hermeneutical revolutions, and historicocritical transformations, there would be no need for all the people who are very expensively trained to engage in just such things. Those who resist the efforts of such talented people are perceived to be anti-intellectual. Frequently they are anti-intellectual, but in larger part they are perceived and condemned as anti-intellectual because most of the people who are paid to be intellectuals are on the other side. In many, perhaps most, instances they are on the other side because, despite all their reductionist theories, they believe the other side to be closer to the "truth." And they are on the other side, not least of all, because that is where the jobs are. It is thought to be impolite to point out this rather obvious consideration. Those of us intellectuals who most relish exposing the "real" reasons people do things, as distinct from the "good" reasons they give for doing things, are too inclined to exempt ourselves from the critical scrutiny we apply to others.

Social scientists have in recent years devoted great attention to the development of a "knowledge industry" in modern societies. Those who make their living in the knowledge industry—in minting and marketing ideas—are described as belonging to the "new class." It is a class in the classic sense of the term, with its own interests, habits of mind, occupational guilds, and struggles with other classes. In religion the knowledge industry might better be described as the gnosis industry. But here too the "new class" phenomenon is at work, although some might dispute whether it is that new. After all, there have always been those in the church who had power, status, and occasionally wealth, by virtue of their role in instructing the faithful. Irenaeus, Augustine, Benedict, Catherine, Thomas, and a host of others had great status by virtue of their learning, and power in the sense of influence, albeit not wealth. But these figures hardly belonged to the "new class" of their times.

The new class is new. It is a concomitant of the much-discussed information and communication explosions of modern postindustrial society. Those earlier figures undoubtedly belonged to an elite, their status and influence being derived from the community of faith that they served. Most contemporary theologians work in the Religion Division of Knowledge Industries Unlimited with the academy serving as their guild. There is, in addition, a confusing overlap between academic guild and community of faith. For many theologians, certainly most Roman Catholic theologians still today, their primary share of the market is defined denominationally as the Roman Catholic community of faith. From that community they also receive their certification, perhaps their jobs too, as theologians of the church. But they are credentialed as professional theologians within the guild by their academic peers and professional associations. The pressures, incentives, and criteria of professional success are all skewed to giving priority attention to the guild rather than to the community of faith. Indeed, the Roman Catholic, or Lutheran, or Eastern Orthodox theologian who "makes it" in the larger theological world, or even in worlds beyond theology, usually enjoys enhanced status also within the church by which he or she was initially certified.

This is not to say that the distinction is between theologians who have a particularistic confessional identity and those who are more universalistically defined simply as theologians. True, that may seem to be the distinction. One may be a noted theologian at, say, the University of Chicago or Harvard without being identified as a Presbyterian or a Methodist or a whatever. In such cases there would seem to be a liberation, so to speak, from denominational identities. But, in fact, the identity in such cases is no more "universal" than is the identity of one who is known as a Roman Catholic theologian. Such universalism is in truth nothing more than another particularism. In this instance the particularism is the amorphous denomination known as liberal Protestantism. It is, and for the foreseeable future will continue to be, the dominant sector in the theological division of our society's new class. In other words, in theology as in any other enterprise, everyone belongs somewhere, nobody can take a stand everywhere. We shall later consider what Cardinal Ratzinger has set forth as his vision of a "church theologian." It is a vision that cannot help but strike many as regressive, premodern, and thoroughly out of touch with the American church's problems with theology as part of the knowledge industry.

That there is a new class, also in the worlds of religion, seems to this writer to be beyond dispute. The conventional response to those who point out the existence and ramifications of the new class is that they too belong to it, which is also beyond dispute. They are traitors to their class. They can be viewed as dangerous because they are inclined to debunk the gnosis by which other members of the class debunk what ordinary people think they know to be true. Sigmund Freud did the psychoanalysis business no good when he observed that sometimes a cigar is just a cigar. One might want to conjecture, along with this writer, that a cigar is usually just a cigar. But the important thing is this: a cigar is always *at least* a cigar. Most new class theologians are in the business of pointing out that things are not what they seem, that there is more here than meets the eye. The problem, of course, is that the "more" usually turns out to be less. A friend reports reading a semipopular Catholic theological work. "The author was talking about angels and demons," she said, "and at first I thought he was talking about angels and demons, but then it turned out that this was simply the church's code language for libido and super-ego and oppressed and oppressor and things like that. How very uninteresting."

In suggesting that things are not what meet the eye and the ear and the mind and the soul of the believer, theologians end up losing their audience. If talk about God is not really about God but about something else, it would seem to make sense to talk about that something else in a less indirect manner, and to continue the conversation not with a theologian but with someone especially qualified to speak on that something else. If theology is really anthropology, one might prefer to take one's anthropology straight, without the theological trappings and all the bother about orthodoxy and heresy that those trappings carry with them.

On the other hand, many serious Christians do want to talk about God and become understandably impatient when told that talk about God is really talk about something else. The irony is that theologians (and many pastors) try to be very "creative" in "interesting people in God" by demonstrating the pertinence of the subject to matters in which people are presumably interested, when in fact it is because people are quite bored with those matters that they are so interested in God. At times and for some people, theology has to be "legitimated" and made interesting by reference to questions of everyday life in which people are presumably interested, but in our churches today it is at least as common that people are searching for a theological reason to be terribly interested in everyday life. Popular and much academic theology has it exactly backward, which is probably a result of the cultural lag to which religion is prone. It is worthy of more than passing note that those churches, mainly conservative evangelical and fundamentalist, that are growing today are the churches that speak most unabashedly about God and salvation and heaven and hell and the healing power of the Spirit. Some among them have even discovered the delights of contemplating angels in relation to heads of pins, a subject ever so much more intellectually compelling than revolutionary praxis or accommodating the teachings of Jesus to sexual liberation.

The new class of the diffuse denomination that is Catholic-Protestant Liberalism is, like Langdon Gilkey, supremely confident about the implausibility of what millions of Christians believe. "A Christian in the modern world can no longer believe such and such," they authoritatively declare. But of course there are all kinds of Christians in the modern world who believe precisely such and such. The new class ploy in response to this embarrassing reality is that such Christians are simply stupid. Or, if such Christians are indisputably very smart, it is said that they are living in the nineteenth century. (A most inappropriate time in which to put them, to be sure, since the nineteenth century was the apogee of the liberalism that still prevails in much of Protestantism and is being discovered with lively enthusiasm in much of Roman Catholicism.) But of course such Christians cannot be dismissed by educated derision or gotten rid of by chronological relocation. The assumption that people who are fully participant in the modern world find the supernatural implausible, the assumption that ours is or is rapidly becoming a secular society—these assumptions have everything going for them except the empirical evidence. (For the pertinent survey research data, and an enlightening discussion of the same by diverse scholars, see *Unsecular America* (1986), edited by this writer.) It does no good to tell people that something is no longer believable when they know from their own experience that it is eminently believable. On second thought, it perhaps does some good. It helps to undermine the credibility of experts on what is and is not credible.

When theology becomes anthropology, when talk about God is just another way of talking about ourselves, then the question of authority in the church takes center stage. The reason this happens is not hard to discover. As a consequence of the aforementioned "geological shift," Christian doctrine and ritual become mere "symbols" that, like Silly Putty, are marvelously plastic in response to what we human beings think about ourselves, how we are and how we ought to be. First we make our decisions—political, ideological, social, cultural, psychological—and then, *mirabile dictu,* we discover that Christianity is in wondrous agreement with what we decided, thus once again demonstrating the "relevance" of the faith. It is important to be reminded that orthodox Christianity has demonstrated a remarkable flexibility, that orthodoxy itself is a brilliant synthesis of Jerusalem and Athens, that it was the genius of Thomas to "baptize" Aristotle, and so forth. Contemporaries who ever have this reminder on the tip of their tongues, however, move with unseemly haste from observing that, since Thomas "came to terms with" Aristotle, we must today "come to terms" with Marxism or the Playboy philosophy. This hasty move skips over a number of considerations that may be germane. First, most of us are not Thomas. Second, Marx and Playboy are not Aristotle. Third, in its two thousand years, the Church has frequently "come to terms" with new ideas by refuting and repudiating them. Fourth, the most touted of today's new ideas are, with few exceptions, time-tattered items on the list of the refuted and repudiated.

18. AUTHORITY AS POWER

Enter church authority. In the Roman Catholic Church this often comes to a question of who owns the copyright on the symbols and who controls the distribution of franchises for the marketing of them. There is no denying that theological discourse has been grievously debased when what passes for theological controversy comes down to questions such as these. One response to all this is that the church should let a hundred flowers blossom and celebrate its theological, spiritual, and moral "pluralism." Jack Cashill, a New York advertising executive, presumably with tongue in cheek, has recently proposed that that might be the way to go. He believes that since Vatican II the church has not paid enough attention to what is called market segmentation. He has done some testing and discovered that "the name that truly caught consumer fancy was RC Light, a bit trendy perhaps but nevertheless a catchy and telling way of summing up contemporary Roman Catholicism. Phil Donahue [a television personality] has already agreed to endorse this product." But what to do about the Catholic traditionalists? RC Classic, of course. Then there's another group. "My idea here is to pioneer the radical segment and to shape a sect around the needs of those young people more interested now in liberation theology than in Papal Bulls but whose potential earning power cannot be ignored. My choice of brand name: RC Free. The attractive diversity of these new product lines should transform Catholicism from a warehouse of equity to a viable, ongoing contender."

Some readers will no doubt think such frivolity to be impertinent, if not blasphemous. That is understandable, for the questions at stake are indeed solemn. And yet our advertising executive helps expose the fatuity of claiming that the answer to confusion and anarchy is to call it pluralism and acclaim it as progress. Theology that is worthy of the name requires continuing conversation and exploration, but the conversation must be disciplined and the exploration guided. Conversation that is not disciplined is mere babble, and exploration that is not guided is mere adventurism. In the past in Roman Catholicism, the disciplining and guiding task, in other words the shepherding task, has been exercised by the magisterium, meaning the bishops acting in concert with the bishop of Rome. This is where the teaching authority resides, it was believed, although it certainly did not mean that the bishops were the only ones who were to be teaching in the church. That approach did not produce the desired conversation prior to the Council and since Vatican II there have been radical changes in the understanding of the magisterium.

We have already discussed the theologian within the context of the new class, and the emergence of Roman Catholic theology into academic respectability and the constriction of specializations and peer group guilds. These are structural questions and are amenable to sociological analysis. It is doubtful that anybody decided one day that this is the way that Catholic academic theology should go, although it is certain that many people failed to think through carefully enough what the future of theology as a discipline, and Catholic higher education as a whole, should be in the American context. Many Catholic universities and colleges were "secularized" in the 1970s in a bid both for government funding and for acceptance by a larger academic world that looks with suspicion upon institutions with a credal commitment. At the same time, such schools wanted to maintain a "Catholic identity" in order to draw students and retain the allegiance of alumni. By the mid-1980s some educators here, joined by authorities in the Vatican, were worrying out loud about the possibility that Roman Catholic higher education might be going the way that most church-related Protestant colleges went long ago. In such cases, the church connection became so attenuated over the years that the initiating religious purpose is now little more than a footnote in their institutional histories. But even if Roman Catholic institutions manage in form and substance to remain distinctively Roman Catholic, individual scholars, also in theology, increasingly find their primary world of discourse in academic specializations that are not specifically Roman Catholic or even Christian. Quite apart from the responsiveness or unresponsiveness of particular theologians to church authority, the magisterium is challenged by a structure that divides the vocational loyalties, and perhaps the souls, of many theologians.

But the magisterium is challenged more frontally by those who insist that authority means authoritarianism, that all relationships in the church are preeminently relationships of power, and that the great struggle in the church, as in the world, is the liberation of the oppressed from the yoke of the oppressor. Those who promulgate this interpretation of reality routinely declare that theirs is a radical and revolutionary program of change. On the other hand, when accused of insurrection against the leadership of the church, they just as routinely plead innocence. First, it is said that theology is anthropology. Second, that the question of anthropology is political. Third, that the "symbols" of the faith are to be retranslated in service to the revolutionary struggle. Fourth, that theological authority belongs to those who are in solidarity with the struggle, and that they therefore have as much right, indeed more right, than anyone else to define the meaning of Catholicism. The radicality of this proposal is not simply in its defiance of the existing magisterium but in its establishment of a new magisterium of revolutionary authenticity.

At times the reasoning involved becomes quite convoluted and perplexing. It is argued, for example, that the new magisterium is in fact the old magisterium in its authentic form. Juan Luis Segundo, a leading liberation theologian, would seem to suggest as much in his 1985 book, *Theology And The Church,* bearing the portentous subtitle, *A Response to Cardinal Ratzinger and a Warning to the Whole Church.* After making the by now conventional theological moves described above, Segundo concludes on this note:

These pages will have fulfilled their task if they convince the reader of the necessity to reaffirm the solemn magisterium of the Church which, after so long a time of immobility and absenteeism, returned, as Paul VI said, to place the Church at the service of humanity. This book will have achieved its purpose if it convinces the reader that the implementation of the Council has not gone too far; that, on the contrary, it has been blocked midway in its journey. Finally, this book will have been worth the effort if it shows that the same Spirit who helped the Council speak the truth also helped it to speak clearly. Fidelity to that Spirit does not allow *the opposite* to be spoken on the pretext of explaining the Council better or of preventing it from being misunderstood. If this occurs, then this book will achieve its goal. In case of doubt, it will always be better to wager on what Cardinal Henri de Lubac expressed in a prayer: "If I lack love and justice, I separate myself completely from you, God, and my adoration is nothing more than idolatry. To believe in you, I must believe in love and in justice, and to believe in these things is worth a thousand times more than saying your Name."

For one who, like the present writer, is looking in on Roman Catholic disputes, the above declaration is in its audacity, in its naked chutzpah, so astonishing as to be admirable. Leave aside what Henri de Lubac might think about the end to which he is invoked by Segundo. The striking thing is the assertion that he, Segundo, is affirming the authentic magisterium. One must try, in charity, to believe that the author is not simply being disingenuous. In sorting out "the councils of Vatican II," he sets forth the true council, appealing to a deceased Paul VI against the all too lively Cardinal Ratzinger who, as he recognizes, speaks with the full support of John Paul II. He does not say that the magisterium of the church is divided. He does not say that the magisterium may be misguided and he has some questions he would like to take up with whomever is in charge. He claims rather that the magisterium is under attack by those who claim to represent the magisterium, and he issues "a warning to the whole church" against their perfidy. With his warning he offers the assurance that he, Juan Luis Segundo, will not abandon the defense and exercise of the church's true magisterium.

With others who claim to have a radical agenda for theological change, there is no suspicion of disingenuousness. Rosemary Radford Ruether, for instance, is nothing if not candid in her assault on the "Vatican conservatives" who are attempting to squelch what she believes to be the authentic church. A feminist devoted to the Father/Mother God and sundry goddesses, Ruether makes no secret of her hope to capture the church institution for the purposes of global liberation. Writing, for example, in 1986 in the Jesuit journal *America* on "Crises and Challenges of Catholicism Today," she frankly acknowledges that the leadership is determined to resist what she believes are the three great challenges that have emerged since Vatican II: "1) the challenge of democratic values and human rights in the church's institutional life; 2) the challenge of feminism and the crisis of sexual morality in church teaching; and 3) the challenge of third world liberation struggles." It is on the sexual questions that conservatives are most unbending. "Although historical-critical thinking and social justice issues generally are on the hit list of these groups, the chief victims are those concerned with sexual rights, namely, reproductive rights, equality for women both in the church and in society, gay rights and optional celibacy." For Ruether there is nothing to discuss with respect to the justice of her positions. Abortion and acceptance of homosexuality are matters of elementary human rights, and as for the question of ordaining women to the priesthood, her answer is unqualified: "Either ordain women, or stop baptizing them."

There is a winsome plainspokenness in the position advanced by Ruether and others. They readily acknowledge that their theological project is in conflict not only with today's church leadership but with much of the entire Christian tradition of two thousand years. Nonetheless, they have accepted Vatican II's invitation to "read the signs of the times" and are pledged to moving the church toward the right side of the revolution that is, they believe, the inexorable course of history. Not surprisingly, many critics are perplexed and irritated that people who admit to being in fundamental disagreement with the church do not simply leave. But that is too simple. Asked at a symposium why she does not leave a church that she believes to be inherently, and not just accidentally, oppressive, Ruether responds, "You can't make a revolution without xerox machines, and the church has the xerox machines." In a more considered vein, Ruether elaborates in *America:* "One might then ask, why even bother to try to reform it, if we are already doing 'our thing'? It is at this point that Catholic liberal-leftists need to gain greater respect and understanding of the function of historical institutions. Because we have been so deprived of meaningful political participation in church leadership, we easily become naive anarchists. We forget that no matter how great our living-room liturgy may be, it is going to last only a few years. The parish will go on and will continue to be the main vehicle for gathering and socializing Catholics throughout the world and down through the generations. Unless we manage to insert what we are doing in more autonomous settings back into these main institutional vehicles of ministry and community, breathing new life and activity into them through sharing the fruits of our work, it will have no lasting historical impact."

That is a remarkably straightforward statement of what the radicalisms of the sixties called "the long march through the institutions." To be sure, it may increasingly seem to be based upon a forlorn hope. While many "liberal-left" Roman Catholics feel free to "do their thing" in liberated corners at the margins of the church, and while people such as Rosemary Ruether will continue to be invited to conferences in order to "balance" the program with a "radical perspective," there is a growing awareness that the party is over. It is now the wee hours of the morning, the band has packed up, the streamers are down, the bar is closed, and most of the revelers have gone home. Having damned everything but the circus, the circus itself has now finished its run. For self-professed radicals who have been on a euphoric roll, the scene cannot help but seem depressing. And yet, for those who take the long view, for those who are secure in their confidence that they act in solidarity with the logic of history, the situation is not all that depressing. There are hard radicals and soft radicals and people who just play at being radical. Those who were just playing are now going straight, and the hard ones need not be disconsolate so long as the soft ones are still doing their work. The most important piece of that work is the further insinuation of the belief that theology is simply anthropology, that the symbols of transcendence are to be harnessed to the immanent concerns that in fact produced them in the first place, that the words and gestures of otherworldliness are but poetically heightened statements about this world, the only world there is.

19. THE PLASTICITY OF SYMBOLS

As mentioned before, in 1975 an ecumenical and unofficial group of theologians, meeting in Hartford, Connecticut, issued what was called "The Hartford Appeal for Theological Affirmation." Their argument that Christian theology across the board was suffering from "a loss of transcendence" attracted widespread attention. The Hartford theologians did not anticipate, however, the ways in which others would then assert transcendence with a vengeance, and would end up reinforcing many of the positions Hartford intended to counter. Among liberation theologians, especially those of the feminist persuasion, it became the pattern to say that, yes indeed, God is transcendent. He/She/It is so transcendent as to be ineffable, beyond the possibility of human imagination or expression. Therefore, since there are no words or metaphors that can approximate the being and purposes of god, which are beyond our understanding, we must select and devise the words, metaphors, and gestures that serve our own being and purposes, which we can understand. Far from reducing God to our human level, God in his/her/its transcendence and ineffability is thus glorified into irrelevance. This is essentially the argument advanced in the explanation accompanying *An Inclusive Language Lectionary,* which was produced under the auspices of the National Council of Churches and has been warmly acclaimed also by Roman Catholic feminists. It is an argument that does an end run around the Hartford critique and returns to the point from which it started. The result is not the loss of transcendence but the declared irrelevance of the transcendent.

Of course, the idea that we can select, invent, and reshape religious symbols that "work" according to our purposes tends to overlook the claim that the ineffable God, who is indeed beyond our capacities of expression, has expressed himself in Jesus the Christ. Consequently, there are words, metaphors, and paradigms that have a normative status because they are, as orthodox Christians say, revealed. In addition to slighting revelation, the approach described above may misunderstand what is indeed the "convergence" of theology and anthropology. Wolfhart Pannenberg, possibly the most important systematic theologian of our time, shares an interest in doing theology "from below." We human beings can only think humanly. When we say "God says" or "God has revealed," or even when we simply say "God," it is unquestionably we who are speaking within the limits of human language and understanding. But that does not mean we are thinking and speaking alone. It does not mean that there is no referent, that there is no "other," to which such language refers. In fact, it may be that there is a conversation and the conversation was initiated by the other. It may be that these symbols of language and ritual are not projection but response. It is precisely by attending to anthropology, suggests Pannenberg, in *Anthropology in Theological Perspective* (1985), that we encounter a transcendence that is not an empty transcendence, a mere vastness to be filled by our religious speech and gestures.

Christianity, and the subspecies of Christianity that is Roman Catholicism, is a thematic grasping of an anthropologically discovered "prior reality" in the particular form of dogma, doctrine, liturgy, and churchly order. Much Roman Catholic theology is still in thrall to the heady discovery that the particular form is not in all its particulars divinely established and unchallengeably normative. That discovery, or the permission to proclaim that discovery, was the great liberation of Vatican II. Theological books beyond numbering, both scholarly and popular, effuse excitements about "historical contextualization" and other hermeneutical relativizations of what was previously taken to be unchangeable revelation. Theology, it is asserted, is no longer to be done "from the top down" but "from the bottom up." And the bottom, so to speak, is defined by experts in the bottom sciences, whether anthropological, sociological, psychological, or political-theoretical. In this view, theology and the church possess an inherited "system" of symbols and beliefs that is employed in distinctively Christian talk about what everyone else may be talking about in the language of their quite different set of symbols. There are no singular Christian truth claims by which other constructions of reality are challenged. Religious symbols, it is suggested, are simply the hypercharged form preferred by *homo religiosus* in talking about reality, and some of these religious people happen to be Christians and many of those happen to be Roman Catholic Christians.

The above is admittedly a too-brief, but not, I think, inaccurate, description of a reductionist understanding of theology and Christian belief that has deeply influenced influential sectors of Roman Catholic thought since Vatican II. The presumed collapse of the possibility of modern belief in the supernatural is characteristic of this development. The result is that Christianity, and the Roman Catholic Church in particular, is seen as a vast resource of spirituality and formidable organizational strength to be recruited to our various projects. The projects may be as different as revolutionary class struggle, the creation of an androgynous society, the advancement of democratic socialism, or the free world's defense against communism. But in self-consciously progressive Roman Catholic thought since Vatican II, the movement has been from the absolutizing certitudes of the Tridentine church to the relativizing certitudes of nineteenth-century Protestant liberalism. Ironically, both before and after, the focus is on the question of institutional authority. Before the Council, authority regulated what may be publicly thought and said; after the Council, when almost anything can and is publicly thought and said, the dispute is over who has the authority to deploy Roman Catholic teaching and devotion to what end.

At the Council and since, much effort was expended on relativizing the absolutizers. Now the task is, in Peter Berger's happy phrase, to "relativize the relativizers." In view of the earlier stifling of the modernist impulse, it was perhaps necessary, even inevitable, that post-Vatican II theology return to the problems posed by nineteenth-century liberalism. One cannot bypass or simply leap over that great intellectual and spiritual enterprise. As the philosopher Alfred North Whitehead observed, the only simplicity to be trusted is the simplicity that is on the far side of complexity. Or we may invoke Karl Marx's wise dictum (playing on the name of Feuerbach) that one has not understood the modern mind unless one has passed through the "fiery brook of Feuerbach." At the risk of pressing the image too far, much of contemporary Roman Catholic theology is wallowing in the marshes on the near side of the fiery brook, while some theologians are center stream and a few seem to have arrived on the far side.

The present Roman Catholic preoccupation with church authority is theologically debased and ecumenically sterile. It is theologically debased because it fixes attention not upon the truth claims derived from God's self-revelation but upon who is authorized to set the rules for addressing such truths, if indeed they are truths. This tends to confirm the cynic's view that theology is not a deliberation about truths but a contestation over power. And the preoccupation with church authority is ecumenically sterile because it is for the most part a dispute over in-house Roman Catholic prerogatives. Thus, despite the Council's "opening to the Church," Roman Catholicism may again be turning in upon itself. The dispute over the magisterium—over the varieties of teaching authority possessed by theologians, by bishops, and by the pope in the exercise of his "Petrine ministry"—could make a great ecumenical contribution. In different ways, the question of teaching authority is of great moment to all the churches. But today the dispute is usually conducted in a manner that is of limited interest to Roman Catholics. Fundamentalists, cleaving to the authority of their inerrant Bible, and liberal Protestants, having largely abandoned the issue of authority altogether, both smugly view from afar the curious contretemps of intra-Catholic quarreling.

Within the Roman Catholic Church it would seem that both traditional-ists and progressives contribute to this unhappy circumstance. Tradition-alists—who are often, perhaps typically, indifferent or even hostile to the ecumenical mandate of Vatican II—frequently seem to be saying that the only theological question is the question of authority. Once the question of "obedience to Peter" is settled, everything else falls into line. Progres-sives find themselves playing by the rules set by the traditionalists and become embroiled in endless discussion about the "limits" of obedience. For example, when a theologian at Catholic University is censured by the Vatican, he defends himself by claiming that he has not dissented from any "infallible" teachings of the magisterium. Here theological discourse is debased, since the distinction between "infallible" and "ordinary" teaching is an essentially mechanical and juridical one subject to institu-tional definition. If, in the power plays between dissenters and authori-ties, that way of putting the issue is pressed hard enough, it can only invite the authorities to fudge the distinction altogether, declaring (fallibly?) that every teaching that is official participates in infallibility.

The consequence is not only ecumenically sterile but potentially disas-trous, for it can only compound existing anxieties about Rome's claims with respect to infallibility—claims that have been since Vatican I happily ambiguous. And, of course, such a direction leads away from theological conversation and back to what we have called a package theory of Catholi-cism that ends up in haggling over how much or how little is required to be a Roman Catholic in good standing. It is a question of professional interest to those who must be certified as Roman Catholic in good stand-ing, of personal interest to those who, for whatever reason, want to be Roman Catholic in good standing, and of political-cultural interest to those, Roman Catholic and other, who think a lighter or heavier Catholic package will advance the social purposes they favor. But it is a question of almost no theological interest whatever.

20. A TRIED AND TIRED ECUMENISM

In this second part we have surveyed, then, "the councils of Vatican II." The survey is by no means exhaustive. Books and monographs interpret-ing Vatican II will be produced for years to come, popular impressions of the spirit and letter of the Council will continue to change from time to time, and all the while the various levels of officialdom will be setting forth their interpretation of what the Council said and what it means today. Confusing though it may be, these are necessary parts to the "reception" of what may be the most important religious event of the century. Analysts of the Council recognized early on that the process of reception would not be easy. The progressives who dominated the Coun-cil knew that they had a once-in-a-lifetime chance to set a clear course toward renewal. That renewal—theological, liturgical, pastoral—might have taken hold more effectively had the Council fathers built into the documents safeguards against some of the more mischievous interpretations of subsequent years. But the climate of that moment, to which the Council impressively contributed, was not friendly to cautionary notes. In addition, the opportunity for advance seemed so singular, and resistance to the advance so formidable, that it was feared that even the most carefully crafted cautions would play into the hands of "the prophets of gloom."

Disputations over the meaning of Vatican II have produced recognizable parties who, as mentioned before, sometimes seem to be settled down into trench warfare. There is the party of continuity and the party of discontinuity, there are those who would discard traditional understandings and those who would deploy them to contemporary ends, plus those who think traditional understandings should be sustained just because they are true. And, of course, there is dispute over how to define the tradition that is to be defended. Those who would renew the faith and life of the church by reference to Scripture and the early fathers are hardly opponents of tradition. At the same time, many traditionalists are in fact defending as *the* tradition but one small slice of the Christian and Roman Catholic experience, namely the shape of American Catholicism in the first half of the twentieth century, notably under the pontificate of Pius XII. In this respect, some traditionalists are like Protestant fundamentalists who champion "that old-time religion," which is in fact a rather novel definition of the faith dating from the fundamentalist-modernist controversies of less than a century ago. In addition, the Council, no doubt inadvertently, gave encouragement to utopianisms, both hard and soft. Thesis 8 of the proposed Catholic moment (see Part 6) underscores the urgency of challenging the imperiousness of the political. Dominant interpretations of Vatican II, regrettably, have typically done just the opposite.

A pervasive soft utopianism, with its heart set upon reordering the world in accord with the brotherhood/sisterhood of humankind and the fatherhood/motherhood of God, can also be very useful to hard utopians. Soft utopians, given the disappointments following the euphoria of the Council, can conclude that the Kingdom of God has but been delayed for a while longer. Hard utopians, as Our Lord observed, would take the Kingdom by force. Hard utopianism is gnosticism with an inhuman face. It is most clearly represented, but not exclusively represented, in varieties of liberation theology. The collapse of the transcendent into the immanent can, in the safe confines of Theology 101 at your local Catholic college, provide the pleasures of nihilism without the abyss. Elsewhere the abyss is all too real, as sacred symbols are used to pave the path toward revolutions that, again and again, devour their children. And, it is said, if the church that surrendered itself to the revolution is itself oppressed by the revolution, it is, by the inherent logic of the revolution, because the church has become counterrevolutionary. It must then be displaced by the true church, the people's church, which lives obediently under the magisterium of the revolution until the revolution is secured and churches are needed no more. When oppression is at last ended, when Marx's "kingdom of freedom" is established, there will be no occasion for religion, which is the sigh of oppressed humanity, and the church will then disappear in the final fulfillment of its mission. This, it is said, is what it means for the church to walk the way of the cross.

Such ideas, in both their soft and hard versions, are not new in the history of religion or of Christianity. The new thing is that they have taken hold as they have in the Roman Catholic Church. And, because of the size, influence, and variety of that church, old ideas are given new direction and new vitality. Further, the embrace of these ideas by sectors of Roman Catholicism has breathed new life into the same ideas in parts of Protestantism where such ideas were thought to be exhausted and discredited. This, it might be suggested, is one kind of ecumenism, and it is surely welcomed by many. The dominance of liberation theologies in, for instance, the World Council of Churches is in large part attributable to Vatican II. One scholar, writing on the relationship between the World Council and the Vatican, argues in effect that the World Council has had the courage of Vatican II's convictions. That is to say, hard utopianism in Roman Catholicism has been promoted chiefly at the "grass roots" and, at a theoretical level, in academe, apart from and increasingly against the formal church leadership. The top leadership of the World Council, on the other hand, has boldly thrown its energy, resources, credibility, and somewhat secularized blessings into partisan struggles to get Christianity "on the right side of the revolution." The World Council, however, is hardly comparable to the Roman Catholic Church. For one thing, it is not a church but a loose federation of churches that represent a declining minority of Protestantism in the world, plus Eastern Orthodox churches that participate in the Council for reasons that are, at least in those cases where church leaders have no choice but to be agents of their governments, primarily political. The irony should not be missed that many ideas that grew up, grew old, and almost died in liberal Protestantism have been given a second life through the vibrant example of their first life in Roman Catholicism.

21. A DIFFERENT ECUMENISM

But there is another ecumenism, and it could be the source of renewal not only for the Roman Catholic Church but for world Christianity. This is the "confessional ecumenism" described by Cardinal Willebrands of the Secretariat for Christian Unity. (See Thesis 4 of the Catholic moment in Part 6.) It is quite the opposite of the old formula of ecumenism once championed by liberal Protestantism and now embraced by many progressive Roman Catholics: "creeds divide, deeds unite." Today, divisions over deeds—over how to read the signs of the times and make the appropriate political, economic, and ideological commitments that will advance God's transformative purposes in the world—are as deep, and often deeper, than divisions over creeds. Such divisions find extreme expression in what some theologians call "the partisan church," which is "the true church" defined by its solidarity with the struggle of the poor and oppressed. In fact, however, the only Christian unity that is distinctively Christian and therefore worth advancing is a unity based upon creed, upon common confession of faith.

Such a common and uniting confession requires a different reading of the text and spirit of Vatican II. The reading that is required focuses upon Christ and leads to what Joseph Ratzinger describes as a Christological definition of the Church as his mystical body. In addition, it lifts up the "People of God" as a category both inclusive and eschatological. It is inclusive because it comprehends the reach of divine grace and covenantal fidelity beyond the boundaries of any religious institution, and it is eschatological because it keeps the community of faith ever under judgment. The smug claim to be the People of God simply because of sacramental participation or of solidarity with God's putative purposes in the world is a boast that is tantamount to blasphemy. The Church is daily called to die to itself and to be born again as it responds to the Gospel with the words of Mary, "Let it be done to me according to your word." The Gospel, the message of God's forgiving and reconciling work in Christ, is not created by the Church; the Church is created by the Gospel. The Gospel is not so much a possession of the Church as the Church is possessed by the Gospel. These are fundamental Reformation insights, but they are in no way the exclusive property of the Reformation. Today they are asserted with more clarity and forcefulness by some Roman Catholics than they are in the churches that lay claim to the Reformation heritage.

In sorting out "the councils of Vatican II," it will not do to simply go through the texts making a count of statements favoring one reading or another. The "spirit" of the Council must be discerned. Presumably the charism of the Holy Spirit, which guided the institution that convened the Council, has not abandoned that institution in its interpreting of the Council. It is really not very convincing to "de-contextualize" the Council, to treat it as an isolated moment of revelatory authority. The complaint is heard that too many Roman Catholic theologians talk about the "pre-Vatican II church" and the "post-Vatican II church" as though these are two quite different churches. The complaint has considerable merit. The even more remarkable development, however, is the widespread habit of speaking about post-Vatican II church*es*. There is, it is suggested, the authentic post-Vatican II church that has "truly" incorporated the Council, and the false post-Vatican II church that is trying to undo the

Council and become again the pre-Vatican II church. The result is a multiplication of churches tenuously related to one another by communal Catholicism. The result is sectarianism. One is reminded of the supraorthodox Scottish Presbyterian who concluded that "the true church is composed of thee and me, and I am not sure of thee."

There are, to be sure, objections raised to the argument suggested here. It may be objected, for instance, that non-Roman Catholics who are committed to Christian unity call for a more coherent Roman Catholicism for which Roman Catholics will pay the price. It may be ecumenically important to know where the Roman Catholic Church "stands," but it is the Roman Catholic theologian who dissents from that stand who will be penalized. The objection cannot be lightly dismissed. Certainly it would serve neither the purpose of Christian unity nor the renewal of Catholic theology were the church to return to the "manual theology" of its more monolithic past. Nobody who cares about the nature and mission of the Church in the world can want that. At the same time, both reconciliation between churches and renewal within churches are ill served by the sectarian chaos that marks much of Roman Catholic life today and is misleadingly called pluralism. Roman Catholicism contributes nothing to the larger Christian community by demonstrating that it can be as diverse, confused, and normless as are some other communities.

The mark of a pluralism that is worthy of the name is not indifference to disagreements but the engagement of disagreements within the context of mutually respectful conversation. What non-Roman Catholics look for from Roman Catholicism, among other things, is the demonstration of the possibility of that kind of conversation. Without that, the theological contretemps in Roman Catholicism are little more than petty battles over institutional authority. It is of slight interest to other Christians that Roman Catholics are as free as, say, United Methodists to believe and teach whatever they wish. Such a situation is, on the other hand, of great and morbid interest to those who are convinced that Christianity has nothing that it believes, teaches, and confesses to which the modern world need pay the slightest attention.

It is illogical to the point of being ludicrous to isolate and elevate Vatican II as having granted a general release from church authority. Apart from the continuing context of the church's teaching about the authority of a council, Vatican II has no authority to grant such a release. It would seem to make little sense to appeal to the authority of the church (e.g., John XXIII and Vatican II) in order to delegitimate the authority of the church (e.g., John Paul II). Of course there are differences and tensions, and one might argue that John XXIII understood the tradition better than does John Paul II, but it is all part of a continuing tradition. It may seem impertinent for a non-Roman Catholic writer to comment in this way on how Roman Catholic thinkers conduct their business; unless, of course, ecumenism means that the business of each is the business of all; unless, of course, what is happening in Roman Catholicism has import far beyond the boundaries of that communion. To this writer, and I daresay to many Protestants, Roman Catholic debates to date about theology and teaching authority have been disappointing in their institutional insularity. In this critical respect, voices on the Catholic Left and the Catholic Right seem equally determined to maintain an essentially insular Tridentine church quite untouched by the ecumenical vision of Vatican II.

But here another objection must be heard. It is commonly said that the current leadership of the church, notably John Paul II and Joseph Ratzinger, are in fact voices of the Right who care little about ecumenism and are concerned only about reestablishing their own power and authority. Such claims, although widespread, are manifestly nothing more than ad hominem attacks aimed at discrediting the person and motives of these leaders and those who sympathize with them. Such claims are, quite simply, violations of Christian charity and distortions of the relevant evidence. One need not believe that these men are spiritual heroes or the greatest theological minds of the century. One need not think they have transcended temptations to pride and petty self-interest. Both have spoken often and movingly about sin and ambiguity in the lives of Christians, and there is no reason to believe that they think they are exempt from the reality they describe. But only the churlish or the partisan fanatic would deny that both are superior theological minds. Both have repeatedly professed their deep devotion to ecumenism. Indeed, as a regular reading of the bulletins from the Secretariat for Christian Unity amply demonstrates, this Pope, much more than any of his predecessors, has spoken frequently, forcefully, and forthrightly on the imperative of ecclesial reconciliation and what is required to advance that goal. John Paul has left no doubt that, in the words of our Thesis 4 (Part 6), ecumenism is for orthodox Roman Catholicism "inherent and irreversible."

It is truly odd but it is oddly true that one must today present a defense for taking the Pope and the prefect of the Congregation for the Doctrine of the Faith seriously as theological interlocutors. In numerous conversations one discovers that it is a defense frequently required in speaking to Roman Catholics and non-Roman Catholics alike. The lively interest in "what is happening in Catholicism" is often focused on what is happening at the margins. A person may argue that what is happening at the margins may in some cases be more true and may finally prevail. But it is beyond dispute that, on the eve of the third millennium, Roman Catholic teaching and life is formally defined with increasing effect by the Pope, the Curia, and, when put to the question, the overwhelming majority of bishops throughout the world. One may not like their definition. This writer has many questions to raise about it. But it is the dominant definition. At least it is a definition so influential that not to engage it is not to be talking about Roman Catholicism today at all. Here the intuition expressed by

Rosemary Radford Ruether is surely correct, although the question goes far beyond her concern for the parish. Long after the passing of the myriad figures who are today "doing their thing," the institution of the Roman Catholic Church as formally defined by its leadership will be shaping the faith and life of generations of Christians to come.

Among the "councils of Vatican II," then, we take with particular seriousness the Council depicted by John Paul II and Joseph Ratzinger. In response to critical challenges to Christianity in our time, they are proposing answers that may not always be helpful but must always be heeded. In contemporary Roman Catholic discussions, it seems to this observer, the arguments are too much about John Paul II and Joseph Ratzinger and too little about the arguments they advance. We need to engage those arguments. One form that engagement takes is to explore the ways in which they are proposing an understanding of "church and world in paradox" that is consonant with Reformation insight and fruitful for reconciliation between the churches. If this understanding is as promising as it appears to be, then *this* Vatican Council II will turn out to be in consequence what it claimed to be at the time, namely, a genuinely ecumenical council speaking from and to the entire Church of Christ.

PART III

The Hard Road to Renewal

In 1981 Paul Johnson, the noted British historian, published *Pope John Paul II and the Catholic Restoration.* Is "restoration" really what this pontificate is about? And, if so, what is it that is to be restored? The situation prior to Vatican Council II? The term "restoration" has been seized upon by many Roman Catholic conservatives and is, with at least equal passion, excoriated by progressives. The latter believe the term smacks of regression, of an effort to reestablish the *ancien regime.* It does not help, in the liberal view of things, that the term has frequently been employed by Cardinal Ratzinger in describing the task at hand.

Henri de Lubac suggests in the interview quoted earlier that, especially among the French, the controversy over the term may be much ado about little.

There are some patriots among us French who cannot imagine that the world is vaster than our own hexagon and that others have the right *not* to shape their language or their experience on the basis of our little political history. Further, . . . this word, which has suddenly become so controversial, is a conciliar word. It's the French translation—and the only one possible—of the word *instauratio,* which occurs in the very title of one of the council constitutions and several times afterwards. Moreover, the word is so far from being backward-looking that it fits in well with another expression in the conciliar text, translated in French by "progress": *ad instaurandam atque fovendam.* . . . It even seems to me that this pair would make an excellent motto: *Restore* (re-establish), where necessary, the true meaning of the council, and *progress* in its application.

Without disputing de Lubac's lexicology, it might be suggested that the better word for the intention he endorses is renewal.

And yet "restoration" is in fact closer to what some people think Pope John Paul is doing and should be doing. Paul Johnson writes about what he views as the illusions and reckless experimentations of the 1960s, followed by the disillusionments and declines of the 1970s. The question now is how "to base the new realism . . . on a firm foundation of reassurance, the rediscovery of ancient truth, the reassertion of fundamental values, the redefinition of what is good and what is evil, not relatively but absolutely, always and everywhere." According to Johnson and many others, John Paul is just the man for the moment.

It might seem an impossible task for one man. But of course John Paul has at his command a matchless instrument, which might have been expressly fashioned for this purpose. It came into his hands just in time. There was a moment, in the mid-1970s, when the Roman Catholic Church seemed in real danger of inflicting grievous injury on itself, to the point of destroying those characteristics which are its greatest strengths: its self-confidence, its internal order, its unchangeability. With the coming of John Paul that moment passed. The damage has now been contained. It is being repaired. The instrument is being fashioned for service again. It is much required.

Unlike some Roman Catholic writers, Johnson is not reluctant to criticize Vatican Council II itself. "From the perspective of today, the Council can be seen as merely one manifestation of the world-wide challenge to authority in every field which was the outstanding characteristic of the 1960s. It was a decade of illusion, in which eager spirits were led by long-continued prosperity to believe and propagate many utopian notions: that poverty could be abolished, cruelty and violence legislated out of existence, every freedom infinitely extended and voraciously enjoyed, and some kind of democratic and egalitarian paradise established on earth." The vastly expanded institutions of higher learning, he writes, poured on to the scene "countless armies of young graduates, who shared these fantastic hopes and set about elbowing aside the obscurantist and authoritarian elders who alone, it was argued, prevented their realization." It is perhaps stretching the point to see the Council fathers, many of whom were elderly, as extensions of the youth revolution of the 1960s, but, as earlier noted, there was a "spirit of the times" to which the Council was by no means immune.

This spirit found even more forceful expression in other parts of the Christian community. The 1968 assembly of the World Council of Churches in Uppsala, Sweden, approved resolutions calling for most of the cosmic transformations listed by Johnson. The belief was proclaimed that all is possible if only we have the will for it. The convergence of post-Vatican II Roman Catholicism and the Protestant main line was evident also in the 1968 establishment of a joint Vatican-WCC Society for Development and Peace (Sodepax). It was a time when Roman Catholic membership in the World Council was desired and confidently expected by many, and was given formal consideration by the Vatican's Secretariat for Christian Unity. But according to Thomas Derr, by 1970 or 1971 "the curtain fell" on such hopes (*Barriers to Ecumenism*, 1983). The Vatican would continue to cooperate with the WCC's Faith and Order Commission, which deals more seriously with the theological and confessional dimensions of ecumenism, but was clearly withdrawing from cooperation in the "praxis" of social transformation and had declared the question of

WCC membership to be, in the words of Paul VI, "not yet mature." "Sodepax" lingered in a long half-life and then expired. What Johnson and others see as the necessary damage containment was under way long before John Paul was elected to the chair of Peter.

The spirited, even polemical, tone of a Paul Johnson is perhaps explained in part by disappointment with illusions that he once shared. A neoconservative, it is said, is a liberal who has been mugged by reality, or a cultural radical who has a daughter in high school. In 1974 Johnson published a biography of John XXIII that is at least as admiring, at times adulatory, as his later writing about John Paul. Of course, to live is to change, as Cardinal Newman observed. The Protestant theologian Reinhold Niebuhr wrote that he was never so inclined to stridency in criticizing the faults of others as when they were the faults he suspected in himself. There is an unmistakable scent of embittered disillusionment among some who champion "the Catholic restoration." The experience of the unhappy consequences of an uncritical opening to the world can prompt a similarly uncritical closing to the world.

Under Pope John Paul, Paul Johnson writes, "Nervous and agitated hands will not be permitted to dilute the essence of Latin Christianity, that potent concentrate distilled over two millennia, which has provided spiritual intoxication for the elite and daily comfort for grateful millions over a huge arc of human history. [The Roman Church] is the one fixed point in a changing world; and if it changes itself (as from time to time it must), such transformations must be as imperceptible as a glacier's, moving with majestic gravity along a path preordained by its own nature. Catholicism has the time-scale not of fashion but of geology." (One remembers the "geological shift" referred to earlier by Langdon Gilkey and Richard McBrien.) Permanence, says Johnson, is 'the salient truth of Catholic sociology."

To say that Johnson's understanding of Roman Catholicism is reactive is not to say that it is wrong. There is much in the world and in the church to which reaction is the only intelligent response. And yet the above understanding of Roman Catholicism does seem as inadequate (well, almost as inadequate) as the understanding that it would counter and, in fact, largely mirrors. It conveys a feeling of relief that at last somebody, John Paul, is calling the church to order, is seizing a few unruly adolescents by the scuffs of their necks and knocking some sense into their heads. In short, there is a sense of being fed up, of having had enough, of refusing to take it anymore. No doubt many Catholics, along with church authorities, feel they have been subjected to extreme provocations. When, for example, at the end of the 1970s the Vatican finally withdrew from the European theologian Hans Küng the license to represent himself as a Roman Catholic theologian, the response of many Roman Catholics was to wonder why it took so long.

It is not that figures such as Küng, Schillebeeckx, Curran, and others do not understand "the salient truth of Catholic sociology." It is rather that they were perceived as playing fast and loose with Catholic faith, without which Catholic sociology is but a residual tribalism. These "dissidents" (a most honorable word) seemed at times to be taunting the authorities, daring the Vatican to act against them, until the Vatican at last called their bluff. Küng in particular had for years been proclaiming publicly that, on a host of issues, his position was not the official position of the church. It can plausibly be argued that, in withdrawing his credentials as a Roman Catholic theologian, the Vatican was doing no more than formally declaring that it agreed with Küng, that he was right in saying that he did not represent official Roman Catholic teaching. There was, it must be admitted, an unseemly whiff of arrogance in many of Küng's pronouncements. "My inquiry into infallibility gave rise to the greatest debate among Catholic theologians since Vatican II." "I can always be convinced by reasons, but I am still waiting for them." "What may perhaps distinguish me from others is simply that I am looking for a clear, honest and consistent solution." "The more gentle notes of my previous works had not aroused those in responsible positions in the church, so I had to sound the alarm. . . . There are cases, and this is one of them, where it is expedient to engage in polemics."

An American theologian who, after years of futile conversations with the Congregation for the Doctrine of the Faith, has been censured by the Vatican holds a news conference portraying himself as a martyr to truth, depicting Cardinal Ratzinger as the Grand Inquisitor, yet reaffirming his fidelity to the church and commending his case to God, "in the confidence that she will prevail." Although effective in eliciting partisan applause, such expressions do not bespeak a seriousness about the theological dialogue that dissidents typically claim they are denied by church authorities. As a Lutheran, the present writer would not disallow the legitimacy of polemics. Blessed Martin, as Roman Catholics do not ordinarily call him, was a master of the art, even by the standards of a most polemical age. But there were very big differences. Luther was not filing a job complaint against unfair employment practices. His Ninety-five Theses of 1517 were not an act of defiance but an invitation to theological debate and were framed in a manner exceedingly deferential—by today's standards, almost servile—toward church authorities. But after his concerns were roughly and relentlessly rejected, he would reach the point of declaring the Roman authorities in question to be apostate and claiming they had become the enemies of the truth. And that is the biggest difference, namely, the truth at stake. Luther polemicized against Rome, as Søren Kierkegaard polemicized against the established church of Denmark, as Karl Barth polemicized against nineteenth-century liberalism, because he believed that the Gospel was at stake. The issue was not academic freedom or the permissible limits of dissent, but the Gospel that alone makes the Church the Church.

One does not sense that same life-or-death urgency in the way the issues are posed by today's dissenters. This is not to say that they are not serious people. It is, for instance, a serious thing to be caught in conflicting loyalties to different establishments, ecclesial and academic. Each establishment has its own canons by which integrity and fidelity are measured. Each has its own orthodoxy, its own doctrines, and even dogmas. What is viewed as dissent from one establishment may also be viewed as obedience to another establishment. But at least in some celebrated cases of dissent from church authority, there seems to be less of a life-or-death struggle and more of a tactical and sometimes coy testing of the ecclesial limits. Particularly troubling is the way in which the plaudits of non-Roman Catholics and the general media are welcomed and indeed solicited. The liberal Protestant divinity school that lionizes Hans Küng does not, in all probability, care very much about the integrity of Catholic theology. On the contrary, it is reasonable to suspect that there is more than a touch of anti-Catholicism in such gleeful celebration of the opponents of putative papal tyranny. The administrator of one Protestant school that has enthusiastically hosted Hans Küng allowed that they would probably not invite Cardinal Ratzinger to lecture since he is "too controversial." Protestant illusions about what constitutes the "mainstream," and the prejudices that accompany those illusions, die hard. It is, among other things, a sobering comment on how superficial has been much of the ecumenical advance of recent decades.

One must quickly add that some forms of contemporary dissent do have about them that quality of life-or-death seriousness associated with the sixteenth-century Reformers. While there is an element of self-dramatization in cooperating with the media in portraying oneself as a martyr, people do reach a point at which, rightly or wrongly, they believe they are required in conscience to take a stand. Admittedly, one person's "Here I stand" may look to another person like "There he goes again." But today's disputes with church authorities do at times go beyond questions of individual freedom and engage issues of momentous import for the faith and life of the church. This is notably true in those cases where liberation theologians are quite solemnly, and quite accurately, saying that the Gospel is at stake. The life-or-death urgency of their position is not primarily because they dwell on questions of life and death in the revolutionary struggle. Rather, the urgency of their cause is in their admitted retranslation of the Gospel in a manner much more radically at variance with the Christian tradition than anything envisioned by Luther or Calvin. Indeed, those classical Reformers understood themselves to be retrieving and renewing a Christian tradition that had been largely abandoned or distorted by Rome. As we will have occasion to examine more closely in the next section, the gravamen of the liberation theology project is (as its proponents accurately claim it is) an utterly fundamental challenge to what John Paul, Joseph Ratzinger, and in fact most orthodox

Christians of all denominations understand to be the Gospel. These dissenters are not testing the limits of church authority but are redefining legitimate authority within the context of a radically reconceptualized understanding of the Church.

22. AN EMBARRASSING POPE

Much more is involved in John Paul's restoration or renewal than knocking a few heads together in an effort to establish some order out of apparent chaos. To depict John Paul simply as a "law-and-order" pope is, I believe, to miss the gravity of the questions now joined. Of course church order is part of the debate, but the much larger part has to do with the theological truth claims that "legitimate" the order of the Roman Catholic Church, and indeed of the Church itself. Paul Johnson is on firmer ground when he suggests that the project of this pope is not to preserve the Roman Catholic Church as it is or once was, but to resist the forces of modern accommodationism. Accommodationism can take the form of tailoring the truth to serve the civil religion of liberal democracy, or to gain respectability in the eyes of secularized academe, or to advance the revolutionary struggle. In these and other forms, accommodationism denies the scandal of Christian particularity, disguises the embarrassment of the supernatural, and "creatively retranslates" otherworldly hope into this-worldly enterprise. In order to resist effectively the forces of accommodationism, persuasive alternatives must be proposed. One such alternative that is now discernible is the growing accent upon the paradox of Christian existence in the world, and indeed within the human condition itself. "Above all," writes Paul Johnson, "John Paul shares Pascal's astonishment at man's divided nature: 'What a chimera is man! What a novelty! What a monster, what a chaos, what a contradiction, what a prodigy! Judge of all things, imbecile worm of the earth; depository of truth, a sink of uncertainty and error; the pride and refuse of the universe!' "

Although the Pope undoubtedly believes that he is Peter's successor and attention must be paid, his great concern does not seem to be the importance of restoring order in the church. Nor, as some observers would have it, does he so forcefully identify with traditional popular piety in order to pander to the demotic everyday sentiments of "simple Catholics" who are confused by all the changes of recent years. He seems rather to be suggesting that "simple Catholics" may have a better grasp of the Christian reality than their intellectual betters. In this respect, some of John Paul's statements and actions are reminiscent of the playful polemics of, say, G. K. Chesterton or C. S. Lewis. Surely the author of *The Screwtape Letters* was cheering from the celestial galleries when, in the summer of 1986, John Paul devoted his Wednesday afternoon audiences to a series of lectures on the reality of guardian angels, cherubim, and seraphim, and included some sobering thoughts about Old Scratch himself.

The Italian press had a field day, noting what seemed to them the incongruity of a pope arriving from Castel Gandolfo in a helicopter to discourse on the livelier locomotion of spiritual beings. But discourse he did in a series of 40-minute talks in which he explained, among other things, the ranking of the angels. The leftist *La Republica* snidely reported, "The Pope tells pilgrims, 'Even among the angels there are chiefs and Indians.' " As to the devil, John Paul noted that the church is extremely cautious in attributing phenomena to diabolical possession but made clear that "in principle, one cannot deny that Satan can arrive at these extreme manifestations of his superiority in his effort to harm and lead to evil." He allowed that the devil might have something to do with the pervasive unbelief of our times, at which the dailies accused him of being unfashionably gloomy and even apocalyptic. In the last talk, the Pope asserted that the devil, "being only a creature with all the limits of a creature, and therefore subordinate to the desire and dominion of God, is destined to be totally defeated." With a mock sigh of relief, the papers headlined, "The Devil on His Knees" and "Wojtyla Envisages Defeat of Evil."

Once again the Pope had succeeded in embarrassing more respectable theologians. The Jesuits, once known as the pope's army, explained through their weekly that reference to the devil is but an outdated way of talking about certain unpleasantries in history. "The devil cannot have a proper name because he represents nothing," explained an editor of *Civilta Cattolica.* The list of names by which the devil is called "is only a useless sequence of names, born of tradition and popular fantasy. No serious Christian must think of monsters, of dragons, of being possessed. One thing is fantasy, another reality." And Screwtape was no doubt cheering from the infernal galleries. But this Pope seems to understand that no serious Christian is very seriously Christian if he shuts the windows to the worlds of which this world is part. Theologians without an angelology usually have a grievously flawed anthropology, since it is by reference to angels that we know what man is a little lower than (Ps. 8). In any event, reality is considerably less interesting in the absence of the playful angels *(angelici ludi)* so luminously affirmed by Dante in Canto XXVIII of the *Paradiso.*

Angels are a part of the restoration project. (See Thesis 3, Part 6.) Chesterton once described modern consciousness as being comparable to the awareness of a middle-aged businessman after a somewhat too-ample lunch. It is a curiosity of our time that precisely when the sciences—biology, astronomy, physics, theoretical mathematics—are stretching our minds toward mystery, much academic theology seems set upon the dulling down of human consciousness. The social sciences, the most dismal of dismal pseudosciences, are taken to be an explanatory framework by which we can make some sense of revelation. This season, for instance, brings a scholarly tome from a respectable press containing essays on "Body Language in the Book of Revelation" and "Grid Analysis and Group Dynamics in John's Gospel." It is little wonder that the *angelici ludi* are given to fits of uproarious laughter. And it is little wonder that the terrain of contemporary intellectuality contains vast social-scientific witchcraft zones where there reign elaborate conceptual devices for explaining phenomena much more straightforwardly addressed by common sense, abetted by a healthy respect for the workings of devils and angels.

A jaunty readiness to challenge the hegemony of stifling secularisms is helpful to understanding a book that in 1985 stirred a storm within Roman Catholic circles. The book, of course, is *The Ratzinger Report* and is based on several days of interviews of Cardinal Ratzinger by Italian journalist Vittorio Messori. The book has become a veritable vade mecum among supporters of "the restoration" and, in the eyes of others, a symbol of all that is odious and threatening about the pontificate of John Paul. Although tending toward the choleric and strident at points, it is an astonishingly candid statement from someone who is the perfect of the Congregation for the Doctrine of the Faith. One of the demands since Vatican II has been for an "open church." The persistent call for openness has been directed most vigorously at the Congregation, which had been notoriously secretive in its inquisitorial doings. At the Council itself, Joseph Ratzinger, then a peritus, had offered the most trenchant criticisms of the workings of what was then called the Holy Office. Among those who applauded him then he has earned slight thanks for having now acted upon his own advice. In their view, the cardinal is altogether too open in engaging the theological disputes of the time.

A brief examination of *The Ratzinger Report* is in order. Before doing that, however, it is necessary to lay to rest several questions that have been raised about the *Report*. At first, some of those who thought the theological shoe described by Ratzinger fit them disturbingly well expressed doubts that the cardinal had actually said what he is reported to have said. That question has been laid to rest by the best of authorities, namely, Joseph Ratzinger. Then the ploy was ventured that the cardinal was out of line with papal thinking. John Paul, it was rumored, was very upset with the book. While John Paul has not to date written a rave review of the *Report*, there is no public evidence that he disagrees with it. On the contrary, his own independently stated views and his public approval of Ratzinger's subsequent statements and actions—which are fully in accord with the *Report*—all lead to the conclusion that while Ratzinger was not speaking on behalf of the Pope, he certainly spoke with an intimate understanding of the mind of the Pope. Then it was said that the *Report* should not be taken too seriously because it was, after all, the rambling rumination of a man caught with his guard down. But that point cuts two ways. The book is certainly not the kind of systematic treatise to which

Ratzinger the theologian is otherwise given, but it may be that its very informality makes it an even better indicator of what this man is really up to. In any case, no one denies that Ratzinger is a very circumspect man and is not likely to give extended interviews and approve their publication without knowing quite precisely what he is doing.

The programmatic impact of the book, as we shall see, was dramatically evident in the results of the Extraordinary Synod held toward the end of 1985. Finally, another criticism of the book is that Ratzinger indulges in broad generalizations about theological directions and misdirections but fails to name names. This, it seems to this writer, is a criticism as frivolous as it is frequent. One can imagine the outcries of injured innocence had he named names. To be publicly named and criticized by the prefect of the Congregation is automatically to come under official shadow. The naming of names must be, and is, done most judiciously. For better or for worse, then, *The Ratzinger Report* cannot be ignored or belittled by anyone who wants to understand the intentions of this pontificate and what some people mean by "the Catholic restoration."

23. CARDINAL RATZINGER REPORTING

"It is incontestable that the last ten years have been decidedly unfavorable for the Catholic Church," declares Ratzinger. He cites many evidences, including both the loss of missionary urgency and the inclination to pander to the modern marketplace of ideas. The point is that, to the extent that Roman Catholics are unapologetically Roman Catholic, both the distinctiveness and the attractiveness of the faith will be enhanced. Ratzinger agrees with Paul VI that dissension in the church has moved from self-criticism to self-destruction. The result is a pervasive sense of boredom and discouragement.

Against what he calls a new triumphalism, Ratzinger asserts, "So long as the Church is in pilgrimage on the earth, she has no ground to boast of her own works. . . . The place of the Church on earth can only be near the cross." Such a theology of the cross (*theologia crucis*) is not pessimistic but looks with hope to the final triumph signaled in the death and resurrection of Christ. This radical hope has been largely obscured by theologians who are "stamped by the typical mentality of the opulent bourgeoisie of the West." In their "laboratories," other utopias are "distilled" that confuse and mislead "the humble people of God." Such theologians, while claiming the brave title of dissident and claiming to speak for the poor and oppressed, act on behalf of the establishments of the age. Here a reversal of the dramatic script comes into play. The story is that of David and Goliath. In the usual telling of the story, people such as Hans Küng and Leonardo Boff are cast as David. The Vatican, especially in the person of Joseph Ratzinger, is Goliath. In Ratzinger's telling of the story, however, these presumably brave dissidents are in fact people who have gone over to the side of the Goliath of the contemporary world against the David of Christian truth.

"The world waxes indignant when sin and grace are called by their names," says Ratzinger. In urging that Christians not be conformed to "the spirit of the world," Ratzinger's language is virtually identical to that used by Kierkegaard, Barth, Bonhoeffer, and others in their criticisms of *Kulturprotestantismus*. We are again reminded that Ratzinger has been deeply immersed in the experience of the German churches and readily identifies his cause with that of "the confessing church" under Hitler. At the heart of what he repeatedly calls "the crisis" is ecclesiology, the understanding of the Church. Many Roman Catholic theologians, he says, are sub-Protestant in their doctrine of the Church. Ratzinger is sensitive to the criticism that he seems more concerned about the Church than about Christ. To that he responds: "Without a view of the mystery of the Church that is also *supernatural* and not only *sociological,* christology itself loses its reference to the divine in favor of a purely human structure, and ultimately it amounts to a purely human project: the Gospel becomes the *Jesus-project,* the social-liberation project or other merely historical, immanent projects that can still seem religious in appearance, but which are atheistic in substance."

Ratzinger is also well aware that his argument rubs against the ethos of a democratic age. "The Church of Christ," he says, "is not a party, not an association, not a club. Her deep and permanent structure is not *democratic* but *sacramental,* consequently *hierarchical.*" Ah, says the skeptic, so there you have it; it is a matter of power after all. Part of Ratzinger's "so uncomfortable" position is that he is indeed defending an authority in which he participates. To those who choose to view it that way, his defense may be dismissed as self-serving. A measure of the corrosion of trust within Roman Catholicism today is the number of people, including theologians and bishops, who choose to view it that way.

The Cardinal believes the decline in priestly vocations is closely related to the decline in the perceived authority and identity of the priest. "The very situation of the priest is singular, alien to modern society," he says. "A function, a role, that is not based on the consent of the majority but on the representation of *another* who lets a man share his authority appears as something incomprehensible. Under these conditions there is a great temptation to pass from that supernatural 'authority of representation' . . . to a much more natural 'service of the coordination of consensus,' that is to say, to a comprehensible category, because it is only human and, besides, more in consonance with modern culture."

Ratzinger's countercultural understanding of priesthood affects every aspect of ministry, and he cites the practice of confession and absolution in particular. Today, he says, confession too often turns the priest into a therapist. "Rather it is much more necessary that the priest be willing to remain in the background, thus leaving space for Christ, who alone can remit sin."

Bishops, too, forget their awesome responsibility to represent Christ. Thus they are inclined to subordinate their role to organizations such as national episcopal conferences. The charge is routinely made that, by emphasizing the "ordinary" and "immediate" authority of bishops in their dioceses, Ratzinger is not so much interested in enhancing the role of bishops as he is trying to discourage bishops from acting together in national conferences in a way that might pose a challenge to the authority of the Vatican Curia. And so in this "realistic"—or, as some would have it, cynical—view, the real question is not theology but, once again, power. But Ratzinger's argument is that bishops' conferences have only a limited pragmatic function and are devoid of theological basis or authority. He says flatly: "No episcopal conference, as such, has a teaching mission; its documents have no weight of their own save that of the consent given to them by the individual bishops." The Cardinal makes no secret of his skepticism about bureaucracies and is determined that bishops should not become managers of branch offices, whether the headquarters be in Rome or Washington. The church, he insists, is not "a federation of national churches." Rather, it is based on the balance between *community* and *person,* and in each place the bishop is the person linking the church to the universal communion. He notes that under Hitler it was not the national conference but individual bishops who spoke out against Nazi atrocities. The church needs bishops of imagination and originality who are at the same time "profoundly obedient." "The Church, I shall never tire of repeating it, needs saints more than functionaries."

The Germans and Americans like rational organization, but Ratzinger has come to appreciate "the Italian spirit." It does seem probable that there are ever so many more *angelici ludi* in Florence than in Hamburg. Although the rhetoric of Roman authority is heavy, the spirit, suggests the Cardinal, is one of great patience and even whimsy—so long as there is no direct challenge to the authority of Rome. Ratzinger presents himself as the champion of churchly freedom. He seems to be saying with Chairman Mao, "Let a hundred flowers blossom." To which some respond that we all know what Mao did to the flowers that took his invitation at face value. Ratzinger's point, however, is that the freedom to play variations on a theme requires that the theme itself be established. But much contemporary Catholic teaching lacks a theme of "all embracing formation in the faith." Rather, the people are offered bits and snatches of "insights" regarding not what is true but what is "meaningful." He does not think his proposal should be thought strange, since from the catechetics of the early Church up through Martin Luther, Christians have had little difficulty in understanding the basic structure of the faith that is to be transmitted.

While affirming historical-critical study of the Scriptures, Ratzinger believes that much contemporary biblical scholarship is making the Bible irrelevant. "An exegesis in which the Bible no longer lives and is understood within the living organism of the Church becomes archaeology: the dead bury their dead." In his critique, Ratzinger reinforces concerns expressed by Protestant scholars, such as Brevard Childs of Yale, about the way in which biblical studies have been divorced from the living tradition of the community of faith. Obviously, the sixteenth-century's heated debates about the connections between Scripture and tradition have not been resolved. But now those debates cut across ecclesial boundaries. There is a growing ecumenical consensus that Scripture and tradition are not to be set against each other, that Scripture is the singularly authoritative part of the tradition. But that hardly answers the questions about how the Church is held accountable to Scripture, and in what ways the magisterium of the Church authoritatively interprets Scripture. In the *Report,* Ratzinger does not venture detailed answers to such questions, but he does note the ways in which the questions are being confused or evaded by current patterns of theological thought.

Patterns of theological thought too are distorted by sin, and it is to the question of sin that Ratzinger returns again and again. "If Providence will some day free me of my obligations," he says, "I should like to devote myself precisely to the theme of 'original sin' and to the necessity of a rediscovery of its authentic reality." Modern notions of social, economic, and psychological "alienation" simply cannot comprehend what Christianity teaches about sin. And, without that teaching, "one no longer understands the necessity of Christ the Redeemer." The cardinal's repeated concern is for "the structure of faith." Once that is in place, there is ample room for theological variation and exploration. He is therefore more concerned about presuppositions than about conclusions. The focus on presuppositions marks his criticism of movements such as liberationist and feminist theologies. Proponents of such theologies sometimes protest that they are not saying what Ratzinger says they are saying. To which Ratzinger responds, in effect: "Perhaps not, but that is what you would and should be saying, were you consistent with the presuppositions you affirm." Some describe this approach as a defect of a lamentably rigid Germanic mind-set; others see it as the virtue of clear thinking.

Ratzinger and, for that matter, John Paul are not intimidated by the charge that they are out of sync with the modern age. Indeed, they seem to exult in the "cognitive dissonance" created by the Gospel. All ages are under the judgment of the definition of reality asserted by the cross and Resurrection of Christ. Those who do not begin from and return to this presupposition, Ratzinger suggests, are not necessarily heretics, but they are metaheretics in the sense that they are not even part of the framework or the structure of Christian faith. Christians must rediscover, he says, "the courage of noncomformism." The *Report* ranges wide and far in specifying where authentic Christianity is being smothered by the spirit of conformity, and gives particular attention to liturgy. Clergy who have been trained to experience something like a loss of transcendence, says Ratzinger, are going through an identity crisis. The result is a kind of "neoclericalism" in which they impose their problem upon the laity. But the people are not eager to be liberated from the "sacred taboos" that the clergy have discarded. "The drama faced by our contemporaries is rather that of living without hope in an ever more profane world. Nowadays the really widespread demand is not for a secularized liturgy but, on the contrary, for a new encounter with the sacred through a worship that manifests the presence of the Eternal." Whether or not that is really what people are looking for, Ratzinger's more basic point is that the encounter with God in Christ is what the Church has to offer.

Surveying the state of the church in 1972, Paul VI remarked, "I have the feeling that the smoke of Satan has penetrated the Temple of God through some crack or other." Ratzinger denies that this is a "pessimistic" reading of reality. "If we look closely at the most recent secular culture, we see how the easy, naive optimism is turning into its opposite—radical pessimism and despairing nihilism. So it may be that the Christians who up to now were accused of being pessimists must help their brothers to escape from this despair by putting before them the radical optimism which does not deceive—whose name is Jesus Christ." Many Roman Catholics, who were previously prevented by their own church from entering into other worlds of theological discourse, now think that in liberal, optimistic Protestantism "they will find a path already blazed for the fusing of faith and modern thought."

In fact, according to Ratzinger, many Roman Catholic theologians are Protestants. The questions that must be raised with them, he says, are the same questions that would have to be raised with Martin Luther. An oddity in this digression by the cardinal is that he comes back to focusing on church authority, apparently abandoning the presupposition that *the* root question is that of the structure of the faith. Thus Ratzinger the theologian, who wants to engage and moderate the conversation about the truth that constitutes the Church, oscillates with Ratzinger the prefect of the Congregation, who wants to control the conversation. Here perhaps is the reason why he finds his position, as he says, "so uncomfortable," and why so many theologians, Roman Catholic and other, hesitate to accept his invitation to enter into conversation. Ratzinger also speaks witheringly of the "static" and "petrified" state of Eastern Orthodox theology, and assumes an idea of "the true Church" that is hard to square either with Vatican II or with his own theological writings. In sum, the discussion of relations with other Christians is marked by a certain petulance and arbitrariness. Of course, critics say that is true of the entire *Report,* that it is little more than a catalogue of things that Joseph Ratzinger doesn't like about the post-Vatican II church. That, I believe, is inaccurate and unfair, but it is a criticism that Ratzinger too often invites in the course of this somewhat rambling statement.

The argument with which Ratzinger concludes is the *cantus firmus* of the entire statement, namely, we must not surrender "the connection which the New Testament creates between *salvation* and *truth,* for as Jesus explicitly affirms, it is knowledge of the truth that liberates and hence saves." A close associate of Ratzinger says that the *Report* "is the most important book published since Vatican II." That is arguable, but the book is certainly without precedent in modern Roman Catholicism. Indeed, such plain speaking by a top leader in any major church body is, to say the least, exceedingly rare. Ratzinger's position requires that he be theological patrolman, his vocation requires that he be theological participant. Both roles are evident in the *Report,* but it must be admitted that the patrolman is dominant. At times the document sounds like the ramblings of an off-duty police officer frankly, and sometimes wearily, talking about the difficulties of his beat. The negations of the book, however, are the obverse of Ratzinger's positive program for theological renewal. To be sure, the positives are evident in the *Report,* but are much more evident in Ratzinger's theological writings and in documents issued by the Congregation. He undoubtedly knew that the *Report* would be as controversial as in fact it has been. Perhaps he thought a certain bluntness, even an element of shock, was required to concentrate the mind of the church. If so, he succeeded dramatically, as became obvious at the Extraordinary Synod of 1985, to which we now turn.

24. AN EXTRAORDINARY SYNOD

"This is not a synod about a book, it is a synod about a council!" declared Godfried Cardinal Danneels, archbishop of Brussels, not even trying to conceal his irritation. It was late November 1985, and the Extraordinary Synod was just getting underway. In the pressroom at the foot of Saint Peter's Square, one reporter after another was asking about the influence of *The Ratzinger Report* on the synod's deliberations. The irritation in the response was understandable. After all, Cardinal Ratzinger is not pope, his Congregation for the Doctrine of the Faith is not the Congregation for the State of the Church, and the synod had been called to consider more than theological disputes. Exactly twenty years after the conclusion of Vatican II, the synod was, according to John Paul II, to "relive the spiritual climate" of that great event, to evaluate its impact upon the entire church, and to point directions for the future. The synod therefore was about more than theology, but theology was at the heart of it, as indeed theology—reflecting upon and articulating Christian truth claims—is at the heart of the Church. Without theology, without the transmission of the doctrine, the Church is little more than tribal attachment, moral uplift, high cultural drama, and a big religion business. At least that is what Cardinal Ratzinger believes, and that is what the Extraordinary Synod came to affirm.

But all those gathered for the synod did not necessarily agree that "the crisis" of Catholicism was chiefly, or even importantly, a crisis of faith. The approximately two hundred bishops, ecumenical observers, and special guests seated around Bernini's high altar in Saint Peter's Basilica, plus the more than ten thousand others looking on, would undoubtedly describe the crisis (if indeed they thought there was a crisis) in maddeningly diverse ways. The most common version of the crisis—a version favored by the general media—focused on social, cultural, and political "challenges" to the church's institutional leadership. Twenty years earlier, however, the media version of the crisis was the crisis of belief. Throughout the Christian world the news then was about "the death of God." Perhaps the crisis of belief faded from attention as it became obvious that more and more people, and not only Christians, found it increasingly difficult *not* to believe. Or maybe religion, including Roman Catholicism, had demonstrated its ability to assimilate the loss of faith and still go on as though nothing very important had happened. Cardinal Ratzinger seems to think that that is what may have happened. If that is what happened, it may be that the media story of twenty years ago was closer to the truth than the way the media tell the story today. In that event, the real question facing the synod was the question that faces the Church until our Lord's return in glory. It is the question he himself posed: "When the Son of Man comes, will he find faith on earth?" (Luke 18).

But in most reports that question was lost in a welter of other questions that constituted "the crisis of Catholicism." Since the Council, the church had lost well over a hundred thousand priests and nuns. Religious orders previously noted for their loyalty, the Jesuits, for example, seemed locked into a pattern of barely controlled rebellion against papal authority. A majority of married Catholics in the developed countries say they do not follow, and maybe believe they should not follow, the church's teaching on artificial birth control. Feminists are storming the gates demanding ordination to the priesthood, Catholic colleges and universities shelter theologians who seem to delight in what even some of them call their heterodoxies, and proponents of revolution explain how Karl Marx revealed to them a gospel worthy of proclaiming.

Before the synod the several episcopal conferences were asked to submit written evaluations of how the reforms of Vatican II had fared in their territories. Some of the conferences were sanguine, even blithe, in their evaluations. The bishops of England and Wales, for instance, acknowledged that the church was experiencing problems, but the problems were chiefly due to changes over which the church had little control. Technological change, unemployment, pervasive economic injustice, the breakdown of the family, and a "collapse of moral consensus" were cited. They did not dwell on how the church might have contributed to such problems, notably the collapse of a moral consensus. But what some perceive as chaos and a loss of unity in the church, others see as a blossoming of diversity. What some deplore as institutional decline, others acclaim as a new modesty that is more appropriate in a community that professes to follow the simple Nazarene. Basil Cardinal Hume of England said immediately before the Synod: "The image the church has of itself nowadays is no longer that of Solomon's Temple, massively fortified, set foursquare against the secular world, rich in beauty and furnishings. It is rather the image of Abraham's tent because the whole church—like the patriarch of old—is on the move through history and is making a pilgrimage of faith." It is a winsome vision, and at the synod, Cardinal Hume was seen as being in the forefront of the forces of progressive influence.

One big change, which almost no one would deny is positive, is the growth of Roman Catholicism in the last two decades. The growth is not so impressive when compared with worldwide population growth, and it is not so spectacular as the growth of conservative Protestant and "independent" churches around the world, but it is impressive nonetheless. When Vatican II closed, there were less than 600 million Roman Catholics in the world; today there are over 830 million. The strongest growth has been in the underdeveloped countries, especially in Africa and Latin America, tipping the demographic balance of Catholicism away from Europe and North America and toward the Southern Hemisphere. Much more impressive to this writer than the pageantry, the copes and the miters, was the cultural catholicity of the synod. A majority of Roman Catholics are now in the underdeveloped countries, and their bishops are typically drawn from the flocks they guide. Numbers, however, do not translate directly into influence.

The hegemony of "European Catholicism" is frequently decried as cultural imperialism. If, according to one way of thinking, it is discovered that a phenomenon is historically and culturally "conditioned," then it is not to be "imposed" upon others. But of course every phenomenon— every idea, ritual, moral judgment, and manner of behavior—is historically and culturally conditioned, including the notion that the historically and culturally conditioned is not of universal validity. This touches on the core scandal of Christianity, namely, that the revelation of the universal, God's revelation of himself, happened in the embarrassingly particularistic circumstance of the itinerant rabbi named Jesus. Contrary to some allegations, the "crisis" of Catholicism is hardly to be located in the fact that there is now "a majority vote in the Third World." Roman Catholicism, like Christianity itself, is not voted into or out of existence. The Spirit blows where it will. For centuries it blew through European civilization, giving particular form to Western Christianity. It was at least theoretically possible that Africa or Asia might have played the primary role in giving shape to Christianity in our time. But, for many reasons, that is not how it happened. Catholicism's (and indeed Christianity's) numerical shift to the Southern Hemisphere will over time work greater changes than it already has. Many anticipate the time when, for example, the direction of the missionary enterprise will be reversed, with Africans going to the dark continents of Europe and North America to evangelize their previously Christian peoples. But that is for a possible future.

At present the "encounter with the Third World" is less a matter of crisis than of accommodation. Enculturation is the term commonly used, and it was much discussed also at the synod. Few Africans or South Americans, it would seem, want to start their own church. There are already plenty of other churches available. They do not want an indigenous church but an indigenous expression of a universal church. One gets the distinct impression that talk about cultural imperialism and the imposition of European Catholicism is in large part an anxiety exported by Europeans and North Americans. Roman Catholics outside the North Atlantic orbit are, to be sure, not content to be passive receivers of a Catholicism already definitively shaped in all its parts. They will increasingly contribute to the development of a living tradition. But they seem to understand better than some of their northern cobelievers that in order to change a tradition, one must be part of a tradition. The only way to supersede the past is to incorporate the past.

The "crisis" of Roman Catholicism in Europe is a well-worn subject. And, of course, it is not only Roman Catholicism. In Germany, France, the Netherlands, England, and Scandinavia, the older theory that modernization and secularization are somehow causally linked still seems credible to many. In France, historically "the eldest daughter of the church," it is estimated that no more than 6 percent of the population is to be found at Sunday mass. Some say it is because the church in these European countries is still associated with the *ancien regime,* an association that gave rise to a vigorous tradition of anticlericalism. Others say it is because, unlike the situation in the United States, the church never had to prove it belonged. The church was always there, it was the taken-for-granted reality. The church proved nothing, everything new had to be proved against the church. Except in places such as Poland, where the regime is hostile, and Czechoslovakia, where the regime is vicious. There is a paradox forced to the surface by oppression: it is hard to be a Christian where it is easy to be a Christian, and easy to be a Christian where it is hard to be a Christian. Of course, in this case "hard" and "easy" refer not to the price exacted but to the understanding of what it *means* to be a Christian.

But Catholicism in Western Europe seems exhausted. Even its protests against the authority of Rome, as for example in the Netherlands, have been made frivolous by repetition. Also in religion, the Dutch have mastered the art of trivializing the crises of the time. The Pope talks about cosmic destiny, and punk rockers burn his pornographic effigy in the streets of Amsterdam. It is not the kind of thing that seems deserving of a sincere bull of excommunication. There is something fundamentally unserious about the "crisis" of European Catholicism, which perhaps makes it more serious. Looking to situations such as Poland, Czechoslovakia, and Lithuania, some West European Catholics suggest that a whiff of Communist persecution might have a bracing effect on their church life. But that seems a strong poison to take as an antidote to whatever it is that has infected the church in Western Europe. In any case, the doldrums of West European Catholicism constitute a continuing crisis about which little can be done at the moment, except to be aware of it and to fan whatever small flames of renewal appear here and there from time to time.

25. RELIVING THE COUNCIL

Rome and the United States are the central influences in the global church today. Of course Rome—for reasons historical, institutional, and theological. And the church in the United States because, for better and for worse, the United States is the dominant power—economic, cultural, and, perhaps, military—in today's world. In Christian history, there is nothing new about a church being elevated by its association with an imperial center, as witness the elevation of Rome and Constantinople. The church in America has the additional good fortune of being at a center that has been conducive to the church's prospering. After his installation in New York, John Cardinal O'Connor visited the Pope. "Welcome to the archbishop of the capital of the world!" exclaimed John Paul. Coming from the bishop of Rome, that is a statement of no small historical significance.

The United States is unquestionably the communications center of the world. The church here has and uses the resources to maintain contacts with other parts of the church throughout the world, thus bypassing what had been the coordinating center of Rome. The church here, located in the ostensible "lead society" of world-historical change, gives definition to the "modern world" to which the "Church in the Modern World" is to relate. The church here disseminates "the Third World viewpoint" and, by selecting the voices from other nations that will be amplified, plays a large part in deciding what that viewpoint should be. The American church has not been noted for its theological creativity. It still draws on European theology and on European theology as refracted through "the Third World perspective." But the American church gives currency to the ideas that will make a difference. To "make it" in the Roman Catholic Church today is to make it either in Rome or in America, and to make it in one place is to be in tension with the other. That has been the pattern since Vatican II. There are those who believe that that is changing now, as John Paul advances American bishops who would turn from tension to trust (or, as others prefer, from innovation to conformity). But the changes in personnel had not yet changed the pattern that was evident at the Extraordinary Synod.

The *Sala Stampa Della Santa Sede,* the press office of the Holy See, reported that more than six hundred reporters had registered for the synod, in addition to the several hundred on regular assignment in Rome. True, many of the "reporters" were experienced partisans representing the newsletters of their various causes. The concluding mass was a splendid affair, designed, like the opening of the synod, to parallel the ceremonies that opened and closed Vatican II. Leaving Saint Peter's, I fell into conversation with one such partisan, a prominent American traditionalist. "It was a clean sweep for us," he declared. "Now we'll have to convince our people not to crow about it too much, or else we could end up being guilty of the partisan spirit that we accuse the opposition of promoting." That seemed a sweeping judgment of what the Extraordinary Synod had done. And yet, given all the ambiguities in what is meant by "conservative" and what is meant by "liberal," the synod results should have heartened those who call themselves conservatives. It is hard to exaggerate the degree to which discussions in and about the Roman Catholic Church have been politicized into often-crude divisions between Left and Right. It is almost an embarrassment to report, until one remembers that it is hardly new in the history of Christianity. At least the bishops and their partisans today do not resort to fisticuffs, as we are reliably informed did happen in some of the early councils of the Church.

In the formal proceedings of a synod, the bishops almost painfully exemplify the civility and mutual deference that is called "collegiality." The United States Senate, with its vaunted protocol, seems rowdy by comparison. But in the receptions, dinners, interviews, and informal encounters that swirl around a synod, greater candor sometimes prevails. The Extraordinary Synod may not have been about a book, but much of the talk surrounding the synod was about the author of the book. Not only in the newspaper columns and cartoons is Cardinal Ratzinger the subject of sometimes witty, often vicious, caricature. Some of those who do not like what he is doing, and they are legion, routinely refer to his department as the Holy Office. The Holy Office, they are pleased to explain, used to be called the Inquisition. That is not the particularly nasty Spanish Inquisition, they admit, but, on the other hand, the mindset is much the same. The instruments of torture, we are invited to believe, are stored in the cellars of the Congregation and have been recently cleaned and polished. Late at night the cardinal visits them there. "Soon my pretties," says he, rubbing his hands in happy expectation, "soon we will have work for you again." Of course such things are said humorously, but the fun is laced sometimes with malice and sometimes with honest fear of what Ratzinger's ascendancy may portend.

It is reluctantly acknowledged that, as a theologian and peritus, Ratzinger—like Karol Wojtyla—was a "man of the council." But that was a long time ago. In the view of his enemies (and the intensity of feeling frequently does warrant the term *enemies*), Ratzinger has moved from being a moderate, perhaps timorous, progressive to having become today's scourge of open inquiry. As one American theologian put it: "I don't know why you're puzzled about it. His is a classic case of selling out." And, of course, he sold out for power. The Pope called the synod, but it soon became apparent that the agenda had been shaped by Cardinal Ratzinger's way of asking what are, and what are not, the authentic teachings of Vatican II. On that question the voice of Ratzinger—given the mix of personality, competence, energy, and, not least of all, office—is more equal than others, with the exception of the Pope. After the synod, it was insistently stated by the Pope and others that there were no losers, only winners. That is a mandatory and healing statement; at a very profound level, it is undoubtedly true as well. But at the synod itself, the alignments of contending forces were no secret. The contentions were often exaggerated by the press and others who make their living by selling melodrama. Most of the bishops probably did not belong to any identified "party," but were there to listen, to learn, and to speak their concerns in a way that they hoped would attract the helpful attention of the Pope and his aides. But there were agendas in conflict. Anyone who doubts that the synod was primarily working off Cardinal Ratzinger's agenda has only to make a point-by-point comparison between *The Ratzinger Report* and the interventions and documents of the synod, the most important document being the *Relatio Finalis* ("Final Report").

The institution of the synod itself is an innovation of Vatican II. The gathering of representative bishops from around the world is not a legislative body but is designed to give advice to the pope. Past synods have dealt with more limited questions, and the pope has received their recommendations with thanks and then issued his own statement on the question at hand. Some participants complain that the pope's statement was often unrelated to, and sometimes contradicted, what the synod had said. This time was different. John Paul promptly lent his authority to the results of the Extraordinary Synod, accepting with praise the *Relatio Finalis* and ordering its immediate publication. By word and symbolic action the Pope most decisively put his seal of approval on the work of this synod. Among all the possible, and sometimes improbable, interpretations of Vatican II that had been circulated for twenty years, this synod and this Pope were making some choices. It was less a matter of condemning or ruling out of order some interpretations than it was a matter of lifting up the intrepretations favored. But, of course, positives imply negatives, and much is said by the selection of what is to be included and what is to be omitted.

The *Relatio* is emphatic in affirming Vatican II, as might be expected. With respect to all that has gone wrong since Vatican II, the point is made that simply because something happened *after* the Council, it does not mean that it happened *because* of the Council. And yet, with the deftness that befits such an official document, the *Relatio* does note that "The signs of our times do not exactly coincide, in some points, with those of the time of the Council." The Council was not wrong, and it is not to be thought that the church has changed its mind, but the times have changed. In the *Relatio,* the Council's generally sanguine view of the modern world is replaced by a recognition that the church is confronted by a secularism that is implacably hostile to transcendent truth. An uncritical embrace of this modern world ends up in subordinating the Gospel to the opposite of transcendence, which is an "immanentism" of crude, and frequently cruel, this-worldliness. "This immanentism is a reduction of the integral vision of man, a reduction which leads not to his true liberation but to a new idolatry, to the slavery of ideologies, to life in reductive and often oppressive structures of this world." The weakening accent on the transcendent, and the consequent influence of immanentism, says the *Relatio,* has produced "deficiencies and difficulties" that are "shadows in the post-conciliar period."

The synod was eager to cultivate unity within the church, to rise above factionalisms. In curious ways, this sometimes resulted in confusing, or even transposing, ideas and issues usually associated with progressives or conservatives. For example, nationalism is conventionally thought to be conservative, while a global perspective is deemed liberal. But it was the progressives, notably from North America and the United Kingdom, who pressed to give national episcopal conferences a larger, even quasi-autonomous, role in the magisterium of the church. This was effectively opposed not only by those who are jealous for Rome's prerogatives, but, more importantly, by bishops who wanted to protect their own freedom to teach and lead. As noted earlier, some American bishops are beginning to express misgivings about the growing prominence of the national conference. It is undoubtedly a minority of bishops, but the uneasiness about possible manipulations by national bureaucrats is increasing. In addition, it has not been lost on some bishops that the arguments they make for greater independence from Rome are, at least logically, not dissimilar from the arguments that some priests, religious, and laity make for greater independence from the bishops.

The Extraordinary Synod came down strongly in favor of the teaching authority of each bishop in communion with the college of bishops and, of course, with the bishop of Rome. Aside from acknowledging their coordinating function in certain practical tasks, the synod was exceedingly cool toward national conferences. A study was approved to look into the teaching authority, "if any," of such conferences. A strong majority of bishops from Third World countries clearly did not share the American and British enthusiasm for national conferences. In many parts of the world, Roman Catholics are a small minority. They feel isolated and think their ties to Rome and the universal church are already too tenuous. They want more attention from Rome, not less, as is evident in the exuberant response during John Paul's several visits to the African continent. In addition, in many countries of the world, indeed in most countries of the world, religious freedom is a sometimes thing. Often governments are hostile, and typically they are suspicious, of a church that wants to chart a course that is independent of the government and aligned with a trans-national communion. The idea of the Roman Catholic Church as a feder-ation of national churches is theologically problematic, but it would also be practically perilous for many local churches. The effort to elevate the status of national episcopal conferences was repulsed by the synod for many reasons. The Vatican's concern for its prerogatives and the ques-tions about the nature of the church undoubtedly played an important part. But it seems also that most bishops were saying that they would rather be accountable to Rome than to national church bureaucracies, or to their government's Ministry for Religious Affairs.

The transposition of stereotypes applied to other "progressive" and "conservative" positions. For instance, progressives habitually assume that they are speaking for the poor against the rich, for the powerless against the powerful. This was given an interesting twist at the synod. Several bishops from Africa and Asia wanted it known that they were quite capable of speaking for themselves. In their formal interventions and private conversations, the point was made that the American-British-European agenda was not necessarily their agenda. There is nothing new in the fact that bishops from poor countries blamed "the First World" for many of their problems. The new thing here is that they were blaming the First World churches for a somewhat different list of problems. It was not the usual United Nations General Assembly list of colonialism, neocolonialism, militarism, and economic exploitation. Rather they blamed Americans and Europeans for sowing theological confusions, exporting alien ideologies such as feminism, and generally "imposing" their concerns and interests where they don't belong.

One African bishop complained that the churches in the developed countries were eager to send him help for programs of social change but were unresponsive to his pleas for help with evangelization and the "spiritual" mission of the church. There may also have been an element of anti-Americanism in Third World resistance to some of the positions advanced by American bishops. As mentioned before, there was little enthusiasm for increasing the authority of national episcopal confer-ences. Another African bishop is reported to have said privately, "You Americans have the money, you have the United Nations, you have the power to blow up the world. Now you want the power to blow up the church." It is hard to gauge how widespread such sentiments are among the bishops of Asia, Africa, and Latin America. The synod did provide evidence, however, that the Third World is by no means prepared to march in lockstep with the programs of progressives in America and Europe. The result may be some confusion and hurt feelings among progressives who have understood themselves as champions of the poor. Third World support for Vatican positions prompted one American observer to remark, with a touch of bitterness, that this perfectly illustrated the Roman tactic of divide and conquer. The more accurate reading, however, may be that these churches are now more confident about their role within the universal church and are therefore less hesitant in expressing their mind. If a bishop in a poor nation feels isolated and vulnerable, as many of them understandably do, clearly Rome can provide a more secure bond and sense of community than can a somewhat amorphous movement of "progressive forces" in the United States and Europe. Admittedly, such a bishop should not have to choose between them, since he needs all the help and all the community he can get. But the fortunes of the self-identified progressive forces, which since John XXIII seemed to be carrying the day, are now on the wane. At the Extraordinary Synod, that point was not lost on the bishops of churches outside the North Atlantic orbit.

26. PRIMARY MISSION DEFINED

In contrast to the dominant tone of Vatican II, the synod was extraordinarily modest about the church's role in the modern world. Calling on the church to walk "the way of the cross," it eschewed triumphalism in all its forms. The church's mission is not to reestablish the old Christendom of ecclesiastical dominance, nor to establish a new Christendom by revolutionary transformation. An earlier synod (an "ordinary" rather than "extraordinary" one) had declared in 1971 that "action on behalf of justice and participation in the transformation of the world fully [appears] to us as a constitutive dimension of the preaching of the Gospel, or, in other words, of the Church's mission for the redemption of the human race, and its liberation from every oppressive situation." Following the 1971 synod, the words *constitutive dimension* received most particular attention. The phrase was taken to mean that social transformation and liberation was not simply an appropriate task for the Church but was essential to both the Gospel and the Church's mission. "Constitutive" is a very strong word. The 1971 statement would seem to be saying that where the Church cannot or does not engage in such transformation and liberation, it is not fully the Church and is not fully preaching the Gospel.

Is the Church fully the Church and is the Gospel fully preached in circumstances where it is persecuted and prohibited from social and political action? The question obviously has large ramifications for the churches in the Communist bloc, and in all too many other places in the world. To put it differently, is the way of the Church typically the way of the cross or the way of triumph, of historically effective transformation and liberation? In the Reformation disputes of the sixteenth century, the contest was said to be between a "theology of the cross" and a "theology of glory." Old disputes have a way of coming back in new guise. A cardinal who was a leading participant in the 1971 synod claims that some of these same questions were on the minds of at least some bishops at the time. The "constitutive dimension" clause, he says, was never properly approved by the synod nor ratified by Paul VI. Others, it should be noted, dispute his account of what happened. In any event, the 1971 statement on social and political action has probably been quoted as much as any synod statement since Vatican II. It has frequently been turned to mean that political action is equivalent to preaching the Gospel, indeed that solidarity with the oppressed in the class struggle is the same thing as the Gospel promise of salvation.

The 1985 synod, in contrast, declared that it is the "primary mission of the Church . . . to preach and to witness to the good and joyful news" of God's saving acts in Christ. The Church, it said, points a pilgrim humanity to the "eschatological character" of a promise that awaits its consummation in the return of Christ. Relative to the notion of class struggle, the synod affirmed that the Church is "a sacrament, a sign, and an instrument of unity and of reconciliation, of peace among men, nations, classes, and peoples." The Church was called to demonstrate its nation- and class-transcending universality, to heed the authentic voice of the poor, and to walk the way of servanthood as a pilgrim people shaped by transcendent promise. In all its discussion of the nature and mission of the Church, one word recurred so often and so deliberately that it became the emblematic word of the entire synod. That word is "mystery." The Church is a divinely constituted mystery, not a humanly constructed agent of worldly purposes. It is a mystery that includes all the baptized, as was stressed in the synod's statements on the "universal vocation to holiness." The last emphasis may well have been thought of as a bridge to a 1987 synod on the laity. The emphasis on the vocation of all Christians would seem to challenge what many perceive as a new clericalism as priests and bishops have increasingly attempted to exercise leadership in areas of public policy that Vatican II designated as the special province and competence of the laity.

One Roman Catholic newspaper, perhaps a trifle irreverently, called ecumenism "the dark horse" of the synod. Ecumenism had not been expected to fare well in a synod determined to redirect the church into the paths of orthodoxy. *The Ratzinger Report* had some hard words for allegedly compromising accommodations in the search for Christian unity. And the truth is that most traditionalists look upon ecumenism as one of the chief sources of the post-Vatican II liberalizing and relativizing that they deplore. Immediately prior to the synod, rumors abounded that the Secretariat for Christian Unity was to be sharply downgraded. At a meeting of cardinals preceding the synod itself, however, the Secretariat and its work received a resounding vote of confidence. The synod was very much of the same mind. The *Relatio Finalis* declares that ecumenism has now "inscribed itself deeply and indelibly in the consciousness of the Church." It goes on to emphasize that ecumenism is not simply about improved relations with non-Roman Catholic churches but is premised upon the intention that "the incomplete communion already existing [may] come to the point of full communion."

In an unprecedented ecumenical service at the synod, John Paul flatly declared, "Divisions among Christians are contrary to the plan of God." Those who are the bearers of Christ's reconciling mission, he said, "must themselves be reconciled." With all the intra-Roman Catholic pullings and tuggings going on, the ecumenical dimension seemed to be lost on most synod watchers, both progressive and conservative. I believe that is a serious oversight. The argument might be made that now, for the first time since ecumenism was made an issue by Vatican II, the cause of ecumenism has been firmly claimed by what is self-consciously the party of orthodoxy. Employing the controverted language of the 1971 synod, it might be said that ecumenism is a "constitutive dimension" of the preaching of the Gospel and of the Church's mission. Where Christians do not pray and work for communion with other Christians in order to give fuller expression to the baptism that already makes them one, they are to that extent unfaithful to the Gospel and to the nature and mission of the Church. In the past, both the proponents and opponents of ecumenism have tended to accept the assumption that there is a trade-off between unity and truth. The proponents have been perceived as willing to trim the truth for the sake of unity; the opponents were viewed as eager to protect the truth at the price of unity.

Whether by human calculation or providential guidance, or a mix of both, the synod's statements on ecumenism reinforce the argument repeatedly advanced by John Paul and by Cardinal Willebrands of the Secretariat for Christian Unity: It is precisely the truth that requires unity, and the only unity worth working for is unity in the truth. Theological coherence and confessional integrity are not the enemies but the servants of ecumenism. This may in some respects make the ecumenical task more difficult. At the same time, the task is greatly advanced when it is no longer suspect or marginal but constitutive and mandatory in the eyes of those who, above all, want to be faithful Roman Catholic Christians. Of course, the 1985 synod has not overcome the misgivings that many conservatives continue to entertain about ecumenism. Some of those misgivings have been amply justified in the past. What the Extraordinary Synod did do was to forge an unbreakable linkage in official Roman Catholic teaching between orthodoxy and the mandate to unity. No doubt one can argue, I believe correctly, that Vatican II's "Decree on Ecumenism" had already forged that linkage. But it was by no means universally recognized. In fact, many believed ecumenism to be one of the weaker linkages that would break upon a rigorously orthodox reexamination of the legacy of Vatican II. That reexamination has now taken place, and the linkage emerges stronger than it was before.

As one might expect, there are various and contradictory evaluations of the Extraordinary Synod. At least two Italian dailies thought the outcome was hardly in dispute. "Ratzinger Wins!" trumpeted their headlines. Others suggested that the synod was much ado about very little. Bishop James Malone of Youngstown, Ohio, then president of the United States bishops' conference, declared himself "more than content" with the synod. "What difference will it make in what you'll do when you get back home?" he was asked. "I'll continue to do what I have been doing, except with greater confidence," he responded. On the question of who won and who lost, Bernard Cardinal Law of Boston, who politely but firmly distanced himself from Bishop Malone at several points, diplomatically said, "The Church won."

27. NO TURNING BACK

Those who had grave misgivings about the synod offered different judgments. Some declared it an irrelevant exercise in reaction. Others claimed it had not said anything substantive at all. Toward the end of the synod, I discussed with two very liberal, and very unhappy, priest observers what term might best describe the change signified by the synod. Restoration? Renewal? Redirection? "I don't like any of them," said one. "Why does there have to be a change? What's wrong with the way things have been going?" The response suggests that perhaps another irony of the synod is that it changed the "progressive" position into a defense of the status quo. It was not uncommonly said that the outcome of the synod was "50-50" or "a toss-up." But when those who previously thought themselves to be in the vanguard of inexorable triumph are prepared to split the difference, it seems likely that they know they have suffered a severe loss. The editor of liberal *Commonweal* urged his readers to interpret the synod "with dogged hope." Peter Hebblethwaite, a former priest and Britain's most prolifically vociferous critic of the Vatican, ends his report on the synod by quoting Godfried Cardinal Danneels: "It was like a slight adjustment on a rocket, a touch on the controls, not going into reverse." Hebblethwaite concludes on a note somewhat short of certitude triumphant: "So there is no reason to give up hope."

E. J. Dionne, who was then covering Rome for the *New York Times,* acknowledged the historic significance of the synod. Quoting the synod's statement that it is the church's task "to cooperate for a return of the sacred so that we will overcome the secularism of our time," Dionne observes: "There are few better summaries of John Paul's own priorities. Twenty years after Vatican II opened the Church to the world, this challenge to modernity is emerging as the heart of Catholicism's new agenda." Others note that that may be the Vatican's new agenda, but the Vatican lacks the means to make it Catholicism's agenda. Those who claim that the new agenda will make no difference are in fact saying that there is no effective leadership in the Roman Catholic Church. And, of course, they may turn out to be right. It was once said, "Rome has spoken; the matter is settled." Today a good many bishops seem to say, "Rome has spoken; we appreciate the input." Nonetheless, Rome does have ways to give its words effect.

For instance, the synod commissioned a universal catechism, or compendium, based upon the teachings of Vatican II. The idea was first put forward in an intervention by Cardinal Law. "Don't worry about that," Bishop Malone later told a young reporter. "You won't live long enough to see it completed." That may be, but others say there will "soon" be such an authoritative guide for the development of instructional materials throughout the church. At the synod, one Vatican wag suggested that Cardinal Ratzinger had already written such a compendium. That was thought to be amusing, until a few days later the cardinal announced that he did indeed have a draft that might serve very nicely as the basis for such a universal catechism.

And the Vatican has other ways of giving its words effect. Although it may not be the most edifying consideration, it is obvious that Rome's speaking has consequence when one remembers that the pope still appoints and promotes bishops. It is fair to assume that those who sense a higher calling to leadership will not be inattentive toward the new agenda. These realities were addressed in a straightforward manner in 1986 by a prominent American theologian, Bernard Cooke, writing in the Jesuit weekly, *America*. In the light of the synod and subsequent actions by Rome, it is time to ask, "What is the source and justification of the papal power of appointing bishops?" Cooke recognizes that that question entails another, namely, "the origin, nature and extent of authentic papal authority." Cooke goes on to challenge the notion that theologians and other experts do not exercise a magisterium as authoritative as that of the bishops. Contemporary scholarship, he writes, has considerably broadened the understanding of magisterium. "Yet this is practically ignored in statements by church officials who still use 'magisterium' as a designation for the hierarchy, or even for the Vatican. As a result there is a widespread belief that a bishop (unless he is out of favor in Rome), whether or not he possesses accurate understanding of a given matter, can teach dependably and that others must accept that teaching as true because he occupies official office."

The question is finally the question of truth, says Cooke. "This is not to deny a primacy of the pope; but it is to say that there is prior primacy of truth, of the Gospel, of Christian conscience and relationship to Christ and of the shared faith of truly believing Christians." He believes that the questions he raises can no longer be evaded. "What this means practically is that unprejudiced, structured and open discussion of the matter among thoughtful people in the church, obviously including the highest levels of the U.S. bishops and the Vatican, is needed." Cooke is by no means alone, although there are not many theologians of standing who have publicly questioned the whole idea of papal authority in the governance and teaching of the church. There was no call to question papal authority when that authority was on the side of what was deemed to be progress— dramatically under John XXIII, ambiguously under Paul VI. More precisely, that call came only from the traditionalist Right, from Archbishop Marcel Lefebvre of France, for instance. To the great satisfaction of progressives, he was sharply disciplined by Rome.

It is doubtful, but certainly not impossible, that the head-on challenge proposed by Bernard Cooke will gain wide support. Many who oppose the direction of this pontificate console themselves with the certainty that John Paul will not be pope forever. At least at this point, few seem prepared to raise the stakes so high as Bernard Cooke thinks necessary. And yet Cooke is hardly a lonely eccentric, nor is *America* magazine marginal to accepted Roman Catholic thought in the United States. They may seem eccentric and marginal in the eyes of Rome, and Rome may be determined to make such views eccentric and marginal in the church. But, at present, those who deplore John Paul, Ratzinger, and the Extraordinary Synod are surely correct in their claim to represent the "mainstream" of what has been the most influential thought in the last two decades of American Catholicism. If it really is, as Cooke and others say, a question of the "primacy of truth, of the Gospel, of Christian conscience," then it is not preposterous to see—between Rome and large sectors of American Catholicism—a schism in the making.

It is not preposterous, but neither does it seem probable. On the one hand, especially in reaction to disciplinary thrusts from Rome, there is a multiplication of protests, manifestos, and hurriedly convened conferences on freedom and truth. At the same time, a new climate of sobriety seems to be setting in. Positions and posturings casually indulged in past years are now seen to have potentially grave consequences. To some the new climate is oppressive, to others it is refreshingly serious. What has happened in the past twenty years cannot, as some seem to think, be turned around by a succession of firm disciplinary measures or by getting rid of a few "bad apples." What has happened has for many shaken the foundations. It is evident in taken-for-granted assumptions that "truth" is something quite apart from, or only coincidentally related to, the Roman Catholic Church and, indeed, Christianity itself. To use the language of sociology of knowledge, a cognitive revolution has taken place. Old "plausibility structures" have collapsed, and it does little good to tell people to start "knowing" again in a way that they know they can no longer know.

Because so many have recognized it to be true, it has become a cliche to say that there is no going back to the pre-Vatican II situation. There are professed partisans of orthodoxy who challenge that presupposition and say it is possible to go back. They are the proponents of a kind of Roman Catholic fundamentalism, invoking not an inerrant Bible but an inerrant hierarchy (or at least that part of the hierarchy with which they agree). This species of orthodoxy, however, flirts with the most unorthodox notion that the Second Vatican Council and its official interpretation for two decades are dead wrong on questions such as the "hierarchy of truths," the role of conscience in relation to authority, the magisterium collegially considered, and the Church in service to the Gospel. Traditionalists are not wrong in believing that the pope and church authority are under attack. Nor, in the view of this writer, are they wrong in wanting to come to the defense of an institution that has a singular potential for resisting the relativizing banalities of our time. But the renewal that is required must be on the far side, not the near side, of the transformation represented by Vatican II.

John Paul, Joseph Ratzinger, the Extraordinary Synod—they represent to some an effort to turn back; to others an effort to rescue the institutional remains of an authority that is no longer plausible; to yet others an effort to chart a course of faithfulness in the absence of false certitudes that once put their leadership beyond question. From an ecumenical perspective, one must hope that the last is the accurate reading of what they intend. If they are, as some Roman Catholics now contend, asserting their authority against the Gospel, then they must be opposed. But, if their personal and institutional energies are in the service of the Gospel and in opposition to "other gospels" (Gal. 2), then they are rendering a monumental service to the entire Church. Those of us who are not Roman Catholic Christians have every reason to hope that the present directions in the Roman Catholic Church are in service to the Gospel. In hoping that, we should be humbled by the awareness that our own institutions of theological deliberation and direction have largely failed.

This writer has for years witnessed Protestant church bureaucracies and church conventions in action. We non-Roman Catholics have much to learn from the level of spiritual and theological discourse evident in, for example, the synod of 1985. Of course all the political games and interests are in play. It would be naive to deny that. And yet, as a corporate exercise reminiscent of the first council in Jerusalem searching for "what seems good to the Holy Spirit and to us" (Acts 15), the synod seemed superior to the familiar exercises in the ecclesiastical worlds of Protestantism. To be sure, there is still some distance to go toward the papacy that is called for in ecumenical dialogues, "a papacy reformed under the Gospel." But those Roman Catholics who are most outspoken in opposing what they view as the present oppressiveness of the Vatican seem to have in mind forms of church governance with which the rest of us are all too familiar. Or else they seem to believe that institutions can get along without any governance at all. Which is simply not serious.

Recovery, restoration, renewal—these are among the terms used to describe the directions pointed by the Extraordinary Synod. They are not much more than directions pointed; if renewal it is, it is not a renewal achieved but a renewal promised. We began this reflection on the Extraordinary Synod with the words of Godfried Cardinal Danneels, and he should perhaps have the last word. He said that there had been three phases. Immediately following Vatican II was the phase of "postconciliar fervor." That, he said in words of elegant understatement, was followed by the phase of "a certain disappointment." "The third phase," he declared, "will be one of balance, rereading, and recovery." All Christians have reason to hope that the Extraordinary Synod signaled the beginning of that third phase.

28. THE AUTHORITY OF THE AUTHORITATIVE

One person's recovery is another's repression. To understand Roman Catholicism today, it is necessary to understand why people of intelligence, good will, and undoubted devotion to the church are worried that talk about recovery is little more than code language for a new repression. We have not accepted the jaded proposition that the whole history of religion is a history of conflict over authority. At least it is not entirely a conflict over who has the power to do what to whom. And yet authority is involved in today's religious conflicts, and not only in Roman Catholicism. In our individual lives, the trajectory of growth is from authoritarianism, through autonomy, to an acknowledgment of what is authoritative. As in individual life, so this trajectory is also evident in the life of institutions and communities. As a general proposition, authoritarianism may be viewed as the premodern, autonomy as the modern, and acknowledgment of the authoritative as the postmodern modes of existence. Our subject, of course, is the paradox of the Church in the postmodern mode. Vatican II offered relief from what was widely perceived to be an authoritarian church structure. There followed a period of heady freedom, of release from boundaries. This was the phase of autonomy, and almost nobody denies that it gave rise to many excesses, some of which may have been dangerous, many of which were just silly. Silly and yet understandable, for the excesses of the release were in direct proportion to the excesses of the prior oppression—or at least what some people thought to be the prior oppression.

Much of contemporary Catholicism is still in the autonomy phase. Of course the great moment of liberation, Vatican II, is now twenty years past. Theologians and others who actually experienced the oppression of the preconciliar period and the liberation from it are now middle-aged or older. Many of them seemed locked into the autonomy mode. Their act has been on the road a long time, and the audiences are no longer so large. The excitations of persecution, the frisson of martyrdom, are hard to conjure for a younger generation that only knows a church that is, at worst, amiably confused. The allure of autonomy pales with time. It must be kept alive by the real or imagined threat of authoritarianism. Every assertion of church discipline must be portrayed as a return to the bad old days, and is thus an injection that momentarily restores the intoxication of autonomy. There is a middle-aged cohort of professional Roman Catholics who have made a career of playing counterpoint to church authority. It is not only a career but an entire way of thinking that, at their advanced age, is not easy to change. The decisively formative moment of their lives was and is the tension between the authoritarian and the autonomous. They are fast being left behind as the conversation has moved from the authoritarian, through the autonomous, to the consideration of what is authoritative.

At the more publicized level, the disputes in Roman Catholicism are over "authority in the church." At a deeper and more productive level, the question is "What is authoritative for the Church?" The issue of "authority in the church" is of course an important in-house question of institutional prerogatives and powers, but it is of little theological consequence except as "authority in the church" either serves or hinders "what is authoritative for the Church." In this section we briefly consider some representative voices addressing the questions of authority and what is authoritative. We then give more sustained attention to a new proposal for understanding doctrine and authority in a way that is described as "postliberal." It is a proposal that is free from authoritarianism and yet is decidedly on the far side of autonomy.

Rembert Weakland is archbishop of Milwaukee and formerly head of the worldwide Order of Saint Benedict. He is respected as a theological thinker and was the key actor in the United States bishops' statement on ethics and the economy. In the wake of the Vatican's 1986 removal of Father Charles Curran's teaching license, Weakland distinguished himself among leading members of the American hierarchy by publicly protesting what he perceived as a threatening return to authoritarianism. In a widely disseminated statement, he acknowledged that the Church from its beginnings has had to concern itself with the integrity of the Gospel. From the time of Saint Paul until our Lord's return, the question of aberrations must be addressed. "The problem of orthodoxy is difficult in itself but becomes even more complicated because the church always exists in a particular historical context and not in some abstract world. Civilization continues to raise new problems and challenges that the church must face up to. Repeating old formulas does not answer new problems; they demand new thinking in the light of held truths."

Beginning from that seemingly unexceptionable premise, Archbishop Weakland identifies himself with the tradition of Cardinal Newman. "He knew that the glory of the Catholic church, as distinct from fundamentalism, has been its willingness (at times, it is true, with much hesitation, doubt and reluctance) to accept truth wherever it comes from and to integrate it with revealed truth, but only after a long struggle to work out apparent contradictions." Opposing the reactionary "integralism" that marked the preconciliar period, Weakland embraces integrationism as the genius of Catholicism. He cites the early Church's integration of Hellenic and Roman culture, and Thomas Aquinas's integration of Aristotle. He states that, from the sixteenth through the eighteenth centuries, humanism, rationalism, and the Enlightenment "all posed problems for the church." But integration nonetheless prevailed, also in the alleged conflicts between science and the biblical accounts, conflicts that have been "put to rest in Catholicism."

The great issues today are those issues that got Father Curran into trouble with the Vatican—contraception, abortion, homosexuality, extramarital sexual relations, and the such. "Today's challenges to the church," writes Weakland, "come mostly from psychology and the human sciences. In fact, it is not by accident that the troubled territory today is sexuality and its relationship to the whole of human behavior, that is, moral issues." The question is whether the Roman Catholic Church will be able to integrate new findings in these areas or will return to "the Inquisition and the periodic witch-hunts for heretics" of its unhappier past. He fears there may now be a return to a climate of fear. "In such an atmosphere, amateurs—turned theologians—easily became headhunters and leaders were picked, not by their ability to work toward a synthesis of the new knowledge and the tradition, but by the rigidity of their orthodoxy, so that often second-rate and repressive minds, riding on the waves of that fear, took over. Religion under such circumstances then can become an ideology that tolerates no obstacle and that values ideas more than people."

Weakland cites his own experience and the experience of the Benedictines when, under Pius X, the modernist movement was quashed. Seminaries were closed, faculty were dismissed, journals were suppressed, "informers" were on the loose, "intellectually rigid" bishops were appointed, "and fear and distrust were everywhere." "The theological suppression of the first decade of the century and the fears it instilled resulted in a total lack of theological creativity in the United States for half a century," Weakland writes. "It also left us unprepared for the dramatic changes in the 1960s. We are only now again coming to life and only now producing in the areas of biblical exegesis and theology worldrenowned scholars." Such times may be returning, he suggests, if the "desire to maintain the purity and integrity of doctrine" finds expression in a way that prevents the church from facing up "to the challenges of the times and the new discoveries about the universe and the human person." He invokes John XXIII and his belief that the church "meets the needs of the present day by demonstrating the validity of her teaching rather than by condemnations." Weakland concludes: "Was good Pope John being naive? Many, I fear, think so."

Speaking at the nondenominational Union Theological Seminary in New York in October 1986, Archbishop Weakland raised the specter that the church in America may go the way of the Dutch church. The several disciplinary actions by the Vatican have sent a chill through American Catholicism. "What could evolve," he said, "is what happened in Holland, where a large portion of the church gave up on the institution and said why worry about that and went their own way." He does not expect a schism or a breakaway church, but, like so many in the Dutch church, Americans would simply drift away, feeling that "we don't have the energy to fight with that kind of thing." "The whole of American society is anti-institutional, and they bring that attitude to the church," Weakland said. He noted that there is "a certain disillusionment that the momentum of Vatican II will be lost in all areas."

Our purpose here is not to comment extensively on Archbishop Weakland's argument. One may think him misguided in his understanding of the development of tradition and alarmist in his estimate of current directions from the Vatican, but there can be no doubt about the sincerity of his concern and the very real past experience of heavy-handed authoritarianism that gave shape and passion to that concern. Weakland's position is of great interest because he is not among the now-not-so-young turks who have made a career of defying church authority. His statements, coming from someone in a position of great institutional responsibility, give evidence of how widespread is the anxiety about this pontificate. Perhaps more important, he reflects a response to that anxiety that is archetypically "liberal" in the sense that we will be discussing later. His "integrationism," perhaps less kindly called "accommodationism," suggests H. Richard Niebuhr's model of the "Christ of culture." One might ask Archbishop Weakland what exactly "modern science" has taught us about sexuality and the person that was not known by, say, Saint Augustine; one might challenge the dichotomy between "ideas" and "people," arguing that the "ideas" of the Gospel are precisely what the Church has to offer people; and one might suggest that the disaffection in the Dutch church may be causally related to the long reign of the most latitudinarian theological establishment in Catholicism. But all such questionings, while perhaps valid enough, are less important than the basic model that Weakland presupposes for the relationship between theological truth and truth, between Church and world.

"No church could long stand if every new idea were to be accepted as a part of faith," Weakland writes. The problem arises when we ask how, and by whom, it is to be determined which ideas are not to be accepted. This is indeed a very old question that goes back to the beginnings of the Christian movement. And, as we shall see, theologians of our time, such as Karl Rahner, have ways of addressing that question. No doubt, were he pressed on the point, Archbishop Weakland and those who share his approach have ways of addressing that question. But neither in liberal

Protestantism nor in Roman Catholicism is the "integrationist" model very helpful in this connection. At the popular level, it would seem to invite an autonomy from church authority and, at the same time, a subordination to the authority of modernity. The autonomy experienced is thus a false autonomy. It may end up being no more than the replacement of one authoritarianism for another. Those who subscribe to the integrationist model protest that they are in no way calling for autonomy from church authority, and the sincerity of their protest should not be doubted. And yet the protest is not entirely credible.

29. ECCLESIASTICAL FUNDAMENTALISM

When speaking with Roman Catholics of a certain persuasion, one is frequently struck by the power of what might best be called ecclesiastical fundamentalism. There is an ecclesiastical fundamentalism of fevered infallibilism, whose proponents exult in surrendering mind and conscience to church authority. But there is another ecclesiastical fundamentalism that seems to believe that—after every form of doctrine, discipline, authority, and communal identity has been abandoned—the Roman Catholic Church will endure so long as there is something to call "Catholic." It is a fundamentalism in a pejorative sense of the term, in the sense that it is impervious to critical reason. A priest in charge of ecumenical affairs for a large diocese explained to me, in terms not so temperate as Archbishop Weakland's, why John Paul and Cardinal Ratzinger constitute "a return to the Middle Ages." In leisurely conversation he expatiated on what a "really renewed" church would look like. Women would be ordained, pastors would be elected, academic freedom would be absolute, and all questions would be democratically settled in church conventions with a majority of lay votes. Yes, he agreed, such a church would look pretty much like the Methodist or Presbyterian church down the street. But in what way would it be different, in what way would it still be the Roman Catholic Church? He seemed taken aback by my question. "Well, of course," he responded, "there would still be the bishops, there would still be the pope, there would still be the sacraments and the other things that really matter."

But why should these realities still be there after every reason for being there is gone? That they would still be there, he allowed somewhat defensively, is an article of faith. So it is that we witness at least some Roman Catholics dismantling the house piece by piece while confidently asserting that the house is indestructible. Curiously, this particular priest harshly criticized the pope because "he talks about the church as though it were an abstraction." Yet the church this priest describes—decontextualized, dehistoricized, and deprived of all its thus and so-ness—will, he believes, forever remain the Roman Catholic Church in which he made his first Communion and his ordination vows. It is a touching sentiment. It is, for him, an article of faith. For a surprising number of Roman Catholics today it seems to be inconceivable that any grave and damaging transformations could happen to their church. Of course we have our Lord's word that *the* Church will endure, since not even the gates of hell can finally prevail against it. But, strangely enough, those who call themselves conservatives seem more aware of the possibility that the gates of hell might do a great deal of damage before Christ returns in triumph. They more readily recognize that the particular form of the Church that is Roman Catholicism is a historical construct and can be historically deconstructed. In this instance, Ratzinger's complaint about theologians who view the church "sociologically" rather than as a "mystery" is reversed. An astonishing sense of "mystery" is to found among the ecclesiastical fundamentalists who believe that the Roman Catholic Church can abandon its identifying particularities and indulge any force of transformation and still be the Roman Catholic Church. Their church, to which they are undoubtedly devoted, floats above the mundane, indifferent to the fragilities and contingencies of historical change. Therefore anything can be done, and it does not matter, not really. It is a church for gnostics who, as with gnostics past, have a strong inclination toward antinomianism.

Karl Rahner died, full of years and honors, in Innsbruck, Austria, March 30, 1984. Long before he died, he had been acclaimed as the most influential Roman Catholic theologian of the century, and we have no reason to question that judgment here. He had a keen appreciation of the fragilities and contingencies of historical change, and not only in the Roman Catholic Church. Some critics thought him incautious with respect to the fragilities, and others accused him of being excessively cautious about the promise inherent in the contingencies. But all agree that few theologians, if any, played such a hand in the changes ratified by Vatican II. Until his death in his eighty-first year, he watched closely and wrote prolifically on the legacy of the Council. In interviews and essays he commented on the ascendancy of John Paul and the directions favored by Cardinal Ratzinger. He had a few cautiously caustic observations about the latter, but Rahner refused to satisfy those disciples who wanted him to say that his work was being undone.

Indeed, he was censorious of those theological frondeurs who delighted in provoking what they depicted to be the Vatican monster. Karl Rahner knew all about authoritarianism, and he understood the transitional pleasures of autonomy, but his task was to argue for what was authoritative. Those who have only a passing acquaintance with his work most commonly associate him with the ideas of "anonymous Christians" and "anonymous Christianity." These terms, which he acknowledged to be easily susceptible to misunderstanding, intended to underscore the saving grace of God in the whole of his creating and redeeming work. The absolute mystery, who is God, cannot be captured or exclusively possessed in any theology or religious expression—not in the Roman Catholic Church, not in Christianity itself. Christ transcends Christianity. There were many who understood this to mean that the Church, and the Roman Catholic Church in particular, were matters of little consequence, that the great thing was to be engaged in what God is doing in history, that the Church deserves our loyalty to the degree that it serves humanity's purposes in history. And, it must be admitted, in the many volumes that came from Rahner's pen, one can find statements in support of that understanding.

Rahner was a Jesuit of an older school who did try to look at Church and world in terms of centuries. He had a modest view of this historical moment, and of his place within it. In a 1977 interview he observed:

The relationship of the Church to the culture and society surrounding her was in history generally much more troublesome than we think as we look back. However, the features of this relationship were in general clearer than is the case today. There were times in which the Church was in the very forefront of societal and cultural development. There were times in which the Church set itself with decision and determination against this development. However, it was clear what was going on. If the Church appears to be confused today, it is because society is confused. Both go together. Sometimes I ask myself if, from the point of view of faith, this is all so bad. Why should we Christians and the Church in an age of confusion have answers for everything instead of putting up with the confusion along with our contemporaries?

But the confusion does not mean, Rahner would insist, that what is authoritative for being a Christian and for being the Church is up for grabs. We are to go ahead being Christian and being Church, even when we know it does not always make sense to us or others in relation to everything else that is going on. Faith is exercised in "putting up with the confusion," even when the confusion does not seem to deserve the name of paradox.

Rahner was critical of those, both on the Right and on the Left, who were determined to cut through the confusion. Archbishop Lefebvre and Hans Küng, for examples. Each proposed versions of Roman Catholicism that they thought "made more sense." But Rahner understood that to be a Roman Catholic, as to be a member of any significant community, is to bear with its ambiguities and even its internal contradictions. In this sense, much of Rahner's work is a commentary on Flannery O'Connor's observation that one is called to suffer much more from the Church than for the Church. Asked why Lefebvre's version of traditionalism cannot be accommodated within the church, Rahner responded: "The Church has certainly room for different mentalities. But unlike others who have a quarrel with Rome, Lefebvre contests the authority of the pope. And this is simply no longer Catholic. I repeat: This is not Catholic." This may sound embarrassingly simplistic to those who expect from a theologian of Rahner's stature Germanic systematizations of infinite distinctions. But G. K. Chesterton said that most judgments of consequence finally come down to drawing a line, and Rahner would seem to agree. There was an authoritative line by which to measure whether one was or was not a Roman Catholic. Of course, behind this was Rahner's conviction that it was not such a very terrible thing not to be a Roman Catholic. Being a Roman Catholic was one way of being a Christian, and, for many reasons, he believed it to be by far the best way. But he seemed puzzled by Roman Catholics who wanted to be Roman Catholic without being Roman Catholic.

When it came to understanding the historical reality of his church, Rahner was anything but a gnostic. The mundane, quotidian realities of institutional life did not, in his view, detract from or negate what one might say theologically about the mystery of the Church. In 1976 he was asked whether confusions in the church might not be attributed to the failure of the pope, Paul VI, to lead. Rahner responded: "He might perhaps have a clearer, a more persuasive, a more transparent line of conduct. That may be connected with the pope's personality. Give me the name of a person in an exalted position to whom you may not also address the reproach of a zigzagging course. In matters of discretion they have no other choice than to weigh the pros and the cons and then to decide. And a decision in such matters of discretion is then too conservative for some and too liberal for others." Rahner's wisdom with respect to the historical workings of the church was both tested and exemplified in his response to the Vatican's agreeing with Hans Küng that Hans Küng was not an official representative of Roman Catholic teaching.

When disputes over teaching arise, says Rahner, it is "the Church's faith awareness that has to decide." The official documents of the church's magisterium also manifest that awareness, "even though in varying degrees of obligation." Küng seems to take a different view. "He will probably say that even though the ecclesiastical authorities declare that the First Vatican Council is absolutely binding, this declaration itself is questionable and therefore nonbinding." This inevitably raises another question. "Who then actually decides what can and cannot be taught as Catholic teaching in the Church? Küng would probably say that this matter will be decided by means of disputation in the constantly ongoing history of the Church's faith awareness." Rahner thinks this quite inadequate.

Karl Rahner is not telling theologians who have difficulties with specific teachings to "shape up or ship out." He is not counseling "love it or leave it." He is proposing a nuanced appreciation of what is necessary to the contingent form of Christianity that is the Roman Catholic Church.

With regard to the Catholic teaching—let us speak with great caution—of recent centuries, I am . . . absolutely convinced that there is a competent position in the magisterium (the pope and the bishops) for drawing such a line, to which I as a Catholic theologian feel bound. If I came into a serious conflict with this line that has been drawn and my sense of truth demanded that I make a decisive protest, then I would have to draw the conclusion that I am no longer a Catholic. I would approve the conviction of countless people in the world, especially in the rest of the non-Catholic Christian world, that they are not able to be Catholic in good conscience. All Christians in the world who do not live in unity with the pope say, of course, that the claim of the pope as defined in Vatican I and repeated in Vatican II is not acceptable to their sense of truth. Understandably, one is able to come to such an opinion; otherwise, these countless people would be stupid or of bad will, neither of which can I obviously maintain. . . . The Catholic theologian only remains, strictly speaking, a Catholic theologian when he or she respects the line drawn by Rome.

Rome thought that Hans Küng had crossed the line also on Christology when in his best-selling book, *On Being a Christian,* he seemed to cast doubt upon orthodox teaching with respect to the full humanity and full divinity of Jesus. Karl Rahner is no friend of those who would place restrictions upon intellectual exploration. For all orthodox Christians there have been binding Christological definitions since the councils of Ephesus and Chalcedon in the fifth century. "It is, of course, self evident," Rahner observes, "that these pronouncements, which in the last analysis represent an inexpressible mystery of God in his relationship to the world, must be constantly thought out anew in terms of their understandability and assimilability." Rahner is not sure that Küng had departed from these orthodox formulations, but he is puzzled that Küng did not straightforwardly commit himself to these dogmas and then say, "I am just reflecting to the best of my knowledge and in good conscience how to make Christology understandable and express it in a modern perspective." Küng, says Rahner, should simply "parry the thrust" of his Roman critics. Instead he challenges them head-on, thereby inviting their challenge to him.

That could be interpreted as a somewhat cynical counsel. But Rahner is not suggesting that a theologian should publicly affirm his loyalty to dogma, and then go on to teach and write whatever he will. He is suggesting that a theologian should be very cautious in saying that his expression of an admittedly inexpressible mystery is incompatible with another expression that has dogmatic status. As he does not fully understand the mystery, he should allow that perhaps he does not fully understand the dogma. A little humility is in order, according to Rahner. Theologians are not as different as they may think they are from "simple" Christians. Rahner explains that, if someone comes to him and says, "I can't understand what the Immaculate Conception of the Mother of God means. I can't make head or tail out of it," he would respond: "My friend, you really have no ground to deny this truth. If for the time being you can't make head or tail out of it, and have enough to do to believe in God and eternal life, then you still have the right to live in the Church as the Christian you are." There is, in short, a great deal more flexibility, diversity, freedom, and, yes, even "pluralism" in the church than either the Marcel Lefebvres or Hans Küngs seem to appreciate. Sometimes one must resist the temptation to cut through the confusions, either from the Left or from the Right.

Rahner's understanding has important implications also for ecumenism. In theological dialogues between churches it has become apparent that unity does not require uniformity in the sense that we must all think and feel the same about every teaching, as though there were no hierarchy of truths. "Supposing," says Rahner, "we were to bring about a unity with Protestant Christians. We must not then demand from these Christians that they have the same reverence for the papacy as we were legitimately accustomed to between Trent and Pius XII." The critical thing in Christian unity is the agreement that the teaching of the "other side" does not constitute a denial of the Gospel that makes us one. As Rahner says, "No one would be allowed to say that the pope is the antichrist or to deny the correctly understood dogmas of the First Vatican Council in regard to the papacy. But one could surely have another relationship to the pope than [Roman Catholics have]." Then he adds, one suspects with an impish smile, "Perhaps it would only be something like that of a thirteenth-century Christian like Saint Thomas, who indeed knew that there was a bishop of Rome who had a special importance, without that fact playing all too large a role in his religious thinking and daily church life."

By 1982 Karl Rahner was speaking in more explicitly critical terms about the more celebrated critics of the church. The views expressed in the 1986 volume, *Karl Rahner In Dialogue,* were sometimes disturbing. Not surprisingly, some of those who had for years celebrated Karl Rahner began to speak of him as being old hat, as another "angry old man" who had finally succumbed to the temptation to reaction. Rahner affirms that "criticism of the Church is entirely normal and basically legitimate. At Vatican II the Church confessed that it was always in need of reforming, and again and again it has to say what needs reforming." But he admits to being bothered by some styles of criticism. "It just isn't so that the critics themselves are above criticism. But they often act as if they are. Sometimes they behave as if they're especially wise and holy, and suffer the most from the Church's defects and failings, to which they haven't contributed in any way. They often lack the self-critical eye that should belong to everyone, and especially those who set themselves up as the judge of others and of the Church."

Rahner was repulsed by theologians who talked about why they stayed in the church, as though the corporate and communal dimensions of Christianity were optional. In accord with Vatican II, Rahner understood "Church" in a comprehensive manner not limited to Roman Catholicism.

But here he is addressing the Roman Catholic situation in a passage that reveals much about Rahner's self-understanding as a church theologian. In recent years numerous theologians and others have written statements with the generic title, "Why I Stay in the Church." Rahner thinks it a very odd genre of Roman Catholic writing.

In all honesty, the statement, "Why I remain in the Church," strikes me as abominable. Faith can be attacked; I can also imagine someone losing this ecclesial dimension of faith without feeling any guilt before God. But the real Christian believer can't possibly have a patronizing attitude toward the Church that allows him or her to weigh staying in the Church against getting out of it. Relationship to the Church is at the very essence, an absolute of Christian faith. And one should be able to detect this when people who claim to be people of the Church, members of the Church, criticize their Church. Those who stand outside the Church or for whom the Church is not an integral part of faith but only an enormous sociological accident which they entered by chance, may judge the Church differently. One should be able to tell from the criticism whether it is formulated by someone who does or does not have a real relationship to the Church.

Rahner then concludes: "When criticism flows from the center of the Church's common life, it is justified, even a necessary and sacred responsibility. But only then. We should leave criticisms of another kind to those who have rejected the Church. We should not flatter them."

Between Karl Rahner and Joseph Ratzinger it may seem that a great gulf is fixed. But, with respect to the movement from authoritarianism, through the autonomous, to the authoritative, there are striking similarities. Theology has to do with intellectual freedom and the unfettered quest for truth. But the truth for which we quest and our ways of questing have everything to do with the ordering of our loves and loyalties. The personally gentle and almost courtly Ratzinger was Rahner's junior by nearly a quarter of a century. Rahner was, in Dean Acheson's memorable phrase, "present at the creation" of what has come to be called the post-Vatican II church. Back then Rahner was, with a few other theological pioneers, at center stage. Ratzinger was a promising comer, although not so spectacularly promising as, say, Hans Küng. Ratzinger and Küng, who are almost the same age, belonged to the generation that would be charged with the stewardship of the achievements of the pioneers. Some of the more febrile critics of Ratzinger make much of the alleged rivalry between Ratzinger and Küng, and of the former's supposed resentment of the latter's celebrity status. So far as this writer can determine, the stories related to this alleged rivalry, and they are legion, have all the credibility of a Hollywood gossip column. What can be documented is how these figures have constructed, in dramatically different ways, the meaning of Vatican II.

One may argue about whether Küng or Ratzinger is the better theologian. But there is little doubt that Ratzinger is the more faithful steward of the legacy of the pioneers. In the interview cited earlier, Henri de Lubac, one of the foremost pioneers, says of Ratzinger: "Dr. Ratzinger is an excellent theologian by profession. Just before he left Regensburg, the best doctoral students were still rushing there to place themselves under his direction. He is not afraid to take up in broad daylight either fundamental questions or current problems, always with calm, simplicity, a sense of measure, great respect for people and a smile. His foremost concern is certainly not to please. He does not try to escape from his role, which is occasionally not a very agreeable one." In addition, since ecumenism is the work of reconciliation between churches, and not a matter of private theological preferences, Ratzinger is certainly the theologian of greater ecumenical consequence. It is no denegration of Hans Küng's work to note that much of the attention accorded him by non-Roman Catholics up to 1979 was attributable to his being a colorful test case of how far a Roman Catholic theologian could depart from established teaching and still be an official theologian of his church. When his license as a Catholic theologian was revoked, his work had to stand on its own merits within the theological community, where it has received a decreasing measure of attention. Ratzinger's growing importance derives, of course, from his position as prefect of the Congregation. But it derives also from his determined effort to reconceptualize the roles of theology and church office in defining what is authoritative in the development of the living tradition of the Christian community. Were Ratzinger simply a policeman and not a theologian, he would play an important part in defining what comprises the Roman Catholic "package." Since he intends to be first of all a theologian, however, he has a singular role in helping to articulate the Roman Catholic contribution to the principles by which the entire Church should be authoritatively guided.

30. THE CHURCH AND THE THEOLOGIAN

Joseph Ratzinger, too, insists that theology must be understood within the context of a historical community that is necessarily marked by ambiguity. When Father Charles Curran's teaching license was revoked in 1986, Ratzinger responded to Curran's claim that a theologian was bound only by the "infallible" teachings of the church. Curran and his supporters charged that John Paul and Ratzinger, who advanced a more comprehensive notion of what is binding, were promoting "creeping infallibilism." Ratzinger wrote that the distinction between "fallible" and "infallible" is altogether too narrow and mechanical. This, he said, is a "juridical approach" that "tends inevitably to reduce the life of the church, and its teachings, to only a few definitions." In addition, it is ecumenically dead-ended and historically myopic. "Only in the last century have theologians begun affirming in such an emphatic way the problem of distinguishing infallible and non-infallible doctrine," Ratzinger observes.

"In the early Christian community," Ratzinger argues, "it was clear that to be Christian meant primarily to share in a way of life and that the most important doctrinal definitions did not have any other aim but to orient this very way of life. . . . When it is affirmed that non-infallible doctrine, even when it is part of church teachings, can legitimately be contested, the end result is destroying the practice of a Christian way of life, reducing the faith to a collection of doctrine." In sum, Ratzinger implies, the Curran approach ends up being another version of the package theory of Catholicism. It is worth noting the forensic skill with which Ratzinger attempts to turn the table on his opponents, employing the very arguments they usually launch against church authority. According to Ratzinger, it is the opponents who, with their emphasis upon what is fallible and what is infallible, are locked into a relatively short period of preconciliar Roman Catholic history. In addition, they are the ones who would turn theology into a matter of juridical and mechanical rules, rather than understanding it as a continuing conversation within the living community of faith.

In April 1986, at St. Michael's College in Toronto, Cardinal Ratzinger attempted to lay out in systematic fashion his understanding of what it means to be a church theologian. The lecture is entitled "The Church and the Theologian" and begins, interestingly, by recalling the experience of the church in Germany under the Third Reich. Ratzinger quotes Heinrich Schlier, a Lutheran theologian who later became a Roman Catholic: "No reasonable Christian would dispute the fact that it is the responsibility of the church alone to safeguard the word of God among men." Ratzinger's immediate point is not that Lutherans should become Roman Catholics, but that, unless theology is grounded in the community of faith, it has no protection from those who would use it for alien purposes. The context, of course, is the "church struggle" against Nazism, in which Ratzinger's sympathies are all with the Protestant "Confessing Church," which in the Barmen Declaration of 1934 followed Karl Barth in asserting the Church's corporate obligation to witness to the truth in independence from and, if necessary, in opposition to the state. Many theologians, frequently in the name of academic freedom, resisted this close linkage between the theological enterprise and the believing community.

Much of the Protestant leadership, says Ratzinger, had become "fearful and indecisive and had retreated into its apparent academic freedom only to become the puppet of the dominant forces and open to the invasions of the power of the party." "In this situation it became clear that theology's connection to the church was the guarantee of its freedom and that any other type of freedom was only betrayal for theology and the sacred cause entrusted to it." Ratzinger's argument is that the integrity of theological teaching cannot exist without church teaching. Otherwise theology becomes a private project in ethics or philosophy, perilously vulnerable to the fashions and pressures of the time. It was the liberals, Ratzinger notes, who championed the spirit of adaptation to the times "which quickly became the spirit of service to Nazism." The "church militant," however, knew that it had to make a decision. "This decision was likewise a decision for theology, which had to opt for a creed and thus for a teaching church."

The Nazi experience is, admittedly, a dramatic starting point for reflecting on "The Church and the Theologian." Some might think it melodramatic. But this touches on a critical difference of perspective among Christians. The difference may in part be a matter of disposition or what is called psychological makeup. It is, I expect, in larger part a difference in the readings of the signs of the times. In any event, Ratzinger may be described as being, in some respects, a "crisis theologian." The term "crisis theology" is associated with European Protestant theologians of the 1930s such as Karl Barth and Emil Brunner, and, to a lesser extent, Reinhold Niebuhr in this country. (The journal Niebuhr founded is, not without reason, called *Christianity and Crisis.*) It is a theology that stands in sharpest contrast to a theology of cultural synthesis and accommodation. The latter assumes that the world is, at heart, kindly disposed and receptive to the Christian message. The accommodationist message is, in short, that the world is a friendly place.

To be sure, the crisis theologians would agree even with Teilhard de Chardin that Christ is the alpha and omega, the beginning and the end, of the whole of history's yearning. But this is asserted now by hope, only to be empirically vindicated in the End Time. Meanwhile, the "principalities and powers of the present age" are in unremitting rage against the truth. Barth and his colleagues, who formed what was termed "the dialectical school," launched a journal called *Zwischen den Zeiten (Between the Times)*. There is a great deal of *Zwischen den Zeiten* implicit and explicit in the writings of Joseph Ratzinger. While the black spiritual is surely correct in declaring that the whole world is in his hands, most of the world does not know it or, if it knows it, does not live accordingly. The question that is very much on Ratzinger's mind, as it apparently is not on the minds of many other theologians, is, "When the Son of man comes will he find faith on earth?" Many would define faith so broadly—meaning simply the nobler aspirations of a world of "natural Christians"—that the question is meaningless. The difference is this: Ratzinger believes in the possibility of apostasy; and, without the Word being preached "in season and out of season" (2 Tim. 3), apostasy is a near certainty.

In "The Church and the Theologian," Ratzinger acknowledges that our time seems more tranquil than the 1930s and the lines of battle are blurred. "The line of demarcation cannot be seen with the same clarity" that it was seen (by some) when confronted by Nazism. But the challenge is still there, frequently in the form of presuppositions that insinuate themselves in most friendly manner. In theology, for example, he allows

that Roman Catholic theologians do not reject church authority in principle, but they frequently accept the idea that church authority is an alien
burden they have to bear. Especially if such theologians are in a university
setting, they tend to be part of a world of "science" in which "nothing
counts except the 'reasonable' and 'objective' argument." The idea of an
authority that decides what should and should not be taught "appears as
something contrary to science." "It discredits theology within the university as a serious discipline," Ratzinger says. Thus authority is viewed as
an exercise of "raw and arrogant power" that must be resisted.

He cites a theologian who during the modernist period declared that
his Catholicism was only "liberalism limited by obedience to dogma."
This, Ratzinger thinks entirely unsatisfactory because it divides the mind
and soul of the theologian. Also, it makes Catholicism appear to be "only
chains and fetters, with nothing of its own, nothing positive, nothing
alive, nothing grand in it." If church authority is a "foreign factor" for
the science of theology, then both theology and the church are imperiled.
"For a church without theology is impoverished and blind. A theology
without a church, however, soon dissolves into arbitrary theory." It is for
the sake of both church and theology that the relationship between the
two "must be restudied at its base." Ratzinger invokes a number of
worthies who have wrestled with this question. With a touch of condescension, he notes, "In his own way, even Karl Barth acknowledged that
either theology is within the community of the church or it does not exist
at all. The fact that he called his greatest work *Church Dogmatics* is itself
an admission of this, without which the work itself would never have been
written." Barth recognized, along with such Roman Catholic figures as
Romano Guardini and Heinrich Schlier, the unacceptable limitations of
what Ratzinger calls "a limping academic theology."

31. THE REPLACEMENT OF THE SUBJECT

To get to the heart of the relationship between church and theology,
Ratzinger suggested at Toronto a consideration of Paul's assertion, "I
live, no longer I, but Christ lives in me" (Gal. 2). Paul is in this passage
recounting his life story, the external events, so to speak. But with this
sentence, "as a lightning bolt," Ratzinger says he moves "from the outside to the inside." This is more than what is usually meant by "conversion." "It is a death event. . . . It is the replacement of the subject. The
'I' ceases to be independent and to be a subject existing in itself. It is
torn from itself and inserted into a new subject. The 'I' does not perish,
but in effect it must let itself fall completely in order to be received
within a larger 'I' and together with it be conceived anew." As noted
earlier, this "transposition of the 'I' " is a recurring theme in the statements of both Ratzinger and John Paul. The Christian "must let himself
be given to himself" by two "conflicting elements," the law and the

promise (or, one might say, the law and the Gospel).

"I live, no longer I"—this is the "replacement of the subject" that is not our own work but the grace of God. If it was something that we did, "the subject would still be at work, but in the futile effort of trying to break out of his own subjectivity." The replacement of the subject happens in Baptism. This is the nub of what it means to "put on Christ" and to understand the Church as "the body of Christ." What I Corinthians 12 says about the body of Christ, argues Ratzinger, is not about the Church as such. "Rather, the new subject is 'the Christ' and the church is thus nothing more than the space into which this new subject can move."

For authentic theology, he contends, participation in the church through faith and sacramental grace is imperative. And this is so, he continues, because the Spirit is promised to the Church. For instance, who Jesus really is cannot be determined merely by a scientific study of his origins. Only the Spirit of the Father and of the Son can make him known. "A person can only be understood through himself," says Ratzinger. Pneumatology, the theology of the Spirit, has everything to do with ecclesiology, the theology of the Church. The Spirit provides the community's memory; it listens and teaches us to listen. The Spirit "creates room for listening and remembering" and this space for listening and remembering is the Church; it is the "we" in which we participate in the origins and can thereby reach understanding. Here Ratzinger quotes, of all people, the demythologizing Protestant Rudolf Bultmann. "Bultmann put it very well when he said that the testimony of the Spirit 'is a repetition, a remembering in light of the communion that the primitive community had with him.' " Theology, says Ratzinger, presumes faith. And then we come to another recurring theme, that of paradox. Theology "lives in the paradox of a tie between faith and science." "When a person tries to eradicate this paradox, he eradicates theology itself and should be courageous enough to say so. But whoever, in principle anyway, accepts this paradox must also accept the tensions which come with it. Above all is the Christian claim to truth, that within the complex of the history of religions it is Christianity which is true."

In theology we are not discussing this or that, "but the truth of our very being itself." And what is *the* question about our very being? "We are concerned in theology with the question of how we can become righteous," answers Ratzinger. We find out how to be righteous through faith in Jesus, and that faith is something we cannot get on our own nor replace with something else. This faith is not opposed to reason. Rather, "We presuppose that this truth, precisely because it is truth, will appeal to our reason, that reason must be able to grasp it in order that it might be able to be adapted to the human condition and so that its full power can be displayed." Ratzinger asserts that "rationality is part of the essence of Christianity and in a way which is claimed by no other religion." "Whoever would abolish the path of reason would eliminate an indispensable dimension of the faith." This truth has a bearing on church authority and its limits. "It is here that a frontier is found that the teachings of the Catholic Church must respect as it encounters theology." The magisterium cannot mandate an abandonment or compromise of reason. The fact that Ratzinger describes this as a limiting "frontier" implies, of course, that church authority might try to do what it is forbidden to do.

Faith and thinking are essential to theology, but "the fresh start for thinking" comes from the word that always precedes us. Conversion—the "I, no longer I"—is the presupposition of theology. Ratzinger anticipates the objection that, by so closely connecting theology and sanctity, he is indulging in "sentimental or pietistic speech." He runs through a canon of great theologians who demonstrate this connection and says he "could go on and on throughout the entire history of theology." Neither a "pure and simple rationality" nor a "religiosity timidly closed in on itself" can build "a great Christian theology" that "transcends human limitations and appeals to a new generation of the human family still seeking after the truth." The unity of sanctity and reason that is the product of conversion is always churchly. Conversion means losing one's life. "But lose it where?" asks Ratzinger. "Surely, not just anywhere." "Such a losing of oneself has to have a proper addressee: God." But then the question is, "Where is God?"

We lose ourselves to God, Ratzinger says, when we recognize that God is not an idea or image projected by us but that God was in Christ and is in Christ in the form of his Church. "Obedience to the church is the concrete form of our obedience. The church is herself a new subject, one in which past and present, subject and object touch one another. It is our way of being contemporary with Christ. There exists no other way." That is a remarkable statement and, for many, a troubling statement. Does he mean that obedience to the Church is obedience to Christ? Is the Church in question only the Roman Catholic Church, and is obedience to that church to be equated with obedience to its constituted authorities? For the moment, Ratzinger would seem to be inviting the suspicion that he believes that obedience to Rome—the pope and his aides with the support of the bishops—is obedience to Christ. This would seem to fly in the face of earlier writings by Ratzinger that we have considered. There, it will be remembered, he underscores the limits of speaking of the Church as the body of Christ, since it might suggest that criticism of his historical, and very human, embodiment is tantamount to criticism of Christ. And yet now he seems to be suggesting something very like that. Against such presumption there was once a Reformation. In fact, most people thought such presumption was abandoned in another reformation, namely, the Second Vatican Council.

But, in what immediately follows, it appears that the suspicion momentarily sparked is not warranted. "By her very nature, the church is wider than any individual person, indeed, than any individual generation," he says. At the same time, "the church is not some ineffable spiritual space in which everyone can look about for what he wants. She is concrete and receives her concreteness from the binding word of her faith. She is likewise the living voice that speaks in and through the organs of faith." The Church's faith is her life, and therefore she must be able to speak authoritatively about that faith. In so doing, "what she says is binding on the theologian." Some theologians claim that the Church has the pastoral task of proclaiming for the faithful, but it does not teach for theologians. Ratzinger rejects this as a form of "classism." In that scheme of things, the theologians are the "gnostics," the first-class citizens who think for themselves, while the common folk must take things on authority. Christianity, says Ratzinger, is a "religion of the people," a "faith in which there is no room for a two-class system."

The proclamation of the Gospel in preaching has a "binding force," says Ratzinger. "The homily does not propose some hobby for leisure time." There is a sharp edge to Ratzinger's insistence that the Church does not merely propose some images, metaphors, or hypotheses that we may find useful for "expressing" whatever we want to express. The Church, rather, proclaims the Gospel and "that proclamation in turn is a parameter for theology." "It is the proclamation which is the measure of theology. Theology is not the measure for the proclamation. Theology can change and theologians can come and go but the Lord Jesus is risen from the dead and will never die again. He remains, and faith in him remains and the proclamation of that faith is the church's unchanging task." This is a heated affirmation, reflecting Ratzinger's barely disguised irritation with what he views as the arrogance of much contemporary theology. Against gnostic "classism," he says there is a kind of democracy in church teachings, for such teachings "proclaim and defend the common faith, equally normative and true for everyone."

32. KEEPING FAITH WITH THE COMMUNITY

Nonetheless, these theologians, troublesome though they be, do have some legitimate concerns. Anxieties that freedom of thought be intolerably limited; fears about a renewed climate of suspiciousness and fear; concern that the church, "going beyond the boundaries of her proclamation, will interfere in scientific matters and make all kinds of mistakes"— all these "must be taken seriously." But a church supervision is necessary, and it should not be seen "as merely chains and fetters." "The church and her dogmas should be considered a thundering, powerful force in theology, not a chain. It is in fact this thundering force that can open theology up to its greatest horizons." Ratzinger's particular worry, as discussed earlier, is with biblical study that "emancipates itself from the church" and turns exegesis into an antiquarian enterprise. Too many

scholars do not read the Bible as a unity in order to serve the proclamation of the Gospel. Rather, some biblical scholars, learning more and
more about less and less, ended up in a situation in which "all that was
left were a few dozen conflicting hypotheses." What has happened in
biblical studies is "something totally unexpected." Decomposition of the
Bible has led to a new form of allegorizing. "It is not the text which is
to be read, but rather one searches for the presumed experiences of
presumed communities. When it is not the text which is read, but what
one presumes lies behind the text, the text becomes just the means to get
to this other 'truer' meaning."

Ratzinger's criticism of varieties of biblical exegesis is strikingly similar
to the attacks on "deconstructionism" in American literary criticism.
Proponents of deconstructionism strive to advance a "radical incoher-
ence" in which the text is of no consequence, in which, in truth, there is
no such thing as a text. Within the history of Christian thought, Ratzinger's criticism is the criticism of Martin Luther against an older form
of allegorizing. "Exegesis," says Ratzinger, "becomes a new kind of alle-
gorization and often a very adventurous one which at the end is useful
only to confirm its own self and not the biblical word which it has neglected." The message of the Scriptures is the Gospel or, as Luther said,
the Scriptures are the cradle of Christ. The Gospel is not "imposed"
upon the text. Rather, it is only the faith of the Church, says Ratzinger,
that "protects the historical seriousness of the text and thus permits an
interpretation of the text which does not fall into a sterile fundamentalism." In sum: "Without the living subject which is the community of faith,
the church, the reading of Scripture either becomes a pathetic attachment
to the literal words or else the text evaporates into vagueness and irrelevance."

Ratzinger says he intends not to limit but to liberate theology for its
proper task. He does not suggest that church teaching should be "idol-
ized." "The danger of a mean and cowardly vigilance is by no means a
ghost in a closet." The sorry experience of the reaction against modernism, he says, must not be repeated. But neither must there be a repeat
of the Nazi period when the trumpet of the Gospel did not sound clearly.
Here Ratzinger again quotes Heinrich Schlier who in 1935–36 criticized
a "liberal opinion" that, he says, is all too consistent. "It says that there
exists no such thing as a decision about the truth of a teaching and that
every point of view has some truth in it and therefore any and all opinions
must be tolerated in the church. But we do not share this opinion because
it denies this fact: that God has made a decision among us." Ratzinger
agrees. He acknowledges that church authorities can make all kinds
of mistakes, that freedom of scientific thought must be carefully protected, that many other things must be taken into account, but finally
decisions must be made and there is "an apostolic office in the church"
to do just that.

When in doubt about where the line should be drawn, Ratzinger proposes what he thinks is an imperative rule of thumb for the theologian. "As to the question of the ordering of the various goods in the community of the New Testament, there is an inflexible divine judgment from which the church may never stray: 'Whoever is a cause of scandal to one of these little ones who believes, it would be better for him to be cast out into the sea with a millstone tied around his neck' " (Mark 9). Scandal, says Ratzinger, means anything that would lead the faithful to lose their faith. "The church's main job is the care of the faith of the simple." Critics might suggest that Ratzinger's appeal to the faith of "the simple," a recurring theme in his writings, is itself an instance of the "classism" that he claims to deplore. There are the sophisticated Christians, such as theologians, and then the simple Christians, and the former are to be held accountable to the latter. Is this not an instance of two-class Christianity? Ratzinger would undoubtedly answer in the negative. His entire point is that, with respect to saving and sanctifying faith, there is, as it were, a "cognitive equality" in the Christian community. When it comes to those things that matter most, the unsophisticated Christian "knows" as fully as, perhaps more fully than, his educated betters. Ratzinger comes close to saying that the theologians who worry him are perhaps the ones who are truly simple in the sense of being simpleminded in their uncritical adherence to secular canons of truth.

There is, in addition, a question of what might be called "truth in advertising." Here Ratzinger again attempts to turn the tables on the question of what is meant by the abuse of authority. "When one teaches, not on his own authority, but in the name of the common subject, the church, the assumption is that he recognizes this fundamental rule [caring for the faith of the faithful] and freely obliges himself to observe it." It is, he says, an elementary question of honesty. A theologian should not teach under false pretenses. To do so is an abuse of authority. "Believers have confidence in the church's word and so naturally transfer that confidence to those who teach in her name." But some who teach in the church's name do not teach what the church teaches. Were church authorities to do nothing about such an abuse of confidence, that in itself would be a grave abuse of authority. Church authorities cannot "lend their authority to support positions which the church has no authority, no revelation, no promise, no competence to maintain. The care of the faith of the 'little ones' must always be more important than the fear of some conflict with the powerful."

Many Christians, and not only Roman Catholics, cannot help but be puzzled by Ratzinger's reference to "conflict with the powerful." They are inclined to think that if anyone represents the powerful, surely it is Joseph Cardinal Ratzinger and the forces of the Vatican. Viewed from within the institution of the Roman Catholic Church, that is undoubtedly the case. But the context of the "war of ideas" in which Ratzinger is engaged is much more inclusive than the Roman Catholic Church. He is speaking of the Church in the modern world, and within the kingdoms of the modern world, the Roman Catholic Church is hardly the center of "the power and the glory." Arrayed against the Christian tradition, its faith and its truth claims, are the sociological dynamics of a "new class" backed by the academic, media, and ideological powers of our time. In Ratzinger's view, those who claim to be the bold minority within the church are frequently those who have joined the powerful majority against the church. This view, his opponents claim, returns the church to a siege mentality that had presumably been abandoned with Vatican II. To which it is responded that the church is indeed besieged, but nonetheless confident of its victory in Christ. If that is true, the course of courage is not to dissent from the tradition but to stand firmly with the tradition that is in dissent from the imperious delusions of the modern world.

Theology today has two ways it can go, according to Ratzinger. It can proclaim itself to be something of an autonomous science and then "impose" itself upon the church and the faithful. In that case, theology becomes the *violentia rationis* that Bonaventure described as a malformation of theological thought. Or theology can take another path; it can be a theology "which knows itself to be in service to the faith and which runs the risk of making itself appear ridiculous by trying to put tyranny and arrogance back in their place." This choice is hardly novel, says Ratzinger; it is the choice that must be made by "preachers and theologians of all times." And finally it is not a decision about theology as such, nor about church authority as such. It is a decision about Christ and his embodiment in the community of faith. "I am convinced," says Ratzinger, "that when everyone allows himself or herself to be guided by a conscience rooted in conversion to God, there can be no insoluble difficulties, even though this may not obviate all conflicts." And so he comes full circle, returning to the transposition of the ego in which the theologian is able to say with Paul, "I, but no longer I."

Ratzinger's effort to spell out systematically the relationship between the Church and the theologian may have settled very little. Indeed, many view it as little more than pious obfuscation that fails even to address the "who-whom" questions in dispute: Who can do what to whom according to what rules decided by whom? By not addressing the who-whom questions, it is claimed, Ratzinger leaves existing lines of authority in place. By obscuring the who-whom questions, he actually reinforces the existing "power structure." His whole enterprise, therefore, cannot help but appear to be self-serving, and there is probably little chance that he could exonerate himself of that suspicion in the eyes of his most determined critics. Perhaps because he realizes the futility of answering that suspicion, Ratzinger wants to change the question. He claims that the questions of power and church authority posed by his opponents are simply the wrong questions; at least they are secondary questions. He wants to pose the more radical question about the nature of theology itself. More interesting than the question of how far one can stretch autonomy and still be recognized as a Roman Catholic theologian is the question of what the theologian, in order to be a theologian, recognizes as authoritative.

Ratzinger is not a fundamentalist. That is, he does not see theology as unthinking submission to authority, whether it be the authority of an infallible Bible or an infallible church. This he dismisses as a "juridical" view of theology that inevitably ends up in the morass of who-whom questions and disputes about "how far you can go" and still be a theologian. Theology, rather, is a matter of conversion, of devotion to a community and the truths it bears. If that is really understood, he suggests, the who-whom questions can be worked out; better yet, they will rarely arise. Theology does not begin with submission to authority but rather at that point where one has reached a conclusion about what is authoritative. More accurately, it begins and ever returns to the point of acknowledging the ultimately authoritative Christ, the "I" who becomes our "I." In effect, Ratzinger is dramatically raising the stakes in the dispute with his opponents. In an informal seminar one theologian vigorously opposed to Ratzinger complained, "He is questioning my good faith." To which another added, "He is questioning our Christian commitment." They are almost certainly right. Ratzinger has offended against established protocols in polite conversation and in academic dispute. He has implicitly charged some theologians with not being who they claim to be and who they insist that the church and the world should continue to recognize them as being, namely, Roman Catholic theologians (or, for that matter, Christian theologians).

Ratzinger's is one way of trying to cope with a set of problems that is hardly limited to the Roman Catholic Church. So long as he and Pope John Paul are setting official theological directions, this is the chief Roman Catholic contribution to a thoroughly ecumenical question regarding the relationship between Church and theologian. It is possible to read "The Church and the Theologian" and forget for the moment that it was written by a curial official of the Roman Catholic Church. It contains no exclusively Roman Catholic points of reference. In form and content it is strikingly parallel to non-Roman Catholic efforts to define what it means to be a "church theologian." And the objections to the argument presented are not substantively different when raised by theologians in other churches who protest real or alleged violations of "academic freedom." To respond, as Ratzinger does, with the "rule of thumb" that the faithful must not be led astray hardly stills the protest. On the contrary, it is urged that the only thing that can really offend the faith of the community is any restriction on the unqualified right—indeed obligation—to pursue the truth wherever it may lead. And this brings us to the critical question of how contemporary theology attempts to deal with questions such as truth, tradition, and the authority of the community of faith.

Before turning to those questions, however, it is worth noting in passing some obvious, if not terribly edifying, factors in the current disputes. While Ratzinger is undoubtedly right in saying that they are not *the* questions, the existence of the who-whom questions cannot be denied. As mentioned earlier, in every institution of consequence somebody draws the lines. A Roman Catholic theologian may agree with everything that Cardinal Ratzinger says about the nature of theology and still challenge the cardinal's official application of his rule of thumb. If Ratzinger says some people are being led away from the faith, the dissenting theologian can point to his evidence that many others have been brought back to the fold through his dissenting arguments. There is even one priest today who claims that many have been won to the faith or strengthened in the faith through his salacious novels. So Ratzinger's rule of thumb does not settle the matter. In addition to the theologian's "conversion" and pastoral disposition, there is the disputed question of what is, in fact, the faith. The subjective disposition of the theologian, even when his or her subjective self has become obedient to the community of faith and its Lord, still requires arbitration regarding which truth claims are, and which are not, commensurate with true obedience.

The procedures of arbitration and decision in the Roman Catholic Church, it must be admitted, are flexible and long-suffering when compared with most institutions of consequence. In recent years there have been but a handful of censoring actions, and those typically undertaken after years of "fraternal consultation" with the alleged offenders. The orthodoxy required of a Roman Catholic theologian, it might be argued, is no more restrictive than that which, de facto, prevails in most academic departments of most universities. It is therefore an oversimplification to think that the nub of the problem is that Roman Catholic theologians are only chafing under onerous authority. The junior faculty member working for tenure, the ambitious scholar contending with the fashions and partisanships of scholarly journals, the underpublished teacher coming up against departmental politics—all these know a great deal about restrictions on absolute freedom. And, of course, the thousands of former priests who have entered government and corporate bureaucracies readily recognize that the structure and the actual operation of the church are, by comparison, remarkably relaxed. So it is likely not authority but the nature of the authority that is in question.

In Ratzinger's view, what is authoritative is derived from the constitution and mission of the Church. Authority in the Church, he suggests, is the authority of the Church, not the authority of authorities in the church. The tradition of the community—its doctrines, devotions, and loyalties—contains its own authoritative logic, so to speak. In addition, those sworn to leadership roles within that tradition and community are to have "internalized" this logic even to the point of surrendering the self. In this understanding, it is only in the exceptional circumstance, only at the margins, that "church authorities" should have anything to do. When such authorities are forced to intervene, it is a sign that something much more basic to the life of the church has already failed. If a theologian must be officially corrected, it is because he has failed to understand the internal logic of the tradition or has broken faith with the community. This is, to be sure, a very heavy judgment, but it seems to be an inescapable part of Ratzinger's understanding of "The Church and the Theologian."

It is a heavy judgment that might easily be dismissed by non-Roman Catholics as being peculiar to the heavy-handedness of Roman authoritarianism. And yet, as we have seen, Ratzinger's argument does not intend to be peculiarly Roman Catholic. He insists that he is talking about the nature of Christian theology itself. There are, however, theologians to whom his understanding would not apply. There are people, including committed Christians, who are theologians in the purely academic or philosophical sense. They are theologians by virtue of the subject matter with which they deal; they deal with theologies and with the subjects of theologies, which are the ultimacies usually associated with "God." However, for theologians who are in any sense church theologians—who understand themselves to be teachers and explorers within and for the community of faith—Ratzinger's argument is persuasive, although not necessarily conclusive. Far from being a peculiarly Roman Catholic argument, it links up with both classic and current discussions about the meaning of truth, community, and tradition among theologians of whatever denominational identity. It is to those discussions that we now turn briefly in order to better understand Roman Catholic disputes within an ecumenical context, and to gain a firmer hold on the significance of the authoritarian, the autonomous, and the authoritative in Christian life and thought.

33. KNOWING AND TESTING THE TRUTH

The ways in which Ratzinger and John Paul address the question of theology and authority is frequently described as "integralism." They are accused of integralism, needless to say, by their opponents, for *integralism* is a very unpleasant word in the history of Roman Catholic thought. *Integrisme* was the motto of a particularly virulent campaign that championed, and carried to extremes, Pius X's 1907 condemnation of modernism. The campaign was centered in France, which was also the center of Roman Catholic scholarship at that time, and aimed to preserve integrally the teachings of the church against critical studies in Scripture and doctrine. Smiting its opponents hip and thigh, the integralists succeeded in casting a shadow over the work of Europe's most distinguished theologians. Among other "reductionisms" they attacked was the "heresy" then known as "Americanism," about which more in due course. In any event, within a few years it was apparent that the zealots had gone too far. In a 1914 encyclical *(Ad Beatissimi Apostolorum)*, Benedict XV noted that the word *integral* is something of a tautology, since the corpus of faith is accepted entirely or not at all. Within that acceptance, research and debate are not only permissible but mandatory, said Rome. The secret society that promoted integralism, the Sodalitium, was suppressed by Rome in 1921, and that was the end of integralism. Whatever remnants of that way of thinking that still lingered were effectively exorcised by Vatican II. Or so it was thought.

It is the farthest thing from our purpose to put in a good word for integralism. From all that the historians tell us, the movement was narrow, nasty, anti-intellectual, fanatical, fideistic, and generally disagreeable. And yet, had the word not been so thoroughly discredited by its champions, *integralism* speaks of a concern that is of continuing and intense interest among theologians in all the churches. The question of what is integral to, what is inherent in, what makes for the wholeness of the faith can hardly be avoided by thoughtful Christians. The connection between *integral* and *integrity* is more than an etymological curiosity. To be sure, concern for theological integrity is not everybody's cup of tea. That is to say, many theologians are more practiced in speaking about the "relevance," or even the "possibility," of theology rather than about its integrity. But if the identity of Christian theology (What is it that makes Christian theology *Christian?*) is not to be dissipated, and if the search for a theologically grounded ecumenism is not to be abandoned, the fear of integralism must not dissuade us from a fresh examination of what makes for integrity in Christian thought.

In almost every field of thought today there is discussion about what it means to be postmodern or postliberal. Theology is no exception. (See especially George Lindbeck's *The Nature of Doctrine: Religion and Theology in a Postliberal Age,* 1984.) It is important to see how Cardinal Ratzinger's understanding of the theological task and its integrity may be related to this larger discussion. Large parts of his argument would seem to fit a type of theology that is aptly described as postliberal or postmodern. It is an approach that is on the far side of modernism, including the modernism peculiar to an earlier phase of the Roman Catholic experience. In speaking of different "types" of theology, one is reminded of E. M. Forster's remark that there are two kinds of people in the world—those who say there are two kinds of people in the world and those who don't say that. Much the same may apply to saying there are three kinds of theologians in the world. But we will say it nonetheless: there are preliberal, liberal, and postliberal theologians. Then the language becomes heavy going, but the terms sort themselves out after a while. Very briefly, the scheme is this: preliberals take a "cognitive-propositional" approach to doctrine, liberals take an "experiential-expressive" approach, and postliberals favor a "cultural-linguistic" approach.

In other words, there are three different answers to what doctrines are and what they are for. Preliberals assume that doctrines are propositions that express revealed and therefore unchanging truths. Liberals assume that doctrines are symbolic expressions of universal and unchanging religious experiences. Postliberals incline to the view that doctrines are essentially "rules" reflecting the "grammar" of specific religious traditions. Postliberals tend to be more critical of liberals than of preliberals. That is because postliberalism shares preliberalism's suspicion that liberalism ends up in robbing doctrines of their normative status. On the other hand, postliberalism is convinced that, even if we wanted to, there is no going back to preliberalism. In the case of the postliberal, as in the case of the postmodern, the "fiery brook" has been crossed.

The approach suggested here can be related to many issues in current dispute. It is pertinent also to misgivings expressed by Cardinal Ratzinger and others regarding ecumenism. Liberalism has proved to be of little help in attaining ecumenical agreement or disagreement. That is because liberalism typically claims that apparent doctrinal disagreements are just that and only that—apparent. Different doctrinal formulations are, in this view, only different ways of saying the same thing. Liberal ecumenism thus tends to produce a type of lowest-common-denominator dialogue that is depressingly vacuous. Successful ecumenical dialogue must produce not a synthetic new tradition but a confession in which both parties to the dialogue can recognize their own tradition. Preliberals, on the other hand, view the ecumenical effort itself with grave suspicion. Put more bluntly, they suspect that all ecumenical agreements must be the result of one party or the other (or both) selling out. After all, if it was agreed that there was a doctrinal disagreement, and then it is later said that there is reconciliation, it would seem that somebody must have changed his position. That does not necessarily follow.

To say there are three types of theologians does not mean that all or most theologians are "pure types." Many Roman Catholic theologians, for instance, seem to be "mixed types," frequently being liberal in their theological method but preliberal when it comes to a crunch with church authority. A postliberal "rule theory" of doctrine would seem to be more promising. In an important sense, this idea is not all that new. From earliest times, the Christian notion of *regulae fidei* has underscored the similarity between doctrines and rules. Doctrines set limits. This is a limit setting not by institutional authority but by the inherent (were it permissible, one might say integral) logic and language of doctrines themselves. If we understand doctrine as church teaching, then the purpose of doctrine is to set the *range within which* theology goes about its business of propositional statements and symbolizing activities. (Of course doctrines are more than formal church teachings and play very different roles in evangelism, catechesis, liturgy, and the devotional life. But here we are primarily concerned with church teaching, which is the question to which

Joseph Ratzinger addresses himself in his reflections on the church and the theologian.)

Critical aspects of Ratzinger's argument, I believe, are consonant with this postliberal understanding of doctrine. The most critical aspect is the relationship between theology and the Church, which includes also the grammar of the community of faith. The postliberal approach can be fruitful for ecumenical reconciliation, for example, because reconciliation can happen when each party to the dialogue acknowledges that the other party's statement is within the communal grammar, within the limits set by the doctrinal "rules." Within each tradition there are truth claims that are described as "encoded propositions." What is positively affirmed in encoded propositions need not be agreed upon by the other party, so long as it is recognized that what is encoded does not violate the "doctrinal code" of the larger and shared tradition.

A useful example is the early Church's controversies over christological and trinitarian doctrine. Consubstantiality was an important issue, the doctrine that in the Trinity, the Father and Son are of one and the same substance or being. Athanasius, the champion of orthodoxy, asserted a regulative or "rule theory" understanding of credal statements. He said that consubstantiality means that whatever is said of the Father is said of the Son, except that the Son is not the Father. Positive affirmations about the relationship between Father and Son can then take many forms, so long as they do not violate this doctrinal rule. There is something powerfully liberating in this approach. As Cardinal Ratzinger emphasizes, in theology, as also in liturgy and indeed in all serious life activities, freedom is made possible by rules. Such activities are anxiety ridden and paralyzed when nothing is established, when nothing is "in place." Skating on a lake where the thin ice has not been marked is a dicey venture, and the almost infinite variations of skill and experiment in baseball are possible only when the game itself has been defined. Thus words such as *doctrine, dogma,* and *orthodoxy* lose the oppressive connotations they carry in contemporary culture. To be sure, dogma sets limits, but the limits are set in order to clear space for the free play of the best that we can bring to the enterprise at hand.

Of course, Christians may still disagree about the grammar of doctrine. But those disagreements are not likely to arise along existing ecclesial boundaries. In addition, it is probable that those disagreements will be more theologically fruitful than contestations over different propositions. For instance, people may believe different things about the proposition that the Blessed Virgin was bodily assumed into heaven (as indeed those who now say they "believe in" the Assumption undoubtedly mean different things by that statement), but they can be agreed upon the rules of doctrine by which the Assumption may be believed. The postliberal approach being proposed is not without difficulties, but it would seem to be a great advance over prevailing liberalisms in Roman Catholicism and elsewhere. In the postliberal approach, as in Ratzinger's argument, the regulating accountability is to the community and its tradition. This is in sharp contrast to the lines of accountability in conventional liberalism.

The liberal strategy and sense of accountability reflect a vulgarized form of what the Protestant theologian Paul Tillich termed *correlation*. That is to say, it is claimed that there is a correlation between the questions thrown up by the culture and the symbolic answers provided by the Christian tradition. If the purpose is to "market" Christianity, this liberal or experiential-expressive approach has distinct attractions. Liberalism might be described as a supply-side view of Christianity. The demand side is the "real world" and the questions it poses. The supply side is the rich lode of symbolic meanings provided by the Christian tradition. In this marketing strategy, Christian teaching becomes an optional aid to individual self-realization rather than a bearer of normative realities to be internalized. Theologians run the design department and are in charge of wholesaling the symbolic meanings retailed in the pastoral care division of the Church's mission. But the market finally determines what is, as they say, "meaningful."

Different religious statements, rituals, and allegiances are then but different ways of expressing a universal and underlying truth. In the second life of nineteenth-century Protestant liberalism that is now thriving among Roman Catholics, that underlying reality is frequently referred to as "mystery." There is a nice irony here, for, as we have seen, "mystery" is also an important term in the thinking of Joseph Ratzinger. One difference is that Ratzinger speaks of mystery with respect to particularities, while liberalism sees the mystery in universals. We earlier considered the ways in which talk about the transcendent and the ineffable can be turned in ways that escape reference to anything in particular. Any specific religious statement, it turns out, is inevitably about something else. Consider the statement, "In Jesus, God became man." Precisely *that*, in one view, is the mystery. In the liberal view under discussion, however, that is but the symbolic expression of some other and presumably deeper reality.

With Karl Barth, among others, Joseph Ratzinger insists that the Christian Gospel is not one symbolic expression among others of the universal phenomenon of religion, but is the controlling statement of truth by which all reality, including the phenomenon of religion, is rightly understood. And this returns us to the question of community, tradition, and how we come to understanding. In the postliberal or postmodern view, it is evident that one can no more be religious in general than one can speak language in general. "Religion in general," in other words, is but another particularism. The liberal tendency to dismiss traditions as being culturally and historically "conditioned" is itself as culturally conditioned as the traditions it presumes to transcend. One of the great intellectual shifts of our time is the recognition that the search for the "universal" place to stand—an Archimedean point to which particularisms can be brought to judgment—is elusive and final illusionary. This does not mean (as some preliberals may be tempted to think) that we have license to assert any truth claims whatsoever, no matter how arbitrary, in complete freedom from reasonable discourse. It does mean that significant discourse is shaped by community and tradition. Liberalism continues to treat religion as the phenomenon, of which Christianity is an epiphenomenon. George Lindbeck perceptively compares this with trying to learn Chinese by reading translations from the Chinese. Liberal marketing, in its version of correlation, offers translated Christianity, which is something very different from the Christian tradition of which it is a translation.

Our understanding of "authority" in theology changes when we recognize that we can only know a tradition by immersing ourselves in a tradition, by submitting ourselves to the doctrinal, ethical, and liturgical "rules" of a tradition. Christian theology does not begin its work with the "limit questions" posed at the boundaries of universal human experience. It begins at the center of reality, which is Christ, by which the limits are set. Being Christian is a scandalously particular way of being human by which "being human" is defined. Christianity is not a brand name product on the "symbol systems" market that offers exchangeable goods. Jesus cannot be exchanged for Vishnu, nor Vishnu for Jesus. This is not to downplay the importance of interreligious dialogue, but it is to say that only those who have interiorized a normative tradition will have much to contribute to the dialogue. Even the goal of interreligious peace, which is a very great good, is best secured when it is grounded theologically. We do not kill one another, not because we agree that nobody really knows the will of God, but because we know it is the will of God that we not kill one another over our disagreements about the will of God.

As Ratzinger emphasized at Toronto, so the postliberal understanding stresses the external word, the *verbum externum.* According to the Christian tradition, God has entered into the deliberation. The liberal derives the external features of a religion from inner experience; the postliberal does not neglect the internal word but understands it as the capacity to recognize the true external word. In other words, the internal word is the acknowledgment of the authoritative. It is not authoritarianism, for the person fully and freely participates in and internalizes the *verbum externum.* Nor is it autonomy in search of community and simply electing this community of symbolic beliefs rather than another. In sum, it is neither preliberal (authoritarian) nor liberal (autonomous). It is the postliberal "I but not I," in which, in the very moment of our choosing, we acknowledge that we have been chosen.

The connection between theology, on the one hand, and community and tradition, on the other, goes much deeper than questions about "church authority" conventionally understood. Preliberals and liberals are alike in assuming that first you discover a truth (whether through inner experience or revelation) and then you express that truth as adequately as you can. Of course, preliberals of the propositionalist school frequently view both the truth and its expression as revealed. But liberals, although they do not speak of revelation in the same way at all, turn out to have a very similar posture. That is, the fundamentalist (appealing to an inerrantly inspired Bible) and the liberal (appealing to intellectual freedom) both claim to have a universally valid "place to stand," quite apart from their embroilment in the particularities of a cultural-linguistic tradition. They make the same conceptual "moves," as it were. First there is the truth discovered, and then one moves to the expression of the truth.

But the emphasis upon theology and community suggests that the conceptual order may be quite the opposite. Perhaps truth and expression are not separable; perhaps the expression is, in important ways, the truth. (Or, as Marshall McLuhan's mischievously insightful axiom has it, "The medium is the message.") The language of the tradition is not just an instrument for expressing what we know; the language is a way of knowing. Put differently, it is necessary to have the means for expressing an experience in order to have the experience. The richer and more varied the tradition in which we are immersed, the richer and more varied is our experience. Pressing the point just a little, we might say that Paul was in the cultural-linguistic mode when he wrote, "Yet, if it had not been for the law, I should not have known sin. I should not have known what it is to covet if the law had not said, 'You shall not covet' " (Rom. 7). John XXIII, on the other hand, was definitely not in the cultural-linguistic mode when, in his opening statement at Vatican II, he declared, "The truths of the deposit of faith are one thing; how they are expressed is another." That sentence can undoubtedly be understood in many ways, but it has in the past two decades been much invoked as a carte blanche for experiential-expressive liberalism.

The postliberal approach sketched here is akin to the directions that Joseph Ratzinger has been pointing for Roman Catholic theology—akin to, but not identical with. Between theology trapped in preliberal propositionalism and theology awash in liberal expressivism, Ratzinger seems much more exercised about the second. That is undoubtedly related to his reading of the "signs of the times" with respect to the state of Roman Catholic theology. When one considers the theologies and theologians given academic prestige and media attention, his reading may well be justified. But if Ratzinger is not to be misunderstood as embracing a Roman Catholic traditionalist version of fundamentalism, he must make it clearer that the rules of doctrine are not primarily *rules of an institution* but *rules of participation* in a communal enterprise. It would also be helpful if he affirmed more clearly the obligation of theology to engage its assertions about reality with other assertions about reality. In fairness, both these requirements are implicit and frequently explicit in his work. But the polemical edge of Ratzinger's statements is found almost exclusively in his strictures against liberalism rather than preliberal propositionalism. This, as we have noted earlier, may have everything to do with what he describes as his "so awkward" official position.

In any event, to the extent that Ratzinger is correctly perceived as a postliberal theologian, he is not the enemy of theological change. It is preliberalism and liberalism that cannot really cope with change. Preliberals speak much of constancy, and liberals speak much of change. But for neither is there real change, since for one the proposition is constant and for the other the experience is constant. In the postliberal approach, there is both constancy and change; they are not in conflict.

That is, of course, a very attractive prospect. But there are many questions calling for further exploration. One question is whether a preliberal must go through liberalism in order to arrive at postliberalism. For many reasons, one must hope that is not the case. If postliberalism is the happy recovery ward for those who have gone through the catastrophe of liberalism, the entry price is too high. For those who have arrived at postliberalism after having gone through liberalism, liberalism may be viewed as a *felix culpa*. But one would not wish the catastrophe on anyone, nor is the Roman Catholic Church likely to recommend it. At the same time, for those who have arrived at postliberalism on the far side of liberalism, there is no going back to a preliberal cognitive-propositional understanding of doctrine. Here it may be helpful to risk complicating the terminology just a little further. Postliberalism, it may be argued, is really pre-preliberalism. That is implicit in the earlier reference to the early Church's understanding of doctrine in terms of the "rule of faith." The point cannot be made too often that what is today described as preliberalism is really a relatively modern, post-Cartesian, understanding of truth. The "old-time religion" of many Protestant fundamentalists and many Roman Catholic traditionalists is in fact a relatively recent development. Each has isolated and frozen a particular historical moment and confused it with the entirety of Christian truth (the Bible for the fundamentalist, The Tradition for the traditionalist). The definitive historical moment for the Protestant fundamentalist was the fundamentalist-versus-modernist controversy of nearly a century ago. The moment for the Roman Catholic traditionalist was post-Tridentine Rome—usually post-Tridentine Rome as they remember it in the reign of Pius XII.

But for most of us who read and write books such as this one, postliberalism is emphatically and inescapably *post*liberalism. Certainly for this author, it is a position arrived at on the far side of liberalism. Some developments are truly irreversible. After solving a puzzle, for example, one simply cannot return to the way one thought about the puzzle before solving it. After experiencing a place or a person or an idea, it is not possible to be the same person one was when anticipating the experience. And so it is with most of us in our experience of liberal theology's understanding of the threat that doctrinal change poses to doctrinal constancy. If we cannot accept the liberal "solution" that the change really does not matter (because it does not affect the constant of experience), neither can we pretend that we have not seen the threat. The preliberally orthodox will tell us that this is a good argument for refusing to taste of liberalism's forbidden fruit in the first place. To which the first answer is that, however that may be, the experience is irreversible. The second and more important answer is that we are morally obligated to a truth that no existing theological method can adequately comprehend and that will not be comprehended adequately before the End Time.

And this returns us again to the reality of paradox. The emergence of paradox signals not a failure of our understanding but the point beyond which our understanding cannot push, given the limits of our historical moment. Such paradox cannot be resolved; it can only be superseded. This future-directed view of theology as understanding anticipating further understanding is not a liberal or postliberal quirk but is firmly rooted in the eschatology affirmed by all who lay claim to being orthodox. Preliberal, liberal, postliberal—these are time-conditioned terms that make sense only within a relatively small part of Christian history to date and, I suspect, a much smaller part of God's workings in history. That the Spirit is guiding us toward the understanding of the truth that is to be manifested is, on the other hand, an article of faith giving us confidence for the entire sojourn.

The proponents of postliberalism have scouted part of the way ahead on the far side of liberalism. Ratzinger points in the same direction. Those who would join in this part of a thoroughly ecumenical exploration must be pledged to intratextual and intratraditional fidelity, to abiding by the rules of doctrine. Such people must also be pledged to intertextual and intertraditional fidelity, to letting our Christian rules and their truth claims challenge and be challenged by other rules and other truth claims in which we are also immersed. As Ratzinger does make explicit, in encountering the confusion of languages, we must be determined that the "control language" is the Christian tradition. In the process of translation, the priority task is to translate the world into the text, not the text into the world. Those who cannot in good conscience maintain that priority should acknowledge that they are outside the *regulae fidei;* they are no longer within the communal enterprise by virtue of which Christian theology is significantly Christian. It is in intratextual fidelity that we find our ultimate identity and the cause in which we hope to die. It is in intertextual fidelity that we discover the ambiguities and responsibilities of who we are along the way toward that hoped-for end.

This section has been preoccupied with theology, even theological methodology. It perhaps seems somewhat abstract and removed from the urgencies of change within Roman Catholicism and the world. The documents of Vatican II are typically charged with such urgencies. And they are charged hopefully, indeed optimistically. With the dawning of the Council, the world seemed all possibility. Decades later, the accent is on limitation. Talk about theology as a cultural-linguistic enterprise accents limitation. It reminds us that this Christian way of speaking and thinking and acting is one way among others. Gone are the heady universalizing flights in which we thought the Church encompassed everything and encompassed it now. And yet this accent on limits, on the particular and on the distinctive, is not a withdrawal. If this Christian way turns out to be true, it does indeed encompass everything. "The vision of God," said Irenaeus, "is the life of humanity." But that vision is now challenged and contested by other visions. These other visions are not, as traditionalists would have it, simply false. Nor are they, as liberals would have, simply different versions of the same vision. They are different ways of knowing, short of that time in which we will know even as we are known. We have decided for the Christian way of knowing, because we believe that "God has made a decision."

Children of the City of God, we are "alien citizens" of the City of Man. This, as we shall see in the next section, has a strong bearing not only upon doctrine but upon deeds, not only upon our way of thinking but upon our way of being in the world. The patristics scholar Rowan Greer (*Broken Lights and Mended Lives*, 1985) reminds us that the Christians in the Roman Empire also had a very ambitious and confident conception of "The Church in the Modern World." It was a soaring ideal that then, too, led to disappointment. Many scholars say that the ideal was so high that it could not be realized and was therefore not attempted by most. "Perhaps," writes Greer, "that conclusion could be elaborated by suggesting that the ideal itself had become corrupted by losing touch with the paradox of alien citizenship. The ideal became a transformed citizenship and so implied that heaven had been or could be brought to earth. The message of deliverance yielded to a message of reordering, most often reducing heaven to earth rather than drawing earth toward heaven."

Our specifically Christian way of knowing and being in the world stands in a relationship of paradox to other ways of knowing and being in the world *in which we also participate.* A paradox is a very unsatisfactory thing. Yet in its very unsatisfactoriness may be its power. Rowan reminds us that, in earlier ages, Tertullian tried to terminate the paradox of "alien citizenship" by a program that required martyrdom, since only martyrdom could finally sever the ties linking Christians to earthly society. Another church father, Clement, emphasized the other side of the paradox, but his more synthetic course ended in dissolving the radical message of deliverance into simply a new social order. The Christian Empire, claiming to have realized Clement's dream, succeeded only in creating an order more earthly than heavenly, identifying the Christian hope with a social order hardly more satisfactory than the one that preceded it. Greer concludes that perhaps a dialectic is at work. "Indeed, the very impossibility of realizing the paradox may be its genuine value." And that is the thought that will accompany us as we consider the most fevered controversy in Roman Catholicism today, the debate over liberation theology.

PART IV

Setting Aside the Tiara

When John Paul I was installed into his sadly brief pontificate of little more than a month, the remarkable thing was that he was *installed*. He was not crowned. He did not receive the papal tiara, which since the Middle Ages all popes had worn. The tiara signified, among other things, terrestrial or temporal power. It was no little thing to set aside the tiara. And when John Paul II was installed, that too was an installation and not a coronation. Protestants of all sorts have long railed against Rome's pretensions to worldly power. Now Rome seems officially to be abandoning those pretensions, while increasingly politicized Protestants on the Left and the Right seek to demonstrate their power as the world measures power. Liberal Protestantism holds on to its pathetic little tiara, while conservative Protestantism tries on new tiaras for size. Thus is the liberating Gospel grievously compromised as "alien citizens" seek to prematurely resolve the paradox of Christian existence between the times. And, perhaps also paradoxically, thus is the Church's power to influence this provisional moment in time eviscerated by the Church's eagerness to influence this provisional moment in time. Only a Church that knows it is vindicated by the Word of God alone, and ultimately vindicated by nothing other than the vindication of that Word in the coming of the messianic age and the fulfillment of the promise—only such a Church can be of much help in the worldly tasks that are also ours.

I say that the Roman Catholic Church has *officially* set aside the tiara. In fact, that setting aside was most forcefully articulated in Vatican II's "Declaration on Religious Freedom." But old habits die hard. And old habits have a way of returning in new guise. The very aggressive liberation theology of the past decade and more may be such a new guise. An appreciation of irony is required to understand the ways in which a passion for the powerless may include a yearning to retrieve the discarded tiara. The conscious will to serve may disguise the unconscious will to rule. In some streams of liberation theology, as we shall see, the will to rule is anything but unconscious. But the rule desired is, it is insistently said, the rule of justice. Liberation theology is not exclusively a Roman Catholic phenomenon nor exclusively a Latin American phenomenon, but it is among Roman Catholics in Latin America that it has taken most influential form. In this section we examine liberation theology (or, as many insist, liberation theolog*ies*) and the ways in which the Roman Catholic Church is responding to this new/old challenge. Admittedly, liberation theology may not be the most intellectually or theologically interesting enterprise in the Church today. But it is the enterprise that is most pointedly, and sometimes painfully, testing the model of "Church and world in paradox."

We begin not with the challenge of liberation theology itself but by trying to understand something of the person who is most critical to shaping Roman Catholicism's response to it. That person, obviously, is John Paul II. Then we will try to examine carefully, and not without sympathy, varieties of liberation theology and the several responses to it, both official and otherwise. This section concludes with a "cautionary tale" about the churches in Nazi Germany. That may seem to be an improbable connection, but I trust it will seem less improbable by the time we get there. For now, we turn to the mind of Karol Wojtyla, who in 1979 became the Bishop of Rome, Pontifex Maximus, John Paul the Second.

It used to be routinely said in the news that the president of the United States is the most powerful man in the world. Undoubtedly it is still said, but not so often. If with Hannah Arendt we distinguish power from force, noting that power is force combined with moral authority, then it seems reasonable to view John Paul II as the most powerful person in the world today. The point is at least arguable. The president of the United States and the head of the Soviet Union can, of course, unleash more lethal force. But neither can match the pope's capacity to influence the loyalties of hundreds of millions of people around the globe. And, of course, that influence is hardly limited to the eight-hundred-plus million who call themselves Roman Catholic. George Hunston Williams, a Protestant scholar at Harvard, has been studying Karl Wojtyla for twenty-five years and is the author of *The Mind of John Paul II: Origins of His Thought and Action* (1981). He thinks it is quite certain that the Pope is far from indifferent to the power he exercises. In fact, writes Williams, the Pope sometimes speaks "as though fondling the tiara never again to be worn." But, as his years in the papacy increasingly demonstrate, John Paul knows that the power and responsibility that are his have little to do with tiaras.

According to close students of John Paul such as Williams, he is not a pope who happens to be Polish; he is a Pole who became pope. "Of him," Williams writes, "perhaps more than of any other modern Pope, it can be said that he may be understood by what he was before he became Pontiff." He has been shaped by the sufferings and hopes of Poland's tortured history. Through bitter conflicts and defeats since the eighteenth century, especially defeats at the hands of Russia, there emerged in Poland a messianic, almost mystical, sense of national destiny. The "prophetic poets" of Poland interpreted the sufferings of their land in terms of Christ's passion and resurrection. Poland, they testified, would play a most particular role in the salvation—that is, liberation—of the world. That vision included the promise that there would one day be a Polish pope.

Apart from this history, it is impossible to understand the intense, even apocalyptic, hold that John Paul has on the Polish imagination. In the minds of Poles and, no doubt, in the mind of John Paul, the coincidence between his ascendancy and Poland's new impulse toward freedom through the work of "Solidarity" is no mere coincidence. He is the first modern pope to have first-hand knowledge of what it means to live under a totalitarian regime and, as has often been observed, has no illusions about Marxist and Marxist-Leninist pretensions. Some liberation theologians say this is a parochial handicap producing a reflexive anticommunism; others see it as a realism born from hard experience. Beyond the knowledge of totalitarianism, however, this Pope who is not incidentally Polish views the failure of existing social systems as part of a cosmic drama. In his first encyclical (Redemptor hominis) he looked toward the third millennium that is almost upon us and spoke about "the Church that is continually preparing for the new coming of the Lord" and, yet more provocatively, of "humanity's new Advent." The twentieth-century skeptic may see events as one damn thing after another, but John Paul's reading of history includes providential purpose in the light of cosmic fulfillment.

As he is not a pope who happens to be Polish, so he is not a pope who happens to be a philosopher; he is a philosopher who became pope. His vision of history is in sharpest contrast to that of American fundamentalists who cite "Bible prophecy" predicting scenarios for the imminent separation of the saved and the damned. Rather, history is the painful, ambiguous development toward universal freedom for all humankind. Talk about history's movement toward universal freedom suggests the much pilloried philosophical flights associated with Hegel and his votaries. Karol Wojtyla, however, is a "phenomenologist" who is chiefly influenced by Max Scheler (d. 1928). Phenomenology, to put it too simply, is a school of thought devoted to attending to phenomena. Scrupulous attention is paid to the particular, the ordinary, the quotidian, the things that others may consider unworthy of serious philosophical reflection. Ridding itself of philosophical and other presuppositions, the process of sheer intellection, of the mind, encounters reality that is both internal and (primarily) external to the mind. The mind—including intellect, will, and feeling—is able to "mirror" a reality in its essence and thus provide a basis for presuming that reality's existence. Liberation theology emphasizes the "concrete" and "contextual" in the "praxis" of life. As a phenomenologist, John Paul undoubtedly feels that he does not need liberation theologians to remind him to attend to the particular.

34. JOHN PAUL AND THE PERSON

John Paul's prepapal philosophical work focused on the human person. That preoccupation with the person is persistent throughout his numerous statements as pope. In his thought there is hardly a word more important than *person*. This is no individualistic focus, however, for the person is always person-in-relationship. But neither does his work descend into sociologese. He has done major studies in Spanish mysticism and the solitariness of the person in the dark night of the soul. The "horizontal" and "vertical" dimensions of the human person can be sustained because, in John Paul's thought, the person is engaged in transcendent reality. He is in simultaneous relationship to other persons and to the personhood of the absolute, of God. The person-in-relationship, John Paul adamantly insists, can never be reduced to the social and economic relationships of the immanent. Concepts such as the transposition of the "I" and the replacement of the subject keep cropping up in John Paul's writings. As we have seen, these concepts are regularly employed also by Cardinal Ratzinger, who has apparently imbibed them from John Paul, since his own intellectual formation is quite different. Ratzinger, it may be suggested, is more of a cosmopolitan than John Paul; he speaks from the mainstream of Western theological and philosophical thought. John Paul speaks to that mainstream but—and this is certainly not unrelated to his being immersed in a national ethos that in this century has been marginalized—comes at it from an angle that frequently seems slightly off center.

Put more bluntly, John Paul is often difficult reading. His writings, both as Karol Wojtyla and as John Paul, are not for the bedside table. (It is said that he knew long ago that he would become pope and he therefore wrote his books so that he could assign them as penance for wicked priests in purgatory.) Those who have known the Pope over the years insist that to understand him it is necessary to understand his mind, the intellectual patterns by which he puts reality together. For the general observer, there is the public pope—both pastoral and political—and then the vague awareness of Wojtyla the scholar somewhere in the background. But those who know him better are struck by the thorough integration of the man, his thought, and his work. One may disagree with particular positions, but each is part of a whole. The positions and the person form a coherent "presentation of self" (Goffman). A bishop who has worked with John Paul for many years told this writer, "Except superficially, you can't encounter the Holy Father selectively."

In short, this Pope is a formidable intellectual. To say that he is one of the great philosophers and theologians of our time is to say too much. In the first eight years of his pontificate, he has doubtless had precious little time for serious academic work. Were he not the pope, it is far from certain that his writings would attract much intellectual attention outside Poland. Indeed they attract surprisingly little intellectual attention even though he is the pope. But that may be because most people who read his writings do not read him intellectually but institutionally. That is to say, they read not in order to follow an argument or the development of an idea but in order to discover "signals" about authoritative directions of the magisterium on one question or another. That is understandable but nonetheless a pity, for, although frequently dense and convoluted in style, the man's way with ideas is fascinating. "Ideas have consequences," Richard Weaver famously wrote, and this pope unquestionably agrees. To be sure, anybody who reads everything in collections such as "The Pope Speaks" must have a great deal of spare time on his hands. One wonders that the Pope has time to speak all he speaks. Whether at the Vatican or on the road, many statements are routine and prepared by others. But pronouncements such as encyclicals and major pastoral exhortations are, we are assured, laboriously drafted by John Paul. Those who read such statements even cursorily need no assurance on that score.

John Paul keeps returning to the idea of the person, plus the culture that sustains and protects that idea. Against sundry determinisms—economic, psychological, biological—he affirms culture as the human artifact that keeps life truly human. Here again his philosophical position is reinforced by his experience as a Pole. He has written: "I am the son of a nation that has lived through the greatest experiences in history, which though condemned to death several times by its neighbors, has survived and remained itself. It has conserved, regardless of foreign occupations, its national (as distinguished from political) sovereignty, not by depending on the resources of physical power, but uniquely by depending on its culture. As it happened, this culture revealed itself as *being a greater power than all other forces*" (Cited in Williams, emphasis added).

As a Pole, John Paul obviously feels that he does not have to take lessons from Western liberalism on the importance of individual and civil liberties. Devotion to liberty is his by birthright. Williams remarks, "No Pontiff in modern times has come to the See of Peter with greater personal devotion to the principles of civil liberties as the natural and *revealed* rights of man than has John Paul II." That being said, more than one critic has observed that it is a weakness in John Paul's thought that he gives such short shrift to the idea *and institutionalization* of liberty in Western democratic history. It is no doubt a great benefit to have experienced the denial of freedom under totalitarianism, but it is equally a great deprivation not to have known in depth the social orders that have protected that freedom. In a very important sense, Polish culture understands itself to be part of the West, not of the East into which it has been politically and militarily coerced in this century. In the eighteenth century, Poland was in the vanguard of enlightened democratic thought. But that is not the Poland in which Karol Wojtyla came of age. This vexingly confused history no doubt has much to do with the ambivalence in John Paul's observations on Western democracies. Another factor, needless to say, is that as pope he feels some need to be, if not evenhanded, at least not excessively partisan in the tensions between East and West.

In any event, John Paul's understanding of freedom is differently grounded than the conventional democratic understandings in the tradition of John Locke and John Stuart Mill. As the person is key to his thought, so freedom is key to being a person. Freedom, in turn, encompasses what Isaiah Berlin terms "negative" and "positive" freedom. It is freedom *from* but, more importantly, freedom *for*. It is not too much to say that, in John Paul's thought, freedom from is important chiefly because it is instrumental to freedom for. In his anthropology, the person freely wills his own actions according to good or evil and thus fulfills or fails to fulfill his humanity. Freedom consists in choosing truth in one's actions. Such choice must be made without coercion from instinctual or subliminal drives, which are self-disintegrative, or from external social and political pressures, which can only lead to the conformism that is the opposite of freedom. The person acting in freedom is transcendent. That is, the person crosses the boundaries of the self. Put differently, to use self-determination in order to move transcendently toward a goal that is in agreement with the truth is to be fulfilled as a person and thus to become good.

John Paul recognizes that all fulfillment, short of perfect union with God, is approximate. Every life encounters obstacles on freedom's way toward fulfillment as a person. In this respect, the Pope is very much in the "realistic" and "anti-utopian" tradition. Obstacles may be physical, mental, economic, or political. No matter the obstacles, however, freedom remains the way. Ultimate fulfillment is a transcendent hope, experienced in this life perhaps only by heroines and heroes who have traveled the mystical path. But, whatever our life circumstance, the personal and social task is ever to expand freedom's field of action. In this task, religion is the central sphere of freedom's acting and is also freedom's shield. "For religion," John Paul writes, "consists in the free adherence of the human mind to God, which is in all respects personal and conscientious; it arises from the desire for truth. . . . And in this relation the secular arm may not interfere, because religion itself by its nature transcends all things secular."

To be sure, religion itself can become an obstacle. There are, for example, conflicts and divisions produced by religious differences. In such instances, mutual toleration is the minimal but necessary requirement of freedom. But toleration is not enough. As John Paul writes "Progress in the perception of the truth must be desired at the same time, for finally nothing other than the truth will liberate us from the various kinds of separation." The clear implication is that no party perceives the truth perfectly, all are progressing toward that perfect perception. This must not lead to a facile relativism, however. With equal clarity, John Paul insists that we must be faithful to that truth that we do perceive. We are responsible for the acknowledgment of the authoritative, and for ordering our lives according to it. We must be faithful even when such fidelity seems to be a hindrance to the reconciliation that we seek. A reconciliation that is not reconciliation in the truth is no reconciliation at all.

In these connections between freedom, truth, and unity are to be found the philosophical sources of John Paul's approach to ecumenism. Some commentators, while appreciating the Pope's relentless accent on truth, suggest that he fails to acknowledge that, with respect to the unity of Christians, unity is itself part of the truth that makes us free. These are difficult questions that cannot detain us here. The point at hand is that— whether the subject be Christian unity or civil liberties—there is a striving for internal coherence in John Paul's thought. Those interpretations that employ a taken-for-granted spectrum of Left and Right, progressive and conservative, in order to locate this Pope are deplorably superficial. With respect to John Paul, the point is not to locate his position but to follow his argument.

35. RELISHING THE CONFLICT

The commitment to freedom must be maintained also when that freedom is abused. Thus freedom to seek the truth is protected also for the atheist. John Paul makes a sharp distinction, however, between atheism that springs from personal conviction and atheism imposed by an unjust social system. He suggests there is a linkage, though, between atheism, even when personally chosen, and the denial of freedom. "The human being who is an atheist is one persuaded of his own end—if I may so speak—of his 'eschatological' aloneness." In this aloneness is a denial of personal immortality, and "this disposes one to seek a quasi-immortality in the collective life. The question is whether collectivism favors atheism more than atheism favors collectivism." Later in his pontificate, John Paul would feel the need to become ever more explicit about the connection between atheism and the particular form of collectivism that is Marxist in its presuppositions. But in his earlier writings, he is relentless in exposing the misdirected transcendent yearning that is at the heart of the totalitarian impulse. However doleful the consequences of atheism, the free society must nonetheless protect the right of persons to choose the atheism that would deny that freedom.

The Pope is keenly aware that this philosophy, which sees every person as possessing a vocation to transcendent freedom, is under attack on many fronts. He seems almost to relish the conflict. Speaking specifically of the need to protect the unborn, he declares, "We are in the front line in a lively battle for the dignity of man." Societal protection for the unborn is viewed as anything but a conservative position, in the sense of traditional resistance to modernity. The "new thing" is freedom, but freedom cannot make its way unless grounded in a transcendent understanding of the person. Many Roman Catholics, including some influential bishops, make no secret of their wish that John Paul would not be so unremitting in his emphasis upon abortion. Yet others, recognizing the overriding importance of the debate over abortion, wish John Paul would not tie the question of abortion so closely to that of contraception and other issues addressed in Paul VI's *Humanae Vitae*. Here Karol Wojtyla the philosopher may get in the way of John Paul the "politician of ideas." His preoccupation, again, is with the internal coherence of the argument, even if that gets in the way of a more ready acceptance of what he wants to say about, for example, abortion. If communication is made more difficult by setting forth the entirety of the argument, then, he seems to believe, that too is part of "the lively battle."

In speaking of the human condition, John Paul cultivates a suspicion of vague generalities. As a good phenomenologist he returns again and again to the specific, the concrete, the particular, the historical person. He is robustly skeptical toward the abstract "man" of Marxist theory and the abstract "humanity" in the tradition of the French Revolution. Warnings against these twin distortions are a constant in his statements as both philosopher and pope. There seems to be little awareness of a democratic and republican tradition that takes seriously the particularity of persons and communities in their transcendent dimensions. There is, for example, no evidence that John Paul has ever read de Tocqueville on democracy in America. In fact, it is not evident that he has ever read John Courtney Murray's *We Hold These Truths*. Those who have taken the measure of the threat of Marxist-Leninist totalitarianism have good reason to be cheered by John Paul. Those who recognize the need to set forth the positive case for historical experiments in "ordered liberty" are less satisfied.

There are critical elements of the American democratic experiment that are strongly congruent with John Paul's understanding of freedom. He emphasizes that human thought, science, and culture all have a "legitimate autonomy" from the tutelage of religious authorities. Precisely out of concern for persons, and out of profound reflection upon what it means to be a person, John Paul cautions against "a humanism that is *closed*, limited to a purely earthly horizon and exposed consequently to decidedly inhuman developments." Closed humanism imprisons human life in a cramped and fetid secularism. The denial of the religious impulse toward the transcendent results in bestowing an absolute or religious legitimation upon a human condition defined by "a purely earthly horizon." That act of closure, which characterizes totalitarian systems, requires the denial of freedom, which is the ultimate sin against the human person. In discussing questions such as these, John Paul frequently sounds like a philosophically freighted partisan of those who polemicize against "secular humanism" and against the "humanism" that John Dewey candidly declared to be the "new religion" of the enlightened.

John Paul's understanding of freedom meets with resistance on several fronts. Champions of democratic freedom express the wish that John Paul would more unequivocally take the side of the West in the ideological conflict with communism. Advocates of a more Marxist-oriented brand of liberation theology wish he would be more flexible about his idea of the person and freedom; bourgeois liberties, they say, may have to be bent a bit in order to achieve a just society. As leader of the most universal of existent communities, the Pope cannot overtly take sides in the many-faceted conflicts between East and West, his defenders rightly point out. He cannot come out for capitalism against socialism, even were he inclined to do so. Therefore, they say, in his public pronouncements John Paul criticizes evenhandedly both atheistic totalitarianism and capitalist consumerism.

In fact, his criticisms of communism and capitalism are hardly evenhanded. First, his reservations about Western democracy come from limited observations about a social order in which he has never lived (except in the rather rarefied circumstance of living as pope in Italy). Second, his criticisms of the democracies characteristically invoke abstract principles drawn from the eighteenth- and nineteenth-century European revolutionary tradition, generally ignoring the historical experience of democratic governance, notably in the United States. Third, his criticisms of Western democratic ideas of freedom usually turn out, upon examination, to be criticism of the terrible things that people do with their freedom, and that is a criticism that is undoubtedly and fully warranted. His criticism of communism, on the other hand, is dramatically different on all three scores. He speaks from deep personal experience, he addresses a historically specific system of government, and he asserts that that system is inherently evil in its declared intent, its design, and its practical operation. It is most evil in its systematic denial and suppression of the human person's vocation to the transcendent. John Paul's philosophy of the person and of freedom is expressly in conflict with every form of totalitarian and authoritarian governance. It is an inherent conflict. In Western democracies, on the other hand, he believes that the person-in-freedom is not actualized adequately and is in fact hindered by disintegrative dynamics. That is unquestionably the case. All social orders must be kept under transcendent judgment; no existing or proposed social order warrants the uncritical blessing of the Church. But this does not mean that discriminations are not in order. It is hardly sufficient to count the number of times that John Paul criticizes the East and the number of times he criticizes the West. One must attend to the substance of his argument regarding freedom and unfreedom in order to see that this Pope discriminates very nicely. He is hardly evenhanded; nor, be it quickly added, should he be.

Self-identified progressives in the Roman Catholic Church began to express their disillusionment with John Paul in the early stages of his pontificate. At first it was charitably allowed that he suffered from the parochialism of being Polish (that was when Polish jokes were still told in polite company). Others said he wanted to move ahead but was inhibited by the outmoded patterns of the Vatican Curia. Then it was said that, while he had started out strong, he had, like Paul VI, regressed into a reactionary posture. Now it is a commonplace among very progressive commentators (Peter Hebblethwaite and Xavier Rynne will serve to represent the type) that John Paul is a superstar, a skillful manipulator of the media, who presents himself as the lovable pastor while Opus Dei sets the agenda and Joseph Ratzinger does the dirty work. (A useful dissertation may one day be done comparing the ways in which John Paul and Ronald Reagan have been depicted in a substantial part of the prestige media. The similarities, one expects, would turn out to be impressive, although a notable difference is that almost no one suggests that John Paul is not very bright.)

These superficial understandings of John Paul should not surprise us. Roman Catholicism is a large and raucous community of communities in which many agendas for change are being pressed. A pope, no less than a president, is widely judged by whether he advances or hinders one's favored agenda. For the vast majority of Roman Catholics, it is probably enough that John Paul is the Pope. As for those pressing specific agendas for change—whether "forward" or "backward"—only the naive would expect such people not to interpret what the Pope says through the filter of the causes they espouse. But I believe a better interpretation begins with the recognition that this Pope does not just "happen to be" a man of ideas. He is that most essentially, and what he most essentially is he most urgently does, within the limits and imperatives of being pope. He tirelessly sets out his argument that the Church is not properly defined either as antimodern or as the avant garde of changes that modernity deems inevitable. Rather, moving beyond the modern and antimodern antinomies, he calls the Church to be a company of clear and even heroic identity that bears in history the transcendent hope for the actualization of the person in freedom and community. Because such a call cannot be fitted into currently competing ideologies, because it does not conform to thought slots on the prevailing spectrum of popular opinion, it is no surprise that John Paul has been widely misunderstood by both critics and admirers.

He surely has reason to feel misunderstood both by many who condemn him and by many who claim him as their champion. Popes being no more than human, he likely finds the misguided who are admirers somewhat easier to take and is less inclined toward diligence in correcting their misunderstandings. Such understandable bias aside, however, this Pope appears to be inexhaustible in his determination to argue us beyond established contentions and confusions. To the extent he succeeds in doing that, he demonstrates himself to be, in fact, the most powerful man in the world. Nowhere has this pope without a tiara had a harder time in doing that than in his encounter with conflicting ideas of what Christians mean by power.

36. THE WORLDS OF LIBERATION THEOLOGY

Proponents of liberation theology typically respond to their critics that generalized criticisms are out of order since there are several liberation theologies. If the critic illustrates a theme of liberation theology by citing Hugo Assmann, defenders promptly note that Juan Luis Segundo puts the matter differently, and Enrique Dussel has yet another view. There is some merit to this response, for within the world of liberation theology there are significant diversities. But there is also an element of disingenuousness in this response, for the project of liberation theology is in most important respects a single project. It is described as such by its proponents, and its main proponents are routinely identified as participants in a common enterprise in numerous books surveying and introducing liberation theology in the singular. To write an "Introduction to Liberation Theology" and to then respond to critics by saying there is no such thing as liberation theology but only liberation theolog*ies* is something less than candid. It makes mutually respectful and rational discourse about this phenomenon very difficult.

There is Latin American liberation theology, African liberation theology, and Asian liberation theology. In addition, in North America there is feminist liberation theology, black liberation theology, Hispanic liberation theology, environmental liberation theology, and even male liberation theology. Borrowing a useful distinction from Reinhold Niebuhr, some liberation theology is "hard utopian" and some is "soft utopian." Some advocate violent revolution—insisting that such violence is really counterviolence against the violence of systemic social evils. Some limit their advocacy to consciousness-raising with respect to gender relations or the nuclear threat or endangered animal species. Our immediate concern is with Roman Catholic liberation theology as espoused primarily within the Latin American context. This has been, and will likely continue to be, the focus of debate in the Roman Catholic Church. Keep in mind that liberation theology is, as theological innovations go, relatively young. Beginning in the late 1960s, it is hardly twenty years old. The full story about liberation theology cannot yet be told. Liberation theology is "on the way" to becoming what it will become. True, that is a debatable opinion. There are those who believe that the official response of Rome, combined with impressively growing criticism within the theological community, indicate that liberation theology is already a failed and fading experiment. They may turn out to be right, but I expect that judgment is premature.

Liberation theology in the years ahead may become something quite different from what it was in its first decade. The changes may be so dramatic that little but the name "liberation theology" remains. Quite possibly, present critics of liberation theology may become more sympathetic to it, for liberation theology does highlight some themes that are crucial to an understanding of the Church in the world. But here, too, continuities are likely to be more striking than discontinuities. Liberation theology in its present contours will, I expect, be with us for some time. Too many people have identified their thinking and their work with the form of liberation theology that has been set forth in the last ten years. Its texts are to be found throughout the curricula of theological education in North America among Roman Catholics and mainline Protestants alike. A small but influential sector of evangelical Protesantism has also been "radicalized" in its embrace of liberation theology. In short, liberation theology is viewed as "what is happening now," and that view is so entrenched in theological education and religious activism that it will continue to be held long after the current project becomes what was happening then.

The long-distance prospects of liberation theology rely, in large part, upon factors that have little to do with theology. The themes of South versus North, of Third World versus First World, of socialism versus capitalism, of the oppressed versus the oppressor—in sum, all the themes of national and global liberation—were hardly invented by liberation theology. Moreover, the generative themes of liberation theology may have a utility long after they have been discredited in other worlds of discourse. Writers such as Peter Berger (*The Capitalist Revolution: Fifty Propositions About Prosperity, Equality and Liberty*, 1986) may conclusively demonstrate on the basis of empirical evidence that democratic capitalism is the best hope for the poor of the world. But it is the strength and weakness of religious thought that it is largely impervious to trial by evidence. Utopian visions are immune to the manifest disasters of all Marxist-Leninist, social democratic, and democratic socialist experiments to date. Through the ruins of disappointed hopes, through rivers of blood and across the killing fields of utopias run amok—the Soviet Union, Cuba, China, Vietnam, Cambodia, and, very likely, Nicaragua—political pilgrims press on toward the great experiment that has still to be tried. One is not easily diverted from the quest when at stake is nothing less than the Kingdom of God.

The influence of liberation theology in North America is largely due to the prodigious efforts of Orbis Books over the years. Orbis is the publishing arm of the Catholic Foreign Mission Society of America, better known as Maryknoll. The Maryknollers were established many years ago to win the world to Christ and his Church. Many remember Maryknollers chiefly for their heroic mission work in China. Afficianados of irony will appreciate that years later, during the rule of Chairman Mao, the Maryknollers would be promoting the view that China was the most Christian nation in the world, albeit without Christ and his Church. Carrying Karl Rahner's notion of "anonymous Christians" to an extreme, it is the triumph of the missionary enterprise by fiat. Certainly it is much more convenient than the heroic but apparently misguided course of Maryknollers of old who gave their lives to winning unbelievers for the Gospel one by one. So also in the supposed contest between atheism and Christianity, between totalitarianism and religious freedom, contemporary Maryknollers have again and again declared victory by redefinition.

Yet the seemingly inexhaustible energy of Maryknollers in promulgating this new version of the historic faith is deserving of respect. For years, the presses of Orbis Books never rested. After a while the titles seemed to be generic: *Marxism and Christianity, Christianity and Marxism, Theology of Liberation, Liberating Theology, The Promise of the Powerless, The Powerlessness of Power, The Power of Powerlessness, Religion and Rebellion, Religion in Rebellion, Religion of Rebellion, Salvation and Struggle, Struggle and Salvation, Communism in the New Testament, The New Testament and Communism.* The search for new titles must have strained editorial ingenuity. Through Orbis, supplemented by other publishers, the ringing of the changes on the themes of liberation theology seem almost infinite.

The Latin American division of the industry also has its staple authors, some of whom are stars. Here, for example, is a recent Orbis listing of some of the key names in the liberationist project: Gustavo Gutierrez, Juan Luis Segundo, Rubem Alves, Leonardo Boff, Hugo Assmann, Jose Porfirio Miranda, Jose Miguez Bonino, Jon Sobrino, Jose Comblin, and Enrique Dussel (thirteen others are listed, but enough). The listing of names is important. The Vatican is frequently censured for not naming names when it addresses liberation theology. Of course, if it did name names, it would almost certainly be accused of recklessly casting a shadow over the work of specific theologians. The immediate point is that the liberation theologians are self-identified; they and their agents attend to the naming of names. The names above, for instance, are described as those responsible for "exploring the major themes" of liberation theology. At the risk of laboring the point, it is not only possible and necessary to speak of liberation theology in the singular, and to address the specific themes and writers that demarcate the enterprise, but we are actually invited to do so by the participants in the enterprise. Liberation theology presents itself as a movement and has a right to be acknowledged as such. While due attention should be given to diversities within the movement, we should not make the famous mistake of failing to see the forest for the trees.

The movement did not spring full grown from the presses of Orbis Books or from a socialist workshop in Santiago, Chile. In the conventional telling of the story, there were a number of precursor events,

beginning with Vatican II. Directions pointed by the Council were reinforced by papal encyclicals from John XXIII and Paul VI, and by the
important Medellin meeting of Latin American bishops. The formation
of "basic Christian communities" were both cause and effect of liberation
theology, as were various floating international seminars on "Christians
for Socialism" and "Third World Theology." The whole enterprise was
surrounded by the aura of "charismatic" figures such as Ernesto Che
Guevara, Camilo Torres, and Dom Helder Camara, and of course the
enterprise was in large part a religious reflection of political and ideological churnings in the world that liberation theology desired to serve.

The liberation theologians in question are insistent in situating their
effort within the mainstream of Roman Catholic social teaching. They
stress the continuity from *Rerum Novarum* (1891) and *Quadragesimo Anno*
(1931) through Vatican II and John XXIII's *Mater et Magistra* (1961) and
Paul VI's *Populorum Progressio* (1967) up to their present liberationist
program. At almost every point along the way, critics of liberation theology protest that it is a grave distortion of the church's social teaching, but,
as we have noted, there is ample language in these official documents,
notably from *Populorum Progressio* onward, to which liberation theology
can appeal in justifying its interpretation. Admittedly, it may frequently
be a case of tearing statements out of context, but the statements are
nonetheless there to be torn and, just as frequently, it is not clear that
the context precludes the purposes to which liberation theologians put
them. *Populorum Progressio,* for example, speaks of "the scandal of glaring
inequalities" in the world's distribution of wealth and blames "a type of
capitalism that has been the source of excessive suffering, injustices, and
fratricidal conflicts." Almost each phrase in such assertions—and such
assertions are abundant—practically begs for another title from Orbis
Books.

In 1968 the General Conference of the Latin American episcopacy
(CELAM II) met in Medellin, Colombia. Medellin is hailed by some
theologians as "the Vatican II of Latin America" and the birthdate of that
continent's liberation theology. "By its own vocation," declared Medellin, "Latin America will undertake its liberation at the cost of whatever
sacrifice. . . . The Lord's distinct commandment to 'evangelize the poor'
ought to bring us to a distribution of resources and apostolic personnel
that effectively gives preference to the poorest and most needy sectors."
From Medellin came the famous formulation, "preferential option for the
poor," and from Medellin was received the magna carta for the "radicalization" of the church in the liberationist struggle. Liberation theologians
acknowledge that the statements of Medellin contain considerable ambiguities. Some of the bishops, maybe most of the bishops, had no intention of giving an uncritical blessing to the liberationist proposition.
Medellin left aspects of Christian teaching and spirituality "untranslated"
into liberationist praxis, but the intensive energies of the liberationist

movement immediately went to work to resolve those ambiguities in favor of the struggle. Medellin was quickly and effectively ensconced in the scriptural canon of liberation theology.

Closely connected was the formation of *communidades eclesiales de base* or "base communities" in which "the poor and oppressed" found a new form of church, and from which their mentors were to develop a new ecclesiology. There are now hundreds of thousands such base communities, more than fifty thousand in Brazil alone. Some are grass-roots associations for prayer, Bible study, and mutual support. Many are centers of intense ideological indoctrination in which the poor undergo a process of "conscientization." The process is much indebted to Paulo Freire's *Pedagogy of the Oppressed* (1970), which shows the way from a religion of consolation to a religion of confrontation. "The central problem," writes Freire, "is this: How can the oppressed, as divided, unauthentic beings, participate in developing the pedagogy of their liberation? . . . The starting point for organizing the program content of education or political action must be the present, existential, concrete situation, reflecting the aspirations of the people." The strategy calls for the intensification of discontents as alienated humanity ("unauthentic beings") are guided from resignation to revolution in becoming "the artisans of their own destiny."

Like other movements of visionary force, this one too has its canon of saints. The hagiology of liberationism routinely includes Ernesto Che Guevara, hero of Fidel's revolution in Cuba, who in 1967 died in Bolivia leading a ragtag effort to spark insurrection among the poor and oppressed of that country. In liturgies of the more ideologized base communities, Che's pronouncements are read as sacred writ: "Our every action is a battle cry against imperialism and a call for the peoples' unity against the great enemy of mankind: the United States of America. Whenever death may surprise us, it will be welcome, provided that this, our battle cry, reaches some receptive ears, that another hand be extended to take up our weapons and that other men come forward to intone our funeral dirge with the staccato of machine guns and new cries of battle and victory." In the last decade there have been numerous setbacks for the liberationist struggle as one Latin America nation after another has moved toward ("bourgeois liberal") democracy. But guerillas in places such as El Salvador and Guatemala, and the government in Nicaragua, continue to intone the dirge as Che envisioned, frequently with "Christ the Liberator" wielding the machine gun in the lead of the battle charge.

Then there is Camilo Torres, son of a wealthy Colombian family who was "radicalized" while studying sociology with Gustavo Gutierrez at Louvain. Back in Colombia, he left his university post, dropped his priestly duties, and joined the insurrection. "I have ceased to say Mass in order to practice love for people in temporal, economic and social spheres. When the people have nothing against me, when they have carried out the revolution, then I will return to offering Mass, God willing. . . . I think that in this way I follow Christ's injunction . . . 'Leave thy gifts upon the altar and go first to be reconciled to thy brothers.' " Torres was killed in 1966. Usually included in the canon is Dom Helder Camara, archbishop of Recife in northeastern Brazil until his retirement in 1985. Dom Helder adopted a simple way of life ("I am becoming one of the voiceless poor of Brazil") in which he became a familiar figure and leading voice of the movement also in North America and Europe. According to a recent book from Orbis, "He was one of the first to appreciate the creative possibilities to be found in a socialist system of government, noting as early as 1956: 'The union of socialism and democracy means . . . that authentic human construction of socialism is not possible without the simultaneous implantation of a real socialist democracy.' " It is said that Dom Helder's credo can be summarized in one sentence: "The protests of the poor are the voice of God." After the failed uprisings against the creative possibilities of socialism in Hungary and Czechoslovakia, Dom Helder and his coworkers would tirelessly promote the prospect of "socialism with a human face."

In 1971 Christians for Socialism brought together eighty priests from throughout Latin America to Santiago, Chile. There themes were set forth that remain more or less constant in the literature and pedagogy of the the liberationist movement.

As Christians we do not see any incompatibility between Christianity and socialism. Quite the contrary is true . . . it is necessary to destroy the prejudice and mistrust that exists between Christians and Marxists.

Or again:

The economic and social structures of our Latin American countries are grounded on oppression and injustice, which in turn is a result of our capitalist dependence on the great power centers. . . . We commit ourselves to the task of fashioning socialism because it is our objective conclusion . . . that this is the only effective way to combat imperialism and to break away from our situation of dependence. . . . There is a growing awareness that revolutionary Christians must form a strategic allegiance with Marxists within the liberation process on this continent. . . . Socialism presents itself as the only acceptable option for getting beyond a class-based society.

The economic analysis is radically dependent upon "dependency theory," a theory that holds that participation in the world economy means slavery to the world economy, of which the United States is the imperialistic master. The moral-theological reasoning is simple and inexorable: the Christian Gospel is a message of social justice; social justice is measured and established by the role of the poor; identification with the poor means identification with their struggle for justice, which is a struggle for socialism. The failed socialisms of the past, with their disastrous economic consequences and their success in creating varieties of the Gulag Archipelago, are irrelevant. The socialism that *we* are building, it is said, has never been tried before. Thus one of the most persistent themes of liberation theology is the claim that it is "truly indigenous."

Critics of liberation theology claim that the North American understanding of it is based on bad English translations of bad Spanish translations of bad German ideas. Whatever the merits of the translations, it is difficult to defend the claim that liberation theology is in any way indigenous to Latin America. The intellectual geneology is almost entirely European, beginning with Karl Marx and running through Ernst Bloch, Jurgen Moltmann, Paulo Freire, and Johannes Metz. There is hardly a prominent concept in liberation theology that cannot be directly traced to a European source. In their footnotes, the more scholarly liberationist writers make the connections quite explicit, including, interestingly enough, the sources of the idea of indigenization. In addition, any complete account of liberation theology would have to pay major attention to the degree of ecumenical cross-pollinization with the activities of the World Council of Churches and North American writers such as Richard Shaull of Princeton. This certainly does not mean that there is nothing original in liberation theology. But it does alert us to the painfully divided mind of many liberationists in their attitude toward the North Atlantic "imperium."

Note also that there are some scholars who today claim that liberation theology is in its "second phase." This second phase is said to be, among other things, more Christianly orthodox and much less Marxist than the liberation theology of the first phase. The evidence of such a major shift is still very sparse, but much has happened since the late sixties and early seventies and it would be surprising if these changes were not reflected in liberation theology in the years ahead. For example, it is generally acknowledged that the base communities have frequently resulted not in the revolutionary radicalization of the poor but in self-help movements of upward mobility toward middle-class achievement and traditional religious and moral allegiance. Further, the last decade in Latin America has witnessed a widespread movement toward democratization, and that has resulted in understandable changes in views of oppression and the revolutionary imperative. Then, too, Roman Catholic liberationists who are serious about being Roman Catholic cannot help but be affected by the determined critique of liberation theology issuing from John Paul and the Vatican. All this means that something like a second phase of liberation theology may well be in the offing. Talk about a second phase, however, should not divert attention from the fact that it is the first phase that is widely disseminated through Roman Catholic and Protestant seminaries and activist networks in North America today. That is also the liberation theology to which official Rome has responded with such clarity and firmness. So even if what is now called liberation theology will in the future be replaced by something else called liberation theology, the present state of the controversy will serve as a benchmark in Roman Catholicism's effort to give new definition to the paradox of the Church in the postmodern world.

A Theology of Liberation by Gustavo Gutierrez first appeared in 1971 and came out from Orbis in 1973. It is, quite simply, the classic text of the movement. Gutierrez, a native of Peru, was at the time professor of theology at the Catholic University of Peru, chaplain to the National Union of Catholic University Students, and advisor to the Latin American Bishops Conference. With this book he became, almost instantly, a figure of stature in world theological discourse. The noted North American Jesuit Avery Dulles declared at the time "Gutierrez shows in this book that 'liberation theology,' far from being a frivolous or irresponsible movement, arises out of deep compassion and critical reflection on the situation of the poor and oppressed. . . . This new theology builds on, and in part surpasses, the neo-Marxism and the secularization theology of Western Europe." The "in part" in that last sentence should not be overlooked. Gutierrez clearly intended to do something new, something truly indigenous, and yet something grounded in a universal tradition and engaging a universal world of theological discourse. It was an ambitious and honorable attempt, not untouched by nuance and internal contradictions.

37. ARTISANS OF A NEW CHRISTENDOM

As is the case with pioneers in any enterprise, Gutierrez is not uniformly appreciated by those who follow in the path he has cleared. While acknowledging him as the godfather, some liberation theologians feel Gutierrez is somewhat too cautious, too eager to demonstrate a breadth and erudition that would make liberation theology respectable in the eyes of the North Atlantic theological establishment. Other workers in the field— Juan Luis Segundo, for example—are held up as exemplifying a more radical and indigenous liberation theology. Segundo's five-volume *A Theology for Artisans of a New Humanity* (1973) does indeed make explicit at many points what remains implicit in the work of Gutierrez and others. It is a rich resource for understanding the common and controlling themes that characterize the liberation theology project. (At the risk of littering the text with bibliographical references, I will in the following pages indicate where in Segundo's opus the reader may find reference to the issues discussed.)

The five volumes of *Artisans* come out of as many years of dialogical (some say dialectical) process at the Peter Faber Center in Montevideo, Uruguay. The process has Segundo presenting some major article of Christian faith and the presentation is then revised in light of several days of extensive exchange with laypeople and clerics. The whole thing is then put together with additional documentation and "clarifications" that are intended to respond to questions raised. It is an intriguing exercise in the doing of theology. While there is no evidence that the group challenges the basic directions posited by the leader, he is forced to address problems he might not have anticipated in solitude. The result of the process has been praised by some as being engagingly complex and nuanced. Others complain that it is a muddle of confusions. That complaint, however, is routinely dismissed as reflecting the bias of academic theologians who are not in touch with the sensibilities and struggles of the people.

Segundo himself begins by distinguishing his "new type of theology" from a theology that treats "the avatars of a doctrine laden with the accumulations of twenty centuries." His is not, he says, a conventional theology so much as it is a statement of "faith-in-crisis." Nine hundred pages later (893 to be precise) he expresses the hope that what has been said might contribute to the whole Church and indeed "to the positive evolution of humanity." "We in our poverty, and precisely because we are poor, may have something new and worthwhile to say. That at least may serve as our excuse." Between these winsome statements of modesty at the start and at the end, Segundo exhibits few inhibitions in taking on most of the problems that have preoccupied Christian thought for two millennia.

In writing a theology for "the new type of human being" now emerging, Segundo has, says the Protestant ethicist John C. Bennett, gone far "in transcending the differences between Catholicism and Protestantism." He has, we would suggest, gone that far and much further. Segundo seizes upon the battle-wearied Protestant dichotomies between the priestly and the prophetic, the cultic and the ethical, the institutional and the functional, the called and the elect. He aligns himself with the left wing of Reformation thought in his emphasis upon the Church as an "aristocracy" of true believers (belief being "orthopraxis") against the notion of a Church encompassing the masses (I, 90f.) At other points he strongly identifies with Karl Barth in opposing "religion" to "Christian faith." While regularly invoking statements of the Roman Catholic magisterium, on substantive questions Segundo typically puts himself on the side of themes that are characteristic of a Protestantism far to the left of Calvinism, not to mention Lutheranism. Although he may add little to the development of these themes, his is a useful demonstration of how malleable are the pronouncements of the magisterium, including the documents of Vatican II.

Like some in the sixteenth century and many since, there is for Segundo no salvation apart from the establishment of the earthly city. Ecumenism must therefore reach beyond ecclesial boundaries to all who are engaged in that task. Segundo affirms a more or less inexorable process of secularization, citing Harvey Cox and others in support of an analysis that in recent years seems increasingly untenable with respect to developed countries and almost totally implausible with respect to what is called the Third World (I, 94f.). The fellowship that is the true body of Christ (II, 105) is seen to include all who are committed to the struggle of liberation, for faith depends not upon a person's "religious situation"—whether or not he calls himself a Christian, for example—but upon "service to man" (II, 112). The universality of the Gospel means not a proclamation to be shared but simply that the grace that the Gospel declares is already present in all efforts toward humanization (V, 96). Segundo does not explore the questions this raises about why it is important to be part of the community that explicitly celebrates the Gospel, although it is clear that this community is to be enlisted in the tasks of humanization.

Segundo's hope is to help Christians "justify" their faith in view of the questions being asked by the world (I, viii and passim). The possibility that the world's agenda should be challenged by Christian faith, that the truth claims of Christianity might throw the world's questions into question, simply does not arise. Perhaps one reason for this is that Segundo defines "the world" selectively as the elite that has through consciousness-raising broken with the illusions of the masses. This elite is the "new type of human being" in service to whom Christian faith must be justified. At one point (III, 48), Segundo challenges the notion that "the modern mind" has no place for the transcendent. At another (III, 91f.), he movingly affirms his need for an I-Thou relationship with a Christ that is more than the depth of his own being. But this seems to be something of an aside, a confession of a personal and even private need that is unrelated to the social and programmatic argument he is making. Segundo perhaps recognizes that this personal need is hard to square with the insistence that "the absolute" has been completely "integrated into the active work of liberation." There, is, he says, no other epiphany of God (II, 163; III, 16f.). The doctrine of the Trinity, for example, means that "God is society" (III, 66). He is not just society in general but the society we struggle to become. What has been revealed is "God's plan for the universe. And this plan is strictly social." The revealed goal is "a society in which each individual person directs his creative potentialities toward the common good" (V, 111).

Lest that seem too general, Segundo makes clear that the society he, and presumably God, has in mind was defined by the Medellin conference of 1968 (III, 15f.). While much of *Artisans* was written well after Medellin, Segundo nowhere comes to terms with the euphoric and mistaken assumptions of 1968 that Latin America was in a prerevolutionary situation. This no doubt helps to maintain the consistency of the programmatic epiphany of God that requires a break from capitalism through revolutionary change. Indeed, such a break is required if we are to "know God" (III, 36). The evolution that is "God's plan for the universe" calls for liberation from every bondage of the masses, for "mass man is sin" (V,

38). Segundo is relentless in his assertion that the whole of the life of the Christian community can be "justified" only in terms of its being instrumental in this liberation struggle (IV, 7, 20). The sacraments, for example, are meaningful *"solely"* (his emphasis) in terms of contributing to community building (IV, 38). The meaning of the sacrifice of the Mass is discovered in sacrificial commitment to the cause, as exemplified by Karl Marx and others (IV, 36). Any notion of sacramental grace that is not justified within this functionalist framework is, quite simply and devastatingly, "magic" (IV, 60, 61).

Since the sacraments and Christian worship are justified by being instruments of consciousness-raising (IV, 111), it remains unclear why other techniques of group dynamics might not serve better than these quaint rites of bread and wine and water and words from a distant past. The answer would seem to be that, while effective grace is available to all and manifest in the liberation struggle, Christians still have a particular need for the ritual signs to which they have grown accustomed (IV, 79, 101). This might be construed as a kind of weakness that other liberation fighters have either outgrown or never needed. Similarly, the theological tradition of the Church is useful, at least for people who happen to be Christians, in shoring up commitment to the struggle (I, xi). There is, in this view, no reason why the life and teachings of the Church should have any claim on *public* attention. The implication is that the best the Christian hopes for is acceptance as a comrade by those who are advancing "God's plan for the universe."

By the midseventies, some liberation theologians were pressing very hard the idea of "the partisan church." In *Artisans,* Segundo still exhibited some hesitation in taking a hard line on this question. At one point (I, 78–88), we are told that the doctrine of the Church should not be so devised as to exclude from the Christian community those who are not part of the liberation struggle. Later (III, 78, 79) we are told that it is foolish to try to hold the Church together, as though it were possible to keep in the body of Christ those who oppose what God is doing in the world. Still later (IV, 10) Segundo writes, "Clearly enough the Church is not an army or a political party," but just as clearly it is not possible to maintain "communion" among people who "think and do things that are completely different or even opposed to each other." Such communion in the sacramental realm is an illusion that causes the Church "to lose any and all specific import or signification." Finally all wraps are removed and Segundo urges the Church in Latin America to throw its declining resources unequivocally on the side of the revolution while there is still time and not to worry about false and distracting notions of Christian unity (IV, 132f.).

Segundo acknowledges, at least in a brief aside (III, 132), that there may be problems once the revolution is successful. If the Church's task is to debunk all stereotypes of the establishment, there may come a time "when this course comes into conflict with the direct effectiveness of the revolutionary movement." His hope is that then "the revolution and its leaders will manage to maintain sufficient breadth of outlook to appreciate and preserve" the critical role of the Church. The Church will have made friends of Mammon while there was still time and will therefore, he hopes, not be cast aside when its role is no longer convenient to the new rulers. If this happens, writes Segundo, "then Church and social change will have taken a considerable step forward." Segundo and others thus envision a church-state relationship dramatically different from that in, say, Cuba or Nicaragua. In their hoped-for revolution, the Church will neither be suppressed nor displaced by a regime-sponsored "people's church." Rather, it seems that the Church will be permitted space within the New Society, and may even get to share the tiara from time to time. In this connection it might be suggested that *A Theology for the Artisans of a New Humanity* might also have been titled *A Theology for the Artisans of a New Christendom.*

Segundo and others seem surprisingly insouciant about the modern state. We are told (I, 96) that the Church in its present form should eschew political power and should remove itself from institutional forms of social influence for the sake of "pluralism." There is no consideration that, in the absence of countervailing forces such as the Church, state power quickly moves to preclude the possibility of genuine pluralism. Gutierrez is more coherent than Segundo in his treatment of the "two planes" notion, which attempts to distinguish the spiritual from the political. Segundo is reluctant to give up the concept of "two planes," even when it seems possible that the Church's political intervention can be directed in support of the revolution. This confusion, or dialectic, in Segundo may be related to his understanding of history. It is a central theme of liberation theology that history is one—there is no distinction between "salvation history" and "ordinary history," all history is redemptive. Segundo goes further, suggesting that history is the history of revolutionary change and that all of the telling of history must be bent to advance that change. Ironically, with respect to Christian history, this requires history without history. That is to say, all the changes, tensions, and contradictions in the Christian story must be ironed out in order to present a uniform support for God's liberationist project.

This uniform support is the "deep continuity" that marks Christian thought from the Bible through the early fathers and councils and up through Medellin 1968 (I, 23f.). Dissonant notes are overcome by explaining what fathers or popes or councils "really meant." Segundo describes this as "creative use" of the tradition, and it does indeed offer almost infinite possibilities in support of the project at hand. "Mere facts" must be enlisted in the service of higher interpretations (III, 89). Even Augustine, whose dismal prognosis for the City of Man makes him an unlikely recruit to liberation theology, is regularly invoked. The most otherworldly papal pronouncements are readily rehabilitated in this thorough project of historical revisionism. The reconciliation of apparent contradictions is made the easier by the fact that the whole tradition must, at least for Latin Americans, be interpreted in the light of Medellin (III, 15). Some Protestants welcome the way in which Segundo and others seem to have rediscovered the importance of the Bible. In Protestant fashion, Segundo views the New Testament Church as normative for our day and, leapfrogging with great alacrity back and forth across the centuries, discovers, not surprisingly, that the Bible anticipates precisely his understanding of the Church's mission in twentieth-century Latin America. But it is not the Bible, nor the tradition, that is normative. This is made explicit in what is called the liberationist hermeneutic.

38. INFINITELY CREATIVE INTERPRETATION

Those who are preoccupied with "mere facts" charge liberation theology with dishonesty in its treatment of history and, more specifically, its treatment of church teaching. But such a complaint misses a key part of the liberationist argument. Segundo, for example, asserts again and again that history is essentially an evolution of interpretations rather than a succession of events. To critics it seems that "mere facts" are dismissed or distorted. To Segundo, it is a matter of rectifying history in the light of a higher interpretation. The boldness of this enterprise is frequently underestimated by its critics. If a fact gets in the way of the enterprise, it is not allowed. It is not allowed not because it is inconvenient but because it is false. Anything that hinders the work of liberation is by definition false (IV, 54).

"God's plan for the universe" is essentially an evolution of interpretations. Sin is, quite simply, everything that gets in the way of that evolution (V, 27). Yet sin is essential as the dialectical negative that gives birth to new interpretations (V, 84). To paraphrase the Easter Vigil: O felix culpa that has given birth to such a mighty revolution! Since this dialectic is so often appealed to by Segundo, it is puzzling that near the end of his project he notes that the concept of dialectic "is very much in fashion but also extremely vague." He says he does not use dialectic in the conventional Hegelian or Marxist sense, but to define it more clearly "is not part of our purpose here" (V, 130). Such a statement after he himself has used the term hundreds of times in these volumes leads to the perhaps uncharitable suspicion that "dialectical interpretation" is but a rhetorical flourish to cover confusions.

Liberation theology is sometimes, and somewhat misleadingly, described as a politicized version of the "theology of hope." But, as in Segundo, there is frequently a striking absence of eschatological reference. That is to say, Christians are not awaiting any new initiative from God. The future is a future of evolving interpretations, not the breaking in of new events (III, 42). There is continuing revelation, to be sure, but it is contained in the liberation worldview of the present (I, 19). The future is not a matter of eschatological arrival but of evolutionary unfolding. The hoped-for new thing "from the outside" or divine action in history is dismissed as magic (IV, 63). Segundo leaves no doubt on this score: "If some sort of secret 'magic' did exist at some point, then Jesus Christ was the last and ultimate 'magician.' He turned us back again to human tasks and human efficacies because he not only offered but really gave us everything we need from God" (IV, 23). Segundo's understanding of grace, reiterated at many points, is that grace means that we now have everything. No longer need the Church pray, "Maranatha! Come Lord Jesus!" If we pray, we pray simply for the higher interpretation that is in fact Jesus in our time. And, because the absolute has been completely "integrated" into the work of liberation, we must of course answer our own prayer. In short, the culmination of this understanding of history is the relentless exclusion of the traditional understanding of hope for the coming of the Kingdom of God as the eschatological fulfillment of history.

Deserving of more than an aside is the observation that liberation theology in this form is a truly astonishing eruption of unbridled Pelagianism. The denial of original sin, the unequivocal assertion of the freedom of the revolutionary will, the insistence upon human self-justification—all comprise a manifestation of "works righteousness" such as the Reformers hardly encountered in the sixteenth century. In terms of the eclipse of the Gospel of God's saving grace, John Tetzel's peddling of indulgences hardly compares with the peddling of revolutionary nostrums as salvation. Little wonder that at a conference on liberation theology, a Roman Catholic theologian concluded his presentation with, "Martin Luther, where are you now that we really do need you?"

Some admirers of liberation theology do that project a great disservice by toning down the radicality of its claims. Liberationists such as Segundo are patronizingly described as doing no more than giving theological voice to the poor or protesting manifest social injustices. In truth, liberation theology is as radical as its proponents claim it to be. There is, for example, a stunning analogy between the liberationist proposition and Dostoyevsky's Grand Inquisitor. It will be remembered that, after that long night in the jail cell, the Grand Inquisitor dismisses Jesus: "He went to the door, opened it and said to Him: 'Go, and come no more. . . . Come not at all, never, never!' " Thus does Segundo dismiss the Last Magician. If indeed he had any magic back then, that was back then. The Grand Inquisitor explained to Jesus that he had no right to return, that he had once and for all handed over his authority to the Church. Jesus' talk about freedom, says the Grand Inquisitor, can only confuse the people who have been freed from the burden of their freedom by the religious and civil authorities. Segundo argues not that Jesus has no right to return but that, even if he could, we must not expect his return. With the Grand Inquisitor, he insists that everything is now in our hands.

For the Grand Inquisitor it was the established order; for Segundo it is the projected New Order that is the Christendom that Christ failed to establish. Christendom can assume many forms—revolutionary and establishmentarian, left and right, spiritual and secular. Segundo writes: "The Absolute enters the world of man in such a way that he does not take over possession of it; instead he places himself at the disposal of every man, *and each man becomes absolute in turn*" (III, 27, emphasis added). What is salvation? Segundo affirms, with the Protestant ethicist Paul Lehmann, "Salvation is maturity" (ibid). Salvation is the maturity that no longer needs, can no longer tolerate, interference "from outside." The Magician has paid his last visit, he has done his work. His work was to teach us that we do not need a Magician. "Go, and come no more."

There is room, then, neither for outside intervention nor for truth independent of the liberation struggle. "Any orthodoxy that does not essentially point toward orthopraxy is magical" (IV, 64). "The only truth is the truth that is efficacious for man's liberation" (IV, 54). Or, as it was said in an older ideology of Christendom, error has no rights. "Christendom" has various meanings, and not all of them are pejorative. But as it appears in the Grand Inquisitor, in liberation theology, in aspects of the late medieval papacy and post-Trent Roman Catholicism, as well as in various Protestant theocracy projects, Christendom is the perennial temptation of Christian existence. Weary of the pilgrimage, Christians want to "get it all together" and to do so *now*. Christendom in this sense is the premature synthesis by which we seek to resolve the scandal of a horrifying and still-incomplete history, and premature synthesis is another name for idolatry. Christendom is the refusal to live tentatively in the courage of our uncertainties, vulnerable to a future revelation that can alone vindicate what we are and do. Christendom is the substitute for the search for the Kingdom of God. Christendom is an act of closure, a desperate and finally futile bid for invulnerability against the judgment of the future, against the judgment of the Absolute Future who is God. Christendom is the easy and false resolution of the essential paradox of Christian existence.

In its secularized version, Christendom is described as *Humanum*dom. But the ideological structure is the same, since Christ, the absolute, is in fact *humanum*. There can, by definition, be no transcendent referent by which the struggle for liberation, however envisioned, can be criticized. At times that struggle has been embodied in the papal church, at other times in theocracies established by millennarian fanatics, at yet other times in the dictatorship of the proletariat, and now, according to some liberation theologians, in the movement led by the revolutionary aristocracy. In all these instances, the desire is to get it all together before God himself has gotten it all together. Its emergence in presumably radical forms today only demonstrates that the lust for Christendom dies very hard indeed. If those who advance the concept of "the partisan church" are really serious, then there must be a new schism, a thorough realignment, within the Christian community. The differences between those on opposite sides of the new divide will no doubt be many. One notable difference will be between those who say, "Go, and come no more," and those who pray, "Maranatha, come Lord Jesus."

39. RESPONDING TO LIBERATION THEOLOGY

Responses to liberation theology, both positive and negative, tend to be fierce. For many in North America and Europe, liberation theology was a welcome refueling of the social justice agenda of "radical Christianity," just when it seemed to be grinding to a halt after the turbulent sixties. Opponents of liberation theology, on the other hand, sometimes depict it as being no more than a movement hatched by the KGB in the Soviet conspiracy to take over the churches and the world. Few observers have succeeded in analyzing liberation theology so dispassionately as Dennis McCann, a Roman Catholic ethicist (*Christian Realism and Liberation Theology*, 1981). McCann's main reference for understanding "Christian realism" is Reinhold Niebuhr, and, for all his trying, McCann cannot see that liberation theology is much of an advance over a Niebuhrian view of Christianity and the political order: "North American theologians and social activists should not . . . [abandon] the legacy of Reinhold Niebuhr for the false promise of liberation theology. Instead, we should take liberation theology as a sincere but confused protest, a call to conscience that challenges us to rethink the theory and practice of Christian realism in light of the problems that await us in the 1980s."

Many others, however, believe that liberation theology represents something much more fundamental than "a sincere but confused protest." Johann Baptist Metz is one of the intellectual godfathers of liberation theology, having first raised the banner of "political theology" in the early sixties. In Roman Catholicism today, said Metz in the *National Catholic Register* in March 1986, there are three models of thought. The first is the classical, neoscholastic model, which is unremittingly defensive in its attitude toward the modern world. The second is a transcendental and idealist approach, which engages the modern world in the manner of Karl Rahner. "Then there is a 'post-idealist' paradigm, which explores new challenges that can't be addressed by the other two models: the Third World and its poverty, Marxism, Auschwitz. Today's new crises must be taken up by this *political* paradigm of theology. For me this includes, in Europe, political theology; and in non-European churches, liberation theology."

Gregory Baum is also among those who believe that with liberation theology there has dawned something like a "third age" in Roman Catholic thought and teaching. Addressing a Vancouver conference on "Liberation Theology—A Blend of Christianity and Marxism," Baum argued that the "turn to the left" in Roman Catholic teachings has gone much further than many bishops recognize and is now "irreversible." Baum, a former priest who is in the forefront of theologians supportive of liberation theology, complains that bishops frequently sign statements reflecting the themes of liberation theology but then "they go back to their dioceses and nothing really changes." While this can be discouraging, and may suggest that some bishops do not know what they are signing, the important thing, he believes, is that the basic themes are entrenched in the teaching of the church. The move to the Left may slow down, but "the process cannot be reversed," says Baum. The bishops have incorporated the key ideas of liberation theology by adopting "the vocabulary of liberation" on issues such as the "theory of dependency" with respect to capitalist oppression, the need for the "conscientization" of the poor, and the understanding of revolutionary violence as counterviolence against unjust institutions. Neither is Baum discouraged by some of the strictures expressed by John Paul II. While the Pope has retained conservative views on women and sexuality—"topics about which he does not know much"—he is, says Baum, a "radical" on social and political questions. Gregory Baum has for a quarter century been a prolific writer, speaker, and bureaucratic strategist in promoting "progressive" directions for the post-Vatican II church. His estimate of what has happened is not unimportant. Despite momentary setbacks, despite occasional shifts in the signs of the times, his reading is that the influence of liberation theology is irreversible and its cause will ultimately triumph in the Roman Catholic Church. Of course, Gregory Baum and others like him may be whistling in the dark. They may be practicing that "creative interpretation" that overrides mere facts to the contrary. But he is surely right in believing that some of the key themes of liberation theology are, if not entrenched, at least deeply insinuated into both official teaching and popular understandings of the Church in the modern world.

There are other voices on the Left, however, who are not so uncritically enthusiastic about liberationist themes and what they may imply. John C. Cort is a pioneer member of the Catholic Worker movement and coeditor of *Religious Socialism,* which is published by the Religion and Socialism Commission of the Democratic Socialists of America. Cort is deeply worried by the indifference exhibited by Gustavo Gutierrez and others toward democratic freedom. While they typically say they are but "employing Marxist analysis," they are in fact buying into hard-line Marxist prescriptions that most Marxist thinkers have long since abandoned. They speak much about "contextualization" and the importance of praxis in the concrete situation, but then subscribe to ideological abstractions that could hardly be further removed from the realities of the poor whom they claim to champion. Writing in *Commonweal* (July 1986), Cort quotes

Gutierrez commenting in 1983 on the unmitigated evil of private property as the source of exploitation. "This is extraordinary," says Cort, "for Latin America's economy is primarily agricultural and what the Latin American peasants, or the vast majority anyway, want is a piece of land of their own. There is no question about that. And I have yet to see a plea by Gutierrez or any other liberation theologian for the right of the peasant to own land, free from the fear of expropriation by the state."

It is commonly said in defense of liberation theology that, whatever its other weaknesses, at least it is indigenous, an authentic expression of the oppressed of Latin America. But that, argues Cort, is precisely what liberation theology is not. He cites the founding document of Christians for Socialism, meeting in Chile in 1972. The document was largely written by Gutierrez and Hugo Assman and is, in Cort's view, a startling instance of blindness to the social realities it intends to address. Nowhere are peasants mentioned, not even as "farm laborers," but there are many references to "the proletariat" and "the working class." The document reads like a translation from the Rumanian. The Chilean delegation came in with a report that did mention the peasants, but mainly to rebuke the peasants because they are "attached to the ownership of land," and that is a value that is "part and parcel of the dominant bourgeois ideology." The document also chides "many segments of the proletariat" because "they have been led astray by a tradition of labor unionism that is economics-oriented." Presumably a labor unionism that is not economics-oriented would not be deemed counterrevolutionary.

Cort's judgment is straightforward: "I suggest that liberation theologians, including Gutierrez, are doing precisely the kind of thing they accuse the European theologians of doing. They are imposing the European abstractions, or conclusions, of Karl Marx onto the Latin American peasant whose actual 'praxis' cries out for his own land and by no means wants to be submerged in some collective farm owned and operated by the state, exchanging one landlord for another who is even more powerful and impersonal." Court expresses admiration and friendship for Gutierrez and his liberationist colleagues, yet he confesses that, on some critical questions, Ratzinger's critique of liberation theology is too soft. Ratzinger, for instance, says that liberation theology pits the poor against their class enemy, the rich. But, notes Cort, the liberationist proposition is not that someone is a class enemy if he is rich but if he is an employer. The Marxist orthodoxy is that "the employer-employee relationship is of necessity a bad, alienating, enslaving, exploitative relationship." To be against the rich is not such a terrible thing, says Cort. "After all, Jesus had a very poor opinion of the rich. Remember the camel and the needle's eye.

"No, Marx did not merely exclude the rich from his secular heaven. He excluded all employers, rich or poor (excepting only the state). And this exclusion is a far, far more difficult position to reconcile with Christianity than exclusion of the rich. Not simply because it flies in the face of all Judeo-Christian tradition, but even more because it flies in the face of common sense and everyday experience." In addition, Cort suggests that Gutierrez's understanding of the class struggle does indeed require a partisan church in which the "myth" of "community of the faith" must be destroyed. Genuine community is defined by the struggle. And all of this directed toward the end of a "genuine democracy" that is nowhere defined but clearly excludes the bourgeois freedoms and institutions ordinarily associated with democracy. Cort says he writes in sadness, and there is no reason to doubt that, since socialism is also his dream. "The conclusion is harsh, something like the harshness of a jealous lover. I am jealous, envious of Karl Marx because he has won the affections of a lot of learned, eloquent, dedicated Christians whom I would like to see dedicated to a brand of socialism that is more unambiguously democratic." And, he might have added, more compatible with Christian teaching.

McCann, Metz, Baum, Cort—each is representative of responses to liberation theology almost two decades after the launching of the movement. McCann is critical but tentative, viewing it as a confused protest that has yet to find its coherent formulation. Metz takes a world-historical view and seems confident of liberation theology's place in the progression of Christian thought, while Baum declares the irreversibility of its long march through the institution that is Roman Catholicism. John Cort writes in the sorrow of knowing that liberation theology has, for many Christians, preempted and discredited his socialist dream. There is another type of response that is more precisely theological in nature, although in saying that, one must remember that the distinction between theology and politics is one of the issues in contention. This further response may be represented here by Avery Dulles, a Jesuit and premier theologian and ecumenist.

40. THE CHURCH AND THE KINGDOM

In the William L. Rossner Lecture of 1985, Dulles addressed the subject of "Vatican II and the Church's Purpose." Dulles asserts that much, perhaps most, of the theological writing since Vatican II has profoundly distorted the teachings of the Council. Especially is this true with respect to the purpose of the Church, which is often depicted as but one agency among others in advancing the goals of peace, justice, and other good things in the service of the Kingdom of God, which is essentially a secular reality. The Church, it is said, was guilty of a "narcissistic self-preoccupation" from which Vatican II has released it in order to be "servant Church," "the Church for others," or "the decentered Church." That the Council promoted such a radical change in the Church's understanding of itself is an idea that results from the hermeneutical mistake of believing that "the traditional utterances of Vatican II are [to be] subordinated to its alleged innovations." According to Dulles, this "deliberately slanted interpretation of Vatican II" has contributed to a passion for building the secular city and produced a "new triumphalism" in which it is believed that the Church is somehow to solve every human problem. There is a perceptible, but often unperceived, slide from the language of servanthood to the language of triumphalism.

Dulles invokes the ample texts of the Council in support of the argument that concern for the Kingdom of God does not displace the Church. "Since the kingdom of God is the future of the world as well as that of the church, it is in some sense wider than the church. But the heart and center of the new creation will be the company of the blessed as they praise and worship the triune God." Dulles claims that in the documents of the Council, the Church is not just a sign of the Kingdom or a servant of the Kingdom but "is either identical with or at least central to the kingdom." (Others would insist that the Church is not *identical with* the Kingdom. Were that the case, since we have the Church, there would be no point in seeking the Kingdom. But in Dulles's reaction to those who would trivialize or marginalize the Church, some excess may be understandable.) Dulles is convinced that those who say the Church's mission is not salvation, or who define salvation in terms of this-worldly liberation, are deliberately distorting the teachings of Vatican II. "The postconciliar secular theologies are most sharply contradicted by the *Constitution on the Liturgy,* which singles out the public worship of the church as the activity that most perfectly manifests and accomplishes human sanctification. No other action of the church, says the Constitution, can match the liturgy in its claim to efficacy. It is the summit toward which the church's entire activity is directed and the fountainhead from which all its power flows."

Dulles does not want to denigrate, but he does sharply relativize, the role of political and social transformation in the mission of the Church. He reminds us that the Council documents quote with approval the words of Pius XI: "It is necessary never to lose sight of the fact that the objective of the Church is to evangelize, not to civilize. If it civilizes, it is for the sake of evangelization." Dulles knows that if others are flying in the face of the Council, he is flying in the face of what many assume is the established consensus in Roman Catholic theology, especially in the United States. With that consensus, he affirms the responsibilities of the faithful in the social and political arena; against that consensus, he says (and he says Vatican II says) that the Church "has no proper mission in the social, political and economic orders." Much turns on the meaning of "proper." "By a 'proper' mission the Council presumably means that which is specific to the church and would remain undone unless the church existed. To preach faith in Christ and to administer the sacraments are in this sense proper to the church. . . . But to erect a just and prosperous society is not, in that precise sense, proper to the church." It is, he insists, the responsibility of Christians to contribute to such a society "insofar as they are citizens of the earthly community." Service to the world is essential in that the Church must remind its members of their social responsibility. "But it is not essential," writes Dulles, "if that term is taken to mean that the success of the human enterprise is the proper goal or responsibility of the church as such."

Dulles, too, writes in sorrow, in the awareness that something has gone terribly wrong. "In our time, Christians, and perhaps Catholics more than others, are haunted by the fear of loving the church too much. They find it hard to share Christ's own love for the church (Ephesians 5:25) and to accept the maxim of St. Augustine, quoted by Vatican II, that 'one possesses the Holy Spirit in the measure that one loves the Church of Christ.' " Dulles is well aware that the Church is composed of sinners and that their performance "must often be said to conceal rather than to reveal the authentic face of Christ," as Vatican II did indeed say. But in loving the Church one is, nonetheless, loving Christ and those in whom Christ lives and who live in Christ. One should not be careful not to love that Church too much. Dulles's argument is not likely to persuade many who are enamored of liberation theology, however. In their view he is obviously inviting back the Last Magician.

Before looking at the response of John Paul II and the Vatican to liberation theology, we should remind ourselves what is at stake. When a centrist and ecumenical theologian such as Dulles dares to speak of the "proper" task of the Church, and to distinguish it from the tasks of social and political transformation, he is taking on a deeply entrenched consensus in the ideological leadership of the Roman Catholic Church in the United States. It is critically important to make a distinction between the leadership and the Roman Catholic people. Survey research suggests that a gap is widening between leadership and people that could one day approach the vast gap between leadership and people that has long been recognized in old-line Protestant churches. A 1986 survey, for example, asked Roman Catholics whether their church leaders should address political and social questions. Eighty percent of the bishops, priests, and religious said yes, compared with fewer than 40 percent of the laity. Of course churches should not order their mission by opinion polls. And of course the leadership is more educated about the nature and mission of the Church. And of course many laypeople subscribe to a sometimes simplistic notion that "religion and politics don't mix." All that said, however, the prospect of a growing gap must be of concern to leaders who intend to lead. And it is at least worthwhile to entertain the thought that the faithful, as it were by intuition, understand the importance of the distinctions that theologians such as Dulles would sustain.

It is safe to assume that in the eyes of, say, most bishops in the United States, liberation theology is "extreme." One must then ask, Of what is it the extreme? It may be that it is an extreme form of assumptions that are pervasive in "mainstream" American Catholicism. In the jargon of the social sciences, liberation theology is a "pure type" of one understanding of the relationship between Church and world. That understanding may aptly be described as monism. The alternative to it is pluralism. Remember Gutierrez and the "two planes." In Latin America and elsewhere (Franco Spain being the outstanding example), the Catholicism of the old Christendom was monistic. As Gutierrez says, that alliance between church and state, that way of "getting it all together," was viewed as oppressive. Its opponents then urged upon the church the "two planes" theory by which the "proper" task of the church would be distinguished, enabling the church to liberate itself from its misalliance with the regimes of the earthly city. But with liberation theology, when it appeared that the church could be brought into "solidarity" with the new and just regime, Catholicism reverts to its monistic habits of thought and behavior. Whether the regime in question is Franco Spain or Sandinista Nicaragua, the formal relationship is the same, and that relationship is one of monism. Let it quickly be added that such habits are not peculiarly Roman Catholic. Much of the left wing of Protestantism (the heirs of what is called "the radical Reformation") is adamantly monistic, as was the social gospel movement with its ambition to "Christianize America and Americanize Christianity."

The great achievement of John Courtney Murray, strongly reflected in the Council's "Declaration on Religious Freedom" was to present a lively alternative to the habits of monism. Murray retrieved and provided a contemporary and sophisticated theory for what he called the "Gelasian tradition." In A.D. 494 Pope Gelasius I wrote to the emperor Anastasius I: "Two there are, august Emperor, by which this world is ruled on title of original and sovereign right—the consecrated authority of the priesthood and the royal power." To suggest that Gelasius was advocating what we today think to be the proper relationship between church and state in liberal democracy would be absurd. But Murray believed, correctly I think, that there was a Gelasian principle that had the potential for further development. That principle recognized the provisional and, if you will, pluralistic character of the world. That provisionality and pluralism should be reflected also in the governance of the world. Christ the King is indeed lord of all, but until he establishes his rule in the right and final ordering of the creation, there are, as it were, provisional spheres of sovereignty. By asserting the proper autonomy of the Church in its mission, Gelasius was also asserting, at least implicitly, the proper autonomy of state power. This does not mean that God is sovereign over only part of his creation, namely the Church. It does mean that God who is sovereign over all exercises his sovereignty through different instruments and institutions as various as Church, family, state, education, and economy.

41. MURRAY CONTRA MONISM

Central to God's rule is the Church. The Church is central because it is the Church that has the particular commission to bear and proclaim the message of God's rule, to which all institutions, including the Church, are accountable. This does not mean that reality is "divided up" into sacred and profane, religious and secular, with the Church limited to the sacred and religious. The God revealed in Jesus Christ is the one God of the one world. In order to avoid the error of thinking about reality as "divided," it is necessary to accent the eschatological. (In this connection, unfortunately, the eschatological dimension was not sufficiently accented either by Murray or by the Council.) The spheres of sovereignty and their institutions are only provisional. "When all things are subjected to him, then the Son himself will also be subjected to him who put all things under him, that God may be all in all" (1 Cor. 15). The Church, the community of faith, is a community ahead of time. Personally and communally, Christians anticipate now what is to be. But they also live in a world that is not yet what it is to be. The result is to live as "alien citizens" in the world, to be a people experienced in the sometimes painful paradox of living between the times, in the "now" and the "not yet."

Christians try to escape the paradox and its pain, and the desire to do so is perfectly understandable. Some escape by committing themselves only to the church of true believers in which it is no longer necessary to pray "Your Kingdom come" because their church is, they say, the same thing as the Kingdom. Many more escape the paradox by being conformed to the world in such a way that their nominal membership in the Church provides little more than occasional qualms of conscience and moments of religious relief. The course of discipleship, however, is relentlessly to sustain the paradox until we are released from it by God himself. The paradox is the result of the pluralistic character of reality itself. John Courtney Murray wrote that pluralism, especially religious pluralism, is contrary to the divine will but is apparently written into the script of history. It may be, however, that God himself has done the writing. Ultimately, whether in joy or in sorrow, every knee will bow and every tongue confess that Jesus Christ is Lord, to the glory of God the Father (Phil. 2). But that time is not yet.

Many Christians have difficulty entertaining the possibility that pluralism may be part of providential purpose. Surely it would be better, they think, if everybody in the entire world agreed on the truth and articulated it in the same way, in the same community of faith, bent upon the same understanding of the right ordering of the world. But that might not be better at all. That might, rather, be a formula for the disaster of premature closure, to which the Church is always tempted. Why it is that the final consummation is delayed is a question that Christians have pondered from Paul onward. But that it is delayed there should be no doubt. On the one hand, the Gospels persistently proclaim that the Kingdom is at hand and even in the midst of us. The Kingdom is now for the believer, because the King is now with us on our sojourn. But it is still a sojourn toward what is yet to be. Christians are forever oscillating between the twin errors of belittling the "now" or the "not yet." The biblical imperative is to maintain both, simultaneously and without compromise. The pluralism of worlds within the world—of different beliefs, perceptions, authorities, traditions, of ways of being in the world—is the constant reminder of our provisionality, and therefore of the need to live in hope, walking by faith and not by sight.

"Two there are, august Emperor." The Gelasian tradition and its distinction between spiritual and political orders is derided by monists of all stripes. It is condemned for being "dualistic," and in contemporary religious culture the charge of being "dualistic" is very harsh condemnation indeed. In fact, the dualism in this understanding of the relationship between church and state is but one facet of the pluralism of reality short of the final consummation. Monists, whether of the Right or of the Left, cannot wait. Monists of all sorts are forever tilting toward theocracy in their view of how the world ought to be ordered. In various ways, they attempt to collapse the "not yet" into the "now." Joachim of Fiore in the twelfth century, Thomas Munzer in the sixteenth, and today's "Christian Reconstructionist" movement in American Protestantism are all instances of monistic hungers at work in the political realm. Before Vatican II, Franco Spain was viewed as the model, the "thesis," of the right ordering of church-state relations. Other models, especially the American, were thought to be deviations to be tolerated until Roman Catholic influence could bring them into line with the Francoist thesis. Francoism was also a monistic conflation of the "now" and "not yet," collapsing the "not yet" into the "now" of the institution that is the Roman Catholic Church. Vatican II repudiated the Francoist formula for church-state relations and, much more important, the ecclesiological understanding, the understanding of the Church, upon which it was premised.

The argument of much liberation theology is, like Francoism, monistic in character. But its conflation of the "now" and "not yet" moves in a different direction and is for traditional Christian faith more radical in its consequences. In this case, the "not yet" is collapsed into the "now" of the liberation process. The "not yet" is declared to be true only to the extent that it serves that process. Any other hope is derided as "magic." Given the monism of liberationist logic, it makes sense to condemn the Gelasian formula as intolerably dualistic. Any formula of pluralism or of transcendent hope is intolerable because it brings all existent regimes and would-be regimes, including all liberation struggles, under judgment. The pluralistic understanding, contrary to the claims of its critics, does not undermine the unity of the world, of reason, or of God's rule.

It does understand that God's rule is exercised through a plurality of means. It does understand that, given the provisionality of this time in the history of the one world, reason is exercised through a plurality of traditions appropriate to diverse tasks. Today many conservatives and many radicals, unconsciously joined in the bond of their monism, criticize such an understanding for being "relativistic."

And, to be sure, it is relativistic in the sense that it sharply relativizes the absolutist claims of all institutions and movements that present themselves as being tantamount to the Kingdom of God. Pluralism is written into the script of history in order to smash all idols. Roman Catholic traditionalists are tempted to make an idol of the institution and authority of the Roman Catholic Church. Liberation theologians are tempted to make an idol of the liberation process. Of the two monisms, the second poses the greater threat to Christian faith. That is because liberation theology more routinely succumbs to the temptation to idolatry and even insists upon it as a virtue. And that is because the dominant liberation theologians exclude the transcendent as a matter of principle. The traditionalist, no matter how extreme in his ultramontanism, in principle relativizes the church in relation to the transcendent. He may be a practical idolator with respect to the church institution, but in theory he acknowledges that the church is the instrument of the Absolute that it cannot exhaustively contain. Finally, the Roman Catholic Church does not occupy the place in his piety that is occupied by the liberation process in the piety of, say, Juan Luis Segundo. When all is said and done, there are cracks in the monism of even the most relentless traditionalist. And, as we have seen, even Segundo allows in his confessional moments that he may nurture elements of "magic" that ought to be excluded by the principles he espouses. Even the most determined monism is not impervious to grace. One may therefore hope that the Last Magicians of both papal absolutism and the liberation process may yet be relativized by the expectation of the One who is to come.

42. JOHN PAUL FOR LIBERATION

John Paul II's response to liberation theology has been complex, and is still developing. He has variously condemned its errors, praised it for raising legitimate concerns, and redefined it so thoroughly that he is now able to recommend his version of liberation theology to the entire Church. In July of 1986 John Paul visited Colombia and spoke at Medellin, the site from which the famous "spirit of Medellin" was launched in 1968. His visit coincided with some particularly repressive measures against the church by the Sandinista regime in Nicaragua, including the expulsion of a bishop who, said the Sandinistas, "does not deserve to be a Nicaraguan." In his Medellin speech the Pope abandoned conventional diplomatic language in condemning the Sandinistas' action. His words must also be understood against the background of his earlier visit to Nicaragua, where he had been most rudely treated by crowds—some say mobs—orchestrated by the Sandinistas. At Medellin he described himself as "profoundly disturbed in my spirit" and urged the Sandinistas to "rethink the seriousness of such an action, which also contradicts repeated claim of a desire for a peaceful and respectful coexistence with the church. . . . This nearly incredible event has deeply saddened me, all the more so because it evokes dark ages—still not very long ago but that one could reasonably believe to have been overcome."

The "dark ages" to which John Paul referred were not, of course, the Middle Ages. He referred rather to the revolutionary anticlericalism that had marked turbulent church-state relations in Mexico and elsewhere in Latin America. Although he did not use the term, at Medellin the Pope was calling for what Gutierrez refers to as the "two planes" approach to the church and politics. He urged once again, as he has done so often, that the church's proper mission is "spiritual and religious" and not political. This was combined, as it almost always is in his public pronouncements, with a reaffirmation of the church's particular commitment to those who are "tired and oppressed by poverty." But "the preferential option for the poor" cannot mean that the church is taken captive by partisan forces. "The church cannot in any way let the banner of justice, which is one of the prime demands of the Gospel and the fruit of the coming of the Kingdom of God, be seized by any ideology or any political current," John Paul insisted. At Medellin, then, John Paul reiterated themes that have become the trademark of his pontificate. These core themes characterize what may well be called the John Paul II Project. The commitment to the poor and oppressed must be unquestioned. The commitment to justice is inherent in Christian discipleship and is motivated by love for the neighbor. At the same time, he adamantly insists that such commitment must not be motivated by utopian delusions nor become hostage to any ideological or political party. The church must insist upon its own social space, it must have the freedom to act in a distinctive manner appropriate to its own constituting imperatives, and its representatives must maintain a critical distance from every existent and would-be regime.

Critics of the Pope have accused him of operating by a double standard. They say he opposes political activism in Latin America, for example, but indulges and encourages it in Poland. The criticism does not stand up under closer examination. The themes listed above perfectly characterize the role of the church in Poland. It is simply that under totalitarian governments, the insistence upon independent social space and critical distance from the regime becomes a "political issue" because it is viewed as hostility by the regime. The formula of totalitarian, as distinct from authoritarian, government is simple and was first articulated by Mussolini: "Everything within the state, nothing outside the state, nothing against the state." The Pope is remarkably consistent in saying how the church should relate to the political order, but the consequences are dramatically different in different political orders. With respect to activists inspired by liberation theology—especially where such theology is wedded to Marxist-Leninist ideology and program—John Paul's criticism is doubly emphatic. Not only are such activists failing to maintain a critical distance, but they are actually espousing a political ideology that, in both principle and historical experience, excludes the possibility of such critical distance. The Pope has a yet deeper concern, however, which goes beyond his concern about the disastrous social consequences of the course advanced by such activists. His concern, very simply and solemnly, is that many Roman Catholics have come to believe in "another gospel."

A decade after the launching of the "spirit of Medellín," the Pope addressed the General Assembly of the Latin American Bishops gathered in Puebla, Mexico. He sets forth the traditional understanding of the Gospel and the way of salvation and declares that from this Gospel the Church "draws everything that she has to offer to people, without any distinction of nation, culture, race, time, age or condition." That may seem to be a very conventional statement, almost an instance of papal boilerplate, so to speak. But John Paul leaves no doubt that he is convinced that the Gospel itself is under challenge. "This is the one Gospel, and 'even if we or an angel from heaven should preach to you a Gospel contrary to that which we preached to you, let him be accursed,' as the apostle wrote in very clear terms (Galatians 1)." A major newspaper reported that the Pope reprimanded theologians for deviations from official church teaching. The apostolic words he invoked, however, are not a reprimand but an anathema. Nor did he leave in doubt whom he had in mind. He mentions those who depict Christ as a partisan in the class struggle of his day, and declares, "This idea of Christ as a political figure, a revolutionary, as the subversive man from Nazareth, does not tally with the church's catechesis."

In notions such as the "partisan church," the Pope recognizes a fundamental repudiation of the accepted understanding of the community of faith. In his pontificate, he said at Puebla, he is determined "to dedicate my greatest care to the ecclesiological area." After praising the Latin American bishops for their orthodoxy, he notes evidence of "a certain uneasiness" about the nature and mission of the Church. "Allusion is made, for instance, to the separation that some set up between the church and the kingdom of God. The kingdom of God is emptied of its full content and is understood in a rather secularist sense: It is interpreted as being reached not by faith and membership in the church but by the mere changing of structures and social and political involvement, and as being present wherever there is a certain type of involvement and activity for justice." Such a view, he says, ignores the teaching of Vatican II that "the church receives the mission to proclaim and to establish among all peoples the kingdom of Christ and of God. She becomes on earth the seed and beginning of that kingdom."

Much of the Puebla address was taken up with John Paul's view of Latin American history and of the measures that make for economic justice. In the judgment of thoughtful critics, John Paul offers a much too benign version of Catholicism's influence in Latin America, comes close to subscribing to a zero-sum theory of economics in discussing the relationship between rich and poor, and borders on sounding ingenuous when he suggests that evangelization and personal conversion will result in economic development. All these criticisms have considerable merit, and, whether he is right or wrong, on these and related questions John Paul's thought has evidenced little development over the years of his pontificate. It is to John Paul the theologian and pastor that we must attend, however. He is keenly aware, as are the liberation theologians, that the most fundamental challenge is the *theology* of liberation, not the economics of liberation or the politics of liberation. Error in economics or politics may be criticized; the denial of the Gospel is to be anathematized. John XXIII notwithstanding, the Church, if it is to be the Church, can never entirely get out of the business of judicious anathematizing.

A year after Pueblo, John Paul directly addressed some of the foundational themes of liberation theology in his encyclical "Rich in Mercy" *(Dives in Misericordia).* The connections are not always explicitly or exclusively with liberation theology. In many instances the arguments he challenges are culturally pervasive, but, when presented as *theological* arguments, they are characteristically the arguments of liberation theology. Terms such as "charity" and "philanthrophy" are typically scorned by the liberationists. In relation to the real needs of the world, it is said, such terms bespeak paternalistic and "bandaid" responses that do not get at the "systemic" and "structural" evils that oppress the victims of injustice. Not philanthropy but justice is required. John Paul insists, however, that it is precisely in mercy and in love that God reveals himself to us and calls us to relate to one another. "Nevertheless, through this 'making known' by Christ we know God above all in his relationship of love for man: in his 'philanthropy.' " The Pope knows that such a proposition cannot help but seem scandalously countercultural. "The present-day mentality, more perhaps than that of people in the past, seems opposed to a God of mercy and in fact tends to exclude from life and to remove from the human heart the very idea of mercy." A power-oriented world, says John Paul, is more at home with the idea of mastery than of mercy.

Emphasizing the Christian difference, John Paul cites *Gaudium et Spes* on the ways in which humanity is, at the same time, becoming more powerful and more powerless. The obverse of humanity's weakness in its power is the power in weakness set forth in the cross and Resurrection of Christ. Current styles of Christian thought about politics appeal, sometimes almost exclusively, to the Hebrew prophets in order to counter what is perceived as the "softness" of a New Testament ethic of love. But this effort to counter mercy by justice is, according to John Paul, a false move. In the Hebrew scriptures "mercy is in a certain sense contrasted with God's justice and in many cases is shown to be not only more powerful than that justice but also more profound. Even the Old Testament teaches that although justice is an authentic virtue in man, and in God signifies transcendent perfection, nevertheless love is 'greater' than justice: greater in the sense that it is primary and fundamental." Human capacity for justice is limited. No matter how many personal conversions or how many rectifications there are of structural and systemic wrongs, there is still the reality of sin. "In the preaching of the prophets mercy signifies a special power of love, which prevails over the sin and infidelity of the chosen people."

Christian thinkers have for two millennia pondered the relationship between justice and love. John Paul understands the relationship this way: "Love, so to speak, conditions justice and, in the final analysis, justice serves love." The words "in the final analysis" are critical. The love of God for his people is the first and final cause of everything, including our desire and obligation to serve our neighbor in seeking justice. The truth of God's abiding love, once proclaimed to Israel, "involves a perspective of the whole history of man, a perspective both temporal and eschatological." The temporal is not enough, nor are existent criteria of justice enough. It becomes evident, writes John Paul, "that love is transformed into mercy when it is necessary to go beyond the precise norm of justice—precise and often too narrow." This "going beyond," the Pope says, is well illustrated in the parable of the prodigal son. The son had no claim to justice, only a hope for mercy. Such a dependence upon mercy offends cultural sensibilities. Evaluating the relationship between father and son "from the outside," evaluating it structurally, it seems like an unacceptable relationship of superior and inferior. "Our prejudices about mercy are mostly the result of appraising them only from the outside. At times it happens that by following this method of evaluation we see in mercy above all a relationship of inequality between the one offering it and the one receiving it. And, in consequence, we are quick to deduce that mercy belittles the receiver, that it offends the dignity of man." When viewed "from the inside" of our dependence upon God's love, however, such a cultural prejudice is shown up for what it is, a rebellion against our creatureliness and a rejection of the utter gratuity of God's grace.

Justice is a fearful thing and should not be demanded lightly, lest we get it. Ultimately, justice is the justice of the cross. "Indeed this redemption is the ultimate and definitive revelation of the holiness of God, who is the absolute fullness of perfection: the fullness of justice and of love, since justice is based on love, flows from it and tends toward it." In the cross justice is done, as Christ "became sin" for our sake. This is a "superabundance" of justice and is, in turn, the cause of our justification. John Paul insists that any message of justice that is put in competition with the cross, that speaks of salvific and justifying promise apart from that already given by grace, is in solemn fact "another gospel."

43. JOHN PAUL FOR MORE THAN JUSTICE

Only with an eschatological, transcendent horizon firmly in mind can we dare to say that "Christ's messianic program, the program of mercy, becomes the program of his people, the program of the church." Only by relying on God's mercy in the cross and Resurrection and in the "definitive renewal" that is promised can we dare to address the contradictions and dichotomies of the world. Otherwise our efforts are sheer presumption. And that is because "the dichotomy affecting the modern world is, in fact, a symptom of a deeper dichotomy that is in man himself," says John Paul, quoting *Gaudium et Spes*. John Paul again implies that Vatican II did not do full justice to the tensions, threats, and ambiguities of the modern world. In any event, the lessons of the years since the Council "do not permit us to cherish the illusions of the past." The illusions of the past are both about human nature itself and about our ability to achieve mastery over all the forces that impinge upon us.

After listing a number of such forces of "radical injustice," John Paul calls for a response that recognizes that, paradoxically, justice requires more than justice. In looking about the world, he says, "it would be difficult not to notice that very often programs which start from the idea of justice and which ought to assist its fulfillment among individuals, groups and human societies, in practice suffer from distortions. Although they continue to appeal to the idea of justice, nevertheless experience shows that other negative forces have gained the upper hand over justice, such as spite, hatred and even cruelty." In case the reader might miss the specific reference, he mentions those who invoke "historical justice" or "class justice" in the name of which "the neighbor is sometimes destroyed, killed, deprived of liberty or stripped of fundamental human rights." He cites the maxim *Summum ius, summa iniuria* (the greatest justice, the greatest harm), which indicates the awful consequences when justice is not drawn from and conditioned by love and mercy. Those who live from the mercy of God are not conformed to the world's understanding of power but are *in statu conversionis*, in a state of continuing conversion to an understanding of justice as love. In addition, they are *in statu viatoris*, in a continuing pilgrimage of hope toward an eschatological horizon.

In this encyclical John Paul counters other conventional wisdoms that find strong, although certainly not exclusive, expression in liberation theology. The idea of equality, for example, must go beyond "the realm of objective and extrinsic goods" and underscore our encounter with one another as equals in the love and mercy of God. Similarly, there can be no authentic justice without reconciliation and forgiveness. "A world from which forgiveness was eliminated would be nothing but a world of cold and unfeeling justice, in the name of which each person would claim his or her own rights vis-a-vis others; the various kinds of selfishness latent in man would transform life and human society into a system of oppression of the weak by the strong, or into an arena of permanent strife between one group and another." Such a Niebuhrian sense of "Christian realism" (which he undoubtedly did not learn from Reinhold Niebuhr) leads John Paul to a position that he insists is ever so much more radical than that espoused by liberation theology. Some people act in the courage of their reading of the "signs of the times." John Paul calls for a courage to live *in statu viatoris* even when the signs of the times are bleak, "even if in the world evil should prevail over goodness, even if contemporary humanity should deserve a new 'flood' on account of its sins, as once the generation of Noah did." He ends on a note of radical and faith-filled defiance: "No matter how strong the resistance of human history may be, no matter how marked the diversity of contemporary civilization, no matter how great the denial of God in the human world, so much the greater must be the church's closeness to that mystery which, hidden for centuries in God, was then truly shared with man, in time, through Jesus Christ."

Liberation theologians, both Roman Catholic and Protestant, seldom challenge John Paul directly. Indeed, efforts are conventionally made to enlist him in the cause. From a statement such as "Rich in Mercy" they pick out statements about specific injustices in the world and the Pope's admonitions to be active in seeking to remedy them. But, for all the emphasis that liberationists typically place upon structure, and upon the priority of substance over form, they just as typically refuse to engage the structure and substance of John Paul's argumentation. Perhaps this is an instance of that "creative" involvement in "the evolution of interpretations" discussed by Segundo, but, whatever it is, it contributes mightily to the debasement of contemporary theological discourse. Both the general media and the church press seem equally indifferent to, or incapable of, theological thought. Thus throughout this pontificate, news reports and editorials beyond numbering talk about whether John Paul is for or against "the church's concern for the poor and oppressed" (which, it is blithely assumed, is what liberation theology is all about). Thus John Paul is regularly rated as to whether he is moving in a more "liberal" or a more "conservative" direction, the fatuity of political labels being the usual limit of the journalistic imagination. And all the time this Pope keeps insisting that the real issue is the contest between *the* Gospel and other gospels.

John Paul seems at times to be becoming ever more explicit, even polemical, in order to force a recognition that he is making an argument and not just blessing one side or another in existing debates. "On Human Work" *(Laborem Exercens)*, a 1981 encyclical, challenges directly some key Marxist assumptions about labor. As is his habit, John Paul tends to suggest a moral equivalence between capitalism and socialist collectivism, although he speaks also about the errors of "early capitalism," thus leaving room for the acknowledgment that the capitalism under discussion has little to do with the democratic capitalism that prevails in democracies today. Here John Paul appears to have put on his philosopher's hat very firmly, and the discussion tends to become quite abstract. There is, however, a bias against the abstract in democratic capitalism. It tends, perhaps of necessity, to be weak on theory. Socialism, especially of the Marxist variety, tends to be very big on theory. Analyzing it theoretically also tends to be more relevant to historical fact, since ideas such as class struggle are acted upon in, for example, the mass elimination or persecution of "class enemies." John Paul's theoretical description of Marxism should be recognized and affirmed by most Marxists, even by revisionists who say they are only selectively "employing Marxist analysis." His theoretical description of capitalism would be recognized by very few capitalists and probably affirmed by none. One measure of the quality of an argument is whether those whom you are arguing against can recognize their position as depicted in your argument. By that measure, it might be concluded that John Paul's treatment of both capitalism and socialism is a failure. Both parties say they do not recognize their position in John Paul's description. Of course both may be responding disingenuously. It is worth noting, however, that it is the liberationist proponents of socialism who have embraced and announced disingenuousness as a strategy.

Even so, John Paul is not entirely evenhanded in his treatment of capitalism and socialism in "On Human Work." Tracing papal social teachings from *Rerum Novarum* through *Mater et Magistra,* he says that the church's teaching about the ownership of property, for example, "diverges radically from the program of collectivism as proclaimed by Marxism" while it "differs from the program of capitalism practiced by liberalism." There is, to be sure, a significant distinction between diverging radically and differing. In addition, John Paul makes clear that he is talking about "rigid capitalism" in which private ownership of the means of production is "an untouchable 'dogma' of economic life." That description might be pertinent to the capitalism—or at least the caricature of the capitalism—practiced by Jay Gould and J. P. Morgan in the last century. It has little bearing on the democratic capitalism practiced in the United States, Sweden, France, or in the Italy surrounding the Vatican. By juxtaposing a theory of Marxism that is officially taught and practiced with a theory of capitalism that is nowhere taught and practiced, the Pope is less persuasive than he ought to be. Of course his way of being evenhanded is deplored by the defenders of democratic capitalism. But, much more important, it detracts from the theological argument that he would make, an argument that cuts across and transcends polarized positions on lesser questions. It provides encouragement to those who are forever trying to locate the Pope on their political and ideological spectrum, rather than listening to the Pope who understands his mission to be the proclamation of the Gospel.

John Paul moves to the center of that mission in his fifth encyclical, "The Holy Spirit in the Church and the World" (*Dominum et Vivificantem*, 1986). The Holy Spirit is the second Counselor (Christ being the first) who teaches the Church and "brings to remembrance" all that has been revealed by God in Christ. John Paul here addresses the role of the Church as the bearer of tradition, and does so in a manner similar to our earlier discussion of a postliberal understanding of cultural-linguistic traditions. "The Holy Spirit," he writes, "comes after and because of [Christ] in order to continue in the world, through the church, the work of the good news of salvation." The promise of Christ is that the Holy Spirit "will ensure continuity and identity of understanding in the midst of changing conditions and circumstances." This is no mechanical transmission of a tradition but a "leading into all truth" that can only be understood "in faith and through faith." The Church is enabled, by the gift of the Spirit, "to accept with faith and confess with candor the mystery of God at work in human history, the revealed mystery which explains the definitive meaning of that history." Here John Paul touches on the reason why it is not "ecclesiocentrism" when, in the ordering of our loves and loyalties, our primary communal commitment is to the Church. Our devotion to the Church is precisely because of our devotion to human history, and that is because the Church bears in history the "definitive meaning" of history. Thus the Spirit comes "to remain with the church and in the church, and through her in the world."

44. "JUSTICE" AGAINST THE SPIRIT

The encyclical "The Holy Spirit in the Church and the World" is in large part a meditation on, and exegesis of, Jesus' discourse in the upper room (John 14). It is powerfully trinitarian in character, and John Paul stresses again the understanding of the "I" as the reality of the Spirit in the relationship of Jesus of Nazareth to the one whom he called Father. Vatican II, says John Paul, is noted as an "ecclesiological" council, but he thinks it so lifts up the work of the Spirit that it deserves to be called a "pneumatological" council. Jesus said that the Spirit would "convince the world concerning sin and righteousness and judgment." The "judgment" in question, John Paul urges us to believe, is a judgment regarding the "prince of this world." In the present phase of the history of salvation, it is mandatory that, precisely for the sake of the message of salvation, the Church be particularly clear about that which works against salvation. "Satan, the one who from the beginning has been exploiting the work of creation against salvation, against the covenant and the union of man with God: He is 'already judged' from the start. If the Spirit-Counselor is to convince the world precisely concerning judgment, it is in order to continue in the world the salvific work of Christ.''

There are different ways of understanding what is meant by "the world." John Paul cites and affirms Vatican II's rather hopeful description of "the world" and then goes on to underscore a necessary ambivalence toward "the world" in view of the universality of sin. The concept of sin must be expanded "until it assumes a universal dimension by reason of the universality of the redemption accomplished through the cross." It is through the mystery of redemption that we understand both the universality and the radicality of sin in a world that so needed redeeming. Sin is not to be understood just as the transgression of divine law. Sin is disobedience, and disobedience is at the most profound level always "nonfaith." Sin is refusing to believe the promise. Here again John Paul expresses himself in harmony with the Reformation insight regarding the centrality of faith, and faith as a gift of grace, opposing every form of legalism or self-justification. Although in this immediate context liberation theology is not mentioned, John Paul's words are in sharpest contrast to a species of "works righteousness" whereby liberation/salvation is achieved through "solidarity in the liberation process."

The mysterious workings of grace are marked by paradox. At the very heart of the relationship between God and world is the paradox of judgment and salvation—it is both salvation because of judgment and judgment because of salvation. John Paul puts it this way: "Thus there is a paradoxical mystery of love: In Christ there suffers a God who has been rejected by his own creature: 'They do not believe in me.' But at the same time, from the depth of this suffering—and indirectly from the depth of the very sin 'of not having believed'—the Spirit draws a new measure of the gift made to man and to creation from the beginning." A few years ago a prominent psychologist wrote a noteworthy book titled *What Ever Happened To Sin?* That might also serve as the title for a large part of the encyclical at hand. John Paul notes that Pius XII had already observed that "the sin of the century is the loss of the sense of sin." We deny sin, John Paul suggests, because we do not understand the paradox of sin and grace. Without the knowledge of grace, we simply cannot afford to face the reality of sin. Without grace, all of our human projects are threatened and made to look ridiculous by the reality of sin and death. Because we want to trust our projects, we deny that which threatens them; we deny sin and, in so doing, deny the God who forgives sin. In this way the denial of evil becomes the greatest evil.

At the heart of what might be called "the modernity project" is resistance to the Holy Spirit, who would give us the faith to accept God's gift of grace. Of course, John Paul notes, there is nothing new in resistance to the Holy Spirit. But such resistance has today become culturally entrenched and finds expression also in philosophies, ideologies, and programs of action. Then appears one of John Paul's sharpest and most substantive comments on Marxism. "[Resistance to the Holy Spirit] reaches its clearest expression in materialism, both in its theoretical form as a system of thought, and in its practical form as a method of interpreting and evaluating facts, and likewise as a program of corresponding conduct. The system which has developed most and carried to extreme practical consequences this form of thought, ideology and praxis is dialectical and historical materialism, which is still recognized as the essential core of Marxism." That statement repays very close examination. Such materialism, John Paul continues, "radically excludes the presence and action of God, who is spirit, in the world and above all in man." It is "essentially and systematically atheistic." True, Marxism sometimes speaks of the "spirit" and "questions of the spirit" in connection with culture or morality. But "it does so only insofar as it considers certain facts as derived from matter *(epiphenomena)*, since according to this system matter is the one and only form of being." Thus religion is, at best, a kind of "idealistic illusion," John Paul notes. Or, as others say, religion becomes a more or less useful "magic" in the advancement of our favored projects.

Marxism represents in our time the resistance to the Holy Spirit condemned by Paul, says John Paul. Paul wrote, "The desire of the Spirit are against the flesh, and the desires of the Spirit are against the flesh" (Gal. 5). Materialism is, quite exactly, the ideology of the flesh. The contrast between "Spirit" and "flesh" entails the contrast between "life" and "death." "This," the Pope writes, "is a serious problem, and concerning it one must say at once that materialism, as a system of thought, in all its forms, means the acceptance of death as the definitive end of human existence." John Paul's strictures could hardly be more explicit or severe. His words are carefully chosen. Some phrases deserve special attention: "a system of thought, in all its forms"; "both in its theoretical form as a system of thought, and in its practical form as a method of interpreting and evaluating facts, and likewise as a program of corresponding conduct." Such formulations are unquestionably directed at those liberation theologians who say they are not Marxist but are only "employing Marxist analysis." It is precisely the analysis, with its underlying presuppositions, that is lethal, John Paul argues.

John Paul is too much of a philosopher and takes ideas too seriously to accept the notion that a system of thought is like a Tinkertoy set with its many pieces that you can, at will, pick and choose, connect and disconnect. There are no naked, independent facts, says John Paul. Facts are "interpreted and evaluated" by ideas, and ideas presuppose other ideas. To those who are simply toying with Marxism, John Paul says they are toying with death. To those who have deliberately accepted Marxist theory, John Paul solemnly declares them to be the enemies of the Gospel.

One can debate whether John Paul is right in his understanding of Marxism or, for that matter, in his understanding of the Gospel. But the clarity and the gravity of his position is beyond honest debate. We are again reminded how superficial are most discussions of the Pope's attitude toward liberation theology. The impression given is that John Paul is engaged in a dispute over the relative merits of different approaches to helping the poor, or over the limits of church authority, or over the pros and cons of priests in politics. All these questions and others are indeed in dispute, but none of them is at the heart of what John Paul is saying. John Paul makes it unmistakably clear that the contest he is talking about is nothing less than the contest between Spirit and anti-Spirit, Word and anti-Word, Christ and anti-Christ.

The concluding section of *Dominum et Vivificantem* focuses on the coming new millennium. The work of the Spirit is the work of unity, first of unity among Christians. John Paul reflects that the millennium now drawing to a close has been the millennium of the great separations between Christians. The renewal of bold Christian witness must also be a renewal for Christian unity "so that all who have been baptized in the one Spirit in order to make up one body may be brethren joined in the celebration of the same eucharist, 'a sacrament of love, a sign of unity, a bond of charity' " (Augustine). Without becoming apocalyptic about it or presuming to prophesy, John Paul does evince a sense of being hopefully intrigued by "this phase of transition from the second to the third Christian millennium." He suggests that something very big is afoot in the divine scheme of things. The signs of anti-Spirit abound, but so also do signs of the Spirit, especially of new communities of prayer and profound Christian devotion. The encyclical ends on the note of hope. "It is the eschatological hope, the hope of definitive fulfillment in God, the hope of the eternal kingdom, that is brought about by participation in the life of the Trinity. The Holy Spirit, given to the apostles as the Counselor, is the guardian and animator of this hope in the heart of the church." Thus "the church, united with the Virgin Mother, prays unceasingly as the bride to her divine spouse, as the words of the Book of Revelation attest: 'The Spirit and the bride say to the Lord Jesus Christ: Come!' "

In April of 1986 the Pope could write to the bishops of Brazil recommending to them an authentic liberation theology. It is a liberation theology refined and redefined by all the considerations we have been discussing. It is a liberation theology dramatically different from, even diametrically opposed to, what those who call themselves liberation theologians have meant by liberation theology. John Paul underscores that the Holy See has been most particularly concerned about the question of liberation theology, as is evident in "the numerous documents recently published." He singles out the two "Instructions" on the subject from the Congregation for the Doctrine of the Faith that were issued "with my explicit approval." He pointedly adds that these two documents "have an undeniable pastoral relevancy for Brazil." Alluding to the second "Instruction" from the Congregation, the Pope emphasizes the "two constitutive dimensions" of the Christian understanding of liberation. "Whether at the level of reflection or of praxis, liberation is first of all salvific (an aspect of the salvation achieved by Jesus Christ, son of God) and afterward socio-ethical (or ethico-political). To reduce one dimension to the other—practically suppressing them both—or putting the second before the first is to subvert and emasculate true Christian liberation."

These things having been said, John Paul affirms: "As long as all this is observed, we are convinced that the theology of liberation is not only timely but useful and necessary." Some thought the Pope was being a little whimsical in the disingenuousness of endorsing liberation theology after he had quite completely turned it on its head. Others—whether because they are dim-witted or devoted to the idea that the only truth is the truth that serves the liberation process, or both—declared that the Pope had finally come around to approving liberation theology. Yet others—and I expect they are closer to being right—believe the Pope was acting in the hope that what is valid in the language and concerns of liberation theology could be separated from its ideological and theological errors. What is necessary above all, John Paul says here and everywhere, is fidelity to the Church as constituted by the Gospel. The Gospel message implies and empowers Christian discipleship also in the social and political sphere, but what can be done in that sphere is not the Gospel, nor is the Gospel dependent upon it. To "reduce one dimension to the other" is to "suppress both." Politics is not salvation; salvation is not politics. The political has its own integrity. Propositions about what should be done to change the world must be acted upon. But there is another proposition that is "proper" to the Church. It is the proposition about what has been done, is being done, and will be done by God in Christ to save the world. To reduce either proposition to the other is to deny both. The course of fidelity *in statu viatoris* is to hold both propositions in paradox until the paradox is superseded by that final advent when everything, including politics, will be salvation in the eternal *polis* of the redeemed.

45. AN INSTRUCTION ON FREEDOM AND LIBERATION

The most systematic official response of the Roman Catholic Church to liberation theology is the "Instruction on Christian Freedom and Liberation" issued in the spring of 1986 by the Congregation for the Doctrine of the Faith. The Instruction bears the explicit approval of the Pope, an approval that he has strongly reiterated on several occasions, lest there be any doubt on the matter. At least some commentators expressed surprise at the very high level of theological and political argumentation in the document. Such surprise may be explained by the widely broadcast expectation that the Congregation and its prefect were simply out to "get" liberation theologians. The Instruction is marked not only by nuanced argumentation but also by ecumenical tone and substance. There is nothing narrowly Roman about this statement. It attempts to set out "values, lines of thought and patterns of living which are valid for the whole human community." People of all faiths, and none, have reason to ponder the meaning of liberation in a world obsessed by the subject. In that connection, the 1986 Instruction deserves a much broader audience than those immediately concerned about internal disputes in the Roman Catholic Church. It is not too much to say that the Instruction may be the most intellectually impressive and potentially significant statement on theology and politics to have emerged from any official church source in some years. No responsible discussion of these questions can bypass it. No serious discussant should want to.

In September 1984 the Congregation issued an "Instruction on Certain Aspects of the Theology of Liberation." That document was a vigorous critique of the alleged synthesis of Christianity and Marxism. According to the Vatican, the synthesis was lamentably short on Christianity. The 1984 Instruction met with cries of outraged innocence from liberation theologians and their sympathizers. Numerous articles and even books were written "exposing" it as an analytically simplistic and ham-fisted exercise in Roman authoritarianism. Critics deplored its failure to name names and to cite chapter and verse. Of course, had the Instruction been so specific, the cries of protest would have been magnified. As it was, all but the most partisan liberationists acknowledged that the propositions challenged by the Instruction were in fact commonplaces in the literature of liberation theology.

When the 1984 Instruction was issued, the Congregation said that another Instruction was on the way. It would deal more positively with the themes of liberation. Much of the religious and general press interpreted this to mean that some in the Vatican thought that the first Instruction was too negative toward liberation theology and the new statement would "balance" that with a more irenic tone. Indeed, the tone of the 1986 Instruction is generally positive and irenic, but there is not the slightest variation from the earlier criticism of liberation theology. Lest anyone thought Rome was retracting that criticism, the new document said of the 1984 Instruction: "Far from being outmoded, these warnings appear ever more timely and relevant. . . . Between the two documents there exists an organic relationship. They are to be read in the light of each other."

It may seem curious at first that some liberation theologians and their allies promptly hailed the second Instruction as an official vindication of their position. While the second Instruction is clearly not a blessing of liberation theology, it is much more than a bashing of liberation theology.

The sharpest criticisms, as made explicit in the 1984 Instruction, are implicitly in the 1986 Instruction, but chiefly it intended to set forth positively the theological, ethical, and political considerations that must shape the right ordering of human society. That right ordering looks very much like a theory of democratic governance, and is most specifically set against the totalitarian temptation in all its forms. Why the proponents of Marxist theory and friends of Marxist-Leninist movements think this new Instruction is a great improvement over the first Instruction or even an endorsement of their position is something of a puzzle.

The puzzle may have something to do with the fact that the Vatican has in the last two years demonstrated the seriousness of its intention to assert its teaching authority. Faced with an assertive Vatican that cannot be intimidated and is not inclined to wink at aberrations, the aberrant resort to "creative interpretation" of Vatican pronouncements. Thus criticism is interpretively neutralized or even turned into endorsement. One can say that a document does not mean what it says in the hope that it will take another two years for the Vatican to put out another document saying that it meant what it said, which document can, in turn, be interpreted as not meaning what it says, and so on and on until the present pope is replaced by a more "enlightened" successor. We do not say that this is what some liberation theologians are up to, but, were that their strategy, it would help relieve the widespread puzzlement about why they are saying that the "Instruction on Christian Freedom and Liberation" is favorable to their cause. It should be noted in passing that, while we do not say that this is what the liberationists are up to, it is the strategy that some of them have publicly endorsed ("The only truth is the truth that serves the liberation process"). Also, it is what Ratzinger explicitly, and John Paul implicitly, have accused liberation theologians of being up to. The charge, quite simply and solemnly, is that they, or at least some of them, are acting in bad faith.

In the language characteristic of statements by the Pope, the document begins by noting the contemporary "awareness of man's freedom and dignity, together with the affirmation of the inalienable rights of individuals and peoples." "The church of Christ makes these aspirations her own, while exercising discernment in the light of the Gospel, which is by its very nature a message of freedom and liberation." Thus the theme of the Instruction of 1986 is set at the start: The question is not simply freedom and liberation but what do Christians mean by freedom and liberation. Jesus said, "The truth will make you free" (John 8:32) and declared himself to be that liberating truth (John 14:6). Thus freedom is a gift from God, and "the church receives all that she has to offer to mankind." As the document repeatedly asserts, "Through his cross and resurrection, Christ has brought about our redemption, which is liberation in the strongest sense of the word since it has freed us from the most radical evil, namely sin and the power of death."

The truth about redemption is "thus the root and the rule of freedom the foundation and the measure of all liberating action." This is in sharpest possible contrast to claims that the liberationist struggle is itself the measure of truth, and that any truth that would presume to judge the revolutionary truth is counterrevolutionary "false consciousness." The Instruction gives generous credit to understandings of liberation that have not been explicitly Christian in their expression. At the same time, it makes an ecumenical appeal for recognition that the "traditional patrimony" of all Christians is the "first source" of modernity's aspiration to freedom. In other words, the Church does not view the modern aspiration to freedom as alien or threatening. On the contrary, Christianity is responsible for having generated that aspiration, and Christians should therefore accept responsibility for clarifying the nature of the freedom to which humanity aspires. The document sympathetically traces ideas of freedom from the Renaissance, through the Reformation, the Enlightenment, and the French Revolution. Here and elsewhere American readers may wonder why there is no reference to the American experiment in the politics of freedom. This is, in that respect, a very European document and reflects what we have suggested is a blind spot of both Ratzinger and John Paul with respect to the distinctiveness of what Murray termed "the American proposition."

The Instruction asserts that, while "modern liberation movements" guided by the secular Enlightenment have "led to remarkable successes," they are far from fulfilling their original ambitions. In the "new forms of servitude and new terrors" of recent history, the secular movements have revealed the "serious ambiguities" that have plagued their guiding idea of freedom from the beginning. For example, the struggle of workers for their legitimate rights is necessary, "but more often than not the just demands of the worker movement have led to new forms of servitude, being inspired by concepts which ignored the transcendental vocation of the human person and attributed to man a purely earthly destiny." So also poor nations under colonialism struggled for freedom only to be betrayed by "unscrupulous regimes or tyrannies which scoff at human rights with impunity. . . . The people thus reduced to powerlessness merely have a change of masters."

The "deadly ambiguity" of modern liberationisms is the result of an exclusive emphasis upon freedom *from.* Normative morality and, most emphatically, belief in God are viewed as "alienating." "Why do liberation movements which had roused great hopes result in regimes in which the citizens' freedom, beginning with the first of these freedoms, which is religious freedom, become enemy No. 1?" The answer is that such movements cannot tolerate the expression of the transcendent truth by which they are to be held accountable. Among Christians, however, "the little ones and the poor" have kept alive an understanding of the "depth of freedom." Under the worst of circumstances they know the dignity of being children of God. "This sharing in the knowledge of God is their emancipation," and they cannot be robbed of it by any regime nor by "the dominating claims of the learned." The last reference is undoubtedly to those who claim that the poor must have their "consciousness raised" in order to understand their oppression and struggle against it. Here and elsewhere the Instruction strikes a populist note, suggesting that the learned must learn from the faith of the poor, while avoiding any false romanticizing of the very real plight of the poor and oppressed. Ratzinger does not want to enter into a contest over who speaks for the poor. While some of its more noted proponents may work in guarded villas and spend much of their time jetting between international conferences, it is fair to say that most of those in the Third World who embrace liberation theology are in their everyday lives closer to the situation of poor people than is, say, Cardinal Ratzinger. That, says the Instruction, is not the issue. The issue is that those who by their own admission are raising the consciousness of the poor cannot present themselves as the voice of the poor. To the extent the consciousness-raising is successful, it may be argued, the voice of the poor becomes but the echo of "the dominating claims of the learned."

"It is the poor, the object of God's special love, who understand best, and as it were instinctively, that the most radical liberation, which is liberation from sin and death, is the liberation accomplished by the death and resurrection of Christ," the Instruction asserts. Only when this "salvific" gift is firmly understood can the discussion move to the ethical and political. Christian freedom is a given; the question is then "education in the right use of freedom." The right use of freedom begins with the recognition that "the good is the goal of freedom." That good is ultimately, of course, unity with God in Christ. Those who forget the goal of the good "exalt the freedom of man or his 'historical praxis' by making this freedom the absolute principle of his being and becoming." But such theories are lethal, for they are "expressions of atheism or tend toward atheism by their own logic." Here it is indicated that some liberation theologians may be quite sincere in repudiating atheism but nonetheless are entangled in a "logic" that emerges from and tends toward atheism. Once again the assumption is that ideas are not like the pieces of a Tinkertoy set but are inherently related to one another.

The freedom given by God has direct implications for the social order. "In the social sphere, freedom is expressed and realized in actions, structures and institutions." Any liberation struggle that is not premised upon the freedom of the person portends only a new servitude. In addition, most talk and action about liberation are dead-ended because they do not take seriously the reality of sin in the human condition. By wishing to free himself from God and to be a god himself, man "becomes alienated from himself." Here and throughout, the Instruction intends to appropriate Marxist terminology and turn it on its head. In Marxist teaching, religion is the consequence of alienation. According to the Instruction, the heart of alienation is man's turn against God and into himself. "For by rejecting God he destroys the momentum of his aspiration to the infinite and of his vocation to share in the divine life."

In co-opting the favored imagery of liberation theology, the Instruction devotes considerable attention to the Exodus story and its implications. In agreement with many Jewish scholars, and against the habit of liberation theology, the Instruction emphasizes that the Exodus cannot be isolated from the covenant. The liberation is "within a covenant and for a covenant." It is right to underscore the role of "the poor of Yahweh," but always keeping in mind that "for them, the most tragic misfortune is the loss of this communion [with God]," which is established by the covenant. And so it is with Christians today. An evidence of the ecumenical sensibility of the Instruction is the employment of Reformation language in stressing that "the heart of the Christian experience of freedom is in justification by the grace received through faith and the church's sacraments." The ethical and political is not a means toward justification. Justification is a gift, and only when that is firmly established can we move to the ethical and political. "Having been reconciled with him and receiving this peace of Christ which the world cannot give, we are called to be peacemakers among all men."

The political process, then, is not salvific but is motored by the commandment to love the neighbor as we have been loved by God. "Love of neighbor knows no limits and includes enemies and persecutors." That is underscored repeatedly against the dogma of inevitable class conflict. Liberationists who say we must give justice priority over love are wrong. "There is no gap between love of neighbor and desire for justice. To contrast the two is to distort both love and justice." Similarly, the Christian understanding of our final, or eschatological, hope must not be compromised. This is not pie in the sky, the Instruction insists. "This hope does not weaken commitment to the progress of the earthly city, but rather gives it meaning and strength." In awaiting that ultimate liberation, the church does "discern the signs of the times" and point out movements "which advance liberation and those that are deceptive and illusory." But "the political and economic running of society is not a direct part of the church's mission."

At several points the Instruction lifts up the integrity of the political and emphasizes that it is primarily the sphere for the exercise of the vocation of the "faithful laity." Although the term "natural law" is not used, the idea is clearly expressed that Christians have no monopoly on the wisdom appropriate to the political sphere. The purpose of grace and evangelical morality "is to perfect and elevate a moral dimension which already belongs to human nature and with which the church concerns herself in the knowledge that this is a heritage belonging to all people by their very nature." In discussing the earthly and heavenly cities, the order of redemption and the order of creation, the Instruction comes very close to a Lutheran understanding of the twofold rule of God or the idea of "spheres of sovereignty" in some Calvinist thinking. Here and elsewhere, ecumenical theologians will find provocations to further research in the development of Catholic social teaching.

In examining the Beatitudes and other biblical texts, the Instruction finds a basis for the much-discussed "preferential option for the poor." But that is an idea that must be used with great care. "The special option for the poor, far from being a sign of particularism or sectarianism, manifests the universality of the church's being and mission. This option excludes no one. This is the reason why the church cannot express this option by means of reductive sociological and ideological categories which would make this preference a partisan choice and source of conflict." Again and again, the Instruction attempts to cut through the obfuscating jargon of liberationist ideology. For example, "A safe criterion for judgment and action is this: There can be no true liberation if from the very beginning the rights of freedom are not respected." In arguing against a perverse "individualism" and equally perverse "collectivism," the Instruction stresses that respect for freedom means respect for persons in their communities, especially in those communities that are called the mediating structures in society, such as family, church, and other voluntary associations. In sum, totalitarianism in all its forms must be denied because it would deny the "social space" essential to freedom.

The Instruction recognizes that many societies, indeed all societies, fail to conform fully to these norms of justice. Some violate these norms so egregiously and systematically that revolutionary change may be the appropriate course of action. Obviously this is the case with existing totalitarian societies. But in all cases the Instruction counsels that preference must be given to reform measures and the use of violence is a last resort. And some forms of violence, such as torture and terrorism, "one can never approve, whether perpetrated by established power or insurgents." The chief way to development is the proclamation of true gospel freedom, education in citizenship, and the formation of "a work culture" in which human persons exercise their dignity. "Thus the solution of most of the serious problems related to poverty is to be found in the promotion of a true civilization of work. In a sense, work is the key to the whole social question." Max Weber should have lived to see this ringing Roman Catholic affirmation of what he and others viewed as the "Protestant work ethic."

There are other elements in this document that seem to portend a further development in Catholic social teaching; at least some ideas are articulated with unprecedented forcefulness. Of particular interest is the sharp limitation placed on the power of both church and state, and the need for separation of powers within the state. Finally, and co-opting a favored text of liberationists, the Instruction ends with a meditation on

Mary's Magnificat. Far from being a call to revolutionary class struggle, the Magnificat reveals that "Mary is totally dependent on her Son and completely directed toward him by the impulse of her faith; and, at his side, she is the most perfect image of freedom and of the liberation of humanity and of the universe." One detects a note of pained dismay in the Instruction's comment on what it sees as the abuse of Marian piety: "It would be criminal to take the energies of popular piety and misdirect them toward a purely earthly plan of liberation, which would very soon be revealed as nothing more than an illusion and a cause of new forms of slavery."

In the continuing debates about religion and society, it is inevitable that the Instruction will be used for partisan purposes. Liberation theologians and their friends are disingenuous in pretending that the Instruction is a blessing for their enterprise. Their opponents, however, have missed the point if they take the Instruction to be no more than a bashing of liberation theology. Much more important than partisan blessings and bashings, the Instruction is a formidable intellectual and theological exercise in setting forth the Christian understanding of a free and just social order. It fleshes out, in response to a new situation, some of the key ideas of Vatican II, especially the "Declaration on Religious Freedom." It represents a continuing development in Roman Catholic social teaching and is an ecumenical and interreligious invitation to join in a new conversation about connections between transcendent hope and temporal responsibilities. The argument is not convincing on every score, and a number of points might have been developed with greater imagination, but after the Instruction of 1984, and especially that of 1986, only the obtuse or the mendacious will claim that Rome has not articulated its response to current political theologies with great care, clarity, and persuasive force.

46. THEOLOGY AND POLITICS—A CAUTIONARY TALE

In examining liberation theology and responses to it, it becomes obvious that the stakes are very high indeed. This is no squabble within the theological professoriat, nor simply a dispute about where church authority draws the line. The most consistent liberationists and their most consistent opponents agree that in this contest almost everything is at stake. The contest is over the continuity and identity of Christian teaching; in fact it is over salvation, and one cannot get more ultimate than that. The questions raised by liberation theology, however, are not entirely new. Whether we think in terms of centuries or concentrate on this century, striking parallels are to be found in disputes of other times and other places. As we discussed at the very beginning of this study, when it comes to concrete situations Christians have always been more than a little confused about what it means to be in the world but not of the world.

And, just when they think they are getting the hang of it, the situation changes, and they have to start all over again. In this section we examine some of the ways Christians have tried to cope with this confusion, especially as it applies to political commitment—and to the limits of political commitment. We end up with a story from this century. It is told as a cautionary tale. The story is true, and very sad. The story has been formative in the thinking of Joseph Ratzinger, and he often refers to it. It should be formative in the thinking of anyone who thinks very hard about the political dimensions of being in the world but not of it.

Most Christians—that is to say, orthodox Christians—have known that politics is not an end in itself, unless, of course, one is speaking of the ultimately "new politics," which is the right ordering of reality in the coming of the Kingdom of God. Politics is directed beyond itself toward a public or common good. But we live in a time in which many educated people doubt that there is such a thing as the good, and therefore the common good is at best a useful myth. The common good without reference to the good results in a politics that has no transcendent goal; it results in a politics that assumes that man is the best thing in the world. Indeed, it assumes that man is the only thing in the world, or at least the only thing that matters. (If other things matter, they matter only because man has decided that they matter.) The consequence is that there is then no "ought" in politics. This poses a severe problem if one agrees with Aristotle that *the* political question is finally the moral question: How ought we to order our life together? But without some understanding of the good, there is no "ought" other than the "ought" that results from the interaction of human interests and desires. What will be, will be; and what will be, will be declared to be what should be. The "ought of results," however, is no "ought" at all, for it lacks the prescriptive force of the word "ought."

Without the prescriptive "ought," there is finally no politics in the classic sense at all. Regardless of how they felt about Aristotle, or whether they ever heard of Aristotle, most Christians over the centuries have agreed that there ought to be an "ought" in politics. Even New Testament Christianity, with its minimalist expectations of politics, assumed that political power should have something to do with the punishment of the wicked and the reward of the good (Rom. 13). By the fourth century, Christians such as Eusebius of Caesarea would promote a much more intimate connection between politics and the good. And so it continued through Aquinas and Calvin, and through the Protestant social gospel movement in this country, with its celebration of the "holy trinity" of Progress, Democracy, and America.

The good to which the "ought" is related in Christian thought is finally the Absolute Good who is God. That is, politics, along with everything else, ought to be in accord with the will of God. The ways in which the will of God is known are variously stated in the several traditions of

Christian thought: in Jesus above all, in Scriptures, in divinely guided tradition, in natural law, in the orders of creation, in common grace, in general revelation, in human reason. Most Christians have conditioned their political expectations by an "eschatological proviso" that makes clear that everything will not be ordered according to the will of God short of the End Time. Only the End Time can satisfy what the "Instruction on Christian Freedom and Liberation" calls our "aspiration to the infinite." On this nether side of the End Time, Christians have tried in different, and frequently contradictory, ways to relate the good and the common good. In what is called the "sectarian" option, Christians have seen a very close connection between the good and the common good, but the commonality in that case is limited to the "new humanity" of the community of faith, which is sharply marked off from "the world." Apart from the politics of its own community, the sectarian option is typically apolitical or antipolitical, and is therefore somewhat marginal to our present considerations.

The more classical traditions have employed concepts such as natural law in order to affirm a convergence or congruence between God's will as perceived by faith and as perceived by reason. In this sense the classic or catholic tradition is a more truly public tradition. Within the Church, humanity receives by grace a further measure of fulfillment, but it is emphasized that this humanity is the common humanity of all, believer and unbeliever alike. In other words, grace does not destroy but crowns nature. It is further emphasized that the one Lord is Lord over all, so there is a will of God both for the redeemed and the unredeemed. Within the catholic stream, Lutherans have spoken of the "two kingdoms," or, better stated, the "two-fold rule of God." Calvinists in the Abraham Kuyper tradition speak of "spheres of sovereignty" by which the world is to be rightly ordered. And of course Roman Catholics have spoken of natural law. What all have in common is a theologically based understanding of the good that gives substance to the "ought" of Aristotelian politics and makes it possible to speak of the common good.

What all have in common is a theology of politics. A theology of politics affirms the political enterprise itself and gives assurance that the "ought" that is pursued in that enterprise can be congruent with the will of God. A theology of politics means, in the present context, something different from a political theology. The term *political theology* has been variously employed. By political theology I mean theology that entails a political direction or course of action. A political theology is more closely tied to political ideology. A theology of politics grants a large measure of integrity to politics itself; it speaks more of creation and preservation, of the public rules by which social life is to be ordered and which are accessible to all rational actors. It is with this understanding of a theology of politics that Luther could say he would rather be ruled by a wise Turk than by a foolish Christian. A political theology, as we have seen, is something else.

A political theology speaks more of "reading the signs of the times" than of obedience to abiding definitions of the good. Put differently, the good is not so much that which God has decreed as it is that which God is doing. History is the story of the "God who acts," to use the phrase from an older school of biblical theology, and it is the Christian's responsibility to get with God's action. Political theology readily becomes politicized theology and theologized politics. It is susceptible to confusing whatever is happening—or whatever we think is happening—with God's acting. Thus the slogan, "The world sets the agenda for the Church." Such political theology frequently turns into the paths of enthusiasm and fanaticism.

All that said, however, political theology has been with us for centuries and is not likely to disappear before the Kingdom Come. And that for very good reasons. Whatever the specifics of its politics, political theology speaks of change in a world that manifestly needs changing. In addition, almost no Christian has such a static understanding of God's will for the world that he does not believe that God is still acting in history. Believing that, he seeks to discern and participate in God's acting. Even the most convinced proponents of natural law or of God's twofold rule have at times read the signs of the times and discerned God's judgment and leading in the events of history. Thus the common good is to be determined not only by eternal rules but also by the active ruling of the One who is the Absolute Good.

We have been examining today's heated controversy among Christians over political theologies. Almost nobody today advances the political theology of the earlier social gospel movement as represented by, for instance, Walter Rauschenbusch. The afterglow of that movement is still evident in the fussy benevolence of old-line Protestantism, but seldom is substantive theological argument mustered in its defense. A more vibrant, if not very persuasive, political theology is advanced in the United States by the religious Right today. Here one encounters strong theological assertions about God's law for the ordering of society and lively apocalyptic readings of how God is acting, as revealed by "Bible prophecy," in the contingent events reported on the evening news. In other quarters there are also today cautious probings toward a political theology of democratic capitalism and of liberal democracy. But these are likely to remain very cautious indeed, since those who are sympathetic to the effort have been made suspicious of political theology itself.

One reason for their suspicion is the influence of the most aggressive form of political theology today, namely, the liberation theology we have been discussing in these pages. We owe a great debt to the liberation theologians for forcing us to think again and more clearly about the difference between a theology of politics and a political theology, about the connections between the common good and the Absolute Good. And this brings us to that very instructive story. It might be called "The Case of Emanuel Hirsch." But of course it is not just about Emanuel Hirsch. It is an instructive story because it is representative of the case of many a Christian, then and now. Hirsch is little known today, but at one time he was ranked as a giant of twentieth-century German theology, along with such as Barth, Bultmann, Brunner, and Tillich. He was, among other things, a preeminent authority on Kierkegaard and sought with existential urgency to discern and act upon the signs of his times. Born in 1888, Hirsch was, as a student and young teacher, an intimate friend and intellectual soul mate of Paul Tillich. Both were the product of the best of nineteenth-century theological liberalism, and both rejected Karl Barth's stringent reaction to that heritage. They were not prepared to say with Barth that there is an "infinite qualitative distinction" between God and man, between God's ways and man's ways in history. Together they searched for the convergences between the Divine and the human, for the correlations, as it were, between theological theory and social praxis. Although their paths were to diverge dramatically in the 1930s, Tillich and Hirsch were asking many of the same questions and coming to many of the same answers.

Hirsch, Tillich, and most of the leading intellectuals of the time shared a passionate contempt for liberal, bourgeois democracy. This was also the case, although it is often forgotten, with the theologians who produced the Barmen Declaration in 1934 and became the heroes of the Confessing Church in opposition to Hitler. The Weimar Republic, they were all convinced, was a time of deepest crisis, what Tillich termed a "Kairos" of monumental historic importance. Tillich developed what was called a Kairos theology, and Hirsch shared fully his sense of almost apocalyptic urgency. To understand the turn that Hirsch took, one must know that he was a deeply committed Christian, a modern man devoted to reason and unwilling to jettison the fruits of science and intellectual inquiry. In addition, he was politically committed to "the people," the Volk, and sought Germany's liberation from what was viewed as the oppressive yoke imposed by the victorious powers after World War I. Hirsch saw reality from "the underside of history" and thus saw through the ways, or thought he saw through the ways, in which the vaunted "freedoms" of liberalism disguised and legitimated continuing exploitation. Because of the terrible triumph of nazism for a time, we see it in retrospect as a movement of the powerful against the oppressed. But it was not always so, and that is critically important to understanding this story. In its beginning and even in its triumph, the Nazi movement understood itself to be an insurgency of the oppressed against the oppressors, of the little people against the elites, of the native against the "cosmopolitan," of the indigenous culture of the Volk against foreign and alien exploiters (the last being represented preeminently, but by no means exclusively, by "international Jewry").

Hirsch wanted a political ethic rooted in Christianity, although borrowing freely from other sources for purposes of analysis. Liberal democracy, he believed, was riddled with internal contradictions, and, in its chaotic give and take, truth had been reduced to "a party matter." Hirsch wanted a potent truth, a revolutionary truth, that could cut through the debilitating relativities of liberalism. "What we are missing today," he wrote, "is contemplation of the ultimate bases of all our political as well as social historical judgments." A radical struggle was required to discover "guidelines for the life of the individual and the society as a whole." The people are hungry for a sense of purpose, a great cause. The sense of crisis is to be welcomed because "crises make us young," according to Hirsch. The revolution "would be a hard path" but at least it would be "a path which has a destination." The new order that Hirsch desired must agree with the Marxists in rejecting the "old Hegel," who elevated the state to the point where the free act is made impossible. At the same time, it must reject the loose and atomizing individualism of liberal democracy. The alternative is freedom that is in solidarity with the people and thus in the service of authentic community. The revolution must be led by a vanguard that constitutes itself as a "community of conscience" leading the entire society to become such a community of conscience.

In this struggle, violence could by no means be ruled out. Hirsch had little patience for pacifists and others who "sentimentally" distorted the liberating force of authentic Christianity. In any event, violence between oppressed and oppressor is inevitable. "War," he wrote, "is a tool of history," and history has its own laws. Against the socialism of the Left, Hirsch would choose the "socialism" in National Socialism. In this socialism, the state would not disappear but would closely regulate the lives of all its citizens and provide for their needs. (In this respect, the state would do in principle what the state attempts to do in practice where Marxist socialism has come to power, always remembering that the party-state decides what people need.) The struggle must be advanced by people who believe that God is at work in it. Against Barth and his followers, Hirsch declared his refusal to view history "as a region abandoned by God." Hirsch and those who agreed with him had no use for the "dualisms" by which the ultimate questions of salvation were kept at a critical distance from the political and social struggle.

Hirsch underscored faith and action in the concreteness of history. He was suspicious of liberal abstractions and for this reason opposed participation in the ecumenical movement of the time. Whatever the "subjective" good intentions of well-meaning Christians, the "objective" consequence was to distract energies from the struggle of the people. The time, he insisted, was not one for pious univeralisms but for deepened commitment to the concrete cause. The conventional distinction between "the sacred" and "the secular" must be challenged. The Church is indeed holy, but it is not an ethereal and disembodied holiness; it is a holiness that intersects with the tasks of history. The Confessing Christians of Barmen were wrong to set their holiness against history. Those who sought to bring Christianity into alignment with National Socialism, the *Deutsche Christen* as they were called, understood that it is precisely Christian faithfulness that requires taking sides. As for those who say that the Church should transcend partisanships, or offer some kind of "third way," or be a forum for the critical engagement of all proposed ways, this is not possible according to Hirsch. The withholding of commitment, he said, can only result in the continuation of what Kierkegaard dismissively called "the all-encompassing debate about everything."

Hirsch did not claim to know the future. His analytic tools included no "scientific laws of history" by which it was certain that the revolution would succeed in history. The future, he said, "lies in that which comes." He did not take lightly National Socialism's restrictions of freedom, but he dared to believe that "all tensions within our new restrictions upon freedom are tensions of an encounter with God." Hirsch asked, "Is it then true that such an encounter with God is the ultimate secret of the German turning point?" If the answer is yes, then a price must be paid without liberal compunctions. Hirsch read the signs of the times and answered yes. Moreover, those who refused to answer the question were in "objective" fact answering negatively. As Hirsch said again and again in his own way, not to decide is to decide; or, as a later generation would put it, if you aren't part of the solution, you are part of the problem.

Unlike the Marxists, Hirsch had no dogmatic consolation that, developments notwithstanding, he had chosen the right side. "Only in the depths of belief in justification by faith was it possible to allow the ethical involvement of the Christian in the historical community. This is not built on the basis of a law, but out of merciful responsibility based on the general self-testimony and rule of God in nature and history." Political commitment, in this view, is to accept Luther's familiar (and usually misunderstood) invitation to "sin boldly." Although Hirsch urged the Church to be partisan, he did not go so far as today's liberationist proponents of "the partisan church." That is, the true Church and the struggle were not coextensive in Hirsch's view, nor were the grace and mercy of God to which the Church witnessed equated with the doctrine of the struggle. The struggle remained in all its parts always under judgment. It may be *an* encounter with God in history, but, according to Hirsch, there is no theological warrant for saying it is *the* encounter with God in history.

The critical thing, according to Hirsch, is that we make concrete choices in history. Barth, he said, thought the Church could and should proclaim its message "as if nothing had happened." Hirsch rejected this as nonsense. "God does not speak to my heart today as if nothing has happened. . . . He carries the danger that lies therein: He is the Lord and does not need to fear for his truth." Nor, contra the Confessing Church that opposed Hitler, need the Church fear the revolution's encroachment on what had traditionally been Church responsibilities in areas such as education, health care, and tending to the needs of orphans and the mentally ill. None of these activities are integral to the Church's essential mission, Hirsch argued, and were only necessary as Band-Aid ministries so long as the state was not living up to its total responsibility for the society. The Church should not complain but should rather acclaim the revolution's assumption of its proper responsibility in these areas. Indeed, the entire posture and structure of the Church should be changed in order to reflect "leadership as passionate will" in support of the revolution. "If that is not easily understood nor understood by all today, that is because it has not yet gone into everyone's blood that National Socialism, based on the right of historical change, is becoming the self-evident and binding form of life for all Germans." Against the counterrevolutionary Confessing Church, Hirsch tirelessly argued that the *Deutsche Christen* movement was the true people's church of the historical moment. But even then he could not bring himself to explicitly excommunicate from "the true church" those who read the signs of the times differently.

"There exists between German *Volkstum* and Christian belief absolutely no division or contradiction to make it difficult as a German to be a Christian, or as a Christian a German," Hirsch wrote. Those who claimed such a division or contradiction were in fact misusing Christianity against the common good as represented by the people's movement and its führer. Hirsch well understood that his argument required a new theology to accommodate the new historical moment. This requires also a reformulation of the Church's self-understanding; it requires what liberation theologians would a half century later call "ecclesiogensis." "The fate of Christianity in Western civilization depends on this," Hirsch wrote, "that in Protestant Christianity the men do not die out who offer this crisis of reformulation as the path ordained by God to our veracity. In this crisis and with its means, they become bearers of a historical process which will build a new Christian concept of history consistent with the new circumstances and the new understanding." Despite his theoretical statements about the uncertainty of historical outcomes, Hirsch ended up giving a moral and theological carte blanche to the Nazi regime. He did not deny that the revolutionary leadership made "mistakes" nor that the leaders were themselves "imperfect," but to focus on these was to run the risk of being "paralyzed by uncertainty" and thus to miss the historical moment and its imperative, which, it must be remembered, were also God's moment and God's imperative.

Robert Ericksen, author of *Theologians Under Hitler* (1985), believes that between Tillich and Hirsch there was not all that much theological difference. He writes that "Tillich jumped left, believing he had interpreted God correctly, and Hirsch jumped right." Either jump, Ericksen suggests, was not theologically mandated but based upon a prudential judgment of historical contingencies. Of course "the judgment of history" has gone against Hirsch, but, according to Ericksen, neither theology nor reason could at the time have settled the dispute between historical actors such as Hirsch and Tillich. Ericksen seems to suggest that they paid their theological money and made their political choice, and some won and some lost. Not surprisingly, Tillich himself had a somewhat different view of the matter.

Writing from Union Seminary, New York, Tillich addressed a long open letter to his friend and colleague Emanuel Hirsch. It is dated October 1, 1934, and goes on for more than thirty published pages. The letter is at times hostile and at times cordial, reflecting the pain of having come to a parting of the ways with an intimate. Also, Tillich reveals both resentment and embarrassment—resentment because he claims that Hirsch has stolen from his own "Kairos doctrine" without giving him credit, and embarrassment because he implicitly recognizes that his "Kairos doctrine" could be taken in the direction that Hirsch had taken it. Of course Tillich claimed that Hirsch had distorted what he, Tillich, intended to say, and the letter is in large part an effort to clarify just what he had intended to say.

Tillich's basic argument is that Hirsch had collapsed theology into politics, giving an uncritical spiritual legitimation to his judgment of contingent events. "I can summarize my critique . . . in this sentence: *You have perverted the prophetic, eschatologically conceived Kairos doctrine into a sacerdotal-sacramental consecration of a current event*" (emphasis his). Hirsch had, according to Tillich, turned theology into ideology. Tillich quotes Hirsch's claim that true theology is possible only "if it is altogether open from within to the great and the new, which has broken through with the National Socialist movement. Its world view should be the sustaining, naturally historical basis of life for the German man of evangelical faith." In making such claims, Tillich wrote, "you have approximated the year 1933 so closely to the year 33, that it has gained for you the meaning of an event in the history of salvation."

By refusing the Church its own space in which to say both no and yes to historical developments, said Tillich, "you consecrate instead of disclosing." Indeed, Christians must make historical judgments and take the resulting risks, but in doing so they must "acknowledge the relativizing of what is risked in all its consequences." Tillich accuses Hirsch of historical myopia, of apotheosizing a specific historical moment as *the* moment of definitive change, to the neglect of two thousand years of Christian history, to the neglect of the longer reaches of human experience, and, most particularly, to the neglect of *the* definitive revelation in the Christ event.

The question of ecclesiology is also critical to Tillich's argument. The role of "the blood-bond" in Nazi ideology denied to Jews who had become Christians full standing in Church and society. Tillich's point is that unity in Christ must transcend any other bond of race or nation or class.

A partisan church that denies this transcendence is a repudiation of the Church. "Are you, precisely as a theologian, called to subordinate the sacramental consanguinity of Christianity, which is given with the Lord's Supper, to the natural historical consanguinity?" Tillich asks. In other words, does solidarity with "the people" take precedence over the solidarity established by God in Word and sacrament? In asking such questions, Tillich is pressing Hirsch to make explicit the radical ramifications of his position.

In his letter Tillich may also be regretting some of his own strident condemnations of liberal democracy, condemnations that had been a commonplace among intellectuals during the Weimar period. Tillich presses Hirsch on what follows "the destruction of democracy." It is fine to talk about a new order and a more just society, but, by refusing to be specific and believable about the shape of that new order, such talk "drives you into a mysticism from which nothing concretely follows." Or, more likely, what follows is "despotism." It is not enough, writes Tillich, to issue "a declaration of hate . . . against everything democratic." Tillich even asks whether Hegel might not have been right after all when he posited "the Christian-Germanic notion of freedom in opposition to the Asian and pre-Christian principle of despotism." Even the so-called negative freedoms of bourgeois liberalism begin to take on great value when one contemplates the alternatives, Tillich suggests.

But the gravamen of Tillich's letter is not whether Hirsch is right or wrong in his political judgment, as such, but whether he understands what is at stake theologically and spiritually. When the idea of the good is subsumed in a partisan definition of the common good, there is no room for the spirit. In order for the spirit to assert itself, "it must have a space in which it can come to yea-saying through nay-saying." "The first step of spirit is to say no to what is immediately given. Does it not contradict the totalitarian ideas, as you portray it, to provide space for the development of an existential no? There have been states that have denied spirit this space and have destroyed spirit in itself. Has the seriousness of this question never disturbed you in your enthusiastic portrayal of the total state and in the demand of ruthless intervention, which is said to be better than persuasion?" In appealing to historical experience with totalitarianism, of course, Tillich did not have the advantage of knowing the Soviet Gulag Archipelago so massively documented by Solzhenitsyn or the despotisms of Cuba, Vietnam, and Cambodia. And, of course, neither he nor Hirsch knew at the time what the Nazi regime would become. But Tillich did have a larger measure of prescience in understanding the historical consequences inherent in and invited by totalitarian principles.

The principle for Christians, Tillich argued, is that there is both a *reservatum* and an *obligatum*, a no and a yes, in all political commitments. Hirsch, like contemporary totalitarians, was prepared to affirm a place for the *reservatum* in the privacy of the individual's personal relation to God. But he does not grant the right of such a *reservatum* to the Church and its "independent historical place." But in refusing that, says Tillich, Hirsch also cancels the personal *reservatum,* for "you make it impotent over against the *Weltanschauungen* or myths that sustain the totalitarian state." Tillich takes pains to absolve his own version of socialism from this totalitarian crime against the spirit: "Religious Socialism knew, when accepting the doctrine of the *reservatum religiosum,* that the religious can never be dissolved into the socialist, that the church is something quite apart from the *Kairos,* that is, from the promise and demand that Religious Socialism saw in the broadly visible irruption of the new social and spiritual arrangement of the society. You took over the *obligatum* but gave up the *reservatum*—the charge that is basically the theme of my whole letter."

At the end of his letter, Tillich says his hope is that "enthusiasts could be made into believing realists." As an example of enthusiasm, he cites Hirsch's words: "When we have the courage, on the basis of the faith that obeys this truth [of the Gospel], to enter into something human-historical with our yes, then the unfathomable sublimity of the truth accompanies us and, in its way, reigns in this human-historical thing." That claim, Tillich makes clear, is not simply an instance of enthusiasm but of idolatry.

Now many years ago, in *The Origins of Totalitarianism (1966),* Hannah Arendt made the case for the similarities and frequent identities between National Socialism and Marxist-Leninism. Many intellectuals, including theologians, still resist that argument, although it has been reinforced by scholarship and historical experience since Arendt. I believe that Karl Dietrich Bracher, for instance, is correct when he argues in *The Age of Ideologies (1982),* that the significant line of division from the nineteenth century through to the present is between those who support and those who oppose the idea of liberal democracy. But our more specific concern here is the theological contribution to maintaining the tension between the good and all definitions of the common good, between a theology of politics and a political theology. Essential to that contribution, I believe, is what Tillich describes as the tension, even dialectic, between *obligatum* and *reservatum,* always remembering that the *reservatum* is prior and more certain. In the absence of the *reservatum,* the *obligatum* becomes spiritually idolatrous and politically disastrous.

As with Emanuel Hirsch and the *Deutschen Christen,* so with much liberation theology today, the *obligatum* has swallowed up the *reservatum.* As Hirsch believed that the truth "reigns in this human-historical thing," so Juan Luis Segundo declares that faith is "the spirit of *freedom for history, of taste for the future, of openness for the provisional and relative,"* in short a *freedom for ideologies.* The critical distance from all ideologies that makes possible the prophetic witness of the Church is eliminated. As Dennis

McCann puts it, "From Segundo's perspective, this religious reservation represents not an ultimate principle of criticism, but one more outmoded Christian ideology. Since it tends to 'throw a dash of cold water' on the political enthusiasm necessary for 'real-life revolution,' it in turn must be relativized . . ." Segundo rejects the traditional idea of the Kingdom of God as "something metahistorical and a disgusted turning away from real-life history." Segundo favorably quotes James Cone: "There are no universal truths in the process of liberation; the only truth is liberation itself." One might say it is an assertion worthy of Emanuel Hirsch, but Hirsch was a careful thinker and never went so far in eliminating the *reservatum*.

Christian realism, as represented by Reinhold Niebuhr, and liberation theology, as represented by Segundo, "dramatize the current impasse in practical theology," according to McCann. It is the same impasse reached by Tillich and Hirsch. To some political definitions of the common good, Christians must say an unequivocal no. There can be little or no reservation, for example, in our condemnation of National Socialism or the regimes of today's Cambodia or Iran. Such regimes are evil in principle and practice, and we should not hesitate to say so. The tragic truth is that history has thrown up numerous distortions of the common good to which the Church can and must say no. Short of the Kingdom of God, however, there is no politically established definition of the common good—nor any candidate for such establishment—to which the Church can say an unequivocal yes. In the exercise of the political *obligatum*, Christians can and do take risks, but we have no right, indeed it is not too much to say that it is apostasy, to risk the surrender of the critical *reservatum*. Against all despots—whether or not they are totalitarian in principle—the first spiritual and political obligation of the Christian community is to struggle to maintain its space for saying yes and no.

We have, I believe, not done justice to contemporary liberation theology until we recognize that it is indeed as radical as many of its theologians claim it is. A careful evaluation of arguments suggests that, compared with the typical claims of liberation theology, Emanuel Hirsch was temperate in his endorsement of National Socialism. Tillich was right to criticize Hirsch for neglecting the *reservatum* implicit in the "eschatological proviso." Dominant forms of liberation theology do not neglect but explicitly deny both the proviso and the reservation. Indeed the "dialectic" employed in such liberation theology has already anticipated and anulled the criticism that Tillich tried to bring to bear in the case of Hirsch. It is a dialectic that, to use its own terms, has negated the negation. We are surely justified, I believe, in describing this as "the impasse" in contemporary theological thought about politics and ideology.

There are no doubt many reasons why theologians in the United States have failed to address this impasse with greater lucidity and candor. One reason no doubt is understandable feelings of insecurity and guilt about our more-favored placement in the global scheme of things, especially when it is alleged that our economic and political well-being is purchased at the price of the misery of most human beings on earth. Another reason is a laudable sympathy for the social and political crises experienced by the people for whom such liberation theologians claim to speak. Yet another and less edifying reason is that there is a certain condescension among us North Americans. It may be that we hesitate to criticize people whom we do not really view as peers in theological discourse. This is evident when we refuse to take them at their word, even though they insist again and again that they mean exactly what they are saying. And finally we fail to criticize because we are afraid. I suspect that more than a few of us are morally intimidated by their claim that, if we are not more or less uncritically on their side, we must be on the side of their oppressors, real or alleged.

It may seem harsh to speak of moral intimidation. After all, theologians, too, want to be on "the right side" of struggles for justice. Theologians are, at least in some cases, also political actors. As political actors we may be inclined from time to time to excuse an excess of rhetoric if the cause is right. But even in causes that seem almost unequivocally just, we cannot, I believe, suspend our critical theological faculties. Here again it is a question of loyalties, whether primacy be given to the theological enterprise or to the advancement of a favored ideological-political direction. I fully recognize that that distinction is itself disputed by some liberation theologians who contend that the theological enterprise must be defined by political struggle. Thus the necessary tension between the two is collapsed, the courage and the admitted embarrassment of maintaining the paradox is precluded.

On the question of making political judgments, I cannot agree with Ericksen's suggestion that the difference between Tillich's and Hirsch's judgments is quite arbitrary. Hirsch should have known (and liberation theologians should know today) that movements that deny in principle a normative reason by which they can be brought under judgment are not to be trusted. Hirsch should have known (and liberation theologians should know today) that movements that claim a right to do terrible things to people in order to achieve their purposes will more than likely end up doing those terrible things. It is fair—no, it is necessary—to add that Hirsch in 1934 was not as culpable as are theologians who serve as apologists for Marxist-Leninist revolution today. Of course Hirsch should have taken the ominous doctrines of nazism, as set forth, for example, in *Mein Kampf*, more seriously, but there never had been a National Socialist regime before. The principles of nazism had no track record in practice. It was possible, even if recklessly self-deceptive, to accent the positive and hope for the best, as Hirsch did. None of these things can be said of Marxism-Leninism in the twentieth century.

The historical evidence notwithstanding, such historical-political judgments will be disputed by many today. Whatever has been the experience with revolutions past, it is today argued that *this* revolution is different, *this* experiment has never been tried before, *this* will turn out to be the new order based on Marxist scientific analysis and Christian revolutionary hope. The force of our criticism is thus stymied by appeal to evidence from the future, evidence that of course none of us can possess. In 1934 Tillich had to admit that, despite the troubling evidences, he could not *prove* that Hirsch was wrong in his political judgment. It was conceivable, Tillich had to admit, that National Socialism would establish the new and just revolutionary order for which Hirsch yearned. *The gravamen of Tillich's argument, therefore, was not that Hirsch was wrong in his political judgment but that he was wrong theologically.* In making our political commitments, he contended, it is theologically impermissible to let the *obligatum* devour the *reservatum,* to annul or suspend the eschatological proviso. Hirsch denied that he was guilty of such an error. Juan Luis Segundo denies that it is an error.

The impasse is all too real. Some of those on the one side of the impasse will object that the argument presented here makes theology counterrevolutionary, pitting theological truth against revolutionary commitment. One can only say in response that any revolution that requires a compromise of theological truth, or sets itself up as the norm of theological truth, is a bad revolution. It is bad for truth, theological or otherwise, and it is almost certainly bad in its consequences for the people in whose name it is advanced. The painfulness of the impasse is intensified when we recognize that what is at stake is the ordering of our loyalties. For the Christian, the truth of ultimate allegiance is the Gospel of God's justifying grace in Jesus Christ, and the community of ultimate allegiance is the Church constituted and sustained by that Gospel. That community is not a theological abstraction but a concrete, social, and historical reality that must be free to proclaim its truth and define its mission. It in turn is created and defined by a proclamation and a grace that transcends all historical moments and movements.

In its institutional forms the Church can be, and frequently has been, inimical to the well-being, the common good, of society. In such instances the Church must be reformed. What must never be done, however, is to attempt to reconstitute or redefine the Church in terms of a program of social and political change. What must never be done is to posit an ideologically defined "people's church" against the Church constituted by the Gospel. What must never be done is to attempt to replace the Gospel itself with an ideology for social transformation, which we then call the gospel. What must never be done was done by some of the *Deutschen Christen* and is being done today in versions of liberation theology. The painful words of Saint Paul recalled by the Confessing Church in Germany and by John Paul II at Puebla now make a new and urgent claim upon our attention: "But even if we, or an angel from heaven, should preach to you a gospel contrary to that which we preached to you, let him be accursed" (Gal. 1). This is a hard word, to be sure, and it is understandable that we shrink from exploring its applicability to our own time. But, as Christians in 1934 were not called to speak the easy words of their own choosing, so we might ask whether the contemporary impasse does not lay a similar call upon us. Of course we do not want to deepen the impasse by unhelpful polemic, but neither should we disguise what is at stake for Christian theology. As Christians and as theologians we must speak the truth in love (Eph. 4), but, insofar as we have been given to understand the truth, we must speak the truth, as Paul Tillich spoke the truth in love to Emanuel Hirsch, as John Paul and Joseph Ratzinger are attempting to speak the truth in love to liberation theologians in Latin America and elsewhere.

In his study of theologians under Hitler, Robert Ericksen concludes by asking what lessons we might draw for today. "We can best avoid [their] error," he writes, "by heavily stressing the values of the liberal, democratic tradition, humanitarianism and justice, and by conscientiously probing history with a view towards its significance for our contemporary decision making." I believe Ericksen is right, although I also believe he is too skeptical about the possibilities of grounding the liberal democratic tradition in orthodox theology and clear reason. But the latter point is a subject addressed in the next section. Our present discussion of liberation theology can be summed up in one sentence: A political theology is politically disastrous and theologically suicidal when it permits any proposal for the common good to subsume the question of the Good by denying spiritual, intellectual, and social space for the Christian saying of yes and no.

John Paul in addressing the bishops of Brazil, and the Congregation for the Doctrine of the Faith in its "Instruction on Christian Freedom and Liberation," hold out the prospect of a dramatically different liberation theology. Theirs is a yes premised upon a firm no to the constituting themes of liberation theology to date. The new liberation theology, unlike the old, maintains the tension between the *obligatum* and *reservatum* of political commitment. It does so not reluctantly but exultantly, for it begins with and ever returns to the clear ordering of our loves and loyalties in which our aspiration to the infinite is directed to Christ and his Kingdom alone. That aspiration to the infinite, it must be asserted firmly, does not make the finite, including the political, a matter of indifference. Here, I believe, is the core of what might be called John Paul's liberationist revisionism. He has launched a fundamental challenge to the habit of mind that pits the infinite against the finite, other-worldliness against this-worldliness, the eternal against the temporal. The political is urgent, but it is not ultimate. In insisting that the political is penultimate, John Paul simultaneously makes clear that penultimate is by no means to be equated with unimportant. Its penultimacy is derived from, and participates in, the ultimate, but must never be equated with the ultimate.

John Paul has not found the fool-proof way of articulating the relation-ship between eternal hopes and temporal tasks, nor has anyone else. This is a perennial problem arising from the Christian awareness that we are alien citizens, in but not of the world. It is undoubtedly and sadly the case that most Christians do not take as seriously as they should their respon-sibility in the right ordering of the earthly *polis*. It is understandable, but also sad, that in order to encourage Christians to take that responsibility more seriously they are sometimes told that the political task is the *most serious* task, that it is indeed tantamount to salvation. This spiritual infla-tion of the immanent is not only at the expense of the transcendent, but also distorts the limits and possibilities of the immanent. Such super-charged political engagement can be sustained only by the promise that politics can deliver much more than in fact it can. This false promise is a particularly cruel lie when told to the poor, oppressed, and marginal who—more often than not—have very limited possibilities of bringing about political and social transformations on the grand scale often im-plied by "liberation." If the meaning of existence is to be established through participation in such transformations, as some theologians are suggesting, then it is to be feared that the masses of the poor are con-signed to living meaningless lives. To be sure, it can be claimed that meaningful existence is achieved by participating in, even dying for, "the struggle" that will some day be vindicated in the New Order. But it must be allowed that, on the basis of the historical record and a reasonable understanding of human possibilities, those who make that claim are in a weak position to accuse traditional Christian piety of offering "pie in the sky."

Marx declared that religion is the sigh of an oppressed humanity. When the oppression is overcome, there will be no more need for religion. This is a common theme that runs through a species of modern political thought that Eric Voegelin has described as "the immanentization of the eschaton." Religion's sigh is the sign of an alienated humanity, and that alienation will give way to *authentic existence* in the kingdom of freedom and justice. This is the presumably scientific theory that is disputed by the critiques of liberation theology offered by John Paul and the Vatican instructions. John Paul not only recognizes but emphasizes the pervasive-ness of alienation under all existent social systems. As we have seen, he lifts up the alienation of humanity from nature, of the laborer from his work, of corporate power from communal purpose, of governments from their people. Some of these alienations can be remedied, or at least tempered, by human action in the worlds of culture, politics, and eco-nomics. As I understand the argument being advanced by John Paul and by the Vatican generally, it is no way to be associated with fatalism, passivity, or resignation to injustice. John Paul has no truck with a carica-ture of a Lutheran "two kingdoms" doctrine which holds that authentic existence is to be found exclusively in the realm of redemption where the Gospel rules, while the rest of existence is consigned to a civil realm untouched by grace and redemptive possibility. At the same time, John Paul is adamant that we should not tell lies to the people of God about what is possible through political and social transformation. To both the rich and poor, the strong and weak, the Church must issue the unremitting reminder that the human aspiration toward the infinite cannot be satisfied by *any* new order short of the ultimate new order that is the Kingdom of God. In refusing to compromise on this truth, John Paul seems well aware that he invites the criticism that he favors some form of "dualism"—and dualism is deemed to be among the most devastating criticisms available to a modern world ruled by the monistic hunger to "get it all together," and to do so here, and to do so now.

John Paul's argument is that the assurance of an eternal destiny is not distraction from but empowerment for worldly tasks. In Poland, in June of 1987, he spoke about the "eternal meaning" of the Solidarity movement. He did not say that Solidarity as a political movement is indestructible, for that is obviously not the case. Rather, the eternal meaning of Solidarity is that it is animated by the truth of ultimate freedom, which is derived from humanity's aspiration toward and promised destiny in communion with the Absolute. Some of John Paul's public statements are marvelously elliptic in manner. In Warsaw he declared that Poland's bishops must commit themselves to proclaiming the "truth about man and his rights," including "the principle of participation in deciding about the matters of one's own philosophy even in the political sphere." That may seem like an innocuous generalization, and spoken in Milwaukee it may have been just that. In Warsaw, however, its very pointed meaning was not lost on either the regime or those oppressed by the regime. As the outlawed steering committee of Solidarity declared in a statement issued at the end of the Pope's visit, "We do not live in a free country and our voices cannot always be heard and therefore the Pope spoke about us and to us and—as he himself underlined—for us."

Earlier in the same year, on his visit to Chile, John Paul drew from this transcendent truth very specific lessons challenging the regime of General Augusto Pinochet. With unusual sharpness, he made connections between transcendent freedom and democratic governance. As he told reporters on this journey, "Yes, yes, I am not the evangelizer of democracy, I am the evangelizer of the Gospel. To the Gospel message, of course, belongs all the problems of human rights, and if democracy means human rights it also belongs to the message of the church."

In short, John Paul's affirmation of transcendence, even of traditional other-worldly piety, is falsely depicted as vacuous or escapist. He is, as we have seen, the Christian humanist *par excellence,* with an understanding of the *humanum* grounded in the Incarnation and our participation in the life of the Triune God, and always directed toward eschatological promise. The dispute with prevalent forms of liberation theology is not, then, over the elevated status of humanity and its possibilities but over the reasons why one thinks so highly of human beings and how one envisions their consummation. John Paul, of course, is not only a man of ideas but also, as befits his position, a politician of ideas. The politics of ideas requires that he appropriate and redirect the legitimate impulses and insights that gave birth to the liberation theology of the last two decades, a theology which still commands so much Christian thought, not least of all in North American theology. Nor is it a matter of his taking over ideas that were invented by liberation theology. As he and the Vatican instructions insist, what is legitimate in liberation theology has always been there in the historic Christian tradition. What the Vatican instructions do not acknowledge as fully as they might, however, is that liberation theology has given new shape and urgency to ancient truths. The way in which liberation theology is now being recast under the leadership of Rome might well produce a new form of transcendently attuned and temporally potent spirituality for the entire Church. If this is the result of what some call the second wave of liberation theology, pioneers such as Gustavo Gutierrez might one day be viewed not as deviant but as having contributed mightily to a more vibrant Christian orthodoxy. Stranger things have happened in the historical dialectic of the Spirit.

The story of liberation theology is not yet completely told. One must hope that the repudiation of older forms of liberation theology will open the way to further development. Unlike those in the past who served as theological apologists for new tyrannies, the liberation theologians of today may be alerted to the unhappy fate invited by their abandonment of the eschatological proviso. In that event, liberation theology may yet be turned against all the Grand Inquisitors of history and rejoin the community that *in statu viatoris* awaits the liberation for which the whole creation yearns.

PART V

The Travail of Becoming American

Toward the end of World War II, in 1944, the *Christian Century* published a series of eight articles under the worried title "Can Catholicism Win America?" The articles were written by Harold E. Fey, later to become the distinguished editor of the *Century*, the flagship journal of liberal mainline Protestantism. With the end of the war, wrote Fey, America faced a new era. "What will this new American culture be like? Is secularism to determine its character? Can Protestantism recover the prominent position in molding American culture which it held before the great waves of Catholic immigration swept across this continent? Or is this once Protestant nation destined to pass into another and different cultural phase under the religious and social preponderance of the Roman Catholic Church?" Only in this generation, said Fey, have the 23 million Roman Catholics come to feel "at home" in the United States. Catholicism has learned to speak the "American" language and having "raised up native leaders who are loyally followed by millions, it is for the first time in a position to make history—American history."

Fey is eager to have it understood that he is not appealing to anti-Catholic prejudice. He and the *Century* are aggressively liberal. He recognizes the dangers of awakening "the dangerous and light-sleeping dogs of intolerance and bigotry." As devoted as Fey is to interfaith harmony, however, harmony must not be purchased at the price of blindly ignoring the threatening policies and influence of the Roman Catholic Church. Protestants, he says, are usually "long on tolerance or intolerance and short on facts." Those who want to be both tolerant and informed must understand the "vast organism" of Catholicism which begins with a foreign potentate in the Vatican who has in this country 145 bishops and archbishops for the purpose of "projecting and carrying out Roman Catholic policy." This was not so ominous when these bishops were divided in myriad immigrant groups, but with World War I, they came together in the National Catholic War Council (later the National Catholic Welfare Council, and later still the National Catholic Welfare Conference). Here the bishops came to know and trust one another, and, with the pope's blessing, the NCWC became a formidable agency for the projection of Catholic power. "So effective is voluntary cooperation even in an authoritarian church that the NCWC has done more in the past twenty-five years to unify the Roman Catholic Church in this country than had been previously done in all its history."

Fey does not criticize the hierarchy for "directing the great power of the ecclesiastical body which it heads toward winning the total body of American culture to Catholicism." On the contrary, the hierarchy "has not only the right but the obligation to do precisely this if it can." And, if the thirty six million Protestants cannot rediscover, while there is yet time, "what it is that makes and keeps us evangelical and Protestant Christians," and if they cannot overcome their divisions, the Roman Church will end up doing precisely what it is determined to do. "Catholicism in that event is certain to win America. Not today or tomorrow but the day after tomorrow, the Roman Church will become dominant in American culture." That is not a happy prospect. "Our sixteenth century forebears were compelled to brush aside the priestly facade of medieval Christianity patterned after imperial Rome to recover the central structure of living faith which was given to the world in first century Palestine." With modern scholarship, with a deepened awareness of the dangers of the authoritarian principle for modern society, and with increased Protestant cooperation, Protestants may still be worthy heirs of the Reformers. "Protestants may discover that their greatest contribution to American culture is not in the past but awaits the future." They, and not the Romanists, may yet take the lead in the effort "to christianize America's national life."

That, then, is the Catholic peril and the Protestant challenge. The second article, "Catholicism Comes to Middletown," explains how, under the authoritarian direction of the bishop, the immense resources of Roman Catholicism can take over a typical American town. Through schools, hospitals, and community services—staffed by religious orders and coordinated by the NCWC in Washington—Roman Catholicism soon becomes the politically and culturally dominant force. "Catholicism and the Press" explains how diocesan papers, with a circulation of nine million and stories largely fed through the NCWC network, are "an instrument of great effectiveness which can be and is being used to alter the character of American society." The hierarchy's activism in promoting "decency" in movies has resulted in "the numerous pro-Catholic films now being produced." The fourth article, "Catholicism and the Negro," acknowledges that Rome has taken the lead in race relations, but this too, of course, is a component in its campaign of self-aggrandizement. Fey writes, "Nearly a hundred Catholic institutions of higher learning today admit Negroes. A decade ago the number was not more than ten." (Remember, this is 1944.) He quotes a leader of this apostolate who says Catholicism "offers the Negro an intelligent religion of the kind he will not find in his roaring, ranting, Protestant meeting houses." Fey notes that a great many informed Catholics consider the Negro apostolate "the church's greatest opportunity."

"Catholicism and the Worker" observes that, unlike some Protestant churches, Catholicism has a solid working class base. Fey describes admiringly the work of the legendary Monsignor John A. Ryan in bringing Catholicism to support the labor movement and other liberal causes. At the same time, it is clear to him that Ryan's first loyalty is to the Church of Rome and he lists what he considers Ryan's several "retreats" from liberal principle. One instance has a strikingly contemporary ring. In 1935 Ryan resigned from the national board of the American Civil Liberties Union "simply and solely," he explained, "because the organization had gone into the field of academic freedom." Ryan added, "I called attention to the absurdity, for example, of my membership on the national committee of an organization which might undertake to defend a professor at the Catholic University who has been discharged for teaching heresy." These and other instances of "retreat," wrote Fey, demonstrated how unreliable is Roman Catholic support when it comes into conflict with institutional self-interest. He concludes, "That American industrial workers are ready to sacrifice their heritage of freedom for the unproved securities of the church's economic leadership is doubtful."

"Catholicism Fights Communism" includes a somewhat grudging acknowledgment that the bishops know that you cannot fight something with nothing. "The church is at least not making the mistake of attempting to oppose a well defined economic system with the ambiguities of laissez faire." In order to counter communism, the bishops educate the faithful in alternative understandings of "economic justice" and actively promote labor organizations such as the Association of Catholic Trades Unionists. The penultimate article deals with Romanist plans for rural America, and then Fey gets to "The Center of Catholic Power." The NCWC in Washington is the organizing center of the crusade to win America. Rome knows how important it is to win America. After touching on the troubled state of Catholicism in other parts of the world, Fey writes, "In all the Roman Catholic world the only place where the wealth and stability of the church are not threatened is in the United States." But what does it mean to win America? Fey quotes at length the same John A. Ryan, the "principal architect of the church's present structure in America," to the effect that it means the official establishment of the Roman Catholic Church. "The state," wrote Ryan in an officially approved textbook, "must not only 'have care for religion' but recognize the *true* religion. This means the form of religion practiced by the Catholic Church." Protestant and other false religions "may" be permitted to practice their faith, providing it is "carried on within the family circle or in such an inconspicuous manner as to be an occasion neither of scandal nor of perversion to the faithful. . . . Since no rational end is promoted by the dissemination of false doctrine, there exists no right to indulge in this practice. . . . Error has not the same rights as truth."

Of course, Fey allows, Roman Catholics are talking about the ideal state of affairs. Monsignor Ryan is reassuring in his affirmation that Catholics have an obligation in conscience to obey the Constitution until they accumulate enough power to change it, and that therefore Protestants need not worry for a long time to come. "In other words," writes Fey, "Dr. Ryan tells Protestants not to worry until it is too late to worry." The intention of the Roman church is clear, says Fey. "How seriously should this intention be taken? The answer depends upon how effectively the church is organizing the energies of its 23,000,000 members to capture the power it seeks." Fey thought it was organizing them very effectively indeed. At NCWC headquarters on Massachusetts Avenue "the hierarchy coordinates the mighty energies of the Roman Catholic Church for the winning of America. Here is the great dynamo from which power flows out through the entire Catholic system." And, given the structure of the flow of power, "it becomes clear that the winning of America to the church is conceived in totalitarian terms." Of course, NCWC is but the coordinating center. In Washington alone there are numerous other agencies critical to the campaign. There is, for example, Georgetown University, where "the Jesuits conduct their School of Foreign Service which each year feeds its graduating class into the United States diplomatic service."

In all this, Harold Fey does not allege that there is something sinister and secretive afoot. It is all quite aboveboard; the goal and the instruments for reaching that goal are quite visible. It is no secret, for example, that the NCWC is, with good reason, called "the most powerful lobby in Washington." The end purpose of this entire enterprise "involves a fundamental revision of the Constitution of the United States and a radical change in the character of American culture." The Roman Catholic hierarchy is using Protestant tolerance in order to establish a system of intolerance. "Today," Fey writes, "America includes Catholicism with other faiths and makes them equally at home. It includes them all, however, on Protestant terms." Roman Catholic doctrine and program aim at a radical modification of this basic freedom. "The Roman Catholic hierarchy has launched a program which will, if it succeeds, include other faiths in American culture only on Catholic terms." Without an effective Protestant countereffort, the outlook is doleful. The long series concludes: "Until such [Protestant] unity appears, the answer to the question, Can Catholicism Win America? is—Yes." That was forty years ago. The reader of those *Christian Century* articles today might well respond: "The answer to the question, Can Catholicism Win America? is—so what?"

47. "BALANCING" AMERICAN AND CATHOLIC

Today it is widely assumed that there is a smooth fit between being Roman Catholic and being American. Some of those who are uneasy about that assumption claim that the appearance of a smooth fit is in fact the result, forty years after Fey's frettings, of American Protestantism having won Catholicism. Fey, it will be recalled, saw a third contender for dominance in shaping American culture, namely, secularism. And so other Roman Catholics who are uneasy about the smooth fit say that secularism has indeed triumphed over both Protestantism and Catholicism. As we have seen throughout these pages, there are many versions of the "crisis" of Roman Catholicism, especially in America. But side by side with the sense of crisis is an almost celebratory sense of the success of Catholicism in America. Consider, for example, *The American Catholic People* (1986) by the pollster George Gallup and the journalist Jim Castelli. Here is a book that has warmed the cockles of the American Catholic heart. It asserts confidently and documents impressively that American Catholicism is in the midst of a "religious revival" and is positioned to become the dominant religious group in American within the next fifty years.

"The American Catholic people are an extraordinary bunch," write the authors. "By virtue of being American, they have reshaped the Catholic Church; by virtue of being Catholic, they have reshaped American society." Roman Catholics are healthy, wealthy, and apparently as wise as anyone else around. They are in positions of leadership in every institution of the society; they are well educated, socially tolerant, politically liberal, and all men speak well of them. They have demonstrated that you *can* have it all. (A voice from the gallery: Jesus should have lived to see the day.) They are very, very pleased with themselves and, we are told, have good reason to be. According to this rendering of reality, today's Catholic, while committed to the faith, is more "independent-minded" and quite prepared to challenge both government policies and church doctrine on matters such as birth control and premarital sex. The authors challenge "five major negative stereotypes" commonly held by Roman Catholics about themselves: that religious activity is declining dramatically; that young people are leaving the church; that people leave the church as they become more educated; that women are in a state of revolt; and that Roman Catholics have become more conservative politically as they have become more affluent. Not true on all counts, say Gallup and Castelli. While it is true that not as many people are going to mass each week, many more are participating in other types of religious activity, including Bible study, marriage encounters, charismatic gatherings, and social justice causes. Theirs is an exceedingly roseate reading of the Catholic situation.

Those who are still uneasy about the smooth fit may simply be churlish. Or they may be troubled by the remembrance that this is not how it was supposed to have turned out. Roman Catholicism was not supposed to become merely a denomination among the denominations, another optional way of being Christian, or just religious, in America. Maybe the earlier expectations were wrong. Vatican II said they were definitely wrong with respect to religious freedom and the establishment of Roman Catholicism as the state religion. But were Harold Fey and thoroughgoing anti-Catholics such as Paul Blanshard right in saying that that triumphalist ambition was the essence of Catholicism's mission in America? With the setting aside of that tiara, was it inevitable that Roman Catholics and Catholicism would become like everybody else? These questions are not new. In 1854 the Yankee convert Orestes Brownson, who urged immigrant Catholic groups to shed their nationalities and become American, wrote, "The Americanization of the Catholic body does and will go on of itself, as rapidly as is desirable, and all we have to do with it is to take care that they do not imbibe the notion that to Americanize is necessarily to Protestantize. The transition from one nationality to another is always a dangerous process, and all the Americanization I insist on is that our Catholic population shall feel and believe that a man may be a true American and a good Catholic."

Now that there appears to be no tension between being a "true American and a good Catholic," the inevitable question is: Which definition has changed—being "American" or being "Catholic"? One answer is that there has been a creative synthesis and there is now a new thing under the sun, the American Catholic. Or we may remember George Lindbeck's earlier discussion about the way the question of "compromise" is raised in ecumenical theological dialogues. The critical issue, said Lindbeck, is whether both partners can recognize their own position and the position of the interlocutor in the new formulation that has been reached. So we might ask whether we can recognize in today's "American Catholic" what was "American" in, say, 1945 or 1854. The answer would clearly seem to be in the affirmative. Then, turning the question around, we ask whether in today's "American Catholic" we can recognize what was "Catholic" fifty or a hundred years ago. Some Roman Catholics, and others, answer in the negative; many more are ambivalent. Most probably think it a completely unnecessary question to ask. Among them are those who subscribe to the "ecclesiastical fundamentalism" or "gnosticism" that asserts that, no matter what Roman Catholicism becomes in historical fact, it could not become anything other than Roman Catholicism. In any event, they say, where the gates of hell cannot prevail, there is little to fear from the force of American culture.

For most of our history as a nation, the formulation "American Catholic" seemed to most Americans, and to many American Catholics, to be an oxymoron. The Lutheran historian Martin E. Marty comments on the work of Walter Elliott, who, under the leadership of Isaac Hecker, helped found the Paulist order. In *An Invitation to American Catholic History* (1986), Marty writes, "Think, for a moment, of the delicacy of his mission. On the one hand, he was busy making Catholicism sound so at home in America that it would be attractive enough for people to want to convert to it. On the other, the act of writing thus forced him to make the church seem inoffensive, so at home that the reasons for joining it dissipated. While he and the Paulists set out to make converts, it was the less adapted and sometimes more beligerent Catholics, who portrayed Rome as an unchanging Rock, who won more converts."

According to Jay P. Dolan in his massive *The American Catholic Experience* (1986), this dilemma of being a "true American" and "good Catholic" constitutes the continuing story line of American Catholicism. The year 1989 marks the bicentennial of the establishment of the Roman Catholic hierarchy in the United States, and, says Dolan, by the end of his life it was obvious that the first bishop, John Carroll of Baltimore (1735–1815), knew that the accent would be placed on "good Catholic," meaning subservience to Rome. "Thus, by 1815, two schools of thought were manifest in the American Catholic community," Dolan writes. "One desired to fashion an indigenous church, an American Catholicism; the other wanted to transplant to the new nation a continental European version of Roman Catholicism. These two positions constituted the opposing forces of an ongoing dialectic that would challenge Catholicism in the United States for decades to come. It was clear, at the time of John Carroll's death, in what direction the church was heading; if there was any doubt about this, the massive immigration of European Catholics would decisively settle the issue." Over the next century and more, the leadership of the "One, Holy, Irish and Apostolic Church" would make it clear beyond doubt that Roman Catholicism in America would be very Roman indeed.

In the story as told by Dolan and numerous others of a similar viewpoint, the contest between "progressives" and "conservatives" has been a constant in the American Catholic experience. The progressives give priority to being true Americans, the conservatives to being good Catholics. Dolan quotes a Baptist minister in Rochester in 1894 who, he writes,

captured the meaning of this controversy . . . between conservatives and liberals. The Rochester minister declared: "There are two distinct and hostile parties in the Roman Catholic Church in America. One is led by Archbishop [John] Ireland. It stands for Americanism and a larger independence. It is sympathetic with modern thought. It believes the Roman Catholic Church should take its place in all the great moral reforms. It is small, but progressive, vigorous, and brave. The other party is led by the overwhelming majority of the hierarchy. It is conservative, out of touch with American or modern ideas. It is the old medieval European Church, transplanted into the Nineteenth Century and this country of freedom, interesting as an antiquity and curiosity, but fast losing its power and consequently, growing in bitterness."

Sixty years later, according to Dolan, the situation had dramatically changed, but the terms of reference remain exactly the same. "By the end of the 1950s, Catholicism in the United States had clearly come of age. More accepted by the Protestant majority, Catholics entered the 1950s confident about their place in American society. Being Catholic was indeed compatible with being American." The constant is the question of compatibility. One may question how secure Roman Catholics felt in the 1950s when books such as Paul Blanshard's *American Freedom and Catholic Power* (1949) were selling in the hundreds of thousands; when, as still today, anti-Catholicism was aptly described as the anti-Semitism of the intellectuals; when it was still considered highly improbable that a Roman Catholic could be elected president. For these and other reasons there is considerable dispute about when to date the "coming of age" of Catholicism in America. Much more interesting than the question of dating the coming of age is the question of defining the coming of age. The conventional histories never move beyond the contest of "true American" versus "good Catholic." Dolan writes: "In 1870, Catholics were struggling with the question of what it meant to be an American; comfortably American in 1965 they now struggled with a more fundamental question: what it meant to be Catholic. Just when they had solved one half of the riddle—what it meant to be American—the other half came unraveled."

48. THE RIDDLE REDIVIVUS

So it would seem we are back to Jaroslav Pelikan's metaphor of the "riddle of Roman Catholicism" after all. Except now it is not the riddle that Roman Catholicism poses to others but the riddle it poses to Roman Catholics. Nevertheless, perhaps the riddle supposed by Dolan and others is the result of a basic misconstrual of the story line. Perhaps the tension was not between being a "true American" and "good Catholic." Perhaps, as John Carroll argued two hundred years ago, "American" and "Catholic" are not antinomies at all. That is the argument that John Courtney Murray made in *We Hold These Truths* (1960) and throughout his life. That is the argument being made by younger Roman Catholic scholars today, such as George Weigel in *Tranquillitas Ordinis: The Present Failure and Future Promise of American Catholic Thought on War and Peace* (1986). Perhaps, therefore, the story line is the search for a distinctively Roman Catholic way of being American, and for distinctively Roman Catholic warrants for sustaining the American experiment in republican democracy. In other words, the hoped-for goal is not to "reconcile" being a true American with being a good Catholic. That way lies the almost inevitable reduction of one dimension to the other. That way lies what Dolan perceives to be the present situation, namely, being "comfortably American" and questionably Catholic. The hoped-for goal, it may alternatively be suggested, is being a true American *because* one is a good Catholic. To be sure, this does not resolve the ambiguity in terms such as "true American" and "good Catholic," but it does fundamentally change the way in which the problem is proposed and progress is perceived.

In his 1960 classic, *Protestant, Catholic, Jew,* Will Herberg saw our society's pluralism being resolved in terms of religious identities that are in the service of "The American Way of Life." Yet there and elsewhere, Herberg recognized that Catholicism was not entirely "comfortable" with its place in that religiocultural triumverate. Similarly, Mark Silk, writing in *American Quarterly* (1977), describes Roman Catholic uneasiness with some of the ways of effecting the smooth fit of "American Catholic." In the 1950s, writes Silk, talk about "the Judeo-Christian tradition" became common currency. The concept of a Judeo-Christian tradition was much favored by neoorthodox Protestants such as Reinhold Niebuhr and was welcomed, with some ambivalence, by Jewish thinkers such as Abraham Joshua Heschel. "Yet for all its usefulness to ideological combat and consensus during the fifties," Silk writes, "the Judeo-Christian enterprise of neoorthodoxy had its recusants. The Catholics, especially, withheld the hem of their garment. The *philosophia perennis* required no Hebraic infusion to save it from liberalism, and as for undergirding anticommunism with religion, American Catholicism was sufficient unto the day. 'Hebraic faith,' moreover, contained much that was repugnant to Rome. Its opposition to Hellenic modes of thought (including natural law) extended to Thomism, which was nothing if not Hellenic; and Thomism reigned supreme in pre-Vatican II theology."

Silk believes that Murray himself was cool to the Herberg triumverate and the Judeo-Christian convergence. Protestantism, Catholicism, and Judaism, said Murray, were "radically different" styles of belief, none of which "is reducible, or perhaps even comparable, to any of the others." The best that might be hoped for was "creeds at war intelligibly" under "the articles of peace which are the religion-clauses of the First Amendment." Somewhat more sympathetic to the concept was Jacques Maritain who, in a 1950 *Partisan Review* symposium, wrote that people "are becoming aware of the fact that no real radical movement in politics and no fundamental social improvements are to be brought about without the spiritual energies and the basic humanist tenets inseparable from the Judeo-Christian religious tradition, and that democracy can only live on Christianity." To which Silk adds the acerb observation: "The energies and tenets might derive from Judaism, but the sustaining reality was Christianity." The observation is, I believe, not justified. To speak of the Judeo-Christian tradition is not to imply an amalgamation of existing religions achieved by some superficial splitting of differences. For Christians in conversation with Jews, it is an acknowledgment of Christianity's

Hebraic foundation and continuing responsibility to what Paul described as the "mystery" of Living Judaism. Both Murray and Maritain were, after all, Christians and, more specifically, Roman Catholic Christians. Their effort was to advance the democratic project by drawing on warrants from their own tradition. In addition, given the religious demographics of democratic societies in 1950, the assertion that "democracy can only live on Christianity" might be viewed as historically self-evident. That is, without the support of Christians and core ideas affirmed by Christianity, democracy cannot live. That would unquestionably be the case in the United States at least.

We have seen that figures such as Murray pondered distinctively Roman Catholic ways of being American and distinctively Roman Catholic warrants for sustaining the American experiment. This would appear to be dramatically different from what Dolan means by Catholicism having become "comfortably American." Oddly enough, Dolan's understanding of being comfortably American means being uncomfortable about being an American. In this view, Roman Catholics have not become just like everyone else. Rather, they have become just like that sector of society that feels itself largely alienated from the society. The "American Catholics" described by Dolan are essentially "new class" Americans who are trying to cope with the "riddle" of what to do about the fact that they happen also to be Roman Catholics. The new class, or the knowledge class, that they have joined is frequently viewed as being so alienated from the American proposition and its influence in the world that it is charged with being anti-American. That is to say, with respect to most of the problems of the world, the new class is disposed toward what has been called the "blame America first syndrome." To the extent this is true, the irony is that the American Catholics described by Dolan have become American just in time to become anti-American.

Dissent, in relation to both church and nation, is critical to what Dolan means by becoming American. "As a result of the Council . . . Catholics acquired the authority to dissent. . . . A new Catholicism was coming to life in the United States." (It is a marvelous phrase, "authority to dissent." From what authority does one "acquire" authority to dissent, and what happens to authority to dissent when one dissents from the authority from which it is acquired?) Dissent from distinctively Roman Catholic teaching and practice, Dolan tells us, contributed to homogenization. "By the 1960s, Catholics in the United States were becoming more like the rest of the American population." Whether or not one agrees that that is a great achievement, Dolan notes with satisfaction the sector of American opinion with which Catholics identify. For instance, "as early as 1967, 24 percent of the Catholic population opposed the Vietnam war, while only 16.5 percent of the Protestants adopted such a position." Almost every loss of Roman Catholic distinctiveness is counted by Dolan as evidence of Catholics becoming "fully American." In the past, parish pastors had controlled the Catholic schools, which "tended to retard efforts toward greater standardization and centralization." But now other dynamics, including standardized accreditation and testing, "helped to make Catholic schools very much like their public counterparts." Publications such as the *National Catholic Reporter* helped "to keep liberal-minded Catholics up to date on developments in the church." The main development has been a continuing crisis of identity. "The crisis of identity also deflated the smugness and confidence of Catholics. The 1940s and 1950s crusade to win converts disappeared, and interest in foreign missions declined." Numerous Roman Catholic fraternal, service, and professional organizations "either passed out of existence or acquired a new self-understanding that was deliberately more American and less exclusively Catholic." The process of becoming "fully American," it would appear, has been one success after another.

I recall speaking with a former priest in the early 1970s who assured me that he had not left the priesthood out of a sense of failure. On the contrary, he said at the risk of immodesty, he had been a great success as pastor of a midwestern parish. "After four years routine mass attendance was way down, almost nobody came to confession, and in another couple of years I would have been able to close the school." It is easy to deride this view of progress, but more important to try to understand it. This priest, like Jay Dolan and countless others, believed he was replacing a routinized "devotional Catholicism" with a more spiritual, authentic, and relevant expression of the faith. Important to this understanding is the presumed antithesis between the authentic and spontaneous, on the one hand, and the institutional and normative on the other. Therefore deinstitutionalization is an essential mark of renewal. One may agree or disagree with this understanding of religious authenticity, but there can be no doubt that it is in historical fact a characteristically Protestant understanding. More precisely, it is characteristic of the left-wing among the Reformation traditions and has found most powerful expression in the American "free church" and "revivalistic" experience. This has been the most typical and culturally formative religion in American culture. In its basic assumptions it has understood itself to be anti-Catholic. It is therefore not surprising that those Roman Catholics who have, no doubt unconsciously, embraced it as a paradigm of renewal find that their Catholicism has become something of a riddle to themselves.

"American Catholics are living in a period of transition," announces Dolan, perhaps somewhat unnecessarily. "One model of church is passing away and another is coming to life." The course of progress is complex. It involves, among other factors, deinstitutionalization and free-church authenticity. Prominent among these factors, according to Dolan and others, is the ascendancy of the laity as the church becomes more "democratic" and control is wrested from white male clerics who think it is *their* church. But the story then becomes yet more, as they say, complex. By page 452 of *The American Catholic Experience*, even the most dull-witted reader has come to understand that "clericalism" was one of the chief curses of the pre-Vatican II church. The "comfortably American" church of recent decades is one in which the lay folk come more and more into their own. This is true in their personal lives surely. "There are various ways of being Catholic," Dolan notes approvingly, "and people are choosing the style that best suits them." But, with respect to the running of the church, it now appears there has been a resurgence of clericalism, and Dolan is equally approving of that. "By 1983 the hierarchy had moved to the forefront of the peace movement. . . . For the first time, large numbers of bishops, priests, and laity were involved in a crusade for social justice." (This would seem to be overlooking clerical and lay activism in the labor movement earlier in the century.) But what has it meant for the laity now that Catholicism has become fully American? Dolan answers: "Catholics were now part of the American mainstream. In its search for relevance, the church found its answer in the gospel mandate of social justice. Many Catholics, in fact the vast majority, found this offensive. They wanted their bishops and priests to stop meddling in worldly affairs and leave the cause of justice to other people better versed in politics and business." Thus we are told that "the church" has joined the crusade, except for the "vast majority" of the people who are the church. Similarly, the "American mainstream" apparently leaves out the vast majority of Americans.

49. CLASS CONFLICT REDEFINED

Dolan, like his colleague at the University of Notre Dame, Richard McBrien, is enthusiastic about the new definition of the converging American and Catholic mainstreams. Within a specifiable sector of Roman Catholic leadership, both academic and episcopal, what they call the mainstream is indeed the mainstream. But it may be that that establishment definition of the mainstream is already being eroded by the passage of time. As Martin E. Marty notes, it depends upon a story, a myth, that is increasingly not available even to Roman Catholics who want to think of themselves as progressive. "The Council effected changes that only those who had come to maturity as faithful 'pre-Vatican II' Catholics can appreciate in their brains and bones," Marty writes. "After more than a generation a genre of literature and drama survived in which authors and audiences could revisit the Bad Old Days. These, however, had to be directed to the Senior Citizen generation. Writers first had to create a world that in some ways was as remote spiritually as the Middle Ages." Marty's observation is directed against nostalgic traditionalists who appeal to the Senior Citizen generation, but the observation cuts in several directions. Marty notes that "discontinuities make up the drama of history." But discontinuities can continue to seem dramatic only against the background of continuities. Those who know "in their brains and bones" the alleged oppressions of continuity against which a generation's protests of discontinuity were lodged are fast becoming the senior citizens. The oncoming generation of Roman Catholics, brought up in the now-established "mainstream" definition of Catholicism, may hear the voices of continuity as the new, the exciting, the discontinuous thing. That at least is the hope of those conservatives who believe their position is not an escape into the past but an anticipation of the future.

Marty's pleasing stroll through the history of Catholicism in America arrives at a five-stage analysis that supposes a sanguine, even blithe, reading of the Roman Catholic situation. One can discern, he says, a kind of "Anatomy of Revolution" in Catholicism.

First there is control, restraint, to the point of absurdity. Then there is pressure against the restraints, voiced in a time of discontent and new ferment. In Catholicism, that movement was the eve of the Second Vatican Council, or, in our terms, the [Gustave] Weigel-Murray era. Third is controlled adaptation to change, as in the Council decrees. This is followed by experiment. Now occurs conflict between those who would push the new freedoms to extremes and those who resisted change all along. Most priests, religious, and laity moved now here, now there, but seldom to extremes. A fifth stage sees a kind of synthesis that cannot satisfy these extremes, but that permits the church to move ahead and focus on other agenda items.

In sum, the anatomy of the revolution is that there was no revolution.

Marty may well be right with respect to the vast majority of Roman Catholics who are seeking, if not a synthesis, at least a measure of stability. We have already noted, however, the increasing statistical evidence of a growing gap between the understandings of the laity, on the one hand, and the clergy and religious, on the other. The clergy and religious, in tandem with the official and activist bureaucracies and the credentialed professoriat of progressive Catholicism, seem more aligned with what has come to be seen as the "New Catholic Knowledge Class." The latter is the concept elaborated by sociologist Joseph A. Varacalli in *Toward the Establishment of Liberal Catholicism in America* (1983), a study focusing on the famous "Call to Action" project of the 1970s. "Call to Action" involved hundreds of thousands of Roman Catholics in local and regional meetings, leading up to a massive conference in Detroit in 1976. Almost nobody thought the Detroit meeting a great success. "Ordinary" Catholics resented the aggressive caucuses and special interest groups that dominated the event with what Marty would call their "extreme" agendas, while those who dominated were frustrated at the unwillingness of the leadership, especially the bishops, to implement the myriad resolutions passed. Bishop James Rausch, who was instrumental in the organizing of "Call to Action," angrily remarked at the time, "We wanted to put the conference in the hands of the people, but instead it's in the hands of the experts." That will do as a rough summary of what is meant by the influence of the "New Catholic Knowledge Class."

New class theory does not explain everything. Like any theory, it is subject to abuse. It can be used, for example, to impugn the motives and ideas of members of the new class, suggesting that they are only or primarily, rather than *also,* acting out of class interest. That way lies the further debasement of intellectual, including theological, discourse. And those who employ new class theory must have a nuanced appreciation of the fact that they too belong to the new class, even if they are traitors to their class. As I have written elsewhere, everyone whose social role is the minting and marketing of the metaphors by which they would have people think and behave is a member of the new class. The new class is also called the knowledge class, and is composed especially of those whose business is the production and sale of symbolic knowledge. New class theory should not be understood as a dogma, however. It is an explanatory device that is to be used or dispensed with, depending on whether it helps to make sense of facts. Jay Dolan's history, for instance, does not employ new class theory at all. And yet the theory would seem to be particularly helpful in making sense of the facts he relates. His depiction of the American Catholic present and future is not the "synthesis" that Marty expects but the prospect of continuing class struggle.

In Dolan's telling of the story, the vast majority of American Catholics are opposed to the redefinition of the church and its mission in terms of "its search for relevance in the gospel mandate of social justice." Dolan believes that the work of this "new Catholic church" has hardly gotten underway, but what he calls "the mainstream" is committed to it. To be sure, there are obstacles in the way and even reactionaries who would turn back the clock. Enter John Paul II. It is true that in his visits to the United States "enthusiastic crowds welcomed him," but that does not mean as much as some may think. "A charismatic individual, he had become a genuine hero whom people wanted to see and touch. But, intellectually and spiritually, he was out of touch with many Catholics." (Not, note, with "most" but with "many.") "John Paul II was calling Catholics back to the old church and trying to restore uniformity and control. But it would no longer work. He could utter the command, but the Papacy had lost the ability to enforce it." Historian Dolan does not leave the reader in doubt as to where his sympathies are. The pontificate of John Paul has brought "the official investigation of theologians suspected of unorthodox teaching, the attempted suppression of books, a renaissance of sexophobia with its accompanying denunciation of artificial birth control, the suspension of priests and nuns who held public office, and a reassertion of male supremacy and clerical control."

Dolan accurately represents the self-consciously progressive understanding of the class struggle going on in American Catholicism. Although he does not use the exact language, in his portrayal the struggle is essentially between most of the Catholic people and the Pope, on the one side, and the new knowledge class, on the other. Nor does he evidence any doubt about the outcome of the struggle. Conservative reactions to progress "have hardened the lines of division in the church." Such reactions to progress, however, do not discourage Dolan: "Traditional Catholics welcomed them, while progressive Catholics denounced them. But the ways of the past will no longer work. A new spirit is alive in American Catholicism, and the twenty-first century belongs to it. The challenge of the future still remains the timeless question that people have wrestled with for two hundred years: how to be both Catholic and American. How the new generation of Catholics solves this riddle will determine the shape that American Catholicism will take in the years ahead."

With this triumphal assertion that the future belongs to his party, we come full circle back to Pelikan's "riddle," although now very differently construed. Dolan may be indulging in bravado, or he may be right about the relative strength of the sides in the class struggle he depicts. It is possible, but not certain, that Harold Fey would cheer Dolan's positive answer to the question, Can Protestant America Win Catholicism? It is not certain because, you will recall, Fey saw a third contender for the role of dominant cultural force. That third contender, he believed, was secularism. One might suggest that there is nothing very distinctively Catholic in the "new church" that Dolan hails. But, more than that, there is nothing very distinctively Protestant, either. Certainly there is nothing of classic Protestantism in its Lutheran or Calvinist varieties; and even more certainly there is nothing of the evangelical, fundamentalist, and pentecostal Protestantisms that are now so aggressively attempting to play a culture-formative role in the public square. In short, there is nothing very Christian in this "new church"—at least not in any of the available forms of Christian belief and community. So we expect that, forty years later, Harold Fey would be deeply ambivalent about the way this triumph of Protestant America seems to have come about. It is the triumph of a *Kulturprotestantismus* of a most particular form. It is the triumph of Richard Niebuhr's Christ *of* culture, except the culture in question is the essentially adversary culture that is virulently opposed to what Harold Fey called "the christianization of our national life." And that is not what thoughtful people who once worried about the future of Roman Catholicism in America had in mind. That is not what they had in mind at all.

50. PAUL BLANSHARD LIVES

We will call it the "Blanshard Thesis," in dubious honor of Paul Blanshard, who represents the Americans beyond numbering who have believed that there is a contradiction, or at least a deep tension, between being a "true American" and a "good Catholic." Against the Blanshard

Thesis we will pose what George Weigel calls the "Murray Project." The Murray Project asserts that there is a distinctively Roman Catholic way of affirming and living "the American proposition." We will then examine the ways in which the Murray Project has been neglected, if not repudiated, by American Catholics, in large part because they are disillusioned with the American proposition. This will lead us to ask whether the goal should be not to "depoliticize" but to "repoliticize" Roman Catholic thought in America.

As we have seen, the Blanshard Thesis is widely accepted, not only by anti-Catholics and not only by ecumenically sensitive non-Roman Catholics, but by Roman Catholics themselves. It is a set piece in the way that Roman Catholics and non-Roman Catholics alike tell the story of Catholicism in America. The assumed antagonism between "Catholic" and "American" leads to inescapable dilemmas. One can choose between being one or the other, and many Roman Catholics have felt the need to make that choice. One can compromise, splitting the difference between them, or come up with a new synthesis. But the result of that is likely to be as unsatisfying to the one who does the compromising as it is unbelievable to others. A further possibility is to reduce "Catholic" to "American" or "American" to "Catholic." Many have elected the first reduction; few have suggested the second. Perhaps the most honorable way of responding to the dilemma, if one accepts the Blanshard Thesis, is to hold "Catholic" and "American" in tension, one might even say in paradox.

To be sure, the serious Christian—whatever his or her denominational persuasion—is an "alien citizen" in any order short of the Kingdom. The American order was in many respects designed for such alien citizens. But, as Harold Fey and numerous others have insisted, it was designed "on Protestant terms." That might be called the "Fey Thesis." And that would seem to pose problems enough for Roman Catholics. The Blanshard Thesis is harder, however. Blanshard claimed that the American design is based on secular humanist terms. Thus the Blanshard Thesis poses a very real problem for all Christians. Blanshard allowed that a theologically eviscerated mainline Protestantism could fit well enough into the American order. Roman Catholicism was something else, however. Many Roman Catholics, as we have seen, accepted the Blanshard Thesis, whether or not they knew they were doing so. The Murray Project challenged it head-on. In doing so, Murray was in continuity with earlier strains of Roman Catholic thought in this country. Now, in an ecumenical era, the Murray Project can take the lead in helping all Christians to affirm and renew the American design of a public order for alien citizens who will never be completely at home until they reach the heavenly *polis*.

Two hundred years ago John Carroll rejected the Blanshard Thesis root and branch. The American dispensation, he argued, is good for the Roman Catholic Church, good for civil society, and ultimately good for all of Christianity. "If we have the wisdom and temper to preserve" the harmonious relationship between people of different religious convictions, he asserted, "America may come to exhibit a proof to the world, that general and equal toleration, by giving a free circulation to fair argument, is the most effectual method to bring all denominations of Christians to a unity of faith." In order to prove the point to the world, however, John Carroll, John Ireland, and others of like mind had first to prove the point to Rome. Rome was unpersuaded. In 1895, Leo XIII sent off his apostolic letter, "Longingna Oceani," to Cardinal Gibbons of Baltimore, and "Americanism" was condemned. The condemnation of "Americanism" had to do with more than the right ordering of the civil order, but it had also to do with that. Pointedly and devastatingly, it had to do with Carroll's affirmation of "general and equal toleration." Generations of Roman Catholics would be taught that, in the right ordering of society, "error has no rights." The order in Spain would be held up as the thesis, the American separation of church and state as a deviation (a "hypothesis") to be tolerated as long as necessary. There is no doubt that on this question the otherwise liberal John Ryan spoke for the church, and those who entertained other views, such as John Courtney Murray, were effectively driven from the argument. The Spanish Thesis gave powerful reinforcement to the Blanshard Thesis.

The hold that the Blanshard Thesis had on American thought, including Roman Catholic thought, was dramatically demonstrated in John F. Kennedy's 1960 address to the Baptist ministers of Houston. Hagiologists such as Arthur Schlesinger, Jr., have depicted Kennedy as a closet Catholic intellectual, but in fact there is no evidence to support such a view. More than two decades later it may be hard to remember the impetus that Kennedy gave to a sense of Catholic "arrival" in America. Despite subsequent revelations about his private life (news photographers at the time, for example, agreed not to publish pictures of him smoking cigarettes), the Kennedy myth remains the forceful statement of Catholics having made it in America. But, as exemplified in the decisive Houston speech, Catholics were to make it on Blanshard's terms. With the help of the gifted writer John Cogley, the very model of the "Commonweal Catholic" who later became an Episcopalian, Kennedy's speech succeeded in putting as much distance as possible between the candidate and the church.

Kennedy began by saying that there were "far more critical issues" in the election that the "so-called religious issue." He invited the inference that his being Roman Catholic was something of a nuisance issue and that it was only most reluctantly that he took time from the real questions in order to address it. (The real questions, he said in Houston, were "an America with too many slums, with too few schools, and too late to the moon and outer space.") As George Weigel has put it: "The realm of public policy, and the realm of religious commitment, Kennedy seemed to imply, were separated by a wide chasm: what an historian of philosophy would call the fact/value distinction. Facts we can argue about; values are matters of private concern only." In short, Kennedy powerfully reinforced the concept of what I have elsewhere called the naked public square—the public arena divorced from religiously based moral judgment and discourse.

Kennedy declared:

I believe in an America where the separation of Church and State is absolute—where no Catholic prelate would tell that President (should he be a Catholic) how to act and no Protestant minister would tell his parishioners for whom to vote—where no church or church school is granted any public funds or political preference. . . . I believe in an America that is officially neither Catholic, Protestant, nor Jewish—where no public official either requests or accepts instructions on public policy from the Pope, the National Council of Churches or any other ecclesiastical source—where no religious body seeks to impose its will directly *or indirectly* upon the general populace or the public acts of its officials—and where religious liberty is so indivisible that an act against one church is treated as an act against all. . . . I believe in a President whose views on religion are his own private affair, neither imposed by him on the nation nor imposed by the nation upon him as a condition to holding that office" (emphasis added).

Let it quickly be said that, while such views may have fit Kennedy's personal disposition very neatly, he also had little choice in taking the tack he did. Remember, this was before Vatican II and the "Declaration on Religious Freedom." Had he attempted to challenge the Blanshard-Spanish Thesis, he might have pleased Murray, but he would have found himself in an intra-Catholic dispute for which he had neither inclination nor aptitude. As it was, even those Roman Catholics who rejected "the American proposition" on theological grounds were willing to suspend public criticism of Kennedy for the sake of seeing a Catholic in the White House.

51. CONTRIBUTING TO AMERICA

Murray's understanding of the American proposition was that it is a proposition about the right ordering of society in a world far short of perfection. It is based upon a thoroughly political notion of *tranquillitas ordinis,* derived from a tradition running from Augustine through Thomas, and finding correlates in classical Protestant thought, especially Calvinism. The order in *tranquillitas ordinis* is a provisional order, as is the peace it produces a provisional peace. It assumes the continuation of tensions, interests, and loyalties that are less than universal. It is an understanding that was strongly reflected in Vatican II's statement regarding religious freedom. Whether Murray's views would have any influence on the Council was a close thing. The Apostolic Delegate to the United States thought Murray a very dangerous person. As late as 1964,

Murray wrote to a friend: "The Apostolic Delegate has elected to be my personal enemy and he has made statements about me throughout the country which are libelous. [But] if there should be any trouble in my own case, which is hardly likely, I am sure that his Eminence of New York [Francis Cardinal Spellman] will stand behind me. He is one of the few American bishops who can be counted on to talk back to the Delegate. And he has—bless his heart—elected to be my patron."

Spellman did stand by him, and the declaration was approved in the fourth and final session of the Council. Gerald P. Fogarty writes in *The Vatican and the American Hierarchy* (1985): "The Declaration on Religious Liberty was the American contribution to the council. . . . At long last, the peculiar tradition of the American Church was Catholic teaching. American democracy and ideas of freedom were no longer construed in terms of nineteenth-century European liberalism, but in terms of British and American Common Law, which underlay the twentieth-century constitutional forms of government. The American Church no longer lived in 'the shadow of a hypothesis'." At least officially, the Blanshard Thesis was devastated. It is not too much to say that no other major church body has ever issued an officially approved and theologically informed affirmation of democratic governance, based on the freedom of the person and of persons-in-community, comparable to the "Declaration on Religious Freedom."

Many "traditionalists," then and now, view the Murray Project as a dangerous innovation. But Murray, it might be argued, was the true traditionalist, drawing from the tradition to renew the tradition. Specifically, Murray drew on Augustine, the sixteen-hundredth anniversary of whose Baptism is observed in 1987. And, as noted earlier, he revived the Gelasian tradition with its foundational insight, "Two there are, august Emperor . . ." Augustine is thought to have been excessively dour in his "realistic" approach to human nature, and some have even depicted him as a proponent of "escapism" from worldly responsibility. But in fact Augustine was arguing against those who blamed Christianity for the demoralization and collapse of the empire. He turned the table on such critics, contending that late-classical antiquity was devoid of a philosophy of public virtue that, in fact, Christianity could provide. This combined emphasis on realism and virtue, Murray believed, found expression in the "American proposition" and could be uniquely sustained by philosophical insights drawn from the classical Christian tradition, especially in its Roman Catholic form.

The assertion is frequently made that Vatican II did not issue any condemnations. In a purely formal sense that may be true, but, as George Weigel writes in *Tranquillitas:*

It is hard to imagine a more anti-totalitarian statement than the Declaration on Religious Freedom. . . . If the essence of totalitarianism is to deny that there is any sphere of privacy in the human person, that all matters, even of conscience, are public matters, then totalitarianism is flatly rejected by the Declaration. The Council's insistence that there remains within each person a sanctuary of privileged privacy that cannot be desecrated by "any human power" is a fundamental challenge to totalitarian claims. The Council thus implicitly asserted that the right of religious freedom was the most fundamental of human rights, and that any human rights scheme that failed to acknowledge this (or that qualified it, as in the Soviet Constitution), was spurious.

Moreover, Weigel notes, the Council insisted that this right is not a matter of special revelation but is in principle knowable by human reason, and therefore no person or state had any excuse for violating the right of religious freedom.

Murray's project, in large part canonized by the Council, was ambitious. He intended to provide a moral-theological foundation for the liberal-democratic experiment. It was in one sense an American project, but it also had universal ramifications, for all people, he believed, aspire to live in freedom. The American proposition, in other words, was not a historical accident but the product of principles applicable to all. The enprincipled linking of the particular and universal was key to the construction of the Murray Project, as it would be key to the virtual demolition of the Murray Project in contemporary American Catholic thought. American Catholicism's lived experience of *tranquillitas ordinis,* Murray believed, should equip American Catholics to take the lead in helping America's influence to advance "right order" elsewhere in the world. This notion is so alien to much current Roman Catholic thought that one must immediately add that Murray was no simplistic Wilsonian proposing a Pax Americana for the world. The experiment in the United States must be kept under rigorous criticism, the American proposition is far from being fully realized, and Murray could be as withering as Reinhold Niebuhr in his strictures against national pride and self-aggrandizement. But, like Niebuhr, Murray knew that keeping pride in check should not be confused with denying this experiment's very particular responsibility for the fate of freedom in the world.

As Murray drew on neglected elements in the larger Christian tradition, so also he wanted to build on American Catholicism's lived experience of *tranquillitas ordinis.* He wanted to make theologically and morally explicit the implicit wisdom of the American experience. John Carroll had said that the American founders had "built better than they knew," and so Murray believed that the American Catholic experience contained more wisdom than American Catholics had been prepared to express, lest they be accused of "Americanism." Today it is commonly suggested by Roman Catholic intellectuals that the church in America had been, until the Vietnam War era, mindlessly uncritical in its patriotic affirmation of America's role in the world. The bishops, we are told, were eager to prove themselves "true Americans" in the eyes of their fellow citizens, while never addressing the questions of principle that might raise doubts about whether they were "good Catholics" in the eyes of Rome. In order to be perceived as true Americans, the story continues, the bishops felt the need to present themselves as mindlessly uncritical patriots. Weigel, arguing for the continuity between the Murray Project and the actual lived experience of American Catholicism, sharply challenges that stereotype. Focusing on issues of war and peace, Weigel painstakingly demonstrates that in World War I and World War II, for instance, the American bishops produced sophisticated statements emphasizing what Tillich called the *obligatum* and *reservatum* of national commitment, and of politics itself.

The bishops, like Murray and the classical Christian tradition, understood that one could only be a citizen of a *polis*. Without reference to a specific *polis,* there could be no politics but only sentimental allusions to chimera such as "global citizenship." While there was not, and is not yet, a *polis* on the international scale, the transnational nature of the Church, and of membership in the Church, posed questions of moral and political obligation that sharply relativized the *obligatum* of being American. It is this nuanced understanding of politics as right order, an understanding exemplified in the work of Murray, that Weigel believes has been "largely abandoned by the most influential sectors of the American Catholic elite in a short decade after Vatican II." The unhappy result is that Catholic elites in the United States "became, not the shapers of a new and wiser moral argument, but antagonists in old ones." In terms of our earlier distinction, in becoming "American Catholic," the intellectual and much of the episcopal leadership did not so much join America as it joined America's new knowledge class. Becoming American just in time to become anti-American, Roman Catholics who had implicitly (and often explicitly) accepted the Blanshard Thesis end up joining the Paul Blanshards of today in rejecting John Courtney Murray's moral-theological understanding of the symbiotic relationship between being "true American" and "good Catholic."

We noted above that Roman Catholic thought needs to be "repoliticized." That may sound confusing, since in the last section we examined the doleful consequences of certain varieties of "political theology." Obviously, the way of thinking that reduces theology to politics is not what we have in mind. In fact, it is quite the opposite of what we have in mind. The way of thinking that we have in mind is one in which it is recognized that theology and politics are discrete enterprises and neither is reduced to, or elevated to, the other. Christians think theologically about everything, including politics. But they do so in a way that respects the fact that politics has its own integrity, its own rules, so to speak. It is in that light that one can say it would be better to be ruled by a wise Turk than by a stupid Christian. But, of course, since politics is not an entirely autonomous enterprise, but is interconnected with culture, morality, and tradition, it might be even better to be ruled by a wise Christian. The point is that those matters having to do with the ordering of public life, the *res publica,* are distinct from (not separate from) the discourse that pertains to the ordering of our ultimate loves and loyalties.

It is in that sense, then, that our thought about politics should be properly political. The theocratic mindset, whether of the Left or the Right, cannot tolerate this distinction. Our monistic hungers drive us to order everything according to the revealed will of God, and to try to do so now. And so in America today religious thinkers on the Left and on the Right propose their versions of "biblical politics." Addressing the National Association of Evangelicals, President Reagan pointed to the Bible and said, "All the answers are in this book." Indeed, with respect to the ordering of our ultimate loves and loyalties. But the answers to the right ordering of tax policy, the strategy for peace in a nuclear age, and the reform of the welfare system—such answers are not to be found in the Bible. Politics for the Christian is not an exercise of biblical exegesis, of moving from Bible passage to policy specific, but of prudential reasoning. Nor is politics a matter of Spirit-empowered will to the good. It is frequently said, "We can solve the problem of hunger—or of war, or of global development, or of whatever—if only we have the political will to do so." Such statements are not simply unhelpful; they are positively destructive. They destroy the possibility of truly political reasoning that attends to structures, institutions, interests, and patterns of human behavior. Such statements reflect the "liberal sentimentalism" that John Courtney Murray and Reinhold Niebuhr were joined in attempting to surmount. The situation is not substantively changed by the fact that such sentimentalism is today frequently found also among religious conservatives.

A common characteristic in the refusal to engage in authentically political thought is the conflation of the Church and the public order. That is, it is assumed that the rules governing life in the community of faith are the same as the rules governing public life. And so it is said that a commitment to democracy in the political realm must be accompanied by commitment to democracy in the life of the Church. Or, conversely, that the love and trust that are to mark the community of faith are the key to advancing peace and justice in the world. Of course, if we argue that the virtue of trust is proper to the Church while justice is properly a public virtue, we open ourselves to the charge of promoting "dualism." Acknowledging that virtues are interconnected in complicated ways, we must nevertheless distinguish without separating. And, as discussed earlier, we should not be intimidated by the charge of dualism. Alien citizens are unapologetically dualistic. The alternative to being dualistic is to be monistic.

Employing somewhat different language, Weigel's *Tranquillitas Ordinis* is in large part the story of Roman Catholicism's intellectual descent into moral and political monism in the years following Vatican II. Instead of elevating the level of morally informed and rigorously rational political discourse, Roman Catholic pronouncements increasingly, in the name of Gospel truth, pitted one "peace and justice agenda" against other peace and justice agendas, also advanced in the name of Gospel truth. In the process the declaration of high ideals is mistaken for political wisdom. Weigel tries to put a favorable construction on official, especially papal, pronouncements. But from John XXIII through recent statements by synods and episcopal conferences, Roman Catholic political utterances have more often than not reflected the Protestant propensity for confusing moral discourse with moralism. Thus it is again and again proposed to the nations that they should "trust" one another, that economic justice can be achieved by "mutual love," that disarmament should be advanced by a greater measure of "faith," and that citizenship responsibility is defined by "the global community." When specific policy options are favored, the clear implication is that those who favor alternative policies are lacking in faith, hope, and love. Thus is political discourse debased, thus is political disagreement religiously inflamed, and thus is Murray's (and Thomas's) "cool reasoning" about the *res publica* abandoned.

52. DISILLUSIONMENT WITH AMERICA

Among many Roman Catholics who "came of age" in America during the sixties and seventies, the abandonment of the tradition of reasoned political discourse was combined with what can best be described as alienation from the American experience and the "proposition" undergirding it. In *Bare Ruined Choirs* (1972), Garry Wills described how in his last years at Woodstock, during the "radicalized sixties," Murray was thought to be impossibly passé. Within a few years of his death, those who remembered Murray were talking about the need to go "beyond Murray." David Hollenbach, for example, writes that post-Murray theologians should undertake "a critical re-evaluation of the American civil liberties tradition which Murray brought into creative contact with the Catholic social tradition." Hollenbach argues that "one can no longer suppose, as Murray did, that the American public philosophy is rooted in and supported by the broad theological tradition of Christian history, [for] the missing element in the public ethos of America is the sense of the sacred in history and in society and human interaction." The Murray Project, suggests Hollenbach, was oriented to the status quo and must now be brought to liberation theology's bar of judgment.

A tradition of radical Catholic action, which had always been there, moved to center stage in the sixties and seventies. Dorothy Day and the Catholic Worker movement represented a confused but exciting mix of personalism, anarchism, eschatological hope, and pacifism that seized the imaginations of many. She was acclaimed as a "witness to profound

Gospel simplification." At her death in 1980, the historian David O'Brien wrote that Dorothy Day "was the most significant, interesting, and influential person in the history of American Catholicism." In an indulgence of hyperbolic excess, Vatican II had called for "an entirely new attitude" toward questions of war and peace. More centrist figures than Dorothy Day took the Council's admonition quite literally. An apocalyptic rhetoric flourished, for example, around the United States bishops' pastoral letter, "The Challenge of Peace." The assumption was that ours is an utterly unique historical moment in which all past experience was to be consigned to the dustbin. As Father Theodore Hesburgh of Notre Dame put it, "There were no precedents to invoke, no history to depend upon for a wise lesson, no real body of theology except for that which dates back to pacifism or a just-war doctrine that was first applied in a day of spears, swords, bows and arrows, not ICBMs." Murray would have been astonished by this wholesale, if not hysterical, dismissal of the Great Tradition of Christian social teaching. But this has been a period for astonishments.

The turning was not only against a tradition of social teaching but also against America and, finally, against politics itself. Of course we are not talking about all Roman Catholics. Far from it. We are speaking about a relatively small number who, at a certain time in American history, were acclaimed by a larger elite to represent a perhaps "extreme" but laudably "idealistic" Roman Catholic posture toward politics. They supply the evidence cited by Jay Dolan and others that Catholics had at last entered the American mainstream. Many Roman Catholics, some reluctantly and some with breathless haste, had arrived at the conclusions expressed by Philip Berrigan at the famous "Catonsville Nine" trial.

Your honor, I think that we would be less than honest with you if we did not state our attitude. Simply, we have lost confidence in the institutions of this country, including our own churches. . . . We have come to our conclusion slowly and painfully. We have lost confidence, because we do not believe any longer that these institutions are reformable. . . . I am saying merely this: We see no evidence that the institutions of this country, including our own churches, are able to provide the type of change that justice calls for, not only in this country, but around the world. We believe that this has occurred because law is no longer serving the needs of the people.

At a rally before the trial, Philip's brother, Daniel Berrigan, typically took "the entirely new attitude" not only against a tradition of social teaching, against the American experiment, and against law, but against politics itself. "How many martyrs ever had any practical programs for reforming society? Since politics weren't working anyway, one had to find an act beyond politics: a religious act, a liturgical act, an act of witness. If only a small number of men could offer this kind of witness, it would purify the world. Wasn't there a time in England when every Quaker was in jail? What a great scene that must have been! Perhaps that's where all Christians should be today. . . ." Of course, Daniel Berrigan was a poet, and, it was frequently said, he had poetic license. But the influence of the brothers Berrigan upon Catholic activists in "the peace and justice network" during and after the Vietnam War can hardly be overestimated.

Under the tutelage of Jim Douglass, a Berrigan disciple, Archbishop Raymond Hunthausen would carry a radicalized version of Catholic social teaching into the eighties. Addressing a synod of the Lutheran Church in America in 1981, Hunthausen declared that America's "willingness to destroy life everywhere on this earth, for the sake of our security as Americans, is at the root of many other terrible events in our country." He was particularly concerned about Trident submarines based in his diocese. "And when crimes are being prepared in our name, we must speak plainly. I say with a deep consciousness of these words that Trident is the Auschwitz of Puget Sound." Hunthausen's understanding of a "biblical politics" made possible, indeed imperative, a rapid and radical move from scriptural truth to political decision: "As followers of Christ, we need to take up our cross in the nuclear age. I believe that one obvious meaning of the cross is unilateral disarmament. Jesus' acceptance of the cross rather than the sword raised in his defense is the Gospel's statement of unilateral disarmament." Hunthausen's restatement of the Gospel as political prescription is based upon a judgment about the nature of American life and power. "In considering a Christian response to nuclear arms," the archbishop told an audience at Notre Dame in 1983, "I think we have to begin by recognizing that our country's overwhelming array of nuclear arms has a very precise purpose: it is meant to protect our wealth. The United States is not illogical in amassing the most destructive weapons in history. We need them. We are the richest people in history." An enthusiastic audience at the nation's premier Roman Catholic university cheered the pronouncement that "our nuclear war preparations are the global crucifixion of Jesus."

But surely, it may be objected, these are fringe figures: Dorothy Day, the Berrigans, James Douglass, Raymond Hunthausen, and others. The answer is that they were exceptional in that they "went further" than most. They were not exceptional but archetypical in that they signaled the direction in which to go. In the conventional telling of the story, they are the ones who are cited as evidence that Catholics have, as it is said, entered the mainstream. That mainstream is not, of course, the American mainstream that elected and reelected Ronald Reagan by overwhelming majorities. But it is the mainstream of that cultural elite that, for the culturally ambitious, defines what it means to have arrived in America. These "fringe figures" defined the moral high ground for many Roman Catholics of influence. Joseph O'Hare, then editor of *America*, tellingly describes a meeting of Jesuits in 1972:

Many of the younger Jesuits present, veterans of the peace movement, needed no convincing of the bankruptcy of American society and the evil consequences of its influence abroad. One soft-spoken seminarian, recently released from prison where he had served twenty-two months for draft resistance activities, quietly asked if there was any name for American influence abroad other than murder or genocide. Another peace veteran took a more historical perspective. Was not oppression the American tradition—not simply Asians and Latin Americans abroad, but blacks and Indians at home, and before them, the immigrant waves from Europe? There did not seem too much left to what John Courtney Murray liked to call "the American Proposition."

Paul Blanshard argued that Catholicism and Americanism were opposed to one another. He could hardly have anticipated the form that that opposition would take in the decades following Vatican II. Attitudes, even among Jesuits, are presumably less "radicalized" in the eighties than they were at the gathering described by Father O'Hare. To be sure, some Jesuits and others are saying much the same thing as was said then, perhaps more virulently, in their promotion of liberation theology. But even among those whose views have been tempered by time—who have arrived at something like that synthesis to which Martin Marty refers—are not likely to have much enthusiasm for Murray's American proposition. The critical question here is not what one thinks about America and its role in the world. The critical question is how one relates moral and theological argument to political reason and imagination. The American proposition is but a case in point, although, especially for Americans, an exceedingly important case in point.

A common complaint, at least outside the new knowledge class, is that American religion in general and American Catholicism in particular have been inordinately "politicized." Our suggestion is that in very odd ways Roman Catholic social thought has in the last years been depoliticized. While intensely political on the level of partisan activism, it has been remarkably indifferent to the political work of reason in the right ordering of institutions and interests. Good intentions are mistaken for policies, postures are passed off as positions, and the fervent hope that the world might be a much nicer place is acclaimed as an alternative to the way things are. Biblical metaphors and truth claims are, with unseemly facility, translated into a "biblical politics" in which the invocation of *shalom* replaces the hard work of political intelligence and imagination in achieving an ever-provisional and fragile *tranquillitas ordinis*.

53. THE VERY MODEL OF AMERICANIZED CHRISTIANITY

That the American ethos is profoundly and confusedly Protestant has been evident enough to most observers. When it is suggested that the Protestant hegemony has been displaced, the displacement that is suggested is not by another religious tradition but by "secularization." At the edge of the third millennium, and a few years into the third century of the nation's history, all the evidence suggests that America is not and is not becoming a secular society. "Unsecular America" is the reality that has long been taken for granted by most Americans but has in recent years taken our cultural elites by surprise. The power and pervasiveness of religion in American life catches the attention of the prestige media when it impinges upon the political arena, for much of the prestige media sincerely believe that politics is "the real world." A measure of skepticism is in order when discussing the new visibility of religion in American society, however, especially when it is described as a "religious revival." Some analysts suggest that this religion may not be very religious. That is, what we used to call secular values and attitudes may have been successfully taken over by religion. In this view, secularization continues apace, except now under the auspices of religion. While such skepticism has its uses, pushing this way of thinking very far gets us into a definitional conundrum in which terms such as *secular* and *religious* lose all meaning.

Suffice it that by the usual indices—professed belief, church attendance, prayer, and other activities and commitments identified as religious—the American people are more, not less, religious than they were, say, fifty years ago. This in defiance of the "modernity project" launched by the eighteenth-century secular Enlightenment, a project that envisioned the withering away of religion. It may be that Americans have found the knack of taking their modernity selectively. On the operational and technical side of life, everything must be up-to-date and "scientific." On the passional side of life, where people look for "meaning," Americans increasingly affirm "the faith of our fathers." Nobody wants a surgeon who operates according to "biblical medicine," and nobody, or almost nobody, looks to the National Academy of Sciences to tell them the purpose of living. However wisely or confusedly put together, then, the American ethos continues to be very religious, and religion continues to be very Protestant.

As we have seen, Roman Catholics in America have been keenly aware of this reality, and from the eighteenth century on have worried out loud about whether it is possible to become American without becoming Protestant. The new factor today is not the relative size of Catholicism in America. Already in the middle of the nineteenth century, the Roman Catholic Church was the largest single religious body in America. The new factor is that—as observers such as Jay Dolan note with enthusiasm and others note with greater nuance—"Catholics have become like everybody else." To the extent this is true, much depends on whom is meant by "everybody else." If it means becoming like the Protestantism that has allegedly been secularized, the future would suggest increased secularization under increasingly vague Roman Catholic auspices. That is clearly a prospect that is not unpleasing to all Roman Catholics. After the collapse of the supernatural and the abandonment of the transcendent, an identifiably Roman Catholic "symbol system" and "communal loyalty" can be selectively employed in advancing sundry purposes, both personal and public. This, according to many experts on the subject, is what is meant and should be meant by the "Americanization" of Catholicism.

Talk about being Americanized requires some model for what it means to be American. The very model of Americanized Christianity is mainline Protestantism. The mainline, which is now increasingly and rightly called the old line, or even the side line, is represented by the core member churches of the National Council of Churches—the United Methodists, the United Church of Christ, the Presbyterian Church USA, the Episcopalians, for example. These are the churches to which Roman Catholics looked when they contemplated the prospect of Americanization. Long before Vatican II, when "ecumenism" was neither on the lips nor on the agenda of American Catholicism, these were the churches with which Roman Catholic leadership established cooperative ties. In the early part of this century, "social Catholicism" was undoubtedly in tandem with the social gospel movement of old-line Protestantism. In 1917 the bishops appointed John J. Burke, a Paulist, to head up the National Catholic War Council, and he immediately reached out to the Federal Council of Churches (predecessor to the National Council) as the voice of a uniting Protestantism that was the logical partner in cooperative work.

Like the National Council of Churches, the NCWC saw in Roosevelt's New Deal the embodiment of the church's agenda for social justice. One Roman Catholic historian approvingly calls Monsignor John Ryan a "cheerleader for the New Deal," and Ryan's biography is titled *Right Reverend New Dealer.* The days of the New Deal seemed like a heady culmination of a Catholic social gospel crusade that took its mandate from the 1891 encyclical, *Rerum Novarum.* At the time the encyclical was issued, Bishop John L. Spalding declared its teaching to be that "the mission of the church is not only to save souls, but also to save society." The idea of the salvific nature of the church's social mission brought sectors of Roman Catholic leadership into cordial communion with the Protestant crusade to "Christianize America and Americanize Christianity"—and to save the world to boot.

If Roman Catholics were to relate to "everybody else," it seems they did not have too many alternatives to old-line Protestantism. They gingerly related to Judaism, at least of the Reform and Conservative varieties. But that was chiefly so that Catholicism could take its place alongside old-line Protestantism in the religiocultural triumverate of the American Way. There were the Eastern Orthodox Christians—Russian, Greek, Armenian, Rumanian, etc.—but they were so divided, exotic, and ghettoized that they were unlikely partners in the process of Americanization. There are roughly as many Orthodox Christians in America as there are

Jews, but they are barely perceptible on the religiocultural map. Anyway, the Vatican took care of relations with the East. Then there are the Lutherans. Gallup says twenty million Americans claim to be Lutheran, although the church jurisdictions count only ten million as members. Premier Protestants though they be, the Lutherans are not really American old line. Numerous authorities have pointed out that, in terms of history, sociology, theology, and religious sensibility, Lutherans and Roman Catholics in America are closer to one another than to anyone else. That has produced some very strong ties, especially in places such as Lake Wobegon, Minnesota, and in the last several decades has resulted in theological dialogues that are generally recognized as being the most sophisticated and promising among the many dialogues in which the several churches are engaged. But the Lutherans, too, are trying to find their place on the religiocultural map and, in the absence of decision, show strong signs of drift toward the camp of old-line Protestantism. In any case, Lutherans are not the very model of the American church that many Roman Catholics want their church to become.

Of course there is that very big world composed of the many worlds of evangelicalism, fundamentalism, and pentecostalism. It claims the allegiance of as many as sixty million Americans. It is a very Americanized Christianity and in recent years has eagerly seized the banners of the old-line Protestant crusade to Christianize America. On some questions—abortion, for example—it is at one with the Roman Catholic hierarchy. Abortion is not the only example. On matters of sexuality, family life, a generous reading of the free exercise clause of the First Amendment, and educational choice—all issues with clear public policy ramifications—there is substantial common interest between Catholicism and the evangelical/fundamentalist world. But Roman Catholics who are eager to become American do not have in mind an alliance with this world. Indeed, the very things that Catholicism has in common with this world are viewed by many Roman Catholics as the Roman-European residue of which Catholicism must be shed.

Furthermore, the worlds of evangelicaldom have been in the cultural wilderness for half a century, ever since they were declared to have lost the modernist/fundamentalist wars. Only in the 1970s did they make their cultural and political reentry, and then they did so in an aggressive, even vulgar, manner that was off-putting to Roman Catholics who were eager to present themselves as secure in their own arrival in America. Evangelicals, fundamentalists, and pentecostals who have just arrived in the corridors of power from the rural South were unlikely allies for culturally aspiring Roman Catholics. As though this were not enough, there was a strong and lively strain of anti-Catholicism in this evangelical/fundamentalist world. Old-line Protestantism is in this respect practiced in the arts of discretion, while some fundamentalist preachers still today occasionally let it slip that the pope is probably the anti-Christ. Old-line

Protestants are never heard to say that sort of thing, probably because they do not believe in the anti-Christ. The evangelical/fundamentalist world was likewise once an incubator of anti-Semitism of a coarse variety, as distinct from the usually more refined anti-Semitism of the old Protestant ruling class. Beginning in the 1960s, the leadership of organized Judaism, increasingly uneasy about what they perceived to be the anti-Israel drift of the liberal old-line churches, began to court the leadership of evangelicaldom. The degree to which the evangelical/fundamentalist world has in a few years developed a theologically grounded commitment both to Israel and to Living Judaism is one of the most remarkable religious and cultural stories of recent American history.

Roman Catholic leadership has made no such concerted effort to reach the evangelical/fundamentalist world. It is intriguing to ask, but perhaps impossible to answer, whether Jews were able to make that effort because they were more secure, or had to make it because they were more insecure. In any event, it is certain that one reason Roman Catholics have not made that effort is because throughout their history the concept of Americanization has been tied to the old-line churches. For the churches of old-line Protestantism, the aggressive world of evangelicaldom is simply beyond the pale. For them, ecumenism stops at the cultural edge. It is no secret that much Roman Catholic intellectual and academic leadership is deeply embarrassed by Catholicism's deviations from liberal Protestant social orthodoxy. This has been notably the case with respect to the public struggle over abortion. A good many bishops seem to plead with their Protestant counterparts and with their own elites to please understand that these questions arising from Rome's "pubic theology" (as one prominent Catholic writer terms it) are imposed upon them and there is little they can do about it. Frequently, useful concepts such as "the seamless garment" and "a consistent life ethic" are invoked in effect, if not in intention, to take the edge off the abortion question, making it one question among others, alongside nuclear disarmament, environmental safety, and kindness to whales. So eager are these Roman Catholics not to offend liberal Protestant etiquette.

This description makes no claim to being novel. The syndrome under discussion is fairly widely recognized. The process of Catholics becoming like everybody else (or at least like the right people) is a welcome achievement in the sight of many, whereas the "liberalizing" and "Protestantizing" of Roman Catholicism is the cause of constant lament among those who are viewed as conservatives. The latter, including not a few bishops, say the process has already gone too far, that the challenge is not to be the American Catholic Church but to be the Roman Catholic Church in America. And yet, however painful and ambiguous the process, "Americanization" is inevitable. There is also no reason why it should not be acknowledged as imperative, as is "indigenization" and "inculturation" for the church in Third World countries. What is neither inevitable nor imperative is that Americanization be defined by the model of old-line Protestantism. This does not mean, one quickly adds, that it should be defined *against* old-line Protestantism. The future of the Roman Catholic Church in America will, one hopes, be something quite new. If and when Catholicism becomes like everybody else, one more church among the churches, one more option in the cafeteria of spiritual styles, then it has not only lost its own identity, but it has contributed little to American culture or to the life of the larger Church. For its own sake and for the sake of all of us, the challenge for Catholicism is to demonstrate a new model of ecclesiastical vitality and integrity within the American context. If it is to make such a difference, one expects it will have to be as determinedly Roman Catholic as it is thoroughly American. In short, the Blanshard Thesis must be repudiated in all its forms. It is easier to repudiate, indeed it is already gravely weakened, in its older Protestant form of anti-Catholicism. It is more difficult to repudiate the Blanshard Thesis as it is advanced by Roman Catholics, both liberal and traditionalist, who would force a choice between being American and being Catholic.

The future, to be sure, is uncertain and filled with contingencies beyond any mortal's foresight or control. A measure of leadership, if not control, is possible by understanding the present. At present, Catholicism in America is remarkably imitative of the patterns of thought and corporate behavior that mark liberal Protestantism. We have already discussed the phenomenon of the new knowledge class that dominates the prestige worlds of academe, media, culture, and religion. In the elaborate and entrenched bureaucracies of the old-line churches, the power of the new knowledge class is much more pronounced than it is today in American Catholicism. But the directions are strikingly similar. Of course this is good news if one is a dues-paying member of the new knowledge class. But there are numerous reasons why Roman Catholics should think twice, and then think again, about the desirability of further emulating the pattern of old-line Protestantism. Not least among these reasons is the long, steady, and apparently inexorable institutional decline of old-line Protestantism.

Much has been written about the declining fortunes of old-line Protestantism and the subject can quickly become tedious. But a few figures indicate some of the statistical changes in the religious situation. According to Gallup, in 1947, 69 percent of Americans said they were Protestant, 20 percent were Roman Catholic, and 5 percent were Jewish. The figures in 1985 are 57 percent Protestant, 28 percent Roman Catholic, and 2 percent Jewish. (One in eleven Americans expresses no religious preference.) Within the world called Protestant there is a further statistical breakdown: 20 percent of Americans are Baptist, 20 percent Methodist, 6 percent Lutheran, 2 percent Presbyterian, and 2 percent Episcopalian. In the last two decades, the Baptists have increased slightly, and the

Lutherans have declined somewhat more than slightly. Among the old-line churches, the Methodists and Episcopalians have fallen by 30 percent, and the Presbyterians have taken a loss of 65 percent.

The suggestion is not that a Roman Catholicism that becomes more like old-line Protestantism will experience similar declines. The figures do suggest something about the presence and absence of institutional vitalities in Protestantism. The communal ties in being Roman Catholic are different and in some ways no doubt stronger. As traditionalists routinely complain, "There are millions of Catholics who are not Catholics but who refuse to leave the Catholic Church." So the predictions that by the middle of the next century more Americans will identify themselves to George Gallup's grandson as Roman Catholic than as Protestant may well be accurate. But it may also turn out that the main difference between Roman Catholics and old-line Protestants in terms of institutional loyalty and religious practice is that old-line Protestants leave when they leave.

54. BISHOPS AND ACCOUNTABILITY

In resisting the control of the new knowledge class and its bureaucracy, the role of the bishop in Roman Catholicism would seem to be critically important. Among major American bodies, the Roman Catholic people's manifest sense of identification with, and usually affection for, their bishop is singular. Bishops in other bodies—Methodist, Lutheran, Episcopalian—frequently have as much power, in practice if not in theory, but are more susceptible to becoming managers of the branch office of the national church. This is not to say that many Roman Catholic bishops are not susceptible to that and other ways of becoming mere functionaries. But the Roman Catholic bishop is somewhat less bureaucratically "capturable" by virtue of having diverse lines of accountability attached to his office. He is pastor of the people, leader of the clergy who exercise their office by his authority, responsible to diverse institutions and religious communities in his diocese, and, very importantly, he is accountable to Rome. The last line is theologically and institutionally constitutive of his being a bishop. It might be argued that this is the structural distinction that precludes the Roman Catholic Church from becoming thoroughly "Americanized" along the lines of other churches in America. The prerogative of Rome to appoint, to hold accountable, and, when it deems necessary, to remove bishops may be a relatively late development, but it has taken on a peculiar importance. In the hoped-for ecumenical future, in the Church of reconciled diversity, that papal prerogative will almost certainly not be acceptable to other communions. But for the Roman Catholic communion, it could turn out to be a permanent feature and a permanent strength in enabling Roman Catholicism to continue to be Roman Catholic, and thereby to make an ecumenical contribution that makes a difference.

The importance of accountability to the Holy See was evident in 1986 when the American bishops' conference considered the restrictions placed by Rome on Archbishop Raymond Hunthausen of Seattle. The general media, and some of the Catholic press, set the scene for a major confrontation between the Vatican and the American bishops. Of course no such confrontation took place. As one American bishop explained, "We could and did express our concerns, but the idea that we would interject ourselves between Seattle and Rome was never on, not for a minute. To do so would be to pull the plug on our own authority. After all, we are only bishops because the Holy Father says we are bishops." Such a "centralized" structure is deplored by many as being demeaning and restrictive. On the other hand, it may be one key to the remarkably decentralized vitalities of Catholicism in this society and elsewhere. That, as we saw earlier, was at least how some Third World bishops viewed the matter at the 1985 Extraordinary Synod in Rome. In any event, for an American bishop, Rome is farther away than Washington, and farther away than a church convention, which, as in other church bodies, could bind a bishop by majority vote. While some Roman Catholics press hard for further "democratization," the prospect of such church conventions seems remote. In the view of at least some bishops, however, Washington appears to be getting closer to everywhere.

After World War I, Cardinal Gibbons took the lead in urging that the National Catholic War Council be continued and strengthened in another form. Writing to his episcopal colleagues, he said that "the Catholic Church in America, partly through defective organization, is not exerting the influence which it ought to exert in proportion to our numbers and the individual prominence of many of our people." Though it was well organized locally, "the Church in America as a whole has been suffering from the lack of a unified force that might be directed to the furthering of those general policies which are vital to all." Some bishops opposed the National Catholic Welfare Council (later Conference), fearing the day when it might impinge upon their authority and independence of action. But most welcomed its contribution to an enhanced national consciousness of Catholicism's strength, importantly sited in the nation's capital. According to one historian of the period, it raised the sights of the bishops "and taught them to think about issues that transcended local diocesan concerns." The Bishops' Program of Social Reconstruction in 1919 was an instance of such "grand thinking," and soon numerous statements were issuing forth on questions of national and international moment. As Harold Fey noted with alarm and the historian Jay Dolan notes with satisfaction, the American Catholic enterprise was being nationalized. "This," writes Dolan, in *The American Catholic Experience*, "had the obvious effect of turning the Conference into a super church agency at the national level. Much like its Protestant counterpart, the Federal

Council of Churches, the offices of the Conference in Washington became the national headquarters of American Catholicism."

By the 1970s Roman Catholic complaints about the Washington bureaucracy often seemed to echo the complaints of Protestant laity and
clergy about the National Council of Churches. But there were also big
differences. The National Council does not claim to be a church, never
mind *the* Church. For Roman Catholics, however, the United States Catholic Conference and especially the National Conference of Catholic Bishops do speak for their church, which, they are inclined to believe, is *the*
Church. Conservative resentment of the Washington bureaucracy, therefore, is similar not so much to Protestant resentments of the National
Council as to resentment of the pronouncements and positions of the
bureaucracies of their own church bodies—whether they be Methodist,
Presbyterian, or Disciples of Christ. Roman Catholic traditionalists tend
to see the workings of the Washington headquarters in terms of sinister
liberal conspiracy, and a number of studies have documented how decisions made by functionaries are then ratified by the bishops. Conspiracy
(*com + spirare,* to breathe together) there may be, at least in the sense of
collaboration. But this need be nothing sinister, since officials are paid
to work together. James Luther Adams of Harvard has a simpler, if not
terribly elevated, explanation that applies to churches and other institutions across the board. "History is made in meetings," Adams once
remarked to me, "and the outcome of meetings is controlled by those
who draw up the agendas, arrive on time, stay to the end, and keep the
minutes." A prominent bishop who is not at all happy with the Washington office explained to this writer, "Early on I decided that I would either
have to be bishop of this diocese or try to take a hand in reshaping the
Washington bureaucracy. I can't do both, and neither can the other
bishops. The simple and dismal fact is that the bureaucrats can always
out-meeting us."

A number of scholars have urged that the public policy positions taken
by the Roman Catholic bishops throughout this century have always been
somewhat "left of center." Therefore the conservative agitation about
the bishops' leftward lurch today is unjustified. There is no doubt some
merit in this claim. After all, when Monsignor Ryan was "cheerleading"
the New Deal, there must have been some very unhappy Roman Catholic
Republicans. But it does not take much historical or sociological sophistication to see the difference between cheerleading FDR in 1936 and cheerleading McGovern in 1972 or the "special interest Democrats" putatively
represented by Mondale in 1984. At least the overwhelming majority of
American voters, including most of the Catholic people, had little difficulty in detecting the difference.

Decades ago "left of center" Roman Catholic leadership had a very
different relationship to the Catholic constituency. The historian Mel
Piehl (*Breaking Bread: The Catholic Worker and the Origins of Catholic Radical-
ism,* (1982) is helpful in this connection.

The problem for Protestantism was how to reach a lower class with whom it had little in common; for Catholicism, it was to keep abreast of the pressing demands from a working-class membership eager for its ministrations. American Catholicism's encounter with industrialization, therefore, was more institutional and practical than intellectual or moral, more an unconscious necessity than a conscious choice. Its leaders were not a minority of articulate prophets challenging accepted beliefs, but numerous clergy and laypersons who seldom understood or proclaimed their activities as distinctly religious responses to industrialization. Many Catholics, therefore, had a long experience in coping with social problems before they began to reflect on them.

The difference between Catholic social gospelism then and now could hardly be more dramatic. Today—in national and diocesan offices, in universities and colleges, in networks of activist collaboration—the leaders are "a minority of articulate prophets challenging accepted beliefs." The leadership, or at least key parts of it, has been to Harvard. Many of the Roman Catholic laity have also joined the new knowledge class and are enthusiastic about this leadership, but most Roman Catholics have not and are not. Success for most Roman Catholics means being firmly ensconced in the old middle class, pejoratively known as the bourgeoisie. Varieties of conservative response to the new class leadership may accurately be described as a bourgeois insurgency.

The historian Jay Dolan is again helpful. He is discussing the American mainstream that Roman Catholics have joined. "By the end of the 1970s, the issues of the '60s were taken for granted, and this alone showed how far the nation had progressed. Women's rights, concern for the environment, racial justice, political accountability, and a desire for peace in a nuclear age had become part of the American mainstream." Catholics were intensely caught up in what he calls a "contagion for justice." At the same time, he himself recognizes that "the vast majority of Catholics" were opposed to this contagion and to this definition of justice. What he undoubtedly means to say, or should mean to say, is that certain elites had successfully seized control of key institutions, and this "minority of articulate prophets" was able to present itself as representing the Roman Catholic position on myriad issues in public debate. To those who contend, then, that there is a "left of center" continuity in Roman Catholic position taking during the course of the century, and that therefore conservatives are much exercised about nothing, the contrasting descriptions of leadership offered by Piehl and Dolan provide a powerful counterargument.

There is another difference between past and present, however, and it may well be much more important. It is essentially a theological difference in the understanding of the nature and mission of the Church. Bishop Spalding's remark about saving the world notwithstanding, until ten or twenty years ago almost all Roman Catholics thought it beyond question that the nature of the Church was primarily spiritual and its mission primarily to save souls. Popular Catholicism effectively tempered the world's definitions of "liberation." (See Thesis 9, Part 6.) Social and political change was an additional and generally approved dimension of the Church's responsibility in the world; it was not, as is now said, constitutive of the Church. The difference between past and present, then, is not only that the positions taken have changed, and not only that the class locations of leadership and constituency have changed, but that the nature and mission of the Church have been redefined. In the past, political disagreements could be more easily accommodated within the community of faith because political positions did not constitute the faith. The church's political position taking was, while not marginal, at least not primary to the church's being the Church. Today, however, political and social change is frequently declared to be the primary, sometimes the only, mission of the Church.

In the 1930s, some parishioners no doubt bridled at partisan politics from the pulpit, but they understood that their disagreement did not drive to the heart of what it means to be a Catholic. Today, many such parishioners feel that they are, at least implicitly, excommunicated by virtue of their political dissent. "If the church is not for promoting justice in the real world," a bishop recently told a midwestern conference of clergy, "I don't know what the church is for." In his case, one hopes, it was a careless remark; for many others it is obviously dogma. In this respect, too, developments in Roman Catholicism parallel developments in the old-line Protestant churches. It needs only to be added that those who say that the Church must recover a "transcendent" and "spiritual" understanding of its nature and mission are suspected by their opponents of simply wanting to capture the Church for *their* politics. "Were the conservatives in the saddle," it is said, "the Church would be even more politicized, except in the opposite direction." The suspicion may well be justified in the case of many conservatives. It is sobering evidence of the debasement of Christian community when discussion of the nature and mission of the Church is thought to be reducible to the partisan antagonisms and alignments determined by the world.

As in the liberal Protestant churches, many dissatisfactions cluster around confusions about the relationship between clergy and laity, their respective responsibility and authority. This too is a perennial question that has erupted throughout Christian history, but it is exacerbated today by, among other factors, the politicizing and bureaucratizing of church life. In a 1974 interview with *Commonweal,* Karl Rahner cautioned against the idea that the church could produce theological answers to moral and political questions like "freshly baked breakfast rolls." But if the church goes into the bakery business, it seems uneconomic to let the ovens get cold. It seems to be a law of church life that the felt need for public policy pronouncements expands in proportion to the offices and procedures established for making them. And the law of diminishing effect sets in with a vengeance as such position taking is multiplied. Almost all students of the subject agree that this has happened to an alarming degree in the old-line Protestant churches. Many laypeople have left, many others stay but seethe at what they view as an abuse of church authority, some protest and try to organize a revolt against the church-and-society curia, some cheer their church's promotion of their favored social and political agenda. But studies indicate that the great majority of laypeople have simply stopped paying attention. And this is a great sadness, for it reinforces the suspicion that Christian faith has little or nothing to do with one's responsibilities in the public arena. The resulting indifference or hostility of the laity confirms the officialdoms in their belief that they are being "prophetic," for everyone knows that prophets are unpopular. Thus in the old-line churches a dismal spiral of alienation has set in, and the end is not yet in sight.

The churches in the Reformation traditions have trumpeted "the priesthood of all believers," frequently in a way that sharply diminished the role of the ordained ministry. But the irony is that the oppressive "priestcraft" once associated with Rome has overtaken much of Protestant church life in the form of "the managerial revolution" of this century. It is not surprising therefore that some Protestants looked hopefully to the declarations of Vatican II to revive a sense of the "lay apostolate" in a manner that would not be anti-clerical and would be rooted in a sacramental understanding of the Church that resists the dynamics of managerial dominance. In this connection, the Council's description of the Church as the "People of God" was warmly welcomed, as were specific statements about lay responsibility, especially in the political sphere. The Council fathers declared, for example, that

a vast field for the [lay] apostolate has opened up on the national and international levels *where most of all the laity are called upon to be stewards of Christian wisdom.* In loyalty to their country and in faithful fulfillment of their civic obligations, Catholics should feel themselves obliged to promote the true common good. . . . Catholics skilled in public affairs and adequately enlightened in faith and Christian doctrine should not refuse to administer public affairs, since by performing this office in a worthy manner they can simultaneously advance the common good and prepare the way for the Gospel (emphasis added).

In this and similar statements the Council recognized the integrity of the political. Such statements counter both right- and left-wing versions of a "sacred politics" that it is the Church's mission to promote. In the order of creation, secular wisdom and Christian wisdom converge as Christians ("most of all the laity") exercise their responsibility in serving the common good. Those Roman Catholics who complain that the American bishops in their "new style of social activism" are violating the understanding laid down by Vatican II may well be exaggerating. The bishops, for example in their pastoral letters on peace and on economics, consistently emphasize the public responsibility of the laity and try to distinguish when they, the bishops, are speaking authoritatively and when they are simply offering their prudential judgments on policy alternatives. At the same time, some bishops, too, express concern that lines are being blurred and distinctions are being lost, with the result that the faithful are alienated from the hierarchy's teaching authority and increasingly skeptical about the need or possibility of making connections between Christian teaching and their responsibilities in the political sphere.

Contrary to a common impression, the Roman Church hardly discovered the laity for the first time at Vatican II. It has always been understood theologically that the Church is composed of its baptized members, even if in practice the impression was sometimes given that the *real* Church is composed of pope, bishops, and clergy, to whom the laity are attached in order to "pay, pray and obey." Important in this connection is the centuries-old teaching regarding the *sensus fidelium,* the "sense" or "consensus" of the faithful. This teaching suggests that the faithful are not only to be respected in their own spheres of competence, but are actually a source of theological understanding and of the Spirit's guidance of the Church. Nor is this a peculiarly Roman Catholic teaching. It reaches far back into the Great Tradition, long before Roman Catholicism became a distinct church in the West. The idea of the *sensus fidelium* is evident also in streams of Protestantism, as, for example, in John Wesley's "quadrilateral" understanding of a communal dimension of Christian truth derived from Scripture, tradition, reason, and experience. But Roman Catholics have paid particular attention to the idea of the *sensus fidelium,* and the subject now comes in for increased discussion as confusions mount about the proper parts to be played by hierarchy, clergy, and laity in the teaching and life of the church.

55. CONSULTING THE FAITHFUL

Thomas Aquinas gave a Christian turn to the Aristotelian notion that the best way to moral knowledge is to consult the intuitions of virtuous people. All the baptized people, said Thomas, participate in the divine nature and therefore have an affinity for the faith that disposes them to accept what is in accord with it and to reject what contradicts it. As Eastern Orthodox theologians are fond of pointing out, the faithful sometimes rejected heresies before the theologians recognized them as such. The fourth-century crusade against Arianism, which denied the full divinity of Christ, was largely led by laypeople. Among Roman Catholics today it is frequently noted that the *sensus fidelium* has sometimes been ahead of the official church and the theologians in accepting new ideas. It is less frequently remarked that the *sensus fidelium* has sometimes served as an early warning system against deviations from the faith. The first role of the *sensus fidelium* is emphasized by those who, for example, cite opinion polls demonstrating widespread Catholic dissent from official teaching on artificial birth control. The second role of the *sensus fidelium* is lifted up, as we have seen, by Joseph Ratzinger and John Paul II against what they view as the excesses of liberation theology and other errors. It should come as no surprise that it proves notoriously difficult to determine the *sensus fidelium*, if indeed there is such a consensus.

It is regularly emphasized that the *sensus fidelium* is not a mechanical thing that can be determined by head count. The somewhat elusive nature of the *sensus* was recognized by John Henry Newman in his 1859 essay, "On Consulting the Faithful in Matters of Doctrine." Newman quotes a systematic theologian who suggested that the Spirit arouses in the Church "an instinct, an eminently Christian tact, which leads it to all true doctrine." (An "eminently Christian tact" sounds very English indeed, and far removed from today's raucous disputes about authority in the church.) The Council's "Constitution on Divine Revelation" asserts: "For there is a growth in the understanding of the realities and the words which have been handed down. This happens through the contemplation and study of believers, who ponder these things in their hearts (Luke 2:19, 51), through the intimate understanding of spiritual things they experience and through the preaching of those who have received with their episcopal succession the sure charism of truth." But all this still leaves unclear which believers are to be believed about the *sensus fidelium*.

We should not be surprised that some theologians, being only human, tend to emphasize or belittle the *sensus fidelium*, depending on whether it fits their own dispositions. If "the people" agree with them, then the people are "ahead of" the official church; if they disagree, then the people do not understand the current state of scholarship, or are impossibly submissive to church authority. The question of the current state of scholarship crops up regularly and strongly in connection with biblical studies. The approval of modern, critical biblical scholarship is still relatively recent among Roman Catholics, usually being dated from Pius XII's encyclical on the subject in 1943. The popular understanding of Scripture, it is pointed out, is still precritical, and appeals to that popular understanding by which figures such as Joseph Ratzinger are seen to be potentially threatening to scholarly freedom. Among mainline Protestants the irony is increasingly recognized that Protestantism, having championed the "return of the Bible to the people," has now tended to take the Bible away again and put it in the hands of "specialists," who are alone equipped to discern the true meaning of the text. Something similar may be happening in Roman Catholicism, except that there the Bible was passed from the official magisterium to the specialists, without ever having gone through the hands of the people.

We are cautioned against confusing the *sensus fidelium* with populism.

After all, the people are not theologically trained. In addition, living in both the Church and the world as they do, they are prone to smuggling into the tradition ideas that reflect their own unreflected interests and experiences. Theologians who say this sort of thing are often remarkably unreflective about their own interests and the ways in which their prejudices may be disguised in the language of the tradition. All that said, however, it is agreed that the *sensus fidelium* is not a kind of supermagisterium. As Avery Dulles has written in *America*, "In Catholic ecclesiology, binding judgments on doctrine and authoritative formulations of the faith are the responsibility of the pastoral office, not of theologians or of lay persons." Most theologians would agree, although some would omit the words "not of theologians."

It is Dulles again who summarizes nicely the meaning of the *sensus fidelium:* "The faithful, in the last analysis, are they who discern the Master's voice, and the voice of the Master is the one that the faithful are able to recognize. The discernment, therefore, goes in both directions. If we have identified the word of God, it serves as a criterion for recognizing God's people, and if we know who God's people are, we have a clue for ascertaining the word of God. The faithful discern the word of God, but on a deeper level they are discerned by it. 'For the word of God is living and active . . . discerning the thoughts and intentions of the heart' (Hebrews 4)."

There is an element of circularity in Dulles's description of the *sensus fidelium*, but it is an inescapable circularity. It is inescapable, that is, if center stage is to be held by the discerned and discerning word of God. Because Dulles keeps the word of God center stage, his description of the *sensus fidelium* is thoroughly ecumenical and could be subscribed to by Thomas Aquinas, Martin Luther, John Wesley, and Joseph Ratzinger alike.

The objection might be raised that this brief excursus on the *sensus fidelium* is beside the point of our earlier discussion of bishops, bureaucracies, public policy pronouncements, and the apostolate of the laity. After all, public policy pronouncements are not usually matters of doctrine. Such an objection is understandable but, I believe, wrongheaded. In their public policy pronouncements, the bishops are wrestling with the problem of what might be called the segmentation of authority. In an important article in *America* in 1986, Archbishop Rembert G. Weakland of Milwaukee, chairman of the committee that produced the pastoral on economic justice, writes, "I am convinced that our laity are intelligent enough to differentiate between those occasions when the bishops want to speak with the full force of their moral authority—whether it be on a moral theory or on its practical application—and those occasions when the bishops are still as undecided as everyone else and are in the process of weighing conflicting values and trying to find the right direction." To which some would respond, with respect, that the intelligence of the laity is not the question. Among the real questions is whether episcopal authority is segmented between those instances where the bishops have made up their minds (even on "practical application") and those instances where they haven't, or between statements of "moral theory" and "practical application." A yet deeper question has to do with the discerned and discerning word of God to which all authority is accountable.

56. TAKING POSITIONS

Garry Wills has written that Vatican II let "the dirty little secret" of Catholicism out of the bag. The dirty little secret, according to Wills, is that the church changes. For many Roman Catholics, if the church could change on anything—meat on Fridays, mass in the vernacular, the historical existence of Saint Christopher—it becomes unreliable on everything. Theirs was the package version of Catholicism in which authority was all of a piece—in which authority was integral, so to speak. In the previously mentioned document, Archbishop Weakland condemns an older version of integralism and yet seems to propose a new. In addressing public policy questions, he says, it is not satisfactory to say that the bishops should address the theory while leaving the practical application to the laity. The reason this is not satisfactory is that at some points "compromises" are required, and the laypeople should not be the only ones who "dirty their hands" with compromise. The new integralism implied is that Christian morality should be applicable in its entirety to the political order. When that does not happen, compromise is involved, and compromise is somehow morally compromising. But in the American theory of democratic politics, compromise is not morally compromising; it is rather the very essence of the practice of democratic politics. The new integralism implied is but another version of the old monism that fails to recognize that the political community and the community of faith are distinctly different communities and different kinds of communities. In this respect, too, one sees Roman Catholic parallels with Protestant confusions stemming from the ambition to "Christianize America and Americanize Christianity."

The community of faith and the political community each has its own integrity. In the ordering of their loves and loyalties, Christians unapologetically give priority to the community of faith. That is because, chiefly, the Church is the institutional bearer of the discerned and discerning word of God. The commitment to the Church is not a commitment against the political order, but it is a commitment that relativizes the political order. It is a commitment that is normative for regulating both the *obligatum* and *reservatum* of political engagement. Bishops are by definition responsible for the ordering and nurturing of the community of faith. Such ordering and nurturing includes "equipping the saints" (Eph. 4) for their ministry in the public arena. On the basis of this understanding, some bishops and theologians have proposed a more sophisticated and promising explanation than that offered by Archbishop Weakland. When bishops make judgments about public policy specifics, they say, they clearly are not doing so in the exercise of their formal teaching office. Rather, they are engaged in an *exemplary* exercise of prudential judgment as informed Christians and citizens. Because they are bishops, they reasonably expect the faithful to take their prudential judgments seriously. But the point is that theirs is an exemplary exercise, not to impose political choices upon the faithful but to encourage the faithful to engage in a similar exercise of study, reflection, and judgment. Disagreement with the bishops on these prudential questions is not only permitted, it is welcomed. The goal is not to advance one set of policies or another but to pastorally provoke the faithful to making reflective connections between Christian faith and political responsibility.

This, it would seem, is an entirely unexceptionable, indeed admirable, thing that the bishops are attempting to do. It is exactly the rationale that is frequently offered for political position taking in some old-line Protestant churches. It is not without its difficulties, however, in both concept and application. First, it assumes considerable sophistication, on the part of both leaders and constituency, about which statements are being made in the authoritative mode and which in the exemplary mode. Second, what is being exemplified in this process remains quite ambiguous. For example, in drawing up a pastoral letter, five or more bishops are chosen to form a committee. They work with the assistance of a professional staff (which, as James Luther Adams might observe, knows all about meetings) and spend several years in study and in holding hearings with selected experts on the subject at hand. Then they write a draft, which is submitted to their fellow bishops; criticisms and suggestions are received; the process is repeated two or three or more times; and finally three hundred bishops approve the final version and send it forth in their name. In many ways, it is an exemplary process. Certainly it is far superior to the way in which some churches produce public policy positions like breakfast rolls baked by a few functionaries in their Office for Prophetic Utterance.

And yet the process cannot help but seem unsatisfactory. What happens is that for several years a handful of bishops take huge amounts of time from their pastoral responsibility to enroll in a crash course in nuclear strategy, market economics, genetic engineering, or whatever. They have undoubtedly become well-informed amateurs, maybe even quasi experts, in the field. Even the most conscientious among the majority of bishops in whose name the final statement is issued can give but cursory attention to the bulk of materials produced by the staff and committee. After a draft of the economics pastoral had been approved, one conservative journal had some fun calling up bishops who voted for it. It turned out that most of the bishops contacted had very little idea of what the draft contained, which will not surprise anyone familiar with the sociology of institutions. Some observers cried foul, others recognized that the journal had a point. As thoroughly well intentioned as it is, the process is the problem. One must ask what it is that the bishops have exemplified, and how the faithful are expected to respond.

The members of the committee and those other bishops who made a substantial commitment of time to the project have certainly exemplified great diligence. They have also demonstrated themselves to be quick learners in an area where they presumably possessed no particular competence. And, one may even allow, they have arrived at exceedingly intelligent prudential judgments regarding the policy specifics in question. It is not for nothing that the majority of other bishops have confidence in them and go along with the final result. The responses of laypeople who are experts in subject X will vary. Some will be grateful to the bishops for bringing things to their attention that they had not previously considered. Others will judge that the bishops do not know what they are talking about and should stick to their episcopal competencies. But all will be essentially involved in "giving grades" to the bishops on the crash course they have taken, which seems like a harmless but somewhat odd thing for the faithful to be doing.

Of course the number of experts on subject X among the faithful will be a very small minority. The great majority of laypeople must of necessity respond in a more confused manner. Those who have all along favored the policy directions endorsed by the bishops will be cheered to have "the church" on their side. Those who opposed those directions will protest or seethe. Almost all will be uncertain about when the bishops are speaking with episcopal authority and when they are engaged in an exemplary exercise, and therefore episcopal authority is almost certainly eroded. The law of unintended consquences sets in: instead of being engaged in a new intensity of reflection, as the bishops intended, people on all sides of the political divides come to view the bishops as simply one more set of actors in the familiar play of politics as usual. That at least is what has happened in liberal Protestantism, even where leaders had a sincere and sophisticated intention that their position taking should only exemplify, nurture, and provoke Christian reflection about public responsibility.

The third problem with episcopal position taking designed to exemplify, nurture, and provoke is that it underestimates the power of both conscious and unconscious partisanships. Unconscious partisanships are the more insidious and, at the same time, the more implicitly arrogant. In unconscious partisanship the most formal propositions are assumed to be filled with self-evident content. For example, "The church should promote social justice." That is an entirely formal and unexceptionable proposition, until one starts filling in the policy-specific content of "social justice." People who press such propositions are often entirely unaware that they are being partisan, and are frequently offended when it is brought to their attention. In Protestant circles, and increasingly among Roman Catholics, one hears it said that Christians should rise above partisanship and simply support a "biblical politics." But, of course, when we examine the policy specifics of "biblical politics," it turns out to be eminently locatable on the political spectrum. A Jesuit-initiated and very influential organization in Washington is named, simply and deliciously, The Center of Concern. A leader of The Center of Concern insists—one must assume quite innocently—that the organization is nonpartisan. But even a cursory examination of its literature and program makes clear that the Center is located somewhere between the Jesse Jackson wing of the Democratic Party and the Juan Luis Segundo wing of liberation theology.

Such unconscious partisanship is more frequent on the Left than on the Right. The reason for that is uncomplicated and has nothing to do with the greater morality or intelligence of those on the Right. It is just that those who understand themselves to be going up against the established wisdom are daily reminded of their oppositional partisanship. Unlike those who speak confidently of their being in the inevitably triumphant "mainstream," dissent knows itself to be dissent. Thus, for example, a lay committee writing in response to a pastoral letter of the bishops conference is consciously, or at least less unconsciously, partisan. Such a committee does not need to be told that it is trying to gain a hearing for arguments that it believes are otherwise neglected. Of course the conservative dissent may in fact be in the *numerical* mainstream in American Catholicism. But, as we have seen, the mainstream is defined by the dynamics of the new knowledge class. The mainstream has little to do with majorities and everything to do with perceived momentum. It has to do with dominance in the minting and marketing of the ideas that are associated with the enlightened viewpoint that will presumably shape the future.

Even with the best of intentions all around, conscious and unconscious partisanships slip into the position-taking process. Of course, this is no fault in the sight of those who subscribe to soft or hard versions of "the partisan church." But most ethicists and moral theologians, both Roman Catholic and Protestant, are at least uneasy about the notion of a partisan church. They, together with the bishops, say that the Church's task is moral education. The leadership is to help inform the *sensus fidelium* with respect to Christian responsibility in the public arena. This is done by setting forth principles and goals, and by pointing to the policy options by which such principles and goals may be served. The informed consciences of individuals in conversation with other informed consciences will finally determine decisions reached. And, again, if the bishops indicate the prudential judgments they have reached with respect to specific policies and policy directions, this is but to encourage the process in which all are to be engaged.

In the last decade perhaps no one has played such an important role in guiding and explaining the Roman Catholic relationship to the public arena as Father Bryan Hehir of the Washington staff. Hehir is a formidable intellectual activist and is generally thought to be the person most trusted by the bishops on questions of the church and public policy. In countless forums over the years, Hehir has tirelessly explained what it is that the bishops are attempting to do, usually in terms similar to those sketched above. On some occasions, however, Father Hehir moves beyond the "exemplification model" to the need for advocacy and recruitment. For example, Hehir offered the following explanation at a conference sponsored by "Network," an activist and lobbying organization founded and led by Roman Catholic sisters:

What religious organizations are uniquely equipped to do . . . is to form a constituency of conscience on key foreign policy issues. By a constituency of conscience I mean a body of citizenry in the midst of the larger society which has a specific angle of vision on foreign policy questions involving significant moral content. Such a constituency of conscience has to be cultivated; it cannot be coerced. The cultivation of such a constituency, however, grows out of the very terms of meaning and motivation in life which are the main themes of our religious traditions. The challenge is to cast the meaning and motivation themes in structural terms of policy and politics.

The power of a constituency of conscience approach lies not only in the unique assets religious bodies have to build such a consensus but also in the legitimate role we can play with our own people on these policy issues. As soon as we enter the social field, questions arise about the legitimacy of our role. In the model I propose we are not trying to tell people how to vote but seeking to help people to think and decide. The dynamics of the model, as I see it, involve the religious institutions taking specific policy positions and then going to their constituencies with the position to see if they can garner support. In this approach, we should make no public claims to speak for 50 million Catholics when we take a position. We speak for institutional Catholicism, and we are going to the community of the Church to form a consensus on a given issue.

To say that this model, described with refreshing candor, is identical to the model followed by the church-and-society bureaucracies of the old-line Protestant churches is not to say that the model is wrong. Nor is it necessarily a demerit that the phrase "constituency of conscience" was the theme of the 1972 McGovern campaign and continues to be a code phrase for the most leftward side of the Democratic party. The critique of the model must be more substantive than that. The notion that one represents the constituency of conscience assumes, not so implicitly, that those who do not share our "specific angle of vision" are somehow deficient in conscience. To exploit the "unique assets" of religion and to "cast the meaning and motivational themes" of religion in support of "specific policy positions" cannot help but seem manipulative. And to capture "institutional Catholicism" in order to "garner support" for one's political preferences cannot help but be viewed as larceny by

Roman Catholics of a different political persuasion. Father Hehir, no doubt sincerely, says that he does not wish to "coerce" people, but surely, if one speaks for "institutional Catholicism," that is strong moral coercion, especially for those who most want to be loyal to institutional Catholicism. Father Hehir's model of a clerical campaign—led by bishops, bureaucrats, priests, and religious—to override, neutralize, or direct the judgment of the Catholic people (all under the rubric of "education") would seem to be very hard to square with Vatican II's affirmation of the apostolate of the laity.

There are alternative and more promising ways for church leadership to help bring Christianly informed moral judgment to bear in the public arena and to "equip the saints" to fulfill their public ministry. All of them require a thorough rethinking—and, most particularly, a thorough theological rethinking—of the relationship between Church and world, faith community and political community, the order of redemption and the order of creation, revelation and reason, grace and nature, eschatological promise and temporal responsibility. There are many good places to begin such a rethinking. One good place, for Protestants and Roman Catholics alike, is with the 1986 Instruction on Freedom and Liberation. It is perhaps too much to expect liberal Protestantism to pay much attention to a vision promulgated by the Congregation for the Doctrine of the Faith. One might think it would not be too much to expect of Roman Catholics—unless, more than most Roman Catholics realize, more than their bishops would like to think, "becoming American" means that they have indeed become like everybody else.

57. ADVANCING TO AUTHORITY

The reader may recall Paul Johnson's observation that the entire history of religion is the history of battling over authority. He is right, if by authority is meant the acknowledgment of that which is authoritative in the ultimate ordering of our loves and loyalties. But his conclusion is to be resisted if authority means authoritarianism, the abandonment of reason and personal responsibility, the handing over of our lives to heteronomous rule. Christians live not heteronomous but theonomous lives. In surrendering our lives to God in Christ, we find our lives in him who is the way, the truth, and the life. This, in the image of Saint Paul so favored by John Paul, is the transformation by which his "I" becomes our "I." Roman Catholics, more than most Christians, have affirmed an intimate connection between surrender to Christ and surrender to his Church in a particular institutional expression through history. They are Roman Catholic by virtue of being in communion with, and acknowledging the authority of, the church among the churches that is the Roman Catholic Church. As has always been the official teaching, and as Vatican II made the more lucid, this is not authoritarianism. The ultimate commitment is christocentric and not ecclesiocentric. The authority of Christ cannot be reduced to any institutional form of his Church. The Church in all of its historical manifestations is constituted by, and accountable to, a Gospel that is not of the Church's own creation. This is the doctrine and, except for the emphatic reference to Rome, it is thoroughly ecumenical doctrine.

As is true with all churches, and indeed with all institutions, there is often a sharp contrast between doctrine and reality. The reality of Roman Catholicism is frequently depicted as being relentlessly authoritarian. Many Roman Catholics themselves exult in drawing a caricature of the authoritarianism of the "pre-Vatican II church." It all finally came down to "Sister says." Behind Sister was Father, behind Father was the bishop, behind the bishop was the pope, behind the pope was Peter, behind Peter was Christ, and Christ was God and you couldn't go any further than that. Moreover, what Sister said is what the entire line of command had been saying from the beginning and would be saying forever and ever world without end. God sent Christ sent Peter sent the pope sent the bishop sent Father sent Sister, and if you doubt even a smidgen of it, you will be sent to hell. Such is the caricature, and, as with most caricatures, there was apparently enough reality in it to keep the caricature alive. The surprising thing is that so many Roman Catholics today seem to have a deep stake in keeping the caricature alive.

The only authority in pre-Vatican II Roman Catholicism, we are frequently told, was authoritarian. The process of becoming "American Catholics" is therefore a matter of "balancing" authoritarianism and autonomy. There is no movement beyond autonomy to the acknowledgment of the authoritative. The only meaning of obedience, in this view, is what Ratzinger derisively terms "mere juridical obedience." All the rest is autonomy and liberation. Vatican II released the modern Catholic from Sister's classroom, and life is now out of school, except for "communal Catholics" who stay in nostalgic touch by attending the class reunion called Sunday mass. This, as I say, is the caricature retailed by much contemporary Roman Catholic literature, sociological analysis, and by not a few theologians. The American Catholic who had been infantilized by an authoritarian church has now graduated to the autonomy of adolescence. Any mention of authority is terribly threatening, for it recalls that authoritarianism from which one has so lately and so narrowly escaped. The adolescent American Catholic must constantly be reminded, and must remind himself, how bad were the bad old days, lest in a moment of weakness he regress to infancy.

Vatican II let the American Catholic in on several dirty little secrets— that the church changes; that maybe Christ did not say exactly what the Gospels say he said; that other Christians may not only be saved but may be exemplary in their sanctification; that the reality of the Church is not exhausted by Rome; that the line of command includes loose links, ambitions in conflict, unresolved confusions, and quite a few contradictions. Suddenly "Sister says" means no more than that Sister says it. And, if she is still a sister and if she is like so many other sisters, probably the thing she says with greatest certainty is that nothing can be said with certainty. Therefore it is a whole new ball game, and if you are inclined to playing Catholic at all, you make it up as you go along. As we have seen, an astonishing number of contemporary Roman Catholic thinkers call this progress.

In his history of American Catholicism Professor Dolan lists the traits that, "towering above else," shaped the older Roman Catholic worldview and "set Catholics apart from other people in the United States." "There were four such central traits: authority, sin, ritual, and the miraculous." The story of "becoming American," as told by Dolan and numerous others, is the story of the discrediting, debunking, and demythologizing of these towering traits. The sociologist Andrew Greeley repeatedly claims that the discrediting of church authority was achieved with one stroke, *Humanae Vitae*. He writes that the only way that church authority might be able "to compel Catholics once again to accept the birth control teaching" is to insist "with all the vigor at its command" that a vengeful God "will punish the 'terrible sin of birth control' by sending most of the current American Catholic population to hell for all eternity." And even then the authority of the church would not likely be believed. "It is very difficult," writes Father Greeley in *American Catholics Since the Council* (1985), "to persuade people that ecclesiastical authority knows more about their own personal experiences of God than they do." The last observation obviously applies to much more than birth control. It perfectly illustrates what we have discussed as the "experiential-expressive" understanding of Christianity that is the hallmark of Protestant liberalism. In this view, Church, ministry, tradition, liturgy, and doctrine are all symbolic resources to be selectively employed in order to express the authentic experience of the autonomous individual. Among those writing about American Catholicism today, the predominant view is that in the Catholicism of yesterday the allegiance of the faithful was compelled by superstition and threat. Now that the superstition has been largely dissipated and the threat is no longer plausible, Roman Catholics have become, or are rapidly on their way to becoming, like everybody else. That is essentially how the Paul Blanshards of America understood Roman Catholicism. We must continue to hope that the Paul Blanshards, and those Roman Catholics who have come to agree with the Paul Blanshards, are wrong.

Becoming American is a difficult and ambiguous process for any community. For one thing, there are so many kinds of American to become. John Courtney Murray had a "transformationalist" vision of an authentic Roman Catholicism that, drawing on its intellectual and spiritual resources, might renew the American experiment in liberal democracy. The knowledge class in contemporary Catholicism has for the most part abandoned that vision and that project. Many of that class have turned against the American political experiment while, at the same time, seeking to transform Catholicism in the image of the liberal individualism that is so prominent in the American ethos. Thus the dynamic and direction of Murray's transformationalist project has been precisely and depressingly reversed. It is important to keep in mind, however, that the final story has not been told. The period since Vatican II is relatively short. We are still in an early phase of response to the Council. What has been reversed can perhaps be reversed again. Midcourse corrections are possible on a course that spans centuries. With respect to the Gospel, tradition, and moral community, there may yet emerge an American way of being Roman Catholic and a Roman Catholic way of being American that bear witness to what is authoritative for all of us.

PART VI.

The Catholic Moment

The argument and presuppositions of this book can be brought together in thesis form. (The reader may be pleased to note that there are not ninety-five theses.)

1. This Is the Catholic Moment.

There are of course many moments in two millennia of Christian history and more than four centuries of Roman Catholicism as a church among the churches in the West. Each moment in time is equally close to God's purpose, and God's purpose equally close to each moment. But we are to read the signs of the times to discern the obligations, limits, and opportunities of our moment. This, I have argued, is the moment in which the Roman Catholic Church in the world can and should be the lead church in proclaiming and exemplifying the Gospel. This can and should also be the moment in which the Roman Catholic Church in the United States assumes its rightful role in the culture-forming task of constructing a religiously informed public philosophy for the American experiment in ordered liberty. The first obligation and opportunity is much the more important. Indeed the achievement of the second is entirely dependent upon giving careful priority to the first. The specifically Christian proposition, and the community of faith that it brings into being, must be held in relentless and dynamic tension with all other propositions, including the American proposition. Pope John Paul is this historical moment's most public witness to the truth that if this tension is relaxed, the Church has nothing distinctive or ultimately helpful to offer the world.

2. The Most Important Opening Effected By Vatican Council II is the Opening to the Church.

This opening to the Church is, above all, an opening to the Gospel by which the Church is created and sustained. This is the Gospel that forms and integrates what Joseph Cardinal Ratzinger calls "the structure of faith." In the Council's further development of the tradition, it is made much clearer than it was before that the Roman Catholic Church is vulnerable to the Gospel and to the entire community that is claimed by the Gospel. In subsequent official teaching the primacy of the Gospel is asserted with a force unprecedented in Roman Catholic history. In truth, the Reformation understanding of the Gospel as God's justifying grace centered in the scriptural *kerygma* of cross and resurrection is today more boldly proclaimed by Rome than by many of the churches that lay claim to the Reformation heritage.

3. THE CATHOLIC MOMENT IS TO ALERT THE WORLD TO THE TRUE NATURE OF ITS CRISIS.

The greatest threat to the world is not political or economic or military. The greatest problem in the Church is not institutional decline or disarray. *The* crisis of this time and every time is the crisis of unbelief. With a sense of urgency that the world, and much of the Church, find embarrassing, Rome persists in asking, "When the Son of Man comes, will he find faith on earth?" This Pope is exercised not about dissent but about apostasy. He is attempting to chart a Christian course that is not so much against modernity as it is beyond modernity. The only modernity to be discarded is the debased modernity of unbelief that results in a prideful and premature closure of the world against its promised destiny. This Pope is giving voice to the Christian correlate to the opening to the transcendent that in culture, philosophy, and science is the great intellectual and spiritual event of our time. The Christian correlate, of course, is Christ. In this respect, John Paul is far ahead of those Christians, including many Roman Catholics, who are only now learning to accommodate the faith to a debased modernity that history is fast leaving behind. It is said that John XXIII opened the windows of the Church to the modern world. John Paul has entered the modern world to help open the windows of the modern world to the worlds of which it is part.

4. ECUMENISM, INHERENT AND IRREVERSIBLE, IS ESSENTIAL TO THE REALIZATION OF THE CATHOLIC MOMENT.

The Roman Catholic decision to pursue the more visible unity of the Church is irreversible because it is based upon the understanding that Christian unity is inherent in *being* the Church. The only Christ and the only Gospel by which a community can be the Church is the Christ and Gospel of the entire Church. The only unity that is lasting and worth pursuing is a unity rooted in a shared confession of Christ and the Gospel. Theological integrity is therefore not an obstacle to unity but the servant of unity. Ecumenism is not so much a program with a timetable as a way of living together in the one Church. Unity is to be achieved not by ecclesiastical conquest but by reconciled diversity in obedience to the Gospel. The Roman Catholic Church has a singular ecumenical calling to take the lead in healing the breach between the churches of the East and those of the West. In the West, the foremost obligation and opportunity is the healing of the breach of the sixteenth century between Rome and the Reformation. In America and especially in the developing world, the forces of greatest Christian vitality are Roman Catholicism and evangelical Protestantism. In many parts of the world, notably in Latin America, these forces are at war with one another. Although the obstacles are daunting, the Catholic Moment requires that the ecumenical mandate of Vatican II be extended to evangelical and fundamentalist Protestantism. An ecumenical commitment indomitable and full-orbed is required if Christianity is believably to represent hope for the unity of humankind.

5. THE CATHOLIC MOMENT REQUIRES A RENEWED DEMONSTRATION OF UNITY IN DIVERSITY.

Pluralism is not a fault. It is evidence of the incompleteness of the world and of the Church within the world. Pluralism in the Church should not be the result of dissent from the Gospel but of diverse forms of radical obedience to the Gospel. The Roman Catholic Church is by far the most diverse of churches. With its discrete orders of ministry, its monastic communities, its myriad works of mercy, its multifarious national and cultural traditions, its political and ideological inclusiveness, and even its different patterns of theological reflection, the Roman Catholic Church is the paradigmatic instance of the unity in diversity that other churches should emulate and to which the world aspires. John Paul now declares that unity in diversity is in jeopardy—not because a few dissent from juridical authority but because many have been led astray from the Gospel. He is engaged in a project of restoration that some view as a renewed oppression and others as an effort to restore coherence to a tradition shattered by the assaults of modernity. In Vatican II the Roman Catholic Church kept its long-delayed appointment with modernity. The future of Christianity in the world will be powerfully influenced by whether Catholicism emerges from this meeting with a unity that is not uniformity and a diversity that is not division.

6. THE CATHOLIC MOMENT REQUIRES A RENEWAL OF THEOLOGY IN SERVICE TO THE COMMUNITY OF FAITH AND ITS MISSION IN THE WORLD.

There are inevitable tensions between the magisterium, or official teaching authority, and the theological enterprise. The basic relationship between the two, however, is not one of tension but of mutual service under the Gospel. That at least is the argument of Joseph Cardinal Ratzinger. Theology is a continuing conversation in which the magisterium plays the essentially pastoral part of guiding but not controlling the discourse. This ecclesial understanding of the theological enterprise is radically at odds with patterns of academic theology that have emerged since Vatican II. Like liberal Protestant theology before it, Roman Catholic theology increasingly finds itself torn between two communities competing for loyalty: academe and the church. This competition engages a strong element of class conflict, for most theologians belong to what is accurately described as the new knowledge class whose interests are preeminently served by academe. Continuing disputes about intellectual freedom are typically not about intellectual freedom. They are disputes over which community and which tradition is given priority by the theologian. In a "postliberal" understanding of cultural-linguistic traditions, it is seen that academic freedom is also an imposed discipline, that putative universalisms are also particularistic, and that release from orthodoxies is yet another orthodoxy. The Catholic Moment depends in large part upon whether Roman Catholic theologians move toward a postliberal position of service to the Gospel and the community that bears the Gospel, or, as in most of Protestantism, become stalled in sterile contests between liberalism and traditionalism.

7. IF THE CATHOLIC MOMENT IS REALIZED, IT WILL ENHANCE THE PROSPECT FOR FREEDOM AND JUSTICE IN THE WORLD.

Among world figures today, John Paul is the foremost champion of freedom as the first component of justice. He proclaims the truth that "the free adherence of the person to God" is both the font and foundation, the source and safeguard, of all human rights. Without that transcendent referent, all talk about human rights is, as Bentham declared it to be, nonsense on stilts. Against the propensities of all states, and against the ideology of some states and movements, the Church must contend to secure social space for the personal and communal "aspiration to the infinite." In order to be more effective, however, Roman Catholic social teaching must more thoroughly integrate the moral and political wisdom of specific experiments in ordered freedom and justice. John Courtney Murray's long-neglected exploration into the meaning of the American proposition should be taken up again, and the Council's "Declaration on Religious Freedom" should be further elaborated to illumine the choices facing the modern world.

8. THE CATHOLIC MOMENT CHALLENGES THE IMPERIOUSNESS OF THE POLITICAL.

This thesis follows closely upon the last. The freedom of the person and of persons in community must be secured by right political order. Right political order requires setting sharp limitations upon the political, if political is understood as state power. A wide array of associations, including religion, are "public" institutions and essential to the vitality of the earthly *polis*. The Church makes its greatest public contribution when it is most true to its own nature and mission. In a democracy, the primary political contribution of church leadership is to "equip the saints" for the exercise of their ministry in the public arena. The Church itself is called to be a community of virtue and a zone of truth in a political world of viciousness and mendacity. A "partisan church" is an apostate church. The Church has a theology of politics, not a political theology. A theology of politics requires that pastoral leadership both affirm the political project while, at the same time, keeping all political proposals under moral judgment. The Church in all times and places has never done this very well. Religious leadership, including Roman Catholic leadership, in America today sometimes seems hardly to be trying. The results are that the Church is perceived as but one political actor among others, political discourse is inflamed rather than informed, and the integrity of both Church and political order are grievously violated.

9. The Catholic Moment Will Redirect the World's Passion for Liberation.

With love for its proponents and even greater love for its victims, Christians must repudiate the proposal that politics is salvation and salvation is politics. With John Paul, and invoking Saint Paul, we must reject the now dominant forms of liberation theology as "another gospel." Contrary to certain ideologies, eternal destiny and temporal duty are not opposed to one another. It is empirically probable and logically persuasive that human development is best advanced by transcendent hope. It is historically undeniable that, where transcendent hope is denied, all development leads only to new forms of bondage. Because it is the only Gospel we have been given, and because it is the deepest truth about humanity, the Church must boldly proclaim our vocation to the radically "new politics" of the heavenly city. Short of the Kingdom Come, we are alien citizens. In contending against the idolatry of the political, the Roman Catholic Church is today contending on behalf of the Gospel and therefore on behalf of all Christians.

10. The Catholic Moment is for the Duration.

Even when, please God, all the churches are in full communion in the one Church Catholic, there will likely still be a Roman Catholic Church. By virtue of its size, tradition, structure, charisms, and energies, the Roman Catholic Church will have a singular part in shaping the world-historical future of Christianity. And if the Gospel is true, Christianity bears witness to the future of the world, who is Christ. Therefore the Catholic Moment is encompassed by an eschatological horizon. Before that final consummation the relationship between Church and world will always be problematic. The world is ever prone to premature closure, turning in upon itself and against its transcendent destiny. The Church is ever tempted to join the world in that fatal turning. This is the temptation represented by Dostoyevsky's Grand Inquisitor, and the Grand Inquisitor takes many forms—theological, philosophical, spiritual, political. The Grand Inquisitor would persuade the prodigal sons of earth that they can be at home in a world that is still far from the home of the waiting Father. Resisting that temptation, the Church must often appear to be against the world, but it will always be against the world for the world. The Church's view of reality is premised upon a promise and is therefore in tension with all views of reality premised upon the present alone. The Church too lives in the present, but it lives by a promise that is also the ultimate truth about the present. Thus the Church's relationship to the world is essentially paradoxical. It is a relationship of yes and no, now and not yet. The Church will endure until the End Time, but along the way it is ever being tested as to whether it has the courage to live in paradoxical fidelity. Nowhere is that testing so severe, nowhere is the outcome of that testing so ominous, as in the Roman Catholic Church. This Pope, we all have reason to believe and reason to hope, knows that the paradox cannot be resolved and must not be relaxed. It can only be superseded by the coming of the One who is both the consummation and companion of our common pilgrimage.

Index